DATE		

Language and
Social Identity

Language and Social Identity

Edited by Richard K. Blot

Foreword by Charles L. Briggs

PRAEGER

Westport, Connecticut
London

Library of Congress Cataloging-in-Publication Data

Language and social identity / edited by Richard K. Blot ; foreword by Charles
  Briggs.
      p. cm.
  Includes bibliographical references and index.
  ISBN 0-89789-783-8 (alk. paper)
    1. Sociolinguistics 2. Group identity. I. Blot, Richard K.
P40.5.G76L36 2003
306.44—dc21   2003042887

British Library Cataloguing in Publication Data is available.

Library of Congress Catalog Card Number: 2003042887
ISBN: 0-89789-783-8

First published in 2003

Praeger Publishers, 88 Post Road West, Westport, CT 06881
An imprint of Greenwood Publishing Group, Inc.
www.praeger.com

Printed in the United States of America

The paper used in this book complies with the
Permanent Paper Standard issued by the National
Information Standards Organization (Z39.48-1984).

10 9 8 7 6 5 4 3 2 1

For all who struggle to preserve
the world's vanishing languages

"Le lien du langage est peut-être le plus fort et le plus durable qui puisse unir les hommes."

Alexis de Tocqueville, *De La Démocratie Amérique*

Contents

Foreword

Charles L. Briggs

Once upon a time, studying questions of language and social identity seemed to confer on scholars a satisfying sense of knowledge and power. Received readings of Ferdinand de Saussure's (1959) *Course in General Linguistics* fostered the impression that language was a privileged cultural domain whose special rules could be discovered empirically. Operating in keeping with the nationalist assumption that every individual learned one language early in life and then remained under the spell of its semantic and grammatical categories forever, the Boasian legacy—culminating in Benjamin Lee Whorf's (1956) *Language, Thought, and Reality*—fostered the claim that secret knowledge of the inner principles of language could confer on practitioners the authority to serve as interpreters of how linguistic categories shape the way people perceive the world. Miraculously, only the linguistically initiated were deemed to be free from the distorting influence of a particular set of categories.

Post-structuralist and postmodern thought challenged the basis of this authority and complicated the study of language and identity by introducing a wide range of epistemological and political considerations. After reading M. M. Bakhtin (1981) and V. N. Vološinov (1973), it is hard to take the received notion of "a language" seriously. When one moves from the notion of a bounded, homogeneous, and relatively stable "system" to acceptance of complex, overlapping, dynamic, and heterogeneous discourses that are shot through with ideologies, histories, and collective and individual voices, the desire to map connections between language and identity can no longer be satisfied with simple one-to-one correlations. Pragmatic thought from Peirce (1932) to Jakobson (1957) to Silverstein (1976) similarly withdraws the simplifying assumption that linguistic cartographies can be compiled on purely referential grounds, compelling scholars to see how poetic or metacommunicative "functions," for example, can belie neat characterizations of "here we say X to signify Y." The fairly recent shift to the study of language ideologies confronts scholars with the realization that *all* characterizations of language are shot through with competing ideologies, thereby withdrawing the sense that students of language possessed special knowledge and authority. As it turns out, the linguist's black box, so prestigious in the 1960s and 1970s, performs the same sorts of operations as those undertaken by philosophers, missionaries, bureaucrats, and the proverbial person in the street.

Things are no easier on the identity side of the question. Although many practitioners in social science disciplines share a common interest in identities with students of literature as well as cultural, ethnic, women's, and science studies, substantial disagreements are apparent with respect to the nature of social identities and how successful scholars can be in representing them. Etienne Balibar (1995, 173) succinctly draws attention to the source of many of these difficulties in arguing that discourses of cultural identity are formulated in terms of "four major categorical polarities." Cultural identity appears as simultaneously (1) "objective structures" and "a principle or a process of subjectivization," (2) as an expression of the singularity of "groups" and as part of "the question of universality or universalization," (3) as a facet of scientific, technical, literary culture and popular or mass cultures, and (4) as being both permanent and evolving (174–76). To these I would add a fifth polarity, the way that cultural identities are often presented as self-constructions of the individuals and groups who "bear" them at the same time that they are imposed by dominant institutions.

Given the depth of these contradictions, a social identity that may be characterized in a social scientific account as consisting of a set of objective characteristics that have been adopted by the members of a particular, territorially grounded, and culturally bounded "group" over a long period of time can be challenged by depicting it as an arbitrary imposition of widely circulating stereotypes imposed by a scientific elite for particular, contemporary interests. In a number of recent cases, these sorts of critiques have also run in the opposite direction (see Briggs 1996). These contradictions can be suppressed in producing the illusion of bounded, non-overlapping, homogeneous, and relatively stable identities, or they can be exploited in destabilizing hegemonic, generating emergent formulations or in enabling individuals to place themselves in multiple overlapping, unstable, and heterogeneous discourses of identity. For many scholars, the task no longer consists of telling people who they really are but in presenting critical perspectives that reveal relationships between competing constructions of social identity.

Richard Blot has done us a service by assembling a collection of essays that challenge these received reductionisms in the course of analyzing concrete relationships between language and social identity. One common thread, albeit implicit, that runs through the chapters is the realization that people who are not language professionals think a great deal about language-identity links and that these reflections are often more critical and sophisticated than extant scholarly accounts. The papers adopt a number of strategies for tapping into these situated metadiscourses and re-presenting them for scholarly audiences.

A number of essays document the use of narratives in exploring relationships between contrastive identities, dominant and subaltern; it is interesting that all of these chapters focus on Native Americans. Many of the founding narratives of linguistics and anthropology picture autonomous, bounded, and independent languages and cultures that emerge in splendid isolation, bumping into each other somewhere along the road to history and establishing fortuitous and often superficial relations. But Gossen's work on a Tzotzil story from Mexico and Villalón's analysis of an E'ñapa text from Venezuela suggest that narratives provide subaltern communities with resources for portraying linguistic pluralism as foundational, as shaping identities and relations of social inequality right from the start. Chernela and Leed tell us that Arapaço people in the Brazilian Northwest Amazon credit Unurato, a culture hero, with having worked in Brazilia, having "moved among many people," and, we presume, having learned Portuguese.

That such reflections on language, identity, and power should take narrative form should surprise us not in the least, given the Bakhtinian capacity of narrative to bring multiple voices and epistemologies into relationship with one another and to open up wider imaginative fields in which to explore the ways that they are—and could be—related. Narratives can unlock dominant modes of conceptualizing links between language and identity, thereby fostering resistant perspectives and furthering the search for alternative arrangements. Kelly's study of the circulation of visionary Mayan narratives enables us to see that even when narratives purport to resurrect "traditional" identities in the name of rejecting forms of oppression identified as "modern," keen awareness of contemporary forms of state violence and linguistic domination may guide constructions of tradition.

A second focus in these essays relates to issues that lie at the center of contemporary research in a number of disciplines. Regulating difference, racial and ethnic, has long been a central concern of nation-states. Lisa Lowe (1996) argues that the racial policies of the political system in the United States revolve around a fundamental contradiction: democratic ideologies that promise inclusion through citizenship, rights, and, one might add, consumerism and social mobility do not alter the political-economic importance of racializing some populations as nonwhite, thereby providing a political and cultural basis for labor exploitation and complex forms of exclusion. As George Lipsitz (1998) suggests, the explicit racialization of nonwhites fuels the reproduction of an implicit ideology of "whiteness" that confers real material advantages on persons classified as white. At the same time that many of the contributors to this volume explore the crucial role that language plays in ideologies and practices of inclusion and exclusion, they also point to the profound changes in the way that nation-states regulate difference that are emerging in the course of globalization. As the same time that social inequality is increasing dramatically, both within and between countries, liberal ideologies of democracy, human rights, and self-determination by minority communities circulate nearly as quickly as capital, goods, people, and germs.

These essays provide us with new insights into the shifting relations between language, identity, and political-economic relations. Catalan's transformation from the suppressed core of nationalist sentiment among a linguistic and cultural minority to the official language of economically powerful "autonomous" Catalonia is in many ways emblematic. Speaking Catalan came to afford access to dominant sectors and symbolize social class at the same time that state language planners attempted to sever its ethnic exclusivity in casting it as the language of democratic participation. In Cochabamba, Bolivia, individuals who are subordinated vis-à-vis "Indian" identities are no longer always economically subordinate to "whites." Accordingly, markers of class and ethnic difference that could once be projected as a stable, unambiguous, and perhaps even natural system can no longer directly contain the aspirations of a subaltern population. Nevertheless, the use of Quechua (as opposed to Spanish) and deployment of the campesino "peasant" label can be refashioned simultaneously as tools for regional political mobilization and instruments for maintaining social inequality. Schnepel argues that language planners, promoters of Creole, and scholars have been blinded to the way that changing gender relations help shape the relationship between Creole and French in Guadeloupe and Martinique. Mentore suggests the literacy practices touted by the state as keys to political participation can best be seen as imperialist tools for the suppression of structures of feeling associated with orality, thereby attempting—unsuccessfully—to produce acquiescent citizens.

Other essays explore the changing politics of language and identity in the United States. Dominant ideologies construe language difference as a "problem" created by "minority groups" that upsets a homogeneous, stable, and monolingual linguistico-political foundation. Mike Long challenges this view in suggesting that the "Ebonics" controversy was sparked not so much by recent changes in the relationship between Ebonics, or African-American Vernacular English, and other varieties of English but by the emergence of the New Right and its strategies for undermining challenges to racial oppression. Bonnie Urciuoli traces the way that media-based assertions of Latino upward mobility must control stigmatized images of linguistic diversity in order to avoid clashing with dominant multicultural policies and the rise of the Official English movement. These contributions complement Jane Hill's (1995) demonstrations of the centrality of supposedly private, jocular, and certainly demeaning representations of Latino identities through stereotypical Spanish words and phrases in legitimating whiteness, the "hasta la vista, baby" phenomenon. In an age of heightened attention to rights, political and cultural, efforts to keep identities tightly bounded and neatly arranged in hierarchical regimes find new ways of preserving—or even extending—social inequality.

James Collins examines new strategies for mobilizing Native American identities in the face of historical and contemporary pressures to eradicate Tolowa identities—as well as rights to land and riverine resources—in California. Many discussions of language and social identity preserve Herderian assumptions regarding one-to-one relations between homogeneous, bounded languages and nations (see Bauman and Briggs 2000). Collins points to means of breaking up language and culture conceptually into specific practices that can be used in creating alternative identities, even in the face of violently assimilative pressures. He also touches on a crucial theme, the role of researchers in creating, legitimating, and challenging notions of language and identity. In tracing the centrality of verbal performance in the construction of Rastafarian identities in Jamaica, Pulis similarly traces his involvement in the ethnographic encounters that shape his account. These reflexive moves provide a crucial first step in exposing the fundamental contradiction that underlies many contemporary constructions of scholarly identities—claiming to align oneself with the powerless while at the same time asserting the epistemological authority of a scientific perspective on language and identity. When researchers implicitly advance such claims to innocence and political marginality, they invite rejection or appropriation by ideologists of the status quo—and by members of oppressed communities.

In the age of globalization, emergent schemes of social inequality are often rationalized through rhetorics of language. Accordingly, researchers who focus on questions of language, broadly defined, can once again play key roles in scholarly debates. What they have to offer at present is less an esoteric set of formal models than sensitivity to the heterogeneous array of ideologies and practices that shape contemporary debates on language. The essays published herein are based on concrete cases located primarily in the Americas, including the Caribbean; engaging issues that are of great interest to scholars in cultural, ethnic, and women's studies, they link broad questions regarding the politics of language to specific sites of social conflict and accommodation. Richard Blot deserves credit for having assembled a collection that provides us with a range of perspectives on crucial contemporary problems of global order.

REFERENCES

Bakhtin, M. M. 1981. *The Dialogic Imagination: Four Essays*. Ed. Michael Holquist, trans. Caryl Emerson and Michael Holquist. Austin: University of Texas Press.

Balibar, Etienne. 1995. "Culture and Identity (Working Notes)." In John Rajchman, ed., *The Identity in Question*. New York: Routledge, 1995.

Bauman, Richard, and Charles L. Briggs. 2000. "Language Philosophy as Language Ideology: John Locke and Johann Gottfried Herder." In Paul V. Kroskrity, ed., *Regimes of Language: Discursive Constructions of Authority, Identity, and Power*. Sante Fe, N.M.: School of American Research.

Briggs, Charles L. 1996. "The Politics of Discursive Authority in Research on the 'Invention of Tradition.'" *Cultural Anthropology* 11(4): 435–69.

Hill, Jane H. 1995. "Junk Spanish, Covert Racism and the (Leaky) Boundary Between Public and Private Spheres." *Pragmatics* 5(2): 197–212.

Jakobson, R. 1957. *Shifters, Verbal Categories, and the Russian Verb*. Cambridge, Mass.: Harvard University Russian Language Project.

Lipsitz, George. 1998. *The Possessive Investment in Whiteness*. Philadelphia: Temple University Press.

Lowe, Lisa. 1996. *Immigrant Acts: On Asian American Cultural Politics*. Durham, N.C.: Duke University Press.

Peirce, Charles Sanders. 1932. *Collected Papers of Charles Sanders Peirce*. Vol. 2, *Elements of Logic*. Ed. C. Hartshorne and P. Weiss. Cambridge, Mass.: Harvard University Press.

Saussure, Ferdinand de. 1959 [1916]. *A Course in General Linguistics*. Ed. C. Bally and A. Schehaye, trans. Wade Baskin. New York: McGraw-Hill.

Silverstein, M. 1976. "Shifters, Linguistic Categories, and Cultural Description." In Keith H. Basso and Henry T. Selby, eds., *Meaning in Anthropology*. Albuquerque: University of New Mexico Press, pp. 11–55.

Vološinov, V. N. 1973 [1930]. *Marxism and the Philosophy of Language.* Trans. L. Matejka and I. R. Titunik. New York: Academic Press.

Whorf, Benjamin Lee. 1956 [1940]. "Science and Linguistics." In John B. Carroll, ed., *Language, Thought, and Reality: Selected Writings of Benjamin Lee Whorf.* Cambridge, Mass.: MIT Press, pp. 207–19.

Acknowledgments

In editing this collection of case studies, my goal was that the value of the whole should be judged to be greater than the sum of its individual parts. Whatever degree of success is achieved is due entirely to the fine studies produced by the authors in response to my request for contributions. My greatest debt is to them all. Their patience and goodwill during an unexpectedly long gestation period was certainly without peer. Without the authors' unwavering insistence on the value of the project, coupled with the interest and support of Jane Garry at Praeger, this work might never have reached completion.

Lisa Rowe, production editor, and Marcia Goldstein, permissions editor, were of inestimable help during all stages of production, addressing my many concerns with patience. Patricia Calderwood, a novice to the field of anthropology, graciously volunteered to read through early drafts of a few of the chapters and share her opinion on readability. James Collins provided critical commentary on the Introduction, urging me to keep it short, to state my ideas in a straightforward manner, and to let the authors, through their studies, speak for themselves. John Pulis's encouragement whenever I lost faith that the project would reach fruition cannot be underestimated. David Rose, archivist, took on the task of preparing the index even as his own work was mushrooming. And not least, Charles Briggs, to my good fortune, graciously agreed to contribute the foreword. To all, my heartfelt thanks.

The following chapters, originally published elsewhere, appear here with the permission of the authors:

Mike Long, "Ebonics, Language, and Power," in Fred L. Pincus and Howard J. Ehrlich, eds., *Race and Ethnic Conflict: Contending Views on Prejudice, Discrimination, and Ethnoviolence* (Boulder, Colo.: Westview, 1999), pp. 331–45.

Ellen Schnepel, "The Other Tongue, the Other Voice: Language and Gender in the French Caribbean," in *Ethnic Groups* 10(4) (1993): 243–68.

George Mentore's "Passionate Speech and Literate Talk in Grenada" is an expanded version of "Alienating Emotions: Literacy and Creolese in Grenada," in *Ethnic Groups* 10(4) (1993): 269–84.

A small portion of Blot's Introduction is taken from his "Language and Social Identity in the Caribbean: Editor's Introduction," in *Ethnic Groups* 10(4) (1993): 239–41.

Introduction

Richard K. Blot

Her defects in pronunciation were atrocious. It would have taken superhuman powers to make her say "fragment," "magnificent," "enigma," and other common words. She strived to overcome this difficulty, laughing and emphasizing it, but she could not. Final *s* sounds became *h*'s and she didn't even notice the difference; she couldn't help it. She swallowed lots of syllables. If she had known how pretty her mouth looked when she did it, she wouldn't have tried to correct her charming defects. But Maximiliano had acquired the strictness of a schoolteacher and the conceit of an academic. He didn't give her a moment's rest and stalked after her solecisms, ready to pounce on them like a cat on a mouse.

   "It's not 'deffrence,' it's 'difference.' It's not 'Holly Ghost' or 'indilgences.' Besides, saying you're 'fed up' sounds awful, and calling everything you don't understand 'tiology' is terrible. And saying 'you're damned sure' every two seconds is vulgar."

Galdós, *Fortunata y Jacinta*

Here, in two brief paragraphs, the Spanish novelist Benito Pérez Galdós introduces his presumably middle-class reader to Fortunata, a title character in his masterful *Fortunata and Jacinta*. Galdós captures the sounds and "misuses" of language in Fortunata's speech to signal a significant difference in class. For whom are "fragment," "magnifi-cent," and "enigma" common words, if not to the educated, middle-class reader of novels? Common to the reader, yet presumably uncommon to one of Fortunata's social class.

Although Fortunata's defects are charming to Maximiliano (and to the reader?), they are nonetheless defects in his eyes (or to his ears). Whenever Fortunata opens her mouth to speak, ample evidence of her class position pours forth; her uncultured, "vulgar" use of language marks her for others to judge. Maximiliano, by his tutoring, hopes to help Fortunata overcome her defects, in order to hide, in effect, her origins. If she speaks "correctly," that is, as Maximiliano wishes her to speak, she will have masked those clues to her identity that allow others to adjudge her character as one of the lower orders. She then will be able to pass as educated.

One is surely reminded of other, perhaps more well-known, literary examples of attempts to "rescue" unfortunates from the consequences of their social positions through education, with lessons in the "proper" use of language and speech being paramount. The phonetician Henry Higgins's hopes and claims for Eliza Doolittle in G. B. Shaw's *Pygmalion* are tragicomic. Higgins's efforts to overcome Eliza's vulgar street talk are rewarded when a guest at a formal reception assumes from her comments and demeanor that she is a Hungarian princess. She is, in other words, *judged by her language use*; she remains other to the social elites, those superficial observers who respond, not to her, but to the distinctive features of her speech. In an ironic twist of the phonetician's experiment, the hypercorrectness of Eliza's language puts her outside the very social sphere Higgins has educated her to represent.

In a less well-known example, Alexandre Kuprin's muckraking novel *Yama: The Pit* (1929), we find the young, idealistic student Likhonin taking the young and doubting Liubka from "the gay establishment of Anna Markova" to his modest, single-room quarters, not to keep her for his own pleasure but to rescue her from the weariness and suffering of life in a brothel. She is to be transformed in "mind and soul" through the tutelage of Likhonin and his fellow students. Liubka is not only to learn to read and to write, but also to be tutored in geography, mathe-matics, literature, applied sciences, even metaphysics. Ultimately, and sadly, the effort fails, and Likhonin returns Liubka to the brothel. Likhonin had begun a magnanimous experiment with dubious re-sources. In seeking the assistance of his friends to "do everything to educate her mind a little," Likhonin assured them "that her heart and soul are beautiful, of that I am sure. I've no grounds for the faith, but I am sure, I almost know" (1929, 276). Liubka is grateful to Likhonin and comes to love him. Yet despite her love and despite Likhonin's genuine efforts and sincere protests, Liubka's soul, pure from the start, remains undiscovered; her identity as one out of place in novel surroundings is imposed by Likhonin and his friends. She is judged by them against the standards of an educated middle class. She has none of the social graces of an educated, urban woman; worse, her language, a coarse, uneducated speech, leads Likhonin to revulsion. Likhonin, immersed in a world of scholarly texts, literary masterpieces, and middle-class mores, cannot truly see the heart and soul beyond the appearance of an illiterate, naive, downtrodden backwoods lass and ultimately condemns her to life as a prostitute.[1]

That we judge another's character by reference to language use is not a novel discovery. Language is inescapably a badge of identity. Although the consequences of all such judgments may not be always as dire as those depicted in Kuprin's *Yama*, they are nonetheless significant. Whenever we open our mouths to speak we provide those who hear us, chosen interlocutors and mere bystanders alike, with a wealth of data, a congeries of linguistic clues others use to position us within a specific social stratum. Our particular uses of language may situate us geographically, physically (by sex or age), ethnically, nationally, and, especially in stratified societies, according to class or caste. Sociolinguists, anthropologists, and others concerned with the formal study of the social uses and functions of language are concerned to document the implications of such judging on the lives of the various peoples around the world and among the peoples and classes within their own societies. Questions such as the following focus their work: What linguistic features of speech are used to form stereotypical impressions about the social identity (as well as the character) of others? How are the marks of language, specific linguistic features, linked to ethnicity, to gender, to race, and to class? *How is language employed in conveying one's individual or one's group identity?*

Why link *language* and *identity*? The cultural historian Peter Burke tells us that language is "one of the most important of the signs of collective identity. . . . Speaking the same language, or variety of language, as someone else is a simple and effective way of indicating solidarity; speaking a different language or variety of language is an equally effective way of distinguishing oneself from other individuals or groups" (1993, 70). The linguistic anthropologist Urciuoli echoes Burke: "Language provides an easily objectified and coded set of elements on which to hang other aspects of identity and difference" (1998, 4). Yet while true, in attempting to answer the last and former questions one must avoid the facile reification of *language* and *identity* (the key terms framing the essays here) and guard against employing them as singular, unproblematic terms in any social science equation that links them to nation, race, class, ethnicity, or gender. Collectively such terms as these comprise some of the most used and most elusive categories in the descriptive arsenal of social science. All such categories are, at their base, about sameness (in some formulations, identity) and difference. This holds true whether we employ these categories as social scientists and attempt to affix them definitively (and even permanently) to some (purported) objective social reality, or whether we find them at play in the varied contexts of everyday social existence. They comprise, I believe, what Rossi-Landi would consider a complex "constellation of overlapping categories in social science, categories which cannot in themselves be accounted for fully without resorting to other categories" (1977, 392). The implications of Rossi-Landi's statement are profound: "When we accept the principle that categories overlap, and deal with two or more categories jointly, nothing like the feared collapse of one category under the rule of some other category need take place; all categories in general, and especially categories used in the social sciences, receive instead full light only if their overlapping is given complete attention" (392). The social scientists' search for the defining characteristics that exhaust any category should give way to the study of both the ways and the extent to which categories overlap in concrete circumstances. A concern for categories in use requires careful attention to the ways and means employed by groups of social actors in constructing and communicating the boundaries that mark them (see Smith 1987).

The cases presented in this collection demonstrate the wisdom of Rossi-Landi's statement. They provide current examples of the processes of group formation, maintenance, and demise as they come to grips with the complexities of race, ethnicity, nation, class, and gender. Each chapter, approaching a concrete social circumstance through language, makes clearer the overlapping of traditional categories of analysis. They highlight questions of establishing identity by marking difference in language use where issues of ethnicity, gender distinctions, oral versus literate uses of language, the meanings and uses of myths and tales, all come into play in the collective construction of identity. Collectively the cases here make the argument that any question of social identity entails an understanding of language in use.

It is here we must introduce and underscore a caveat: both key terms, *language* and *identity*, are problematic; they are too often subject to reification, imputing to the concepts and the processes they name an unwarranted stability. Careful examination of the uses to which the terms are put in social science enquiry and description thus becomes necessary. Kroskrity provides a handy starting point with a definition of identity neatly conjoined with language: "Identity is defined as the linguistic construction of membership in one or more social groups or categories" (1999, 111). Yet Handler (1994), for example, has questioned the usefulness of the concept *identity* in any discussion of cultural identity, especially when used in cross-cultural studies, while Silverstein (1998) has argued that the construct *language* is itself inherently unstable. Handler argues against the assertion of a homogeneous, essentialist identity while at the same time warning of the pitfalls of a too-easy acceptance of a constructivist approach to both culture and identity:

> I would avoid—or, at least, refuse to privilege—the discourse of: "who we are," that is, of identity. Groups are not bounded objects in the natural world. Rather, "They" are symbolic processes that emerge and dissolve in particular contexts of action. Groups do not have essential identities; indeed, they ought not to be defined as things at all. For any imaginable social group—defined in terms of nationality, class, locality, or gender—there is no definitive way to specify "who we are," for "who we are" is a communicative process that includes many voices and varying degrees of understanding and, importantly, misunderstanding. (1994, 30)

In light of the papers in this volume, we would add to the brief list of categories employed in the understanding of social identity that of *history*. From the time of Marx up through Hobsbawn in the present the centrality of human agency in the making of history has been much debated (see Miller 1979; Ahern 2001). As humans make their history, within a preexisting sociocultural context, they interrogate their pre-given history, which is narrated, for example, through myth, ritual, political oratory, literature, and so forth, using it to form a current identity within the flux of the everyday. Thus, as Stuart Hall (1989, 15) reminds us, "We now have to reconceptualize identity as a *process of identification*. . . . It is something that happens over time, that is never absolutely stable, that is subject to the play of history and the play of difference." If identity is reconceptualized as a *process of identification*, identity becomes inherently unstable. It is always emergent; it is part of the history (myth, ritual) that is made, and part of the history in the making through its enactment in ritual, myth, and the like.

Kroskrity, in his ethnolinguistic study of the 600 native Arizona Tewa, provides an argument that language, history, and identity are not distinct categories: "for the Arizona Tewa people these notions are unified in their collective and individual experiences in a manner unsurpassed by any other claims" (1993, 3). What outsiders may label as distinct entities for the Tewa is one "experienced unity." Collins (this volume) makes much the same claim for the Tolowa of northern California. On the ground, in the daily experience of people, the categories are not the analytic constructs of social scientists, but the concrete means of group-, and thereby, self-identification. Tolowa (and Tewa) identity is manifestly experienced and conveyed through communicative means.

Kroskrity attends to a series of questions that are very much the questions raised by this volume's authors. Where Kroskrity has Tewa, we may supply Tolowa, or E'ñapa, or Tzotzil, or Arapaço and seek the answers provided by the specific cultural contexts:

> What are Tewa cultural beliefs about their language and about language in general?
> How does the Arizona Tewa language reveal the history of its people?
> How does the speech of individual Arizona Tewa people reveal their biographies?
> How are social identities conveyed by language and ways of speaking?
> How does the use of different languages available—Tewa, Hopi, and English—display a strategy of selection from among a repertoire of culturally available identities?

But although, or rather because language is used to judge others, people may often consciously choose one form of a language or dialect over another to create or to mark a boundary between themselves and others. They may employ one form in acts of resistance against an oppressor's imposition of a colonial language. Clearly this is so because claims that seek to establish or to challenge cultural borders must, in the first instance, be communicated. The choice of language employed in making the claim may be as important to the claim as the claim itself. In other words, by choosing to use one language, dialect, style, or register over another, one is in effect establishing a difference, however tenuously, while simultaneously making a claim for it. Ngũgĩ puts it clearly and succinctly: "The choice of language and the use to which language is put is central to a peoples' definition of themselves in relation to their natural and social environment" (1986, 4). It is not surprising, therefore, that issues of language choice are frequently in the news. A recent article in the *New York Times* referred to the new Europe as "a lingual hodgepodge" (Simons 1999), and noted that "[t]he European Union has created the Bureau for Lesser-used Languages, which finances projects such as developing Internet browsers in Welsh and cartoon books in Alsation (sic)." All this while the same European Union worries that parts of a Latvian language law supported by four political parties that are traditionally at odds will create language problems for investors ("Four Parties Back Latvian Language Law," 1999).

The chapters in this volume address the following two questions: *Under what conditions does it become necessary or desirable, permitted or attempted, for a people to have recourse to a specific language, dialect, jargon to establish a claim to a recognizable identity, sexual, social, ethnic, tribal, or otherwise? What are the consequences resulting from such a claim?* In the authors' responses we find no evidence of reification. Language and identity remain firmly grounded in the concrete. As peoples engage in social and political battles to establish and maintain an identity as a people, they will, of necessity, make claims about language directly or as a means to mark boundaries of class, ethnicity, nation and gender. The claim made by the authors here— that we *must* look to language in use to understand issues of social identity—is by no means radical, but each of the case studies richly demonstrates that in examining the means by which differences of class, of ethnicity, of nationhood, or of gender are communicated, we learn that such means are part and parcel of the differences themselves.

Yet that a particular language choice itself may be an identifying marker of ethnic, tribal, or indeed any form of social identity, that it marks group membership, both for insiders and outsiders, would seem obvious. One could then argue that the social scientists' task is a straightforward one, that is, merely to describe the language in use and map the boundaries of those groups differentiated by language and their struggles for identity. Would that social science enquiry were that simple! For while language may be the means by which ethnicity or class is maintained or reestablished (for example, through ethnogenesis), sometimes it does not serve so easily as an important recourse for peoples for marking (or overcoming) boundaries. Lagos, in her chapter on the relation of language to region or class, undermines any facile equating of linguistic borders with geographic. The ethnographic evidence drawn from her work in Cochabamba, Bolivia, demonstrates that caution must be observed in drawing conclusions pertaining to language use by particular groups. Particular forms and meanings may transect regions and classes, and linguistic borders won't comfortably coincide with geographic borders.

Further, at times an indigenous language is abandoned in seeming contradiction to traditional cultural practices of solidarity in order to maximize communication across borders. Chernela and Leed's chapter deals with an Eastern Tukanoan group, the Arapaço, whose traditional language has been replaced by Tukano or Portuguese, yet they remain endogamous. This in itself is not surprising. Untold numbers of indigenous languages have been abandoned by native speakers in response to the onslaught of conquering tongues (see Hymes 1973). But as Chernela and Leed demonstrate, the case of the Arapaço is unique, since "for Eastern Tukanoan, it is language that marks group affiliation and identity."

Social scientists who, in their attempts to describe and analyze social identity, employ the categories "ethnicity," "gender," "class," "nation," and "nationality" in the abstract and *without any connection to language in use* risk missing an extremely important means that peoples use in constructing and maintaining identity. The chapters in this volume describe the processes by which peoples in vastly different societies use their linguistic resources to construct a social identity, to set boundaries and borders linguistically, to overcome the strong forces, both external and internal, of conquest. They expose and seek to close a theoretical gap in our understanding of the relation between language and culture. No longer will the Herderian equation—one language, one culture— suffice.[2] The need for solid case studies, clear examples by those who have continued down a new theoretical path, is met in this volume. We learn from these cases that what is called for are new ways to frame our analyses of social identity and that any such frames must look to language in use.

The chapters by Chernela and Leed, Gossen, and Kelly deal with myths.The myths are used to explain the status of languages used by the groups involved and why those languages are employed as they are: Spanish/Tzotzil; Portuguese/Tukano; English in the translation of Mayan myths. Myths about language help place the peoples historically and socially, as Gossen so nicely demonstrates. Lagos, Woolard, and Villalón offer good case studies of the importance of attention to language use in the making of class and ethnicity, while Long with Ebonics, Urciuoli with the use of Spanish in advertising, and Schnepel with gender differences deal with language variety and with language difference and power. One might say that these cases illustrate the struggle for voice.

The remaining chapters, those by Collins, Pulis, and Mentore, most clearly illustrate the idea of overlapping categories. Of all of the chapters, these three make the strongest claim of all that language is key, it is the way in, to understand how people view themselves *and* how they use language to construct themselves, their identity. Traditional means of understanding the constructing of social identity no longer serve: Identity is not simply race, or class, or gender. Language practice and identity categories are being constructed simultaneously. What these cases demonstrate is that without careful attention to language we gain much less insight into this process.

In sum, the articulation of identity always and everywhere involves some type of encounter with another. Identity is always and everywhere formed in the dialogue with others, symbolic or real, who are different, whose difference from you and yours from them is made manifest in the claim for identity. In other words, the only fixity in the process of identification is the necessary connection, the relationship, with the other who is different. Identity is made within the claim that is communicated. As Hall so clearly maintains, "Identity is within discourse, within representation. It is constituted in part by representation. Identity is a narrative of the self; it's the story we tell about the self in order to know who we are. We impose a structure on it" (1989, 19). However we choose to construct that narrative, language is essential; the social self, one's social identity, is embodied in the discourse structure created to give voice to a people.

NOTES

1. For a discussion of the linking of dialect variation, termed "vulgar speech," with "moral deviation," see Ramos 1994.

2. The controversy over language laws in Chirac's France regarding lesser-used languages provides a current example: languages other than French were outlawed after the revolution in order to promote and insure equality, and thus strengthen the nation. Now there are moves to strengthen languages such as Breton.

REFERENCES

Ahern, L. 2001. "Language and Agency." *Annual Review of Anthropology* 30: 109–37.

Burke, P. 1993. *The Art of Conversation*. Ithaca, N.Y.: Cornell University Press.

"Four Parties Back Latvian Language Law." 1999, July 7. *New York Times*, p. A3.

Galdós, Benito Pérez. 1986. *Fortunata and Jacinta*. Trans. Agnes Moncy Gullón. Athens: University of Georgia Press.

Hall, S. 1989. "Ethnicity: Identity and Difference." *Radical America* 23(4): 9–20.

Handler, R. 1994. "Is 'Identity' a Useful Cross-cultural Concept?" In John Gillis, ed., *Commemorations: The Politics of National Identity*. Princeton, N.J.: Princeton University Press, 27–40.

Hymes, D. 1973. "Speech and Language: On the Origins and Foundations of Inequality Among Speakers." *Daedalus* 102(3): 59–85.

Kroskrity, P. 1993. *Language, History, and Identity*. Tucson: University of Arizona Press.

Kroskrity, P. 1999. "Identity." In Alessandro Duranti, ed. "Language Matters in Anthropology: A Lexicon for the Millenium." *Journal of Linguistic Anthropology* 9(1–2): 111–14.

Kuprin, A. 1929. *Yama: The Pit*. Trans. Bernard Guilbert Guerney. New York: Bernard Guilbert Guerney, Publisher.

Miller, J. 1979. *From Marx to Merleau-Ponty*. Berkeley: University of California Press.

Ngũgĩ wa Thiong'o. 1986. *Decolonizing the Mind: The Politics of Language in African Literature*. Portsmouth, N.H.: Heinemann.

Ramos, J. 1994. "Faceless Tongues: Language and Citizenship in Nineteenth-Century Latin America." In Angelika Bammer, ed., *Displacements: Cultural Identities in Question*. Bloomington: Indiana University Press.

Rossi-Landi, F. 1977. "On the Overlapping of Categories in the Social Sciences." In William C. McCormack and Stephen A. Wurm, eds., *Language and Thought. Anthropological Issues*. The Hague and Paris: Mouton, 391–403.

Silverstein, M. 1998. "Contemporary Transformation of Local Linguistic Communities." *Annual Review of Anthropology* 27: 410–26.

Simons, M. 1999, Oct. 11. "In New Europe, a Lingual Hodgepodge." *New York Times*, international edition.

Smith, C. 1987. "Culture and Community: The Language of Class in Guatemala." In Mike Davis et al., eds., *The Year Left 2*. London: Verso, 197–217.

Urciuoli, B. 1998. *Exposing Prejudice: Puerto Rican Experiences of Language, Race, and Class*. Boulder, Colo.: Westview Press.

2

Language and Indians' Place in Chiapas, Mexico: A Testimony from the Tzotzil Maya

Gary H. Gossen

The present chapter has as its centerpiece a Tzotzil Maya narrative account of the origins of the linguistic and political inequality between Indians and Ladinos (bearers of Spanish-speaking Mexican national culture). Xun Méndez Tzotzek, a bilingual man from San Juan Chamula, Chiapas, Mexico, wrote this testimony in 1979. My initial translation to Spanish, together with ethnographic notes, was prepared in close consultation with him. I consider this text to be an important document because it records the views of a sensitive Indian observer on the close ties among language, ethnicity, and asymmetrical political power in the highlands of Chiapas, Mexico, one of several states in Mexico that have significant Indian populations (numbering in the millions). Since San Juan Chamula itself is the largest single Indian community in Chiapas, this text provides us with the opportunity to examine, from the Indian point of view, a volatile current topic that is certain to become a hot issue in the state, indeed in the whole nation, in the near future.

I use the word "volatile" advisedly, for the directorate of the Zapatista insurrection movement of 1994—whose constituency is largely Maya Indian peasants—has made numerous demands of the Mexican federal state, none of which has been resolved as of this writing. These demands are not only for political and economic reforms, but also for cultural autonomy. This specifically implies development of public

educational policy and pedagogical materials that treat Indian languages, culture, and history not as afflictions to be overcome but rather
as respected features of Mexico's de facto ethnic pluralism.

Mexico has postponed dealing with this challenge for four-and-a-half
centuries, and the piecemeal solutions that *have* been proposed have
invariably derived from the wisdom and political interests of the con-
queror/tutor/missionary state rather than from the Indian communities themselves. This is not to say that the politics of language and
literacy have been absent from the public forum, but only that Indian
communities have typically been the recipients of these policies, not
consultants in their formulation and implementation.

THE COLONIAL LEGACY

Beginning with the creation of New Spain from the ruins of
Mesoamerica's pre-Columbian civilizations in the sixteenth century
and continuing even as this is written in January 1995, Mexican mestizo
and criollo (white European) authorities have been concerned with
finding ways to assert to themselves and to persuade the outside world
that they preside over a Western polity, in spite of the fact that native
speakers of Indian languages constituted, until approximately 1800, a
numerical majority. Even today, 12,000,000 (about 11 percent) of
Mexico's 90,000,000 people speak one of more than 50 distinct Native
American languages as their first language. Native American biologi-
cal, cultural, and linguistic forms have mingled with European and
African bodies, ideas, and languages to create a modern Mexico that is
truly the quintessential mestizo ("mixed") nation of the Americas.
Everything from the lexicon of Mexican Spanish (which has hundreds
of loan words from Indian languages, particularly Nahuatl) to the food
in market stalls, to the faces on the street, expresses the pervasiveness
of the mestizo roots of this nation.

While it is impossible to imagine modern Mexico without its Indian
past and present, public policy has always treated Indians and Indian
languages as problems to be overcome. Early in the contact period, the
priests faced the challenge of evangelizing the Indian community and
found that they could not do so without learning native languages. If
the sixteenth century produced a pragmatic political and religious
interest in using native languages as a means of facilitating conversion
and subsequent tutelage in Christian doctrine, this interest diminished
in the seventeenth and eighteenth centuries. Deposed native political
leaders became the local agents of Crown policy. Typically descending
from the elite families in the old social order of the Indian communities,
these men were taught Spanish and brought into the colonial power

structure as intermediaries—political *caciques* (local bosses), *sacristanes* (sacristans), and *maestros de capilla* (choirmasters)—who gained exemptions from taxation and forced labor by "facilitating" the delivery of labor and tribute from their Indian compatriots to Crown authorities. These local Indian leaders were also expected to encourage their subalterns to follow daily and annual religious observances in compliance with dictates of priests who often visited the villages only a few times a year to perform baptisms, weddings, and memorial masses for the deceased.

This colonial system was, by design, conceived as a caste system (to be Indian literally carried with it, according to ecclesiastical and civil codes, the legal "duty" to bear the burden of *casta*). This policy effectively segregated Indian communities in the countryside from the Spanish (criollo) and mestizo populations of the town and cities. These two "republics" had separate and unequal tax and legal codes as well as different expectations for religious observance and participation in the sacraments. Until well into the nineteenth century, schooling for other than the local elite leaders was out of the question. When schooling was available, it was, with few exceptions, delivered in Spanish and conceived entirely within the curricular framework approved by the Church. With a number of notable exceptions (particularly those documents numbering in the many hundreds dating from the sixteenth century), works written in and about Indian languages were not widely available in Mexico; with the exception of a few scholars and clerics, native languages held little interest for the rank and file of the colonial establishment. Although thousands of religious, legal, and census documents written in Mesoamerican Indian languages and dating from the colonial period survive today, it is nevertheless true that educated mestizos and criollos held Indian languages and verbal art forms to be inferior human expressions, to be used only as a matter of administrative and evangelical necessity.

To a great extent these colonial social, ethnic, and linguistic attitudes survive remarkably intact in our time. If anything, public policy and local practice in the nineteenth century exacerbated the social and economic asymmetries of Indians in relation to the state. The nineteenth century, with the exception of the period of Liberal reforms in the 1850s and 1860s, saw almost no progress in the education of Indians, even in Spanish. The pattern of local rule continued and, with it, the pattern of local elite bilingualism that served the purposes of the state. Social and economic circumstances of the Indian communities deteriorated to conditions that were decidedly worse than those that prevailed during the colonial period. After independence from Spain, the criollo and mestizo elites who had controlled public life under Crown authority were free to exploit Indian land, labor, and production without any encumbrances in the form of Church and state responsibility for Indian welfare, under what had been called the duties of the Crown as the head of a "missionary state." Indians by the hundreds of thousands were obliged during the nineteenth century to become debt slaves of criollo and mestizo-owned ranches, plantations, and mining operations. This caused a marked depopulation of demographically isolated Indian communities, for the men in particular often had to spend many months a year working as day laborers far from their home villages. Just as often whole families were forced to migrate to the ranches and plantations where they worked under a system that was, in effect, debt peonage.

Against the backdrop of this massive political and economic exploitation, which reached its peak during the long dictatorial regime of President Porfirio Díaz (1871–1910), Indian languages and literatures and Indian education found themselves where the Indians themselves were—at the very bottom of the heap of national priorities. The state found it convenient to ignore the demographically isolated (and linguistically conservative) Indian communities as long as the flow of cheap labor continued. Most Indian villages had no schools or other social services. These thousands of isolated Indian populations became what Aguirre Beltrán has called *regiones de refugio*, suggesting that they were forced—demographically, culturally, economically, and socially— to the very margins of national life (Aguirre Beltrán 1967).

THE MEXICAN REVOLUTION AND *INDIGENISMO*

It is well known that the epic Mexican Revolution (1910–1917) attempted to address many of the social ills that I have just described. The theme of *pan y libertad* ("bread and liberty" or, more generally, economic, social, and political justice) underlay not only the Revolution itself, but also the creation of modern Mexico. This is neither the time nor the place to discuss this theme at length. However, it is relevant to the present discussion to observe the irony that has most recently been noted by the Maya Zapatistas themselves: that although the Revolution was fought in the name of Mexico's poor and oppressed, both mestizos and Indians, many of the structural inequalities that created economic and social misery for millions of the urban and rural poor in pre-Revolutionary Mexico remain in place today. Some observers, ranging from academic historians to Subcomandante Marcos de Maya Zapatista fame, contend that the Revolution never even happened in Chiapas. Indeed, with all of Mexico's golden age of agrarian reform in the Cárdenas era (1930s), its incredible artistic and literary florescence throughout the post-Revolutionary period, and its post–World War II economic prosperity, crowned most recently by the boom years of the

1970s and the passage of the North American Free Trade Agreement (NAFTA) in 1993, it remains the case that the poorest state in Mexico is Chiapas; and it is the rural poor, including hundreds of thousands of Maya-speaking Indians, who are at the bottom of the heap. Mr. Méndez Tzotzek, whose account follows, speaks to us from this social and economic space.

It would be mean-spirited, indeed historically irresponsible, not to recognize that Mexico has implemented literally hundreds of policies and programs in the post-Revolutionary period that have focused on the improvement of the economic and social circumstances of the nation's rural and urban poor. Indian communities themselves have been targeted for special attention in this regard. Indeed, a whole body of policy legislation and related health, educational, and economic programs—known as *indigenismo*—has evolved since the 1920s with the specific goal of bringing the thousands of Indian communities into the cultural and economic space of modern Mexico. Many *indigenista* programs have been enormously successful. For example, the municipio of San Juan Chamula, the source of the text to be examined, did not have a single public school or clinic in 1910. It now has dozens of one- and two-room rural grammar schools, plus an upper school and a clinic in the town center.

However, as noted at the beginning of this chapter, Spanish language, Mexican ethnicity, and social place are still so indelibly linked within national culture that virtually all programs aimed at social and economic "progress" for Indians follow the state-initiated pattern of colonial and nineteenth-century public policy thinking. Indianness and Indian languages are viewed by public policy makers as problems to be overcome (and sometimes as "background noise" to be ignored), not as integral parts of the nation's historical and present identity. In particular, throughout the twentieth century, Indian education has been conceived and delivered with an eye to remedial intervention. The initial goal is always *castellanización*, that is, to teach literacy in Spanish together with the standard curriculum of Mexican schools to liberate Indians from the social and economic disadvantages that are thought (by Mexicans) to be linked to their Indianness. Invariably, Indian language syllabaries and reading materials are abandoned once a child is able to understand, read, and learn in Spanish. Briefly stated, the state retains today many of the same tutorial functions that the Church exercised in the colonial period. There is but one route to social and economic adaptation, and the structurally dominant Spanish-speaking state defines it. Indians can take it or leave it. The subtext has not changed much since the sixteenth century: Indianness is a social, linguistic, and spiritual condition that should be corrected (cf. Lomnitz-Adler 1992:261–81; Modiano 1973).

CHIAPAS IN MEXICO

Along with Caxaca and Yucatan, Chiapas is among the states of Mexico that have the largest and most conservative Indian populations. Perhaps 50 to 100 percent of the populations of half the municipios in Chiapas are monolingual or bilingual speakers of native languages, most of which belong to the Maya family of languages. Among the most important of these languages are Tzotzil, Tzeltas, and Tojolobal. Until the mid-nineteenth century, most of the Indian population of Chiapas lived in the demographically isolated communities described earlier. In large part by colonial design, Indian municipios evolved as unique cultural isolates; each one had its characteristic dialect of an Indian language, colorful traditional clothing, a particular variant of a civil-religious hierarchy of ritual officials, and a particular cycle of public ritual observances in honor of the saints. This pattern survives today in many of the municipios of the Central Highlands. This vibrant ethnic mosaic also, ironically, attracts the national and international tourist trade. Indian traditionalism is thus not only a source of cheap labor and produce; it is also a marketable commodity from which the Ladino community reaps considerable economic benefit.

However, beginning in the nineteenth century, for reasons previously discussed, thousands of Indians emigrated from these closed communities to several sparsely populated regions of the state in search of employment on cattle ranches, coffee plantations, and other commercial agriculture operations. These areas of recent immigration lie to the northeast and east of the Highlands (the valley of Simojovel and the Lacandon jungle) and to the southwest (the Grijalva River Valley and the Pacific coastal strip and foothills). This out-migration pattern has continued unabated in the twentieth century; the reasons for it have been not only the desperate quest for land and economic opportunity, but also political and religious exile from people's communities of origin.

The most recent wave of this exodus has been the result of missionary activity. Protestant evangelical activity began in the 1950s and lay Catholic mission activity (post–Vatican II) began in the 1960s. Even more recently, in the 1970s and 1980s, the more radical Roman Catholic liberation theology movement has been active in these areas of recent immigration. Initially, at least, all of this missionary activity proceeded with the blessing of the Mexican state, for, it was argued (and still is), mission activity shares many of the tutorial goals of state indigenista policy. Missionaries believe as do Mexican state officials, that planned change—e.g., literacy programs, access to modern health care, improved farming techniques—will benefit Indian communities in ways that their traditional lifestyles and customs cannot accomplish. All of these various mission initiatives tend to hold a highly negative opinion of what they regard as the spiritual and political tyranny of traditional Indian lifestyles and community organization. Although the nuances differ from one mission group to the next, the critical theme is similar: that economic and social "progress" is incompatible with traditional Indian customs. Thus, the missionary critique of traditional Indian customs has often gone hand-in-hand with support for modernization and closer interaction with the Mexican state and its social and economic institutions. This has generally been the Protestant and Catholic Action message. Sometimes (as with liberation theology), the focus of the critique is the blatant collusion of traditional Indian caciques with the Mexican state, a pattern of cooperation that enriches the caciques at the expense of their own Indian subalterns. Sometimes (as with the Protestants), the reasons offered for conversion center on the paganism and evil nature of Indian religious practices; they also note that taxes levied for the celebration of village festivals drain limited financial resources that would be better invested in improved nutrition and health care for local families. They are also adamant about the evils of alcohol, its excessive cost, and its relation to domestic violence. Thus, there is the promise of economic progress and personal "betterment" if one abandons core elements of Indian traditional life.

These missionary groups also agree generally on the importance of education and literacy. Protestants have been successful in encouraging literacy in both Spanish and Indian languages (and in providing Bible translations and other religious tracts to read). They all agree, also, on the de facto importance of Spanish as the lingua franca of the nation.

All of these forces for social change have had a particularly strong impact on the areas of recent immigration, beyond the Central Highlands. As for the highland Indian communities themselves, many have reacted violently to these challenges to their local autonomy and related political authority. Many of these traditional municipios, most notably San Juan Chamula, have reacted by purging Protestant converts from their communities at gunpoint, stripping them of their land and property, and quite literally sending them into exile. This has led to decades of conflict and litigation and also to the massive out-migration of Protestant converts to new communities in both urban and rural regions of the state.

In summary, Chiapas today is a region of great social unrest, demographic displacement, and political flux. The 1994 Zapatista Movement expresses the desperate circumstances that thousands of Chiapas Indians perceive to be their lot. By virtually all measures of social statistics, Chiapas is a third-world enclave in a nation that aspires to first-world status. The gap between the rich and the poor is enormous, and this pattern is exacerbated by the ethnic and linguistic diversity of the state.

Any solution to the social and economic problems will undoubtedly have to come to grips with the politics of language, literacy, and ethnicity, for the Zapatistas have made it clear that they are both Mexicans and native peoples, with rights to their own ethnic and linguistic heritage. Social and economic progress cannot come, as state officials might wish, at the cost of Indian identity.

LANGUAGE AND ETHNIC IDENTITY

The number of speakers of Indian languages in Chiapas is growing with each new census. As noted above, massive change has come to the region, but outright acculturation (or Ladinoization) to Mexican national culture is apparently not the strategy of choice for many hundreds of thousands of speakers of Indian languages who live in the state. While bilingualism is undoubtedly on the rise (particularly so in the areas of new immigration, where there is no common language other than Spanish), it is also the case that Indians value their linguistic heritage, for tradition has taught them that their very being as humans and their identity as individuals and members of social groups reside in their language. Indeed, language is the most fundamental marker of Indian identity. It typically continues as the defining attribute of Indianness even when people abandon their traditional dress and traditional customs. This pattern of linguistic conservatism characterizes hundreds of Maya Protestant congregations in the state; their songs, religious services, and community and home activities are conducted in Maya languages. All Maya-speaking people in Chiapas refer to their particular dialect of their language as "the true or real language." It is ironic to note, in contrast, that Ladinos in Chiapas do not typically even recognize Indian languages as languages; they call them *dialectos* (dialects). Indians are well aware of the condescension implied in this designation, for it constitutes but one more gesture of Ladino contempt for Indians and Indian identity. The barriers of *casta* are obviously still in place. Because an understanding of a problem from the point of view of all parties involved often precedes the formulation of possible solutions, it makes sense to take seriously just what Indians think about the history and nature of language and its related verbal art forms.

Language is not, for the Indian community, an easily negotiable or expendable part of their collective and individual being. Chamula Tzotzil sacred narratives pay a great deal of attention to the key role of language (*k'op*) in the evolution of the human condition over the four cyclical creations and restorations that make up the history of the earth and its lifeforms. Mayas (indeed, most Mesoamerican Indian communities) link language and dialogue to the dawn of consciousness in their creation narratives. In time present, as in time past, language, with its wide range of rhetorical, poetic, and musical embellishments, has served as a sacred symbol that allows humans to share qualities with, and communicate with, gods. In effect, beautifully executed speech and song are the only substances that the human body can produce that are accessible to and worthy before divine beings. Ritual speech, prayer, song, and sacred narrative performance share with other sacramental substances—such as liquor, incense, tobacco, fireworks, aromatic leaves, and flowers—the quality of metaphorical heat. They all produce "felt" intensity of message as essence, not substance. All of these sacraments share the quality of transcending substance through heat, smell, sound, smoke, and feeling (as in drunkenness), which are media which Our Lord Sun/Christ and other deities both understand and consume; it is, quite literally, their only "food." In the case of language, it is said to be the "heat of the heart" of the performer (which invariably expresses itself in the intensified messages of couplets and other forms of stylistic redundancy) that makes it reasonable to classify ritual language, song, prayer, and sacred narrative as sacraments (cf. Gossen 1976).

Thus, language matters a great deal to the Tzotzils. Its mastery qualified protohumans for true humanity in the time of the ancestors. In its embellished forms, it serves as food for the sustenance of deities. In the individual life cycle, minimal mastery of its complex art forms constitutes basic competence as an adult. Political and religious officials and shamans must master it with even greater aplomb in order to be credible as community leaders. It therefore makes sense to Tzotzils to cultivate language and to take it seriously.

XUN MÉNDEZ TZOTZEK'S NARRATIVE

The following narrative refers to events in the Third Creation, what might be called the "heroic period" in Chamula historical reckoning. Prior to this period (in the First and Second Creations), the creator sun god (Our Lord Sun/Christ in Heaven) had created humankind a number of times from clay or mud, or sometimes sticks. Although different narrators disagree on the particulars of what happened to these earlier experiments with humankind in the First and Second Creations, all agree that learning to eat corn and learning to speak, sing, pray, and dance were diagnostic of the dawn of human consciousness. It is also remembered in the oral tradition that the failure of early beings to learn these things caused Our Lord Sun/Christ great frustration in his creative labors, so much so that he destroyed his trial beings because they could not do these things adequately.

It is also true of all the narratives that abuse of the gift of food (for example, the use of their own babies as meat filling for corn tamales) and speech (as in the narrative that follows) caused Our Lord Sun/Christ to take radical action in changing the course of human history. In the case of the baby tamales, Our Lord Sun/Christ caught the people in the act of pitching their live babies into a kettle of boiling water and immediately changed them into monkeys, condemning them to live forever without maize, to subsist on fruits and seeds of the forest. In the case of the abuse of language, as documented later, people sought, through the construction of a great cement stairway (a labor facilitated by having Spanish as a common language), to be too close to Our Lord Sun/Christ, even presuming to reach his domain on the third and highest layer of the heavens. In this narrative, which is of course reminiscent of the biblical Tower of Babel story, Our Lord Sun/Christ could not abide the presumption to power and knowledge that derived from people's having a universal language. (Might this historical memory lie behind the so-called linguistic conservatism of the Chiapas Maya? Might it also lie behind their reluctance to commit themselves, once again, to a common language, Spanish, that caused such difficulty for their ancestors in the past?)

The narrative text belongs to a speech genre known in Tzotzil as True Ancient Narrative (*batz'i antivo k'op*). This type of sacred narrative is regarded as a true account of premodern times, that is, it reports events that are attributed to the First, Second, and Third Creations in their cyclical reckoning of human history. The "truth status" of events reported in this story is comparable to that of the historical present (the Fourth Creation), which is reported in accounts known as True Recent Narrative (*batz'i ?ach' k'op*). Thus, the text that follows has the truth and reality status of events that happened yesterday. Tzotzils carefully discriminate in their native taxonomy of speech genres between invented stories (*hut k'op*, "lies," and *?ixtol k'op*, "jokes") and true stories. The narrative is thus, by Tzotzil reckoning, a true story.

Although I intend to discuss the text at some length after it is presented, three further introductory comments are appropriate. First, the translation is rendered in verse couplets and multiples thereof. This translation style and its rationale are described at length elsewhere (Gossen 1985). Here it suffices to say that Tzotzil oral performance is keyed to dyadic structures of speech. This is explicitly manifest in the hundreds of fixed formal couplets used in the composition of ritual language, prayer, and song. The semantic couplet is also, perhaps by extension, the stylistic "center of gravity" used in the composition and performance of important historical narratives. This dyadic style, which is noted by the numbered verses in the text, is characterized by semantic redundancy, which is marked linguistically in spoken Tzotzil by verbal "punctuation marks," known as *enclitics*. The couplet style, therefore, is central to how Tzotzils tell stories. What is missing, of course, is that, at each pause (that is, at the end of each verse), we, the listeners, would be invited to participate in the storytelling with exclamations like "Is that so?", "No way!", "Really?", "Can it be so?", "I don't believe it!", or "Far out!" The reader must imagine these embellishments while reading the text.

The reader may also be interested in knowing something about the narrator. When I first heard Mr. Méndez Tzotzek's recitation of this narrative in 1979, I lost no time in realizing that it was important, both to him—for it revealed in poignant detail how he viewed his life and circumstances as a landless, poor Tzotzil—and to me—for it provided a local history of language and of the close ties of language to the politics of ethnic subordination of Indians to the dominant Ladino, Spanish-speaking social order. Xun Méndez Tzotzek was in an excellent position to comment on these parts of his community's historical memory, for life had not treated him well. Like so many Chamula Tzotzils, he was born into a densely populated, land-poor rural hamlet where he had no hope of ever making it as a subsistence farmer, although this was the ideal. Until he was 45 years old—in 1979, when he wrote this narrative—he had spent most of this adult life as a migrant day laborer on the coffee plantations and large-scale corn-farming operations of the Pacific lowlands. Although he was able to support his family minimally with this income, he never accumulated savings sufficient to allow him to assume a position in the civil-religious hierarchy of the town center. This disappointment notwithstanding, he nevertheless sought local prestige and modest income through the practice of traditional curing. His career as a shaman failed when he became an alcoholic and could not manage to get through the long prayer recitations that were involved in curing rituals. He had enjoyed a brief interlude of economic success in the late 1950s and early 1960s, when he worked as a paid assistant for U.S. anthropologists. It was in this context that he learned to write Tzotzil. However, alcoholism also compromised this employment, and he resumed his usual pattern of migrant labor to the coffee plantations.

Méndez Tzotzek worked with me as an assistant for many months in 1978 and 1979, and during this time I came to respect him for his keen and poetic intelligence. He was particularly patient and adept at explaining during our translation sessions what was obvious to him but not explicitly stated in his written texts. These discussions are the source of most of the ethnographic notes at the end of this essay.

The narrator is typical of most Tzotzil males of his generation in his inability to cope economically at home and in his inevitable decision to enter the migrant labor market. In this context, like virtually all of his compatriots who were obliged to do the same thing, he experienced firsthand the exploitation and humiliation of being an unskilled Indian day laborer in Ladino-controlled economic and institutional settings.

The bitterness of these memories, together with his carefully considered rationalization and understanding of his experiences with the Ladino world, are evident in what follows.

A third proviso is offered as I present this text. The narrative reads like a Tzotzil rendering of Genesis 11: 1-9, which tells the story of the tower of Babel. Is it a Maya account at all? It is and it isn't, as I discuss later. However, there can be little doubt that the Dominican missionaries must have told their version of this story to the Tzotzils and told it well. "Babel" was the Hebrew rendering of Babylon, and it is well known that this city represented everything reprehensible to the Israelites. The Tower of Babel represented the ultimate claim to temporal and secular power on the part of the Babylonians. They had to be foiled. God did so, according to the Bible, with his mandate for the confusion of tongues. However, the Tzotzil rendering of this story casts the Spaniards and their language, quite unambiguously, as the Babylonians of the New World. What hath God wrought? Listen to this story.

The Great Cement Stairway to Heaven

1. Here is an account of long ago about Ladinos,
     Of where they came from.
2. Long ago there were only Ladinos.
     It happened that Our Father Sun/Christ first gave souls to the Ladinos.
     It happened shortly after he had first molded them from clay.
3. When he had formed the first person,[1]
     Only then did he begin to make the second person.
4. After Our Father Sun had formed them from clay,
     The clay came out looking just like little dolls.
     It was then that he began to give to the clay images their souls.

1. ?oy jun lo?il yu?un kaxlanetik to vo?ne,
     bu talik.
2. veno, ti vo?ne lae ?a? li jkaxlanetik
     ti jtotike.
     ja? la ba?yel la jyak'be xch'ulel li jkaxlanetik
     ti htotike.
     ja? la ba?yel las spat ti ?ach'el.
3. k'alal la ti la spat ti ba?yel vinike,
     ja? to la lik spat ti jun tz'akal vinike.
4. k'alal la ti lah spat ?ach'el ti jtotike,
     k'alal la ti lah xlok' ta chak k'ucha?al santo ti ?ach'ele,
     ja? to la lik yak'be xch'ulel ti ?ach'el.

5. This happened at the time when we were being placed on the earth.
    It was then that Our Lord Sun/Christ molded the clay.
    The first of these images to whom he gave a soul was
    the first whom he had made.
6. He began by rubbing and rubbing the molded image, over and over.
    In this manner, he proceeded to place a soul in the first person.[2]
7. When he had placed a soul in the first person,
    It was then that he began to place a soul in the
    second person, the second one he had formed from clay.
    Just as this image was the second one in Our Father
    Sun's order of creation, so it was the second to
    receive a soul.
8. When Our Father Sun had finished giving these beings their souls,
    That which had formerly been only clay began to change
    into people.
    These were the ones whom Our Father Sun had first
    wrought from clay.
9. When the two images began to become human,
    They walked alike.
    They worked alike.
    They talked alike.
10. Indeed, both people spoke only Spanish.
    Long ago, Spanish was still the only language.
    Tzotzil, the true language, did not yet exist.[3]

5. k'alal la ti meltzajtik ta banomil,
        ti ?ach'el spatoj ti jtotike.
        ja? la ba?yel laj yak'be xch'ulel ti bu ba?yel la spate.
6. lik la sjuch' ta ?ox juch'tael,
        ti k'alal la lik yak'be ti xch'ulel ti ba?yel vinike.
7. k'alal la ti laj yak'be xch'ulel ti jun ba?yel vinike,
        ja? to la lik yak'be xch'ulel ti ju tz'akal vinike,
        ti tz'akal spat ti ?ach'ele.
        ha? la tz'akal laj yak'be xch'ulel ti tz'akal vinike.
8. k'alal la ti lah yak'be sch'ulel ti jtotike,
        lik la pasuk ta viniketik ti ?ach'el to?ox.
        lik spat ti jtotike.
9. k'alal la lik pasuk ta kirsano ti cha?vo? viniketike,
        ko?ol la ta xanavik
        ko?ol la x?abtejik,
        ko?ol ta xk'opojik.
10. ta puru kastiya ti cha?vo? viniketik
        ti vo?ne lae jmoj to?ox la ti k'op ta puru kastiyae.
        mu?yuk to?ox la ti batz'i k'ope.

11. The people began to multiply.
     As they multiplied, they talked alike, in just one
     language, Spanish.
12. Since they had but one common language, the people talked
     among themselves and got ideas.
     "Perhaps we should go to find Our Father Sun up
     above?" they wondered.
13. "But how shall we climb up?
     Any ideas?" they asked.
14. "Come, it would be best to make a stairway.
     We can climb up and find Our Father Sun and talk to
     him," said the people.[4]
15. "But how shall we build a stairway?" they asked.
     "It would be best to build a great stairway of
     cement," said the people.
     So they began to build the cement stairway.
16. As they began to make the great cement stairway,
     Some prepared the mortar,
     Some gathered the stones,
     Some put the stones in place, layer by layer.
17. The great cement stairway was still not finished when they
     ran out of stones.
     "Bring more stones!
     Bring more mortar!

11. lik la boluk ti kirsanoe.
     k'alal la bol ti kirsanoe, jmoj la ta xk'opojik, ta
     puru kastiya.
12. k'alal la ti jmoh ta xk'opojike, lik la snop sk'opik.
     "mi xak'anike ba jtatik la jtotik ta ?ak'ole," xiik
     la.
13. "pero k'usi xkutik chijmuy.
     xana? ?un," xiik la.
14. "ja? lek la? jpastik tek'obal.
     yo? chijmuy ?o jtatik ta k'oponel ti jtotike," xiik la ti kirsanoetike.
15. "pero k'usi xkutik xana? xkak'tik ti tek'obale," xiik la.
     "ja? lek jpastik muyel tek'obal siminto pilal," xiik la ti kirsanoetike.
     lik la spasik ti tek'obal simintoe.
16. k'alal la ti ?ocik ta spasel ti tek'okal pilal simintoe,
     yan la ta sjuy meskla,
     yan la ta sa? talel ton,
     yan la ta slatz muyel ti tone.
17. xkechel to?ox la ta meltzanel muyel ti tek'obal pilal
     simintoe, k'alal la ta xlaj ti tone.
     "tzako me tal ton.
     tzako me tal meskla.

18. The stones are all gone!
    Bring some more!
19. The mortar is all gone!
    Make some more!" they said.
20. "Come build it up!
    The mortar is all gone!
    Come build it up!" they said to each other with full
    understanding,
    For the language that they spoke was the same.[5]
21. The stairway they were building quickly grew upward.
    Different people came every day to help build the
    great cement stairway.
22. They all spoke the same language.
    They understood the same tongue.
23. "Well, it simply won't do for them to speak the same
    language."
    So said Our Father Sun when he started to think about
    it.
24. "Just look! They've almost reached me!" exclaimed Our
    Father Sun.
    "No, it won't do for them to talk alike."
    So said Our Father Sun when he started to think about
    it.

18. laj me ton.
    sa?o xa me tal.
19. laj me meskla.
    juyo xa me talel," xiik la.
20. "?ak'o xa me muyel talel.
    lah xa me meskla.
    ?ak'o xa me muyel talel," xiik la,
    jmoj la ti sk'opik ta xk'opohike.
21. ti tek'obal la ta spasike jlikel la muy yu?unik.
    yantik xa la xmuy yu?unik jujun k'ak'al ta pasel ti
    tek'obal pilal simintoe.
22. ja? la ti jmoj ti sk'opike.
    jmoj la xa?ik ti k'ope.
23. "veno, pero le? ?une mu xtun ma li jmoj sk'opik ?une."
    xa la lik snopik ti jtotike.
24. "k'elavil ?un, sk'an xa xistaik ?un," xi la ti jtotike.
    "mo?ohe, mu xtun li jmoj ta xk'opojike."
    xi la lik snop ti jtotike.

25. "It would be better for me to change their languages.
    We'll see if they understand one another when they
    talk now.
    We'll see if they understand one another when talking
    among themselves about what they are doing," said Our Father Sun.
26. When Our Father Sun changed the languages, the people were
    right in the middle of their work,
    Right when they were in the midst of building the
    great cement stairway.
27. When their language changed, they could no longer
    understand what they were saying to one another.
    As they worked, they no longer understood what their
    companions were asking for.
28. Just as they were in the midst of building the great
    stairway, they abandoned it, half-finished.
    This happened because they no longer understood what
    they were saying to each other.
    This happened because Our Father worked great changes
    in language itself.
29. It happened that he started to oblige us to speak nothing
    but Tzotzil, the true language,
    Those of us who are Indians.
30. It is for that reason that we only speak Tzotzil, the true language,
    Those of us who are Indians.

25. "ja? lek ta jelbe ma sk'opike.
    ta jk'eltik mi xa?ik ta sk'opon sbaik tana un.
    ta jk'eltik mi xa?ik k'alal k'usi ta x?albe sbaike
    k'usi ta spasike," xi la ti jtotike.
26. k'alal la shel ta k'op ti jtotite, syakelik la ta abtel,
    ti k'alal la ti syakelik ta spasik ti tek'obal pilal
    simintoe.
27. k'alal la hel ti k'ope, mu xa la xa?ik k'usi la ta x?albe la
    sbaik.
    ti k'alal la ta s?abtejike, mu xa la xa?ik ti k'usi ta
    sk'anbe sbaik.
28. ti k'alal la ta smeltzanik ti pilal tek'obale, te la kechi
    yu?unik smeltzanel.
    ja? la ti mu xa la sa?ik ti k'usi la ta s?albe sbaike.
    ja? la ti lah sjel ?ep k'op ti jtotike.
29. ja? la ti lik yak' puru batz'i k'op chijk'opojtik,
    ti k'uyepaltik ?inyotike.
30. ja? yu?un la ti ta puru batzi'i k'op chijk'opohotik,
    ti k'uyepal ?inyotik lae.

31. You see, it happened their souls entered their bodies second in the order of creation,
    The bodies of those ancient ones, our forefathers.[6]
32. Those of us who were the children of the second person were separated from the others.
    We were left with the name of 'Indians.'
33. It was different with the first person.
    It was this one who was the first to receive a soul.
    It was this one who was left with the name of Ladino.[7]
    It was this one who received the first language.
34. Everyone still spoke just Spanish in ancient times.
    That is why it happened that Ladinos are also called 'Spaniards.'
35. They speak only Castilian.
    That is why we are obliged to learn Spanish.[8]
36. You see, it was the first language that Our Father Sun assigned to the ancestors long ago.
    It is for this reason that there is but one common language, Spanish.
    All are thus obliged to learn Spanish.
37. You see, the Ladinos speak only Spanish.
    That was because Our Father Sun first gave souls to the Ladinos.

31. xavil la ja? la tz'akal ?och xch'ulel,
    ba?yel totik ku?untik la ti vo?nee.
32. ja? yu?un la kich'tik ch'akel ti k'u la yepal snich'nab ti tz'akal vinike.
    ha? la kom ta ?inyo sbi.
33. yan la ti ba?yel.
    ?och xch'ulel ti ba?yel vinike.
    ja? la kom ta kaxlan.
    ja? la yich' komel ti ba?yel k'op.
34. ti puru kastiya to?ox la ti xk'opojik ti vo?nee.
    ja? yu?un la ti ja? la kom ta j?espanyol sbi
    li kaxlanetike.
35. ja? ti ja? ta xk'opohik ta puru kastiya.
    ja? yu?un la ti ja? la ta persa ta jchantik li
    kastiyae.
36. xavil la ti vo?ne ja? la ba?yel k'op la jyak' komel ti
    jtotik vo?nee.
    ja? yu?un ja? no?ox la jun k'op, kastiya.
    ta persa ta x?ich' chanel li kastiyae.
37. xavil la li jkaxlanetike ja? la puru kastiya ta xk'opojik.
    ja? ti ja? ba?yel la jyak'be xch'ulel ti jkaxlan ti
    jtotike.

38. When Our Father Sun changed the languages, people began to
    split up.
    They scattered;
    Some went to the lowlands,
    Others, like ourselves, scattered here and there in
    the highlands.
39. Those who went off together were those who had the
    same language.
    The different groups were divided according to those
    who had the same language.
40. So it is true that different groups do not understand
    each other's languages.
    That is why we remain separate, very separate, those
    of us who still speak Tzotzil, the true language,
    today.
41. In all lands there are those of us who speak our native
    languages,
    All over the earth.
42. It is different with the Ladinos; they all speak but one
    language.
    They speak Spanish.
43. As for those who are Indians, they speak only their native
    languages.
    This is true of all native peoples.

38. k'alal la ti jel ti k'ope, lik la xch'ak sbaik ti
    kirsanoetike.
    tanijik la;
    yan la ?olon,
    yan la ?ak'ol la jbatikuk.
39. ja? la jmoj la xch'ak sbaik ti bu ko?ol ti sk'opike.
    slekoj la xch'ak sbaik ti bu ko?ol ti sk'opike.
40. ja? la ti mu la xa?ibe sba sk'opike.
    ja? yu?un la tana ti sleklekoj ti batz'i k'optik komem
    hasta ?ora.
41. ta jujun lum ti ?oy jbatz'i k'optik,
    ta skotol banomile.
42. k'ajomal jkaxlanetik jun no?ox k'op.
    ta xk'opojik ta kastiya.
43. k'u yepal puru ?indijena ta puru batz'i k'op to sk'opojik.
    skotol ?indijena.

44. So then, when the people split up long ago,
     The different groups of people went separately to find
     land to build their houses.
     So it was that the Ladinos went separately to look for
     land where they could settle.
45. So it was that they found their homelands.
     There they began to build their houses.
     There they multiplied.
46. When they had multiplied, it seems to me that the Ladinos
     began to reflect upon who they were and what they should
     do.
     Indeed, the correct name of those whom we call
     "Ladinos" ought to be "Spaniards."
47. Now, then, soon thereafter, the Spaniards began to harass
     the native people.
     They began to oblige them to do forced labor.
48. When the Indians worked, they were not given rest periods
     when they grew tired.
     Although they were thirsty, they did not permit them
     to drink water.

44. veno, k'alal la ti la sch'ak sbaik ti kirsonoetik to vo?ne
     lae,
     bat la sa? yosilik bu la xu? spas naik to hchop la ti
     kirsanoe.
     jech la ti jkaslanetike slekoj la bat sa yosilik bu
     xu? snakik.
45. veno, sta la ti yosilike.
     te la lik spas naik.
     te la bolik.
46. k'alal la ti bolike, lik la snopik ti jkaxlanetik,
     xkaltike.
     pero li sbi la ta kastiya j?espanyol la sbi.
47. veno, ti j?espanyole lik la yutilan ti kirsano ?indijenae.
     lik la tzakik ta ?abtel.
48. k'alal la ti ta x?abtej ti ?inyoe, mu la x?ak'bat xkux
     k'alal xlube.
     ?ak'o la chak' yuch' ya?i ?o? mu la x?ak' yuch? ti
     ?o?e.

49. Only when their work time was over could they rest from
their labor.
      And if they chanced to fall asleep during their
      assigned work time, they were sure to receive a
      sound beating.
      This was their fate if the Indian workers should fall
      asleep.
50. This was what happened to them in the daily round of their
labor.
      The Spaniards watched over them and tormented them a
      lot while they were working.
51. Their hateful ways carried over into the manner in which
they feigned to "baptize" people.
      They didn't really baptize them in the churches.
      There *were* no churches.
52. Instead, what really happened was that they did nothing
more than brand them, just like horses.
      That was how the Spaniards of long ago humiliated and
      mistreated the Indians.
53. Soon, Our Father Sun felt that there had been enough of
this.
      He didn't want us to be abused and hurt by whippings,
      Nor to be humiliated by threats and scorn from the
      Spaniards.

49. ja? to la mi sta ti ?orae, ja? to la ta xkux ta ?abtel.
      pero k'alal ta ti ta x?abteje, mi vayi la jlikeluk
      ta ?abtel lek la jun majel ta x?ich'.
      k'alal mi vayi la ta ?abtel ti ?inyo vinike.
50. jech la jujun k'ak'al la spasbat.
      ti ?ilbaj ta x?utilan la tajmek ti k'alal la ta x?abteje.
51. jech la xtok k'alal la ta x?ich'ik ?o?e.
      mu?yuk la bu ta x?ich'ik ?o? ta ch'ulna.
      ch'abal la ch'ulna.
52. k'ajomal la ta x?ak'bat smarkail chak k'ucha?al ka?.
      ?ilbaj to?ox la yutilan ti ?indijenaetik ti
      ?espanyoletik ti vo?ne lae.
53. ?entonse ta?lo xa?i ti jtotik.
      mu la sk'an ti ?abol la jbatik ta majel,
      ti ?abol la jbatik ta ?utel yu?un ti j?espanyole.

54. When Our Father Sun felt that there had been enough of this, the warfare began:

> The Spaniards began to make war with the Indians.
> It was they who made war.
> Indeed, it was a war that lasted for perhaps four years.
> It was they, the Spaniards, who made war.

55. It was hard to solve these problems.

> The one who managed to do so was one who suffered through the fighting and triumphed.

56. It was Miguel Hidalgo who prevailed and caused peace to come.[9]

> He stopped the old custom of branding us as though we were horses.
> He began to show them how to baptize us in the church.
> He began to show us how to pray to our Father Sun.
> He began to tell us what we should say in prayers.
> He began to show us how to work.
> He began to show us how to read and write.
> He began to show us everything.

54. k'alal la ti ta?lo xa?i ti jtotike, lik la ti letoe.

> lik la spaik leto xchi?uk ?inyo ti j?espanyole.
> ja? la spasik ti leto.
> laj la spasik chanvikuk ?a?vil ti puru leto lae.
> ja? la spasik ti letoe.

55. vokol la meltzaj ti k'ope.

> ja? la meltzaj yu?un ti kuch yu?un pas leto.

56. ti mikel ?idadkoe, ja? la la skomtzan ta lek ti k'ope.

> ja? la ta xch?ay ti ta to?ox la xkich' jmarkailtik.
> ja? lik yak' ?iluk ta xkich'tik ?o? ta ch'ulna.
> lik la yak' ?iluk ta jk'opontik jtotik.
> lik la yal k'uxi ta jpastik resal.
> lik la yak' ?iluk k'uxi chij?abtej.
> lik la yak' ?iluk chanvun.
> lik la yak' ?iluk skotol.

57. It was Miguel Hidalgo who accomplished these good works:
    It was he who settled the conflict a long time ago.
    It was he who left the problems well solved.
    It was he who hunted and chased the Spaniards back to
    their own ancestral homeland where they really
    belonged.
    It was he who forced them to return to Spain, as their
    country is called.
58. That is why they celebrate his fiesta every year on the
    16th of September.
    That is when Don Miguel Hidalgo was shot to death.
    You see, he left the earth in good condition long ago.

57. k'usitikuk ?abtelel ti mikel ?idadkoe.
    ja? la smeltz'an ti k'op vo?ne lae.
    ja? la la skomtzan ta lek ti k'ope.
    ja? la snutzik sutel to j?espanyoletike ti bu la sta
    ti yosilik ti j?espanyol ti vo?ne lae.
    ja? la ti sutik batel ti ta ?aspanya, sbi ti lume.
58. ja? yu?un la ti ta xlok' sk'inal ta jujun ?a?vil, ta
    vaklajuneb semiembre.
    ti k'usi la ti cham ta tuk' ti don mikel ?idadko lae.
    xavil ja? la la skomtzan ta lek ti banomil ti vo?ne
    lae.

A MORAL EXEGESIS OF ETHNIC AND
LINGUISTIC SUBORDINATION

The reader will undoubtedly have noted themes in this text that link it to the biblical text of the tower of Babel. The narrator also reveals to the listener/reader that he is a keen observer of his own life and times with regard to the asymmetries of Indian and Ladino economic power and social prestige. He is also clearly conversant with Mexico's own mytho/historical accounts of its own history. All of these constitute clearly identifiable and easily understandable strands of historical memory that enter into the composition of the narrative.

Other themes, however, do not lie so close to the surface and are not so easy to comprehend. In particular, although it is never stated here (for it belongs to other accounts of Chamula history), a fundamentally Maya vision of cyclical time and moral evolution informs this entire narrative. I refer to the startling placement of Ladinos and Indians, Spanish and Tzotzil, in precisely the opposite chronological order from that which we assume to be common knowledge.

Don't all of us, Indians and Westerners, know perfectly well that thousands of years of Indian civilization preceded the Spanish invasion and conquest of what is now Mexico? And that no one in the New World had heard of Spanish until it was violently foisted upon Amerindians as a colonial language? Doesn't this muddling of chronology come across as a naive conflation of stories from "our own tradition" that Tzotzils don't quite get right? I answer "yes" and "no" to all of the above, for all knowledge, including our own, is situated in particular historical contexts and social constructs. The Tzotzil Maya world was and is different from our own in terms of the rhythm of historical process. Ours has a dominant linear, progressive theme, with occasional cyclical moments that startle us. For example, the press reminding us of Nazi and Allied parallels to what is happening and not happening in Bosnia. The Maya world, in contrast, is keyed to a basically cyclical vision of historical process, with a secondary progressive, linear theme; the structure of current events inevitably recapitulates the pattern of the past to provide the opportunity to correct past mistakes.

Cyclical time reckoning thus allows for, even invites, human progress if it is understood that old structural grids regulate, condition, and limit this progress. These structural grids also demand a due placement of new historical "others"—such as the Spaniards—in a moral slot that suits them. The narrative text performs this historical surgery quite effectively. Spaniards are banished to the very distant past, a chronological place that renders them morally inferior to, and prior to, Indians in the order of creation.

Maya-derived four-part cyclical time does not posit a mere repetition of former time periods. There is, rather, an orthogenetic thrust, a kind of "moral progress," that underwrites the unfolding of historical experience. In this sense, present-day Chamula Tzotzils believe themselves to be at the cutting edge, the frontier, as it were, of moral progress. This is why they unabashedly classify themselves as the "true people" and their language as the "true language." At one point in their history, as recorded in this text, they shared important aspects (notably the Spanish language and associated human arrogance) with Ladinos. Ladino culture, therefore, figures as a part of their own ancestral lineage, in particular a primitive phase of it. They shared, in times past, the moral weaknesses of their present adversaries. They have "progressed"; Ladinos have not. Ladinos (and, indeed all white Europeans) figure not exactly as ethnic others, but as depraved, primitive versions of themselves.

The theme of relegating morally inferior beings to their own ancestral past rings as a powerful leitmotif to virtually all of Chamula cosmological and historical reckoning, including the ritual representation of these ideas (cf. Gossen 1993). For example, the crime of infanticide, discussed earlier, was not the sin of ethnic others, but of their own ancestors; this crime is dutifully represented ritually in the preparation, exchange, and consumption of "baby tamales" in their annual ritual of solar renewal, known as the "Festival of Games" (cf. Gossen 1986). This ritual constitutes a great historical drama of the four creations of human experience; virtually all of the barbarous behavior and immoral beings, real and imagined, who have crossed their paths over the ages figure as motifs in this festival. These events and beings include the Spanish conquest, Spanish soldiers, Mexican soldiers, Guatemalan soldiers, transvestite campfollowers, monkeys, demons, Ladinos, and European tourists. All of these motifs are placed in their own journey through the trials of moral progress, and they themselves play these parts and reenact these events, which are, for them, morally reprehensible. They triumph over this immoral landscape of the past in the climax of the ritual, which consists of purging these immoral aspects of their lineage in a ritual race through a path of burning thatch grass on the fourth day of the festival. This path of fire represents the solar orbit; in it and through it, the Chamula actors purge the negative aspects of their past and emerge purified, exonerated, and changed from the depravity of their own past. They ritually create a new present in which they are the victors and their adversaries (who also reside within their own genealogy and consciousness as a people) are vanquished.

Language figures prominently in the symbolic content of the ritual I have just described. The monkey characters and other immoral beings speak Spanish, in a manner that can only be described as farcical mockery. Indeed, the charter document that is recited during numerous episodes of the Festival of Games is called the "Spanish Letter." Recited in Spanish by a ritual personage known as the *pixcal* (from Sp. *fiscal*, "public prosecutor" or "district attorney"), this is a call to war, which calls upon the Chamulas themselves to engage, as Spanish soldiers, in the military destruction of their own community. It is precisely this theme of foreign military invasion of Chamula that makes up the nonstop ritual activity of the three-and-a-half days that precede the firewalk. Involved here are not only Spanish soldiers and the theme of the Conquest, but also Guatemalan and Mexican soldiers, specifically named, who were leaders in wars of the nineteenth century. All of these adversaries spoke Spanish, and their human and moral qualities were dubious at best. For example, the common Norway rat—predator, scavenger, and bad citizen par excellence—is known in modern Tzotzil as *karansa*, named after Venustiano Carranza, Revolutionary hero and president of Mexico.

It can thus be seen that the attribution of Spanish language and Ladino ethnicity to the first-made of Our Lord Sun Christ's creation is an elaborate and quite elegant joke; Ladinos were destined to be primitives and must therefore work harder, even harder than Indians, to overcome this affliction.

While the immorality of Spanish-speakers and Ladino culture is unambiguously and scathingly reported in both the Festival of Games and in the text just cited, it is also true that the text speaks charitably of the "good Ladino," Miguel Hidalgo, who is in fact recognized by all Mexicans as the "founding father" of the whole nation. At this point, Méndez Tzotzek seems to buy into Mexican public mythology about its own past in acknowledging that Spaniards (*gachupines*) were in fact evil and that they did in fact exploit Indians mercilessly. Furthermore, one of their own (i.e., Hidalgo) realized that this was so and acted forcibly to correct it.

Thus, Ladinos are not, as an ethnic category, relegated to unredeemable evil. They clearly have in their own genealogy leaders who are capable of acting on behalf of all Mexicans, Ladinos and Indians. It is surely this same logic that accounts for the presence of white gods and saints, including Our Lord Sun Christ himself, as redeeming, compassionate, creative beings in Chamula historical reckoning. Indeed, in deepest antiquity, the creative force of life itself is attributed to deities with shining, white, radiant faces. The problem is that most Ladinos have "forgotten" this opportunity for goodness and redemption in their own lineage, preferring instead to remain mired in their own primitive past, fossilized somewhere between the very dawn of creation and the present. Undoubtedly this same logic makes the mestizo Revolutionary hero Emiliano Zapata and Subcomandante Marcos, also a white Spanish-speaking Mexican, plausible as symbolic and real paladins of the Maya Zapatistas' cry for social justice in our time.

In conclusion, therefore, Chamula Tzotzils and perhaps also all Indian people in Chiapas recognize that their own language and ethnicity share important historical experiences with Ladinos. Ladinos thus have the opportunity not only to become moral beings but also to recognize that they, the Ladinos, share a past with Indians. Neither should be expected to give up the identities embodied in their languages, for as the text tells us, this diversity was part of the creator's plan. Perhaps there is an opening for dialogue here. The final passage in Méndez Tzotzek's text offers a moving appeal for redemption and reconciliation in the centuries-old Mexican chronicle of ethnic, class, and linguistic conflict. The conciliator is not a parochial Indian hero or god; he is Miguel Hidalgo, mestizo parish priest and national hero, one of the central figures in Mexico's own story of itself. Méndez Tzotzek, and through him, Hidalgo, seem to be reminding Mexicans that their diverse languages and cultures belong to all Mexicans as the heritage of their great nation.

NOTES

1. I choose "person" to translate *vinik* ("man," also "twenty"), for although it literally means "man" in contrast to "woman" (*antz*), it is clearly meant here to indicate the general human condition, as in "humankind." Dennis Tedlock solved this problem another way in his recent book on the ancient and modern Quiché (see Tedlock 1993), by translating the Quiché cognate of this word as "vigesinal being," for the attribute of having twenty digits is a diagnostic feature of people in general, as well as being the word for "man" and "twenty."

2. The emphasis on the placement of the soul (Tz. *ch'ulel*) in the newly created being occurs here because it is the most powerful of the three types of spirits or souls that all humans possess. It is responsible for the human capacity for speech and language, among other things. The other two souls are the junior and senior aspects of the animal soul companion (see Gossen 1994). The *ch'ulel* is the invisible essence of the tongue and is the first spiritual attribute each person receives from Our Father Sun and Saint Jerome upon conception. It is also the last spiritual attribute to depart from the body at death. It goes on to live forever in the underworld after death and is said to return to the world of the living each year on the eve of All Saint's Day (Tz. *k'in santo*), November 1. The *ch'ulel* therefore is responsible for human spiritual essence and is manifested in the human capacity for language.

3. *batz'i k'op*, "the true language," is the Tzotzil word for Tzotzil. The word *batz'i* also means "true," "right," "genuine." Thus, a measure of linguistic chauvinism is built into the very name of the language.

4. The placement of this tower in the cosmos was unclear to me as we translated this text. Figure 2.1 is a reproduction of a pencil sketch of the tower drawn by Mr. Tzotzek. The labels on the drawing were placed by the narrator in Tzotzil. These are identified with numbers, which correspond with the translations in the caption. Otherwise, the drawing is exactly as it appeared in my original working text.

5. This series of emotional phrases (verses 17-20) serves to emphasize that all did indeed speak a single language and were thus capable of communicating and working together.

6. The logic of this arrangement—Ladinos first, Indians second, in order of language acquisition—is consonant with the Chamula view that saints, who are the common ancestors of all people, are Ladinos. Like saints, Ladinos have greater power than Indians in most spheres of contemporary life. Furthermore, nearly all Chamula images of the saints, as well as of Our Father Sun and Our Mother Moon, have fair skin and non-Indian features. Paradoxically, it is nevertheless true that Chamulas believe themselves to be morally superior to Ladinos, and that it is Tzotzil, not Spanish, which is the "true language."

7. *kaxlan* is the Tzotzil word that means Ladino, or bearer of the Spanish-speaking Mexican cultural tradition. It comes from *castellano*, which refers to Castilian, or the standard Spanish language. Thus, ethnic and linguistic identity are explicitly tied together in Chamula thinking.

8. For several decades, it has been the goal of Mexican Indian primary education to teach Spanish to Indian children, thereby facilitating their participation in Mexican national culture. This policy is called *castellanización* and has generally used Indian language texts only for elementary teaching of the idea of sounds in relation to written symbols. After the first few years, Spanish is "ideally" the language of instruction. Teaching of literacy in Indian languages has never been a specific goal of Indian education in modern Mexico.

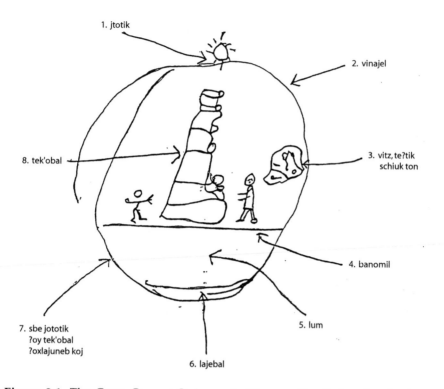

1. jtotik
2. vinajel
3. vitz, te?tik
   schiuk ton
8. tek'obal
4. banomil
5. lum
7. sbe jototik
   ?oy tek'obal
   ?oxlajuneb koj
6. lajebal

Figure 2.1 The Great Cement Stairway to Heaven. Pencil drawing by Xun Méndez Tzotek, traced and enlarged. Translations of captions: 1. Our Lord Sun/Christ. 2. Heaven. 3. A mountain with forest and stones. 4. The surface of the earth. 5. The earth itself. 6. The underworld. 7. The path of Our Lord Sun/Christ. There are thirteen steps or levels (above and below the surface of the earth). 8. The stairway.

9. Father Miguel Hidalgo is also acknowledged by Mexican written history as being the father of Mexican Independence. He gave the famous "Grito de Dolores" ("Long live Our Lady of Guadalupe! Down with bad government! Death to the Spaniards!") on September 16, 1810, which launched the Mexican Independence Movement against Spain. This date is celebrated as Mexico's Independence Day. It may be of some importance to Chamula historical reckonings (though it is not mentioned in this Chamula text) that Miguel Hidalgo was a parish priest who was close to poor village people. He felt a special affinity for mestizos and Indians and in many ways, both theological and intellectual, distanced himself from the Spanish *criollo* establishment. Among other attributes, he learned and used in his parish ministry a number of Indian languages. These aspects of his background, according to fact and legend as recorded in Mexican school textbooks and history books, contributed to his sensitivity to the problems of the poor and oppressed in colonial Mexico. Condemned to death as a subversive, he faced a firing squad on July 31, 1811.

REFERENCES

Aguirre Beltrán, Aguirre. 1967. *Regiones de refugio: El desarrollo de la comunidad y el proceso dominical en Mestizo América*. Mexico City: Instituto Nacional Indigenista Interamericano.

Gossen, Gary H. 1976. "Language as Ritual Substance." In William Samarin, ed., *Language in Religious Practice*. Rowley, Mass.: Newbury House, 40–60.

——. 1985. "Tzotzil Literature." In M. S. Edmonson, ed., *Supplement to the Handbook of Middle American Indians*. Vol. 3, *Literature*. Austin: University of Texas Press, 64–106.

——. 1986. "The Chamula Festival of Games: Native Macroanalysis and Social Commentary in a Maya Carnival." In Gary H. Gossen, ed., *Symbol and Meaning Beyond the Close Community: Essays in Mesoamerican Ideas*. Albany: Institute for Mesoamerican Studies, State University of New York at Albany, 227–54.

——. 1993. "The Other in Chamula Tzotzil Cosmology and History: Reflections of a Kansan in Chiapas." *Cultural Anthropology* 8(4): 443–75.

——. 1994. "From Olmecs to Zapatistas: A Once and Future History of Souls." *American Anthropologist* 96(3): 553–70.

Lomnitz-Adler, Claudio. 1992. *Exits from the Labyrinth: Culture and Ideology in Mexican National Space*. Berkeley and Los Angeles: University of California Press.

Modiano, Nancy. 1973. *Indian Education in the Chiapas Highlands*. New York: Holt, Rinehart and Winston.

Tedlock, Dennis. 1993. *Breath on the Mirror: Mythic Voices and Visions of the Living Maya*. San Francisco: Harper San Francisco.

3

The Deficits of History: Terms of Violence in an Arapaço Myth Complex from the Brazilian Northwest Amazon

Janet M. Chernela
and
Eric J. Leed

How is a collective identity generated and preserved in the vicissitudes of population dispersal and decimation? The myth cycle of Unurato answers this question, placing the figure of the white man in a native context of related identities. It provides some evidence about the way in which categories of personhood are defined by the Eastern Tukanoan Arapaço of Brazil. The myth is posed against a historical treatment of the Arapaço in order to reveal some of the ways that native systems of meaning render coherent the experience of a people who both lived—in Hugh-Jones's words, suffered—that history and constructed it.

Located on the lower Uaupés River in Brazil, the Arapaço are one of approximately fifteen named, patrilineal descent groups of the Eastern Tukanoan family in the northwest Amazon. The "language groups" of the Uaupés form a single, integrated network, united by kin ties and marriage, since the rule of language group exogamy requires that persons always marry into a different language group. Each group regards its own members as kin, and others as in-laws or "in-laws of in-laws" (Chernela 1993). Although the Tukanoan groups of the Uaupés basin

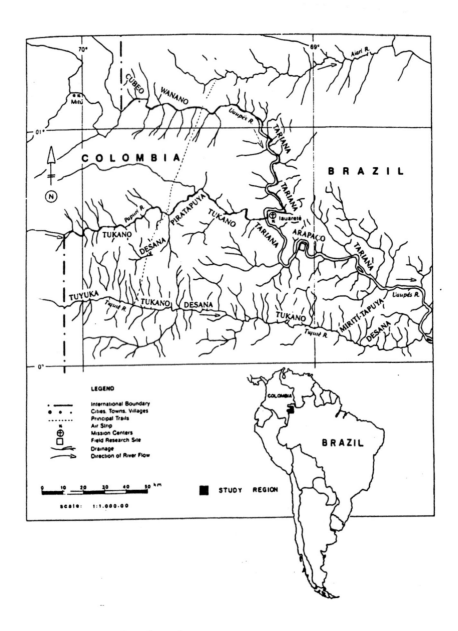

Figure 3.1 Map of study region

share many common features, the Arapaço depart from the pattern in significant ways.

First, the Arapaço remain one of the few exogamous descent groups that do not speak a distinct, identifying language. Language is an important source of social identity for speakers of Eastern Tukanoan languages, as it marks membership in a major descent group. Relatedly, brotherhood is traditionally expressed and demonstrated through common language. On this basis, researchers working with Eastern Tukanoan peoples have referred to the "tribes" or nations of the Uaupés as "language groups" (Jackson 1974, 1983), a convention also followed here. The Arapaço are exceptional among Eastern Tukanoan peoples, however, for they no longer speak their own language. In place of their traditional language[1] the Arapaço now speak Tukano or Portuguese. Yet they continued to identify themselves as one descent group, putatively related through a founding ancestor.

The myth cycle of Unurato narrates the position of the Arapaço between an upriver linguistic "homeland" and a downriver, impinging Western world. It narrates a past, a present, and a future held in suspension.

A BRIEF HISTORY OF THE ARAPAÇO

In the seventeenth and eighteenth centuries, the Spanish and Portuguese competed to establish and hold possessions in the Amazon basin. When, in the mid-eighteenth century, the Spanish moved southward into the Rio Negro system, the Portuguese proceeded northward through the same system in order to "expel the foreign presence." The Portuguese dispatched reconnaissance troops as far upriver as the Uaupés affluent of the Rio Negro. There troops were halted by a set of impassable cataracts—a site known as Ipanorê—then occupied by the Arapaço Indians. The Arapaço were likely the first Uaupés tribe to bear the impact of contact with the white world.

Despite the fact that the explicit intent of the expeditions was to remove "foreign invaders," the result of the expeditions was in fact the removal of large numbers of native inhabitants from the region. Early contacts opened channels of outmigration and recruited native labor. One chronicler estimated that, in the ten years between 1740 and 1750, twenty thousand Indians from the Upper Rio Negro and its tributaries were enslaved (Szentmartonyi, trans. in Wright 1981). The continued presence of Spanish militia in the nearby Orinoco and Upper Rio Negro valleys further inspired the Portuguese to fortify their positions, and in the following decade a number of military outposts were built. One of these, São Gabriel da Cachoeira, established in 1761, was situated below the confluence of the Uaupés on the Rio Negro, adjacent to the area occupied by the Arapaço.

Thus began the *descimentos* (literally, "the descent"). By 1779, Indians were recruited by force to the newly established posts, such as São Gabriel, in order to work for colonists in factories for the production of cloth, indigo, and brick and on large plantations of indigo, coffee, and cotton (Lopes de Sousa 1959, 204). During the especially brutal period between 1780 and 1820, the native population of the Rio Negro was ravaged, enslaved, and dispersed by such recruiting campaigns. By 1820 the indigenous population of the Rio Negro was dramatically reduced (Lopes de Sousa 1959, 205).

According to both Arapaço informants and a number of researchers (Azevedo 1933; Bruzzi 1977; Giacone 1949), the Arapaço were early inhabitants of the lower Uaupés, occupying its margins from the mouth to the Japurá River before the arrivals of other Tukanoan and Arawakan-speaking peoples. Bruzzi (1977), Coudreau (1887), and Lopes de Sousa (1959) all report a once-thriving population, yet when Koch-Grünberg encountered the Arapaço in 1904 he found two desolate longhouses with only 100 persons in all (1909, 20).[2] Bruzzi (1977) attributes the decline in Arapaço population to two principal factors: (1) the removal of males by whites to labor in regions outside the Uaupés basin and (2) the seizure of women as wives and concubines.[3]

This dramatic reduction of population was intensified by the international market for Amazonian rubber. From 1853 on, rubber surpassed all other Rio Negro forest products, monopolizing all extractive labor for the next 90 years. The rubber camps on the middle Rio Negro were particularly lucrative, and São Gabriel functioned as one of the bases from which patrons recruited indigenous labor for temporary service. Once outside the indigenous area, many Arapaço settled in cities. Some became itinerant workers, alternating between temporary residence in the rubber camps and home villages. Many others never returned.

The rubber years brought with them several forms of enforced labor. Reports from the then Indian Protection Service (SPI: Serviço de Proteção aos Indios), written between 1925 and 1951, document several practices of enforced labor associated with the Upper Rio Negro rubber camps. The first practice was to retain laborers by manipulating them into an indebtedness from which they could not be freed. The practice is documented in detail for the Upper Rio Negro in official SPI reports from 1929 to 1941. A second widespread practice was the illegal capture of Indians to work in the more undesirable flooded or malarial rubber collection areas. Rubber continued to be the principal export from the Rio Negro Valley until 1950.

Following a pattern now two centuries old, the rubber era took many people from the Uaupés region, but brought in few long-term outsiders.

After the decline in demand for Amazonian rubber, São Gabriel continued to function as the base of white commerce and bureaucracy. There was little motivation for white settlement in the Uaupés itself, and, except for missionaries and itinerant traders, whites rarely ventured into the area.

No factor more insidiously deranged native identities than the forcible resettlement of Indians to centers where they were schooled in Portuguese language and culture, trained and encouraged in techniques of intensive agriculture, policed, and generally educated in the ways of the whites. The government provided incentives to Indians who would speak Portuguese and take Portuguese surnames (Burns 1980, 48). The Arapaço were moved into such a controlled settlement in 1790 when André Fernandes de Sousa, the parish priest of São Gabriel, gathered Arapaço and other tribal inhabitants from the lower Uaupés into a single large settlement on the island of Ipanorê (Aranha 1907).

A former Arapaço center, Ipanorê was to become the focus of mission and trade activities for the next two centuries. It offered several strategic advantages to administrators, missionaries, and traders. First, its turbulent waterfall was a barrier to deep-draft river boats so that weighty cargos such as construction equipment or agricultural supplies could reach Ipanorê but proceed no further. The import of such technology to Ipanorê allowed the development of a large settlement to which Indians could be enticed with trade goods or brought through forceful resettlement. Ipanorê was a desirable mission center for a second reason. It was considered to be the site where the founding ancestor of all Eastern Tukanoan tribes, an underwater vessel with attributes of anaconda and canoe, surfaced from the river waters and deposited on land the first ancestors (called *Pamori Mahsa*) of the Uaupés peoples. Missionaries and priests could take advantage of this preexisting sacrality of place, overlaying one symbolic system with another.

Ipanorê became so large a settlement that one writer called the Ipanorê of 1883 "the capital of all Uaupés and Paporí villages" (Coudreau, translated in Aranha 1907, 33) and described it this way:

> Ipanorê . . . was the village that possessed the largest number of houses and inhabitants. Besides the church, that was in architecture and proportion the largest and best of any on this river, it also had a cemetery, school, missionary residence, and a jail (Coudreau, in Aranha 1907, 58, author's translation from the Portuguese)

Such settlements were the crucibles of tribal identities. The consolidation of native populations into such large settlements, in order to facilitate increased production, policing, and education, required a specification of ethnicities. Sibs of diverse language groups were moved to inhabit the same settlement. For example, the mission-created settlement at Ipanorê contained the Arawakan-speaking Tariano with members of several language groups of the Eastern Tukanoan family: Tukano and Piratapuia as well as Arapaço. The Arapaço eventually abandoned their language for the lingua franca of Tukano and for the official Portuguese tongue.

In place of their traditional language, known as Konea (Arapaço is a *lingua geral* translation of Konea, and the name by which the group is known in the region and literature), the Arapaço now speak Tukano or Portuguese. Yet they continue to identify themselves as one exogamous descent group, putatively related through a founding ancestor. In remaining exogamous, yet not linguistically distinct, the Arapaço are unique among Eastern Tukanoan peoples.

The loss of an identifying language is a crucial factor in the reading of the myth of Unurato. For Eastern Tukanoans, it is language that marks group affiliation and identity. Following Tukanoan reasoning, the designation "whiteman" refers not to color but to speech; it might be better translated as "speaker of white's language." If you are what you speak (the speech that you "give"), as the Tukanoans believe, then the loss of the Arapaço language and the acquisition of Portuguese, the language of whites, is critical in the transformations of Arapaço identity.

For speakers of Eastern Tukanoan languages, language maintains distinctions. The traditional division of language as marker of descent divides the social unit into those who speak father's tongue (members of one's own patrilineal descent group and speakers of one's own language) from those who speak mother's tongue (the language of one's affines), and those who speak "other" languages. This last group is considered to be in-laws-of-in-laws. Within this tripartite system, the universe of kin and affines is infinitely expandable.

Now that mother and father speak the same language, an essential distinction has been obscured. Moreover, whereas the Arapaço language once distinguished Arapaço speakers from all others, this linguistic indicator of uniqueness and difference is lost. As speakers of Portuguese and Tukano, the Arapaço are cultural mediators. This, it will be shown, is the role played by Unurato in the myth; he embodies mediations between the Arapaço and a variety of others.

The different exogamous "language groups" of the Uaupés recount many of the same myths. For example, according to a sacred myth shared by all the Uaupés societies, mentioned earlier, the first people emerged from a primordial anaconda who swam up the Rio Negro to the Uaupés with the rising waters. Arriving at the headwaters, the primordial "canoe," as the anaconda is called, turned round, and from its body emerged the first ancestors of each language group.

The founding ancestor of a language group in the Uaupés basin is called both "grandfather" and "the people's oldest brother" (Chernela 1982). He is also called "Head," a term that refers not only to his leadership role but also to the anatomical head that leads and "speaks for" the body. On another level, the term refers to the head of the ancestral anaconda, from which the descendants of the earliest (called "first") ancestors originated. Members of each language group conceptualize their relation to one another by virtue of the founding ancestor.

Such "heads" or leaders are perceived by the Arapaço as necessary to the continuity and integrity of the tribe. It is thought that a group's vitality or life force (yeheripona) depends upon the ongoing rebirth of the first ancestors. Only then and through proper "sitting" (continuity over generations in the same locality), breathing, and speaking in the place where the ancestors first emerged can the group persist. Settlement relocation disrupts the correspondence between descent and locality, dividing residents into "those in place" and "those who wander" or "mix with others" (Chernela 1988a, 2003).

In another variation, the snake-canoe contains the patrilineal descent groups, or sibs, that comprise a single "language group." The anaconda represents the body of the brotherhood and each sib a constituent segment of that body. The Arapaço recall fourteen member sibs, although only one of these survives today. The names and ranks of the missing groups are remembered and kept alive through sib litanies and legends recounting their demise. The one surviving Arapaço sib is said to have subdivided, producing 10 sub-sibs.[4]

In a Barasana myth recorded by Hugh-Jones (1988), whiteman and Indian share a single ancestor, Waribi, and emerged in sequential order from an ancestral anaconda. By Eastern Tukanoan reckoning, this common progenitor-anaconda would render the whiteman a kinsman or affine, but as Hugh-Jones (1988) points out, the whiteman's violence precludes any such relationship.

THE MYTH

Although the following text constitutes a single speech performance, we refer heuristically to "parts," where part 1 occurs within the Uaupés region and part 2 outside it. Part 1 is recounted as a totality by all of the tribes in the Uaupés basin.[5] But the Arapaço, who are alone in considering the prominent culture hero their grandfather, continue the myth so that it contains several unusual episodes that take the hero out of the Uaupés basin and bring him into contact with whites. Variants of part 2 are reported from Portuguese-speaking populations along the lower Amazon River, but, apart from the Arapaço version, we have not found the myth among other Eastern Tukanoan groups in the Uaupés. Moreover, only the Arapaço, to our knowledge, regard the water snake as an ancestor. This last elaboration and its meaning to the Arapaço are the particular focus of our concern here. Part 1 recounts the circumstances of Unurato's birth as the offspring of an illegitimate union between a supernatural snake and a human. In part 2 the hero emigrates downriver, out of the native area, and into a city where he is shot by a white man. The "white" in the myth is described as a "Manuara," a person from Manaus.

Text Translation and Organization

The text presented here was told by C. Carvalho[6] in Portuguese in the Arapaço village of Parana Juca (Dia Phosa Yu'uro). Author's inserts include proper names where they are not found in the original and bracketed explanatory material, so that the myth can be easily followed by an audience not familiar with it. Some detail and repetition have been eliminated.

The Myth of Unurato

Part 1

This water snake [anaconda], Dia Pino, our grandfather, lived under the water in a stream across from Loiro in a place called Dia Wekuwi, the House of the Capyvara. Every day when the sun was high he would swim downriver from Loiro, above S. Luis. There he would go into a passageway—it was a kind of corridor for him, for us it was a stream. He would arrive at the edge of the river, and there transform himself.

We are grandchildren of the Anacondas, we are the Arapaço snake children. He was our grandfather. Unurato is our oldest and most cherished brother. He will come back to us; we are waiting for him.

It happened this way. When he crossed the river he saw a woman [Iapo's wife] bathing. On arriving at the river's edge, he transformed himself into a human being and lay with her. She was struck with his startling beauty and his simmering gold ear ornaments. Being bewitched, she could think of nothing else. So he lived this way, having contact with her, each time returning to his underwater house as an enchanted snake. Every day when she returned from the garden, she would go to the river edge and beat her calabash to make the sound "coro, coro, coro." He would hear it and come to meet her. This went on every day.

Her husband [Iapo] became distrustful. He put a companion of his, a bird, in a termite nest high in a tree. Then he hid and waited with a blowgun and poisoned darts.

When it was nearly mid-day, the woman was returning from the garden, and, as was her custom, she carried the calabash to the river. She made the sound and our grandfather heard it and went to her. When he got to the edge, he changed into a human being. He lay with her; and just as he was at *that* moment, as he lay on top of her, the husband blew into his blowgun and sent flying a poison dart which hit the snake in the buttocks. The snake felt almost nothing: he thought it was a horsefly! When a third dart hit him, the termites on which the woodpecker[7] was feeding fell and landed on the woman. She looked up, and there she saw her husband. Terrified, she shook her lover to tell him the husband was watching them. But it was too late. Our grandfather, the snake, had been poisoned. We are the family of that snake; he is the grandfather of the Arapaço.

As he fell into the water he changed into a snake and went rolling downriver. There is an island called Tununi Nuku, and he rolled there. He went rolling until he arrived at Numiani Tuku and there he surfaced. He floated one day, then two days. On the second day, while the wife was making manioc flour, the husband went there to fish. He caught many small fishes. [Wrapping them in manioc bread,] he made a bundle for himself and another for his wife. Then, he cut off the penis of the snake. He mixed the penis into one of the bundles and took them home. When he arrived home, he gave the bundles to his wife to roast. They ate together: he ate his bundle and she ate hers. When he finished eating, he picked up his flute, lay in his hammock and played. He played, "toro, toro, toro." It was enough for her to understand. The melody meant this: "A woman who liked her husband wanted to love. She ended up eating that which she most loved." Understanding the meaning of the music, she took her calabash and ran to the river edge. She dipped it and drank many times. A kind of fish, like a snake, came out of her mouth. She returned home, thinking that the penis had left her body.

I will tell only a part of how our Unurato, our beloved oldest brother, reappeared and is here today. Well, the husband left the woman. He went away and she remained here. She was pregnant. When she was about to give birth, she went to a stream above S. Luis, looking for shrimp to eat. In the leaf debris in the water, she found a little fruit—bacaba—which she wanted to eat. A voice within her would called out: "Mother, I'll climb the tree and get the fruit for you." She said: "Don't speak: you are not people. You cannot speak as a human." He was the son of the enchanted snake. But, in truth, he had the spirit of a human. He answered: "I am a person. I am a man and I can do it. I will get you [the fruit]." He slipped out of her mouth and slithered up the tree. He climbed very high until he was able to reach the fruit. Each time he dropped a fruit, the mother responded "uh, uh." She couldn't escape because his tail was still inside her mouth. She was frightened: he was a human child but he was also a snake.

When she saw the snake, the mother was frightened (we know well that he was really a man).[8] She folded a leaf of the *duhpiapuli* tree into a funnel shape and spit saliva into it. She put a frog called *ditaro* near the funnel to call out "uh, uh."

Then she ran to the port and escaped in a canoe, leaving the stream, crossing the river, and entering another stream [Diya: the Stream of Blood] where she bathed [cleaning the birth]. From there she set out paddling home.

Our grandfather, high in the tree, saw her leaving when a beam of light—a reflection—hit her paddle. He shouted to her. He was a spirit. He flew to the house and lay on top. It was really a hill of earth, but for them a house called Ditabua in Wituriro. She hid in a large ceramic beer vessel as he remained on top of the house shouting. When she was thrown out by her family, she threw herself into the water and transformed into the fish pirarara.

Part 2

Unurato entered the water and there he grew very big. Soon, there wasn't enough water to contain him, so he moved downriver to deeper water. First he went to the Rio Negro, then to the Amazon. In the Amazon he found fishes even bigger than he. So he went to Manaus. He arrived in Manaus at night. As he came on land he transformed into his human form and spent the night drinking and dancing. At dawn he returned to the water and assumed his snake form. After some time he went to one of the whites with whom he was drinking and asked him to meet him at midnight on a beach. The white had whiskey, a rifle, and a hen's egg. He was to throw the egg at Unurato. The white went to the river edge and waited. Suddenly the waters rose and Unurato appeared as an enormous snake. In fear, the white shot him with the bullet instead of throwing the egg. With the blow, his snake skin fell into the water and his human body remained on the beach. The blow destroyed his supernatural qualities. He remained a simple man, on the beach, blinded in one eye. He began to live as any man.

We are his descendants. That's why we are called Pino Mahsa, People of the Snake.

Part 3

Unurato went to Brasilia and there he worked constructing large buildings. He came to know every kind of thing: houses, furniture, taxis—things we don't have here. And he moved among many people.

Last year, the waters rose very high. That was Unurato coming back. He swam upriver. He was a gigantic submarine, but since he is a supernatural snake he passed the rapids. The submarine is here, across from Loiro. It appears at midnight. It is so full of goods, it is impossible to count the number of boxes on that ship. The ship has electric lights. With machines the snake-beings (*Wai Masa*) are building an enormous city under the river. You can hear the noise of these submerged machines when you go near there. Every kind of *Wai Masa* [underwater, supernatural beings] is at work on that ship. Now we are few, but he will give us back our prosperity, and our numbers.

Discussion

In the myth cycle presented here, the river is the primary metonymy. The myth is centered not upon place or wit, but upon a *limen*, a term that simultaneously signifies a boundary and path, a limit and a corridor. Unlike the pan-Tukanoan founding myth that recounts the ancestral anaconda who placed the First Ancestors and constructed the proper "seating" (or permanence) of each descent group, this myth is a vehicle of mobilities used to tell the story of passage, a river descent and a promised return. The myth narrates Unurato's position and origins as "one who wanders," whose home is the *limen*. Unurato mediates between a variety of "others"; and in each of these mediations he is transformed.

It is significant that the myth is centered upon the river, the *limen*, as much a channel of connectivities as it is a boundary between culture and nature, man and animal, the known and the possible. It is at the boundary between water and land, the river-bank, that all of the primary transformations in the myth take place. Here Dia Pino couples with the wife of Iapo, is shot, killed, dismembered, and eaten. It is here that the eldest brother of the Arapaço is born from his mother's mouth, here that he is transformed by the penetration of the whiteman's bullet into a mere man living like others. Across this boundary are projected the expectations expressed in the last section of the myth, a world of potential, impregnating and transforming the Ancestral Anaconda by means of contact with an industrial world.

The union of Dia Pino and Iapo's wife is a crossing of boundaries and a linking of distinct realms: outside and inside, natural and cultural, the wild and the tame, the strange and familiar. This fragment of the myth makes use of the contradiction noted by Levi-Strauss, "the contradiction by which the same woman was seen under two, incompatible aspects: on the one hand, as the object of personal desire, thus exciting sexual and proprietary instincts; and, on the other, as the subject of the desire of others, and seen as such, i.e., as the means of binding others through alliance with them" (Levi-Strauss 1969, 496). Exchange of women, a primary medium of Tukanoan relationship, is the initial metaphor of connection here. In Tukanoan society, if not universally, the relations between men are mediated through women and through the exchange of women.

There is a wide range between the total insider—the consanguineal sib-mate—and the outsider—the enemy or "cannibal." Mediating these extremes is the in-law, a category of "other" with varying degrees of closeness, one that is elastic and subject to the vagaries of history. Through exogamy the "other," the stranger who may be an enemy, is rendered ally (Chernela 1989, 1993). Thus, in principle, in-law status domesticates or transforms a potentially hostile relationship into a relationship of mutuality. A group to whom you give wives or from which you receive wives, the in-law group is not kin, but it is "near" kin—mediating between kin and total "other."

In the exchanges between Unurato and the whiteman the very absence of those female mediations that translate the frictions of sexuality into the fictions of social life is significant. The whiteman comes without women. His means of building a boundary society is by the absorption of Indian women as concubines, slaves, and maids. As wife-seizer, rather than wife-exchanger, the white is the one outsider who does not reciprocate in traditional terms, for whom sexuality is a matter of consumption rather than a medium of enduring relations (1989).

For the patrilineal Arapaço, seizure of women as wives and concubines constitutes the appropriation not only of women as sexual partners, but also of paternal rights over offspring. Where paternity is the basis for group affiliation and self-identity, as it is for the Eastern Tukanoans, illicit paternity by a white man (or other outsider) amounts to a theft of future generations.

Symmetrical events in parts 1 and 2 of the cycle are the structural axes upon which the story turns. Emotions, too, peak at these points, as the ancestor is in each case shot: first with a dart and later with a gun. The shooting is simultaneously a stripping away of doubleness and a process of "manufacture" in which the culture hero is changed and reborn.

The parallels between shooting and sexual exchange are evident here. Shooting and wounding are the means by which men penetrate each other directly, without the mediations of women. Here the act of real or symbolic violence is a boundary-making act that reasserts the integrity of those categories joined in passage.

The act of shooting may also be regarded as what the literary critic Kenneth Burke calls a "fictional death," a death that is fictional rather than real because it uses mortality—a dissolution of form and a solvent of identities—as an identifier, showing what or who the deceased "really" is. The *topos* of the fictional death is used to dramatically different effect in these two shootings. In the first instance, the shooting of Dia Pino by Iapo, the ancestor is changed back into what he was, a snake; while in the shooting of Unurato by the whiteman the culture hero is stripped of his original, snake form. It is necessary to determine what this significant difference means.

Unurato is born from those procedures that rectify the violation of a boundary and "make good" an act of adultery. The violation of the proprietary rights of the husband to the woman is made good by the killing of the intruder. The act removes his human form and reveals him to be actually an anaconda. The body of the ancestor then undergoes a process of dismemberment, repackaging, cooking, and ingestion mediated by the husband. The ancestor becomes impregnating food. According to Goldman (1963), Tukanoan Cubeo women consumed the genitalia of enemies slain in battle. The meaning of this act would appear to be the same: the incorporation of the enemy and enmity into the domestic sphere, which neutralizes the strangeness of the other and incorporates his power into the local group. The exchange of food between husband and wife is a complicated act of love/revenge, an equation that is explicit: "she ended up eating that which she most loved." In a Uanano version of this myth (in which Iapo is called Wanari, the ancestor of the Uanano), the cuckolded husband says, "Is it that a woman who had a good husband, eats the body of her husband who isn't?" (Chernela 1988c, 70), a formulation that suggests the triangularity of the relationships being mediated.

Both the conception and the birth of Unurato occur through the woman's mouth. Unurato's birth is intimately involved with voice and language. Speech signifies a human identity. The mother says to her unborn child: "Be quiet: you are not people." But Unurato speaks in reply, intimating his human nature. As suggested, identity among Eastern Tukanoan is marked by language.

The ancestor is a stranger of double form, alternatively man/animal, human/divinity. In each of the two peak transformative events of the story—the shooting and the killing—this doubleness is cancelled, but each time in a quite different way. In the first instance the shooting of Dia Pino returns him to snake from man. The snake is then dismembered, cooked, and eaten. Only when he is reborn as Unurato does he resume his double form. In the second instance—the shooting of Unurato by the whiteman (the Manuara)—his double nature is cancelled in another direction. The encounter with the whiteman strips Unurato of this double nature (*doppelganger*) and of his capacity for self-transformation. He loses the capacity to become other and is stripped of his divine powers, becoming merely a man and living a common life.

The birth and identity of Unurato are rooted in traditional exchanges that establish the native terms of relatedness and identity—women, food, violence, and words. The distinctiveness of the encounter with the white lies in the absence of all these modalities of exchange but the mediations of violence. The shooting of Unurato is the result of a failed exchange, the substitution of the bullet for trade-goods: whiskey, an egg, a rifle. The white man's goods are substitutions for a prior exchange that renders a stranger an affine: white man's alcohol for manioc beer; domestic animals for feral animals; firearms for blowguns. Each of these carries significance. The egg is seed, a symbol of fertility, conjugality, and reproduction. Drink is a connector between groups that exchange females and goods. The bullet, like the dart of the blowgun, is a connector through violence. These substitutions serve to define the Manuara, the white man.

Though parallel, these "shooting" events contain important dissimilarities that reveal fundamental differences in the relationships the Arapaço bear to a Tukanoan-speaking world, on the one hand, and the white man's world, on the other. The white's character is revealed in the terms of violence he chooses in his paradigmatic exchanges with the Arapaço ancestor.

In rules of Eastern Tukanoan exchange idealogies, you are what you give.[9] In fear, the white man gives the bullet, and this gift defines him just as it redefines the nature of Unurato. Unurato invites the Manuara to hit him with an egg, a vehicle of fertility. The egg is the proper object of mediation, through impregnation, that constructs in-law relations. But the bullet by which it is replaced is not only infertile; it destroys. It is a fatal egg.

Whereas an egg is a symbol of reproduction and regeneration, the white man's bullet accomplishes the opposite. The shooting death/destruction of Unurato's "doubleness" by a white man's bullet is the primal image of nativity and origin for the Arapaço. Its annihilation destroys the possibility of return to those origins, of resuming an identity that links through time. The bullet destroys the mutability of Unurato's identity and deprives him of his capacity for self-transformation. But what does this mean?

This question can only be answered within the universe of signification set up in the myth, which narrates the conception, germination, birth, and evolution of Unurato in terms of a variety of exchanges from which identities are derived and in which they are transformed. Giving and exchanging—food, women, words, myths, blows, trade goods—are the fundamental means of relatedness and indicators of identity among the peoples of the Uaupés. The white man enters into these terms and is defined by them, but he is marked by his exclusive preference for the bullet, for the terms of violence.

This is also the case in the Eastern Tukanoan Barasana myth cycle recounted by Hugh-Jones (1988), wherein the white chooses the gun rather than the bow and ornaments that were chosen by the Barasana. This was a choice that defined them: "The ancestor of the Whites then began to threaten the others with his gun. To keep the peace, the culture hero sent him far away to the East and declared that war would be the White People's equivalent of Indian ritual and that through war they would obtain the wealth of other people" (Hugh-Jones 1988, 144). Equally, in the myth of Unurato, the white man's choice of the bullet defines him.

Strangers in Eastern Tukanoan history are converted to familiars by means of exogamy and ritual exchanges of food and drink (Chernela 1989, 1992). The terms of relatedness defining Unurato's birth are extended to the white, but it is clear that the white man is anomalous within these terms. He becomes a contradiction, one who does not reciprocate in expected ways. Instead, he brings about an end to exchange. It is this contradiction that the final part of the myth attempts to attenuate. The substitution of the bullet for trade goods produces a fictional death, revealing Unurato to be merely a man, half-blind. This diminution, the cancelling of doubleness, produces a loss that must be made good.

Within Tukanoan ideology the world is governed by balance so that a gain in one part of the system always produces a deficit in another (Reichel-Dolmatoff 1971). The converse is also true: a deficit within a transaction builds an "abundance" elsewhere. It is this abundance that is contained within the ancestral anaconda, with house, car, telephone. In the final segment Unurato phones from Brasilia, where he lives among new houses and cars. This transformation of the primal image of relatedness is itself striking and invites interpretation. The anaconda-Unurato has swallowed and incorporated the city; he has ingested the white world.

CONCLUSIONS

For the Tukanoan Arapaço, relatedness and distinctiveness are a matter of specific kinds of exchanges—of women, food, words and languages, myths, and blows. Within these relations, which define identity and the degrees of relatedness, the white man is anomalous not by "nature" or "category" but by virtue of the fact that he does not reciprocate and introduces an imbalance within a structure of reciprocity, an imbalance that defines an experience of history and shapes expectations of the future.

The Unurato myth narrates the terms of mutual penetrations and incorporations, as the bullet of the white man penetrates Unurato and as he penetrates the white world and incorporates it into himself. The return and rebirth of the remade ancestor augments the *yeheripona* (life force) of the collectivity. This "position" betwixt and between has become the proper "sitting" of the Arapaço, the position assigned them by a history of uprootings, migrations, wanderings, and mixings. In the last analysis the myth itself may stand as the most enduring template of collective identity, surviving and even substituting for the loss of languages, kin, place, fullness. "White man," Unurato tells the white and the listener of the myth, "I have a name."

It is perhaps the very position of the Arapaço as a people between worlds, as mediators, that transforms the oppositional self-image into a culminating synthesis. For the culture hero, whose identity is defined in and through relations to a variety of others, himself becomes a connector of worlds and a medium of exchanges. In this role, as inhabiter of the *limen*, the path, the ancestor promises a retribution, a restoration of an imbalance, a future but imminent payment on the deficit of history.

NOTES

A discussion of this myth appears in "Righting History in the Northwest Amazon," in *Rethinking History and Myth: Indigenous South American Perspectives on the Past*, ed. Jonathon Hill (University of Illinois, 1988). The authors wish to thank Crispiniano Carvalho, Miguel Carvalho, and João Bosco for their invaluable assistance in recording and translating the myth and Robin Wright, Terence Turner, Jane Fajans, Ken Buscher, Jonathan Hill, Aracy da Silva, and Nancy Fried, all of whom read and commented upon earlier versions of this paper. The field research on which this paper is based was carried out by author Chernela during intermittent periods between 1978 and 1985. Funding was provided by the Fulbright-Hays program of the U.S. Department of Education; the Social Science Research Council; the Instituto Nacional de Pesquisas da Amazônia; and the Joint Committee on Latin American Studies of the American Council with funds provided by the National Endowment for the Humanities, the Ford Foundation, and the Andrew W. Mellon Foundation.

1. Konea or Korea is the Tukanoan name of the group and language; Arapaço, Arapasço, or Arapaso is the *lingua geral* name and the name by which the group is known in the literature on the Northwest Amazon.

2. Statistics compiled in 1958 by the parishes at Taraquá and Iauaretê show 283 Arapaço (Bruzzi 1977:84). Chernela's census from 1979 shows an Arapaso population of only 202, a decline of 81 persons in only 20 years. The 5 settlements which Chernela encountered in 1979 ranged in size from 11 to 83 inhabitants, with a mean population of 40 persons per village (1988b). Bruzzi's list includes two additional villages, Baia (Wituriro) and Ponta de Mucuim (Umu sua noa), which were abandoned in the twenty years between the two surveys.

3. "Padre João Marchesi, on arriving in 1925 among them, learned from the elder Arapaço, that they had been the 'nobles' and leaders of the Uaupés, [occupying settlements] from S. Jose to the mouth. For having been more sociable and agreeable than the other Indians, many women became wives of whites and many men were carried off to work. Many remained in the lower Rio Negro and others disappeared entirely. From constant cross-breeding with Arapaço, a large population of mixed-bloods evolved in that region. The tribe was greatly reduced. There had been a large group at Pinu-Pinu, on the Uaupés, who emigrated to the lower Rio Negro. On return, they found the Taryana in their place. Not wishing to cede the land, the Taryana aduced that they were many, whereas the Arapaço were few" (Bruzzi 1977, p. 84, author's translation).

4. Informants report 10 sibs, Bruzzi (1977) reports 4, and Beksta (n.d.) reports 7.

5. See, for example a Wakwenai version in Wright 1981, pp. 571–74, and Uanano versions in Chernela 1988b.

6. Crispiniano Carvalho was an invaluable assistant to Chernela between 1978 and 1985. He and his wife were her hosts when she visited their village, Parana Juca.

7. Both Konea, the Eastern Tukanoan name, and Arapaço, in *lingua geral*, gloss as woodpecker.

8. Whereas phrases in brackets are ours, phrases in parentheses were spoken by the narrator.

9. This includes speech, as in the speech one produces.

REFERENCES

Aranha, Bento de Figueiredo Tenreiro. 1907 "Archivo do Amazonas." *Revista Destinada a Vulgarisação de Documentos Geográficos e Históricos do Estado do Amazonas* 1(3).

Azevedo, Soares de. 1933. *Pelo Rio Mar.* C. Medes, Rio de Janeiro. Report compiled by the Salesian Prelacy of the Upper Rio Negro, under the coordination and supervision of Dom Pedro Massa.

Beksta, S.D.B., Padre Casimiro. n.d. "Origem e Divisao das Tribos." Unpublished ms.

Bruzzi, Alves da Silva, P. Alcionilio. 1977. *A Civilização indígena do Uaupés*, 2nd ed. Manaus (Brazil): Missão Salesiana do Rio Negro.

Burns, E. Bradford. 1980. *A History of Brazil*. New York: Columbia University Press.

Chernela, Janet M. 2003. "Language Ideology and Women's Speech: Talking Community in the Northwest Amazon." *American Anthropologist* 105(4) [in press].

———. 1997. "Ideal Speech Movements: A Woman's Narrative Performance in the Northwest Amazon." *Feminist Studies* 23(1): 73–96.

———. 1993. *The Wanano Indians of the Brazilian Amazon: A Sense of Space*. Austin: University of Texas Press.

———. 1992. "Social Meanings and Material Transaction: The Wanano-Tukano of Brazil and Colombia." *Journal of Anthropological Archaeology* 11: 111–24.

———. 1989. "Marriage, Language, and History Among Eastern Tukanoan Speaking Peoples of the Northwest Amazon." *Latin American Anthropology Review* 1(2): 36–42.

———. 1988a. "Gender, Language and 'Placement' in Uanano Songs and Litanies." *Journal of Latin American Lore* 14(2): 193–206.

———. 1988b. "Righting History in the Northwest Amazon." In Jonathan Hill, ed., *Rethinking History and Myth*. Urbana: University of Illinois Press, 35–49.

———. 1982. "Estrutura Social do Uaupés Brasileiro." *Anuário Antropológico/81*, ed. Robert Cardoso de Oliveria. Rio de Janeiro, 81: 59–69.

Chernela, Janet M. and Eric J. Leed. 2001. "As Perdas da Historia." In Alcida Ramos and Bruce Albert, eds., *Pacificando o Branco*. Brasilia: Universidade de Brasilia, 469–86.

Coudreau, Henri, 1887. *Voyage a travers les Guyanes et l'Amazonie, La France Equivoxiale*. Vol. 2. Paris: Challamel.

Giacone, Antonio. 1949. *Os Tucanos e Outras Tribus do Rio Uaupés Afluente do Negro-Amazonas; notas etnográficas e folcloricas de um missionario salesiano*. Associação Brazileira dos Americianistas. São Paulo: Impr. Oficial do Estado.

Goldman, Irving. 1963. *The Cubeo: Indians of the Northwest Amazon*. Illinois Studies in Anthropology, Number 2. Urbana: University of Illinois Press.

Hugh-Jones, Stephen. 1988. "The Gun and the Bow: Myths of White Men and Indians." *L'Homme* 28(2–3): 138–55.

Jackson, Jean E. 1974. "Language Identity of the Colombia Vaupes Indians." In R. Bauman and J. Scherzer, eds., *Explorations in the Ethnography of Speaking*. Cambridge: Cambridge University Press.

———. 1983. *The Fish People: Linguistic Exogamy and Tukanoan Identity in Northwestern Amazonia*. Cambridge Studies in Social Anthropology. Cambridge: Cambridge University Press.

Koch-Grünberg, Theodore. 1909. *Zwei Jahre unter den Indianern: Reisen in Nordwest-Brasilien 1903–1905*. 2 vols. Berlin: Ernst Wasmuth.

Levi-Strauss, Claude. 1969. *Elementary Structures of Kinship*. Boston: Beacon Press.

Lopes de Sousa, Marechal Boanerges. 1959. *Do Rio Negro ao Orenoco*. Ministerio da Agricultura, Conselho Nacional de Proteção aos Indios, Rio de Janeiro.

Reichel-Dolmatoff, G. 1971. *Amazonian Cosmos: The Sexual and Religious Symbolism of the Tukano Indians*. Chicago: University of Chicago Press.

Sorensen, Arthur. 1967. "Multilingualism in the Northwest Amazon." *American Anthropologist* 69(6): 670–82.

Szentmartonyi, Pe. Ignacio. 1753. "Seguentes Notiates de Rio Negro, 1753." In Robin Wright, *History and Religion of the Baniwa Peoples of the Upper Rio Negro Valley*. Ph.D. dissertation, Stanford University.

Wright, Robin. 1981. *History and Religion of the Baniwa Peoples of the Upper Rio Negro Valley*. Ph.D. dissertation, Stanford University.

Giving Voice to the Hill Spirit: Mayan Visionary Testimony in Southern Belize

Jerry Kelly

INTRODUCTION

Since Belize's independence in 1981, teachers and students in Toledo, the country's southern district, have been collecting, transcribing, and printing local residents' traditional and life stories for use in indigenous literacy texts. Both the performance and inscription of these oral narratives are important elements in the process of regional cultural renewal, and a number of contemporary stories have elicited a strong response within the Kekchi Maya population,[1] foremost of which is the visionary narrative of a traveling Kekchi evangelist. Beginning in 1990, Juan, a Guatemalan catechist, began recounting his hill spirit epiphany in an effort to reinstill respect for communal identity, traditional hunting codes, ritual approaches to planting, and the overarching value of the sacred earth.

Based in the Kekchi homeland of Guatemala's Coban region, Juan has extended the geographic reach of his account of the hill spirit's message to Belize's Toledo District, the eastern periphery of the Mayan world. Bypassing any contentious division between orality and text (Goody 1986; Ong 1982), Toledo Mayans are continuing to spread Juan's message beyond traditional ethnic and linguistic borders by promoting its translation, textualization, and further distribution by means of radio

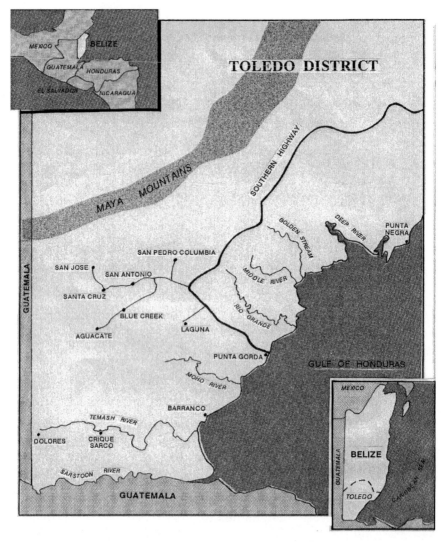

Figure 4.1 Map by Dean Scott

and audiotaping. Thus, his teachings and the enthusiastic response to them in Toledo are manifestations of the contemporary process of Mayan ethnogenesis (B. Tedlock 1992), a reassertion of Mayan cultural identity across national borders.

Emerging from an earlier colonial era of neglect and isolation, as well as a protective furtiveness, Toledo's Kekchi Mayans have begun to take their place in independent Belize's political arena. Centuries of the destruction of signs and stories are ending. Mayans, as well as their

Creole and Garifuna (Black Carib) counterparts, are once again free to dance, drum, celebrate religious rituals, speak, write, act politically, and engage in nation-building. Not only are Kekchi leaders broadcasting in their native language, religious leaders promote the Kekchi bible and vernacular liturgy, and Toledo educators are beginning to develop Kekchi literacy programs.

As with many native peoples, land use and ownership represent a focal issue that has propelled Kekchi voices into Belize's unique multilingual discourse. Since Belize's independence in 1981, Toledo Mayans have begun to utilize their grasp of English to state their case on a number of key land issues. Leaders in Santa Cruz and San José have lobbied for the local management of a national park, the Toledo Mayan Cultural Council (T.M.C.C.) members have begun to promote ecological reserves, and Mayans throughout Toledo have resisted the intrusion of a Malaysian timber concern (Berkey 1995), in each case making use of English as well as Kekchi. In 1990, Juan the Catechist entered this public discourse, giving voice to the hill spirit and the land itself, in his effort to promote the wise use of sustainable resources.

Juan's preaching in Kekchi, as well as his followers' use of English, Creole, and Mopan Maya, offer a communal articulation of an evolving multilingual Kekchi identity in southern Belize. Juan's testimony regarding traditional Kekchi spirituality has had a catalytic effect on many of Toledo's Kekchi. His sense of mission and responsibility to the land have made him a model of the power and wisdom of speaking out forcefully about essential beliefs. Encouraged by Juan and other Mayan leaders, Belize's Kekchi are beginning to make a wider use of the country's classrooms, airwaves, and public forums to assure themselves a seat at the new table of power that is currently being set in independent Belize.

As a teacher/researcher who has collaborated with Belizean educators for the past ten years on the Toledo District literacy text program, I have studied not only the emergence, content, and spread of Juan's vision, but also its translation, textualization, and distribution in English and other local languages. While news of Juan's vision circulates orally among the Kekchi in their native language and while some would urge a decisive return to ethnic first languages in the post-colonial era (Ngũgĩ 1986), Mayan leaders have promoted the narrative's further distribution in an English text, as well as a Mopan Mayan version.

Emerging from the shadow of colonial inattention and silencing (Farris 1984; D. Tedlock 1993), the Kekchi inscription of visionary narratives and other stories for the schools' literacy programs is creating a "new kind of knowledge, . . . a new way of learning called education" (Halliday 1987). This growing body of inscribed Toledo narratives, encouraged and spread by educators, may be considered one experimental form of postmodern ethnography (Clifford 1986; Rosaldo 1989), "a cooperatively evolved text consisting of fragments of discourse" that "attempts to recreate textually this spiral of poetic and ritual performance" (Tyler 1986). These literacy texts present the Kekchi people with both a history and an ethnographic profile that they have composed themselves, as opposed to the constructs of foreign "experts" (Marcus 1986; Said 1993; Tyler 1986). In Toledo, educators are creating their own local literacy that not only enables individual cognitive attainment, but also potentially provides students with the capability to inform themselves about their history, identity, and traditional moral values (Street 1993). By enlightening students about issues such as the Mayans' history of living in sustainable harmony with the earth and their people's resistance to colonial domination, this indigenous literacy program may also provide Belizean students with the emanicipatory tools that are needed to understand and challenge the cultural domination resulting from the former British rule and current U.S. mass media.

As part of the textbook research, I have situated Juan's narrative within the broad Mayan tradition of visionary narratives (Colby and Colby 1981; Fabrega and Silver 1973; Oakes 1951; B. Tedlock 1982; D. Tedlock 1993), as well as Toledo's own local tradition. I will also describe the pedagogical implications for language and identity that may accrue by the use of the rich, generative vocabulary (Freire and Macedo 1987; Kozol 1978; Miller 1985) employed by Mayan narrators. The vibrant language of self-determination, cultural renewal, communal harmony, and ecological knowledge contained within these oral and written narratives offers evidence of the contemporary articulation of Mayan identity in independent Belize.

The bilingual extension of Juan's visionary testimony mirrors the multilingual identity that is currently being promoted and embraced among the Maya of Belize. While reflecting a transnational Mayan identity and providing an opportunity for literacy education, Juan's narrative reiterates a traditional moral code and carries the specific and timely message that all people must work together to avoid waste and destruction. In addition, Juan urges that his listeners return to ritual and to disciplined modes of ecological husbandry now to insure the continued fruitfulness of the sacred earth (Nelson 1983; Taylor 1990). Juan's visionary account gives voice to the earth, a powerful call that is emerging from the mountains and valleys of southern Belize. It is of special significance that the articulation of Juan's message coincides with the historical epoch of independence, a moment when Belize's Mayan peoples are pushing aside a veil of silence and confronting the historical silencing of their voices to enter the national arena as Belize's new national agenda is discussed, negotiated, and enacted.

BACKGROUND: LANGUAGE, LITERACY, AND IDENTITY

Belize

South of the Yucatan Peninsula and west of Guatemala, Belize is a country of mountains, low hills, powerful rivers, and a rich coastal zone. About the size of Massachusetts, Belize (formerly British Honduras) has a population of just over 200,000 mestizos (Spanish-Indian), Creoles, Mayans, Garifuna, East Indians, Asians and Anglo-Americans. Toledo, Belize's remote southern district, has the smallest population, and many of its villages are still accessible only by jungle trail or sea dory. Creoles and Garifuna live in Punta Gorda, Toledo's district center, and along the coast, while Kekchi and Mopan Mayans inhabit most of the inland villages where many villagers practice the subsistence farming methods that have existed since the era of the Classical Maya.

Postcolonial Language Issues

Since 1981, Belizean language planners and politicians have charted a course maintaining British Standard English (B.S.E.) as the nation's unitary language in the belief that this policy maintains a national language stability and provides the best access to international business and economic interests. While teachers may instruct students in B.S.E. (hereafter referred to as English), Belize Creole English (B.C.E.)[2] is the first language spoken in urban areas and the lingua franca used in rural areas (Hancock 1971). Most Belizeans speak B.C.E. (hereafter referred to as Creole), and this language is currently gaining increased formal recognition and acceptance in Belize, as it has in many former British Caribbean colonies. Belize's language managers are also responding to the country's growing Spanish-speaking population in the North, and Spanish language education is newly mandated for elementary schools. Language renewal initiatives are underway in parts of the country, as Garifuna, Kekchi, and Mopan educators are locating and producing texts in their own languages for the first time.

While national planners promote English, it is significant that many ethnic groups have modified their approach to language. In Toledo, many Kekchi and Mopan Mayans use their native languages for domestic and village discourse, while maintaining English and/or Creole as a second language for wider communication and print. This dual language usage parallels the "special diglossia" that Daniel McLaughlin (1992) describes among the Navajo. McLaughlin, who studied Navajo schooling and noted a preference for the use of Navajo in most oral situations, noticed, too, that younger Navajos usually employed English for reading and writing. He considers Navajo literacy to be a model of literacy, noteworthy for this special bidirectionality (19). His study suggests that modern, younger Navajos are "bilingual, biliteral, bicultural and bicognitive" (129).

Though some politicians and educators encourage the complete rejection of colonial languages, Belizean educators are charting a multilingual course that emphasizes English, while giving consideration to Spanish and ethnic first languages. Given their history of raising children in multilanguage home environments, most Belizeans have already embarked on this linguistic journey. In the Toledo textbook project, many Kekchi and Mopan Maya narrators are renewing their use of ethnic first languages, making use of their school-taught English, and employing Creole in appropriate situations. While many Mayan narrators attempt to render their stories in English, some make use of Creole, and the transcription of their oral stories serves as a graphic indicator of Belize's Creole in a state of linguistic expansion. As they listen to mass media, travel more extensively, and meet Belizeans from all regions of the country, Toledo's Mayans are also embracing the new national identity through their expanding use of Belizean Creole (LePage and Tabouret-Keller 1985).

Last, it should be noted that the inscription of Mayan narratives in Toledo's indigenous textbooks demonstrates a new objective equality with the other Creole and Garifuna contributors. Since the oral narration of stories in English, often followed by transcription assistance, results in English texts, there is new and demonstrable evidence that Mayans are not only capable of the articulation of their people's interests in English, but also currently active and assertive about their new and growing English literacy.

Literacy Efforts in Independent Belize

Since emerging from its colonial status, Belize has devoted a substantial portion of its limited monetary resources toward achieving universal literacy as one important building block for expanding Belize's agricultural and subsistence economies. Though most national reports indicate greatly increased school attendance in recent years, standardized test scores and low student matriculation in secondary schools suggest that success in literacy for Toledo's Mayans is still in doubt.

With the coming of independence, E. Roy Cayetano, a member of a Garifuna family dedicated to education, took on the challenging responsibility of trying to effect change in the Toledo school district. Early in his tenure as District Education Officer, Cayetano set out on a walking tour to investigate the educational system in Toledo's vast and often impenetrable outback. Cayetano found a desperate situation, including low teacher morale, rapid teacher turnover, and a deplorable shortage of school facilities and supplies. While noting the deficiencies in his report,[3] Cayetano (1984) did not hesitate to consider a number of powerful building blocks for literacy and community education, particular the widespread popularity of Kekchi radio programming and the spread of vernacular Catholic liturgy. Ever vigilant for active literacy, Cayetano recorded that, "Women and children write letters to Pedro Cucul (a Kekchi radio host) to make their requests for their favorite song, for their favorite people" (6).

A reader of Cayetano's report also learns that there was a "great deal of interest in schooling and education in the villages in the Toledo hinterland" (6). The author points out that certain changes in Catholic church policy that promoted the availability of the Bible, hymnbooks, and other literature in Kekchi were fostering increased interest in literacy.

Concentrating on the positive aspects, Cayetano's initial report suggested a three-prong response to the situation that included the promotion of bilingual education:

1. Materials should be produced to make pupils literate in English as well as Kekchi.
2. Teachers must themselves learn the Kekchi language and become literate in it.
3. Teachers should seriously consider giving adult classes. Some villagers are interested in their English language skills. Others want basic literacy, to learn sound-symbol correspondences. Once they learn these correspondences, they can go on to read Kekchi, since the orthography is more "phonetic" than English, and therefore easier to learn. (8)

As a result of this initial appraisal of Toledo needs and resources, Cayetano and his successor, Fabian Cayetano, became particularly concerned with the remote Kekchi schools. To address the literacy situation, district education leaders created a regional textbook project wherein educators used life stories, expository descriptions of work and crafts production, folklore, and traditional stories in composing texts that demonstrate their own special approaches to literacy. These local texts are also part of an effort to forge a new Belizean national identity. The current Belizean literacy programs are not designed to be neutral technologies, nor do they intentionally serve British interests (Fabian 1986); rather, they were produced to challenge the former structures of power and domination that were once created to shape subservient subjects to the crown (Freire 1973). Roy Cayetano offered his view of Toledo's emergent literacy in a July 1995 interview:

Literacy for me, and this is reminiscent of our friend Paulo Freire, is more than just learning to read and write graphic symbols. Literacy is the ability to read our environment, our social and physical environment, and to take appropriate action aimed at making a better life, aimed at securing our happiness and the happiness of the people around us.

(Taped in Dangriga, 7/1995)

Mayan Cultural Renewal and Identity

Less than ten years after substantial educational reform began in Toledo's hinterland, Juan the Catechist began his mission in this same region. Juan's visionary narrative has struck a resonant chord with both Kekchi and Mopan Mayans in Toledo as they share the news of his vision among themselves. As a Kekchi Maya, Juan is speaking as the current bearer of a tradition that spans millennia in the Americas. His stories are not perceived locally as quaint artifacts for Western appropriation and salvage (Clifford 1986; Rosaldo 1989). Juan is calling for a return to the sacred earth as the source of the moral and spiritual renewal of his people, helping them "remember they are Mayans" (B. Tedlock, 1992, 463).

Juan's urgent message is timely, as today's Toledo Mayans are facing new threats to their traditional life ways. Skidders and D9 dozers are currently slashing their way through the district's high bush en route to Guatemala, and roads will one day link most of the southern villages in a modern transport grid. Rural electrification is taking place on the mainline roads; and today, while children in Laguna still dance to harp music by kerosene lamp, families in San Miguel are watching *Die Hard* on video. Change, however, is not a new experience for the Maya. During the last century-and-a-half they have had to adapt to the Yucatan caste wars, indentured servitude, modern agribusiness, extensive logging, and Belizean independence. Through it all, the Mayans have maintained many of their essential folkways while adapting when necessary to modern times (Canby 1992).

A particularly traumatic experience created a pall over the Maya of Belize as their fellow Maya suffered through the civil war and ethnocide in neighboring Guatemala that began in the mid-1960s. The 1978 massacre of Kekchi in Coban to the West (Stoll 1993) was one of the first manifestations of the Guatemalan government's recent brutality that has exterminated over 50,000 Indian people and eliminated over four hundred Mayan villages (Perera 1993). Many of the Kekchi and Mopan in Toledo have either fled to Belize or know people affected by the civil war. This consciousness undoubtedly affects all Indian peoples in the region as they realize that the extermination campaigns are aimed not just at political insurgents but directly against Indians (Canby 1992; Menchu 1984; B. Tedlock 1992). This recent conflict between the Guatemalan oligarchy and the Indians is based in part on an effort by Protestant evangelicals and segments of the Catholic church to eradicate traditional Mayan religious practices (Perera 1993; Stoll 1993; B. Tedlock 1992).

Barbara Tedlock describes the Mayan peoples' transnational response to the civil war's "violent process of uprooting and dispersion," as an example of ethnogenesis, the "cultural and political regrouping into an ethnic nation within and even transcending the boundaries of established nation-states" (1992, 454). Juan, a frequent border crosser, is testifying against this backdrop of growing ethnic awareness and fear. His vision exposes waste, carelessness, the destruction of an ecosystem, and the turning away from the old ways. His visionary account is a clarion call for renewal and rededication to the practice of the ritual methods required by the spirits of the hills (Chapman 1992). This is part of a much broader cultural process, for as Tedlock, who has also researched Juan's visionary narrative,[4] indicates, "The narration of dreams and visions has long validated Mayan traditional religion and world view" (1992, 453). She notes that the very fact that it is a catechist spreading his dream vision signals a reintegration of traditional Mayan beliefs with Christian monotheism.

Tedlock contends that visionary narratives function "simultaneously to facilitate cultural innovation while sustaining traditional culture" (465). She isolates key aspects of Juan's narrative and compares them to stories collected throughout the Mayan world, indicating both shared traditions and the current process of ethnogenesis. She notes that "The hill spirit, sacred earth, or 'mountain valley,' " is chief among the "conventional set of signs" (464) that interconnect Juan's narrative with the broader Mayan visionary tradition. Tedlock cites other significant, conventional signs, including the child guide, "an old person as the spirit of Mountain-Valley," the call for a return to ritual behavior, and the inauguration of a mission. All three versions collected for the textbook program, emanating from a common source, basically share these essential signs and relate as well to the regional Mayan tradition. Likewise, other visionary narratives recently collected in Toledo also possess most of these conventional signs, indicative of both ethnogenesis and a local tradition of hill spirit apparitions. The commonalty of themes, signs, structural devices, and generative vocabulary (key words that allow people to question their experiences) found in all these stories outlines the foundation for the cultural receptivity and communal identity evidenced currently among many Toledo Mayans.

JUAN'S VISIONARY TESTIMONY

Myths, and the characters whose stories they are, live in the quiet of mountains and valleys, forests and meadows, rocks and springs, until someone comes along and thinks to tell them. They have other hiding places too, inside the language we use every day, in the names and places where they happened, or the names of the trees or days on the calendar. Sometimes myths try to catch our eye, looking at us through the holes in a dancer's mask or the glass eyes in the face of a saint. In dreams they show us their scenes and characters directly, but only long enough to make us wonder, afterward, which story we were in. (D. Tedlock 1993, ix)

February 1991

Standing by the Toledo District Health Office in Punta Gorda, one looks southward across the Bahia D'Amatique to the distant coast of Guatemala poking out into the cerulean blue waters with the mountains of Honduras looming purple in the background. Early one day in February 1991, Thomas Teul, a rural health workers, and I relaxed in the morning's cool and talked as the battered school buses full of Mayan families came down into Punta Gorda for the Wednesday market day.

I had met Thomas on my first trip to Punta Gorda, a visit that offered me my initial exposure to the rich oral lore of the Toledo District. For most of this second visit, as a member of the Belize-NH Teachers Program,[5] I had exchanged and recorded stories of forest and sea with teachers from the outlying schools. That morning, I explained my transcription plans once I returned home. I shared a few tales of troublesome bush denizens, and, as stories often do, these accounts stimulated Thomas to tell a story he had recently heard about a Guatemalan catechist who was recounting his encounter with a hill spirit:

Last year [1990] a Kekchi man from Guatemala came to visit the villages around San Jose and he told his story. This year is the first year of his story-telling mission, and he has six years of his life left to tell his story.

He was a hunter who always hunted in the old ways. Before sunrise, he would burn incense and ask the twelve spirits of the hills to release animals for the hunt. Then he would go into the forest and try to make his kill sure and painless.

One day last year, he was hunting turkey along a steam when something blew into his eye. He rubbed his eye and was blinded to the outside world. He rubbed again and had a dream that he met a small boy. He closed his eye again and suddenly he was taken up by the winds over many hills until he landed on the ground. Standing there was a spirit dressed in the robe and headdress of an ancient chief.

The chief told him that he had been chosen for a special mission and that he had seven years to accomplish his mission, and seven years left to live. Then the chief led the hunter through the bush till they came to a clearing. There were pens filled with wounded and suffering animals. There was a pen of antelopes, their flanks and legs bleeding with broken bones. A smaller pen enclosed wari and peccary [two different types of wild pigs], their wounds covered with flies. Other pens kept in tiger [jaguar], red tiger [puma], and margays. Baboons [howler monkeys] howled cries of pain. These were the animals that were injured and maimed by hunters who did not trust the old ways of hunting but only grabbed their guns and shot at whatever moved in the forest. The chief also showed him rooms filled with corn, beans and rice, wasted by those who were careless in harvesting and preparing food.

The chief then taught the hunter a song and told him that he must return to the villages south of the Maya Mountains and tell what he had seen. He must tell hunters and farmers that they must return to the old rituals.

Even now as you hear this story, Juan the Catechist is visiting villages in Guatemala and Belize, singing his song and describing his vision. He has told his wife that when his seven years are up that he will return to the same place in the forest. She is not to worry for he will live and die in the hills, and care for the same wounded animals who live in the pens. When he is gone, another person will be selected by the spirits of the hills to tell the story of the need to avoid the waste of food and animals.

Thomas narrated this story with pride and conviction and spoke of the need for the children to read about Juan's visit with the spirit chief. As an educator, I was struck by this powerful call for respecting all life and promoting an ethic of sustainable resources. Juan's vision had a progressive, future-oriented trajectory, a forward-looking movement that runs counter to the Western analysis of visions and dreams as windows on the past (Basso 1992, 86). Thomas was telling me that the spirit chief or hill spirit was speaking to the Mayan people in this time. Juan's story represented a special, spiritual form of narrative that described an entry into the sacred earth. Throughout much of the Mayan region the mountains, hills, and caves contain numerous spirits, including the hill spirits that watch over the land and its bounty of games and crops. Meeting these spirits is not without risk, for while neighboring mountains may serve as the homes for the guardians of animal souls (Fabrega and Silver 1973, 260), entry into the earth by means of caves may also signal witchcraft and the selling of souls (261).

Thomas's story crossed over into a class of narratives markedly different from the "hearth and hunting" stories that educators had most frequently collected for the textbook program. His account of the hill spirit's injunction to Juan suggests another, more spiritual category of local narratives, in line with Bierhorst's (1990) analysis of Mesoamerican native terminologies for dividing their stories into two kinds. Thomas's stories were akin to the more serious narratives that Bierhorst describes among the Sumu of Nicaragua, who refer to traditional narratives as "nighttime" stories. Bierhorst likewise notes that the Tarascans call spiritual stories "true" stories, and the Yucatec Mayans describe them as *ejemplos* (exempla). Such traditional stories are contrasted with Sumu "daytime stories," Tarascan "false" narratives, and Yucatec *cuentos* (tales) (2). Clearly, Juan's account exhibited the characteristics of a "true" nighttime story designed to instill or renew community values.

As a leader of the T.M.C.C., Thomas had previous experience with foreigners working cooperatively on T.M.C.C. projects, and in most cases these outsiders responded to local needs and direction. Perhaps because of that prior cooperation, Thomas decided to trust me and other New England teachers with this story in the belief that it was essential that Juan's story find a focal place in the next generation of textbooks in order to affirm many key aspects of Mayan identity for the region's Kekchi and Mopan Mayans, as well as their neighbors.

July 1991

I returned to Punta Gorda with a packet of typed stories from the February teachers' workshop. Finding the storytellers wasn't always easy, and the experience for the narrators of seeing their stories in print was usually so overwhelming that people were often unwilling to edit their work. Considering their prior education, they may have been resistant to or inexperienced with redrafting (Lofty 1992), or they may have feared that any tampering might threaten the very existence of their first printed texts. In any case, narrators have routinely handled their printed stories in a reverential fashion, indicating the high value that many people place on text in the modern Mayan world.

Five days into that summertime visit, as the rainy season threatened to make its entry from the western highlands, I visited with potential narrators in three hill villages west of Punta Gorda. Following the lead of a fellow New Hampshire teacher, I visited with Micala Wewe, the organizer of a women's craft co-op in San Antonio Village. Micala was aware of some taping that I had done with local schoolchildren and, over a meal of tortillas, pork rinds and fried cabbage, she excitedly recounted a story she had recently heard and suggested it for the textbook project. She entitled her story "Juan and the Hill Cave" and said that Mr. Bol, the proprietor of the village's small store, had a tape of the talk that the catechist had given to residents of San Antonio. Though she missed Juan's presentation, Micala recounted with reverence the story she had heard on tape. Her account is essentially the same as the story I first heard from Thomas. In the San Antonio version, the narrator is headed for a wedding celebration rather than a hunting trip. Micala's description of the hill spirit is perhaps a bit more personal and threatening, as the spirit confides to the catechist, "All this hurts me. If I wanted I could kill you right here, but I don't want to kill you." The return of the catechist to the village is slightly different too, as he must respond to accusations of drinking. Juan then claims that he was "closed somewhere that he didn't know, and he had been told to tell the whole story that he saw and what he was told."

Micala affirmed the teachings of the catechist and explained her own positive response with a short reflection of her own.

> This is a strong belief that we all have. Because I remember when I was small, my mother would lash me when we would throw corn all about, walking on them. She said that the spirit of the corn would get mad at us and he would not make the corn bear fruit again. So, I think that it is the strong belief that people still have.

Returning from the village trip, I rushed to tell Thomas about Juan's recent testimony in San Antonio. While not surprised, he was pleased to learn of the existence of a taped version of the narrative. He told me that the members of the T.M.C.C. were monitoring Juan's preaching throughout the region and the widespread interest he had aroused. He asked me to send him a copy of Micala's version as soon as I returned home and transcribed my tapes.

February 1992

Returning to Belize, I found that cholera had broken out in Guatemala and was now threatening people in Toledo. Within two years of the initial outbreak in Peru, the disease had spread across the equator, from the Pacific to the Atlantic, and made a dangerous foothold on Guatemala's Atlantic coastline by the Sarstoon River, Belize's southern border.

One evening Thomas and I sat on the veranda at Nature's Way Guest House,[6] and the conversation shifted once again to the travels of Juan the Catechist. Thomas was excited because he had just heard people speaking of a recent talk by Juan in Crique Sarco, a village on the Temash River. I responded with interest because we were scheduled to leave for Crique Sarco in two days. However, a long sea-dory ride under the latitude-16 sun put me down with too much heat, and I was unable to learn any details of Juan's visit, other than to confirm that he had spoken in the church and aroused the interest of community members, including teachers and students who discussed his testimony during classes.

July 1992

An early meeting with Thomas indicated that the travels and story of Juan the Catechist had continued to spread throughout Toledo. In the late spring of that year Thomas had journeyed to the remote village of Dolores, just after a visit from Juan. Another village health worker had taped the performance, and Thomas made a copy of Juan's speech. He was currently passing the tape around to those members of the T.M.C.C. who had not yet heard Juan in person. Furthermore, Thomas indicated that someone in San José Village also taped Juan when the peripatetic catechist had passed through that hill town. Thomas said that some members of the T.M.C.C. were interested in getting an English transcription of the talk for their archives, as well as for more general circulation. He also believed that it was critical to get an accurate, first-hand transcription of this essential story for the textbook project. He asked me to help the Mayan Council by transcribing the English translation into text.[7] By September our international collaboration in editing worked its way through two drafts, and I sent copies of the following draft, which was presented to the T.M.C.C.

The Story of Juan and the Hill Cave

One day I was on my way home from a village named Mash Cohune. On my return, something happened to me that is incredible for you all to believe. It's a true story; what has happened. It happened just for the sake of you all, concerning our corn food. So, every time I go to my work, I pray to god because he is the one who protects and cares for me. I believe that is the reason I was chosen to be taken to a hill cave.

I left my home on the sixteenth of November and returned on the eighteenth of November 1990. It is five hours walking into the high jungle and hills. I left from Mash Cohune Village at four o'clock a.m. When I reached the high jungle and hills, I stopped and prayed to god for I knew not what I might stop and meet on my way. On the continuation of my journey, reaching the first high, steep hill, going up, I saw a young boy coming in my direction. When I got closer to him, when we were about to pass each other, he spoke to me saying, "Sir, my father said he would like to talk to you."

He was [a] cute, little boy, just as if I knew him before. The little boy said, "Hurry, let us go."

I felt that a piece of dirt got into one of my eyes. I quickly rubbed my eye, and when I took off my hand from my eyes, I opened it. I saw I was in a very strange place.

The person said to me, "You are now here and I want to talk to you but first go in and pass by to observe everything inside."

So, I started to go. First I saw corn wasted, torn away. Then I saw cassava, yams, potatoes, all types of grown food. Into the next apartment I saw different types of animals. First I saw a tiger in the next apartment. I saw a deer, gibnut, squash. They are animals I saw personally with my eyes. I walked among them. It's not a dream. It is a true living thing.

After I finished seeing all these [things], I returned to my place where I first reached, and the person asked me what all I saw. I told him everything I saw.

Now he started to talk to me. He said, "I sent for you. You are to take this message to all the people in the world, young and old. Explain to them about their corn food, how they are very careless with it. The first and second box of corn you saw—see how they wasted the corn food! Now it is getting short [scarce]. Why? Your people, when their farms [are] blessed by god, they have a lot of corn. What they do is, they abuse it. Instead, they should use it wisely. They are short of corn now. All of them are trying to plead to god but their prayers are not answered again."

So, now my father said, "You must go all over the world. Explain to the people. If they need the corn, let them do something very important to get back their food if they want. Don't force them, for you are sent to do this job for seven days only."

Seven days means seven years. So, I am living in this world for seven years only. Who would not feel sad to hear and know that he is living in this world for only seven more years? After that, I am going. It is very sad to hear. After, when I am gone, there will be three more coming who will be chosen to do the same work but I do not know who, where, or when.

When we have hatred in our hearts for each other, sometimes, what we do, we destroy the person, the person's plan for other things he possesses. Everything we destroy or damage, the hill gods see it and take that away from us. Those are the same things he showed me in the hill cave. He has preserved them there.

He said that we should not hate each other for god loves us. He cares for us. What we beg from god, we receive it, here in the hill cave, as well as it is received in heaven also. This is the second [message] I learned in the hill cave also.

First of all, I want to tell you all. Please let us stop to hate and hurt our fellow men or our fellow brothers and sisters. Let us bind each other in love, patience and long-suffering which is acceptable to god. I am sent to tell you all, that we must learn how to use these things, what god gives us. Let us use it wisely. Let's not destroy it or waste it, whatever is thrown away because the person has a lot or may be wealthy. To own anything, instead of throwing it away, we should share it with the one who does not have. It is better to give than to receive. But, we in this world, we like to receive rather than to give or share with someone wise. Pleading to god for what we need is very important. As the words say, "Ask and you shall receive."

When I was inside the cave, a message reached there but I could not see what it was. I just heard it. Someone was asking the hill god for a deer, game. In a short while, I saw the deer jump over the fence and I heard a dog bark. In a few minutes I heard a shotgun. It was the same animal that got shot. The hill god gave that person what he asked for.

Take for example, if you have a chicken and someone comes. He starts chasing it and wants to catch it and take it without your permission. Will you give it? No, no way, because he did not ask for the chicken. It is the same thing we need to do with whatever we want. We have to ask the hill god, which is our tradition of doing, so then he will give it to us. Because the hill god has the relationship to god in heaven, we have to give our offering to the hill god. Whatever we offer to the hill god, god in heaven receives it also. This is what the younger generation is abandoning. In the book of Leviticus of the Old Testament, it says, "Offer your burnt offerings to god with all your heart and soul, not without doubt" [sic].

We need to take the word of god seriously when we give our burnt offerings to the hill god. People nowadays believe that the hills are the places of animals, places of rat-bats, and places of Satan. They don't know that each hill keeps its own property, just like we have our own home where we own chickens, pigs, et cetera. They [the domestic animals] go into our houses. [It is] the same with the forest animals. They go into the hill because that is their home.

This is what I saw inside the hill named Torio Shan god hill. That's the name of the hill god where I was taken in. After that, the hill god, Torio Shan, told me that I most go back. After a while, I was transported back, just how I was taken into the cave, except that it was one more long hour to walk from where I was picked by the little boy. And, I am told to preach this message all over the world. Now that I am returning to my home with my family, I am speechless. People try to talk to me. I am speechless.

The day of my return it was raining but I didn't feel that I am getting wet. When I reached closer to my own house, then I was told that I now reached my home, except that I will [should] not talk until tomorrow at four minutes, which means 4:00 p.m.

My wife didn't know where I was. She thought that I was somewhere. Maybe I had gotten drunk and fallen asleep. She questioned me, "Where were you?"

All I could say was that I was taken into a hill cave. She continued to talk but I was unable to answer and hear clearly. About five o'clock in the evening, a number of people came to my house. They wanted to know where I was but I cannot respond to them. Lots of people asked me, "Say, Mr. Juan, where have you been?"

No answer! I could not be able to say an answer until the next day at 4:00 p.m.

One of the hill gods, named Cho Co thundered and all of a sudden I felt my word come in. So now, two agreeable, older persons came closer to me and said, "Now we believe that you came from the hill god. We heard the hill god thunder just a while ago, and saw [that] you started to talk to us at that minute."

The men started to question me. I explained to them that I am sent to be a messenger, to tell the people what they need to do concerning offerings. He gave me an example of the flower plant. The leaves are the symbols of money, donations. The flowers of the plant are the thirteen [sic] god hills, which I am going to give you all their names: Torio Shan, Cawa Seea, Cana Itsa, Cawa Sha Canet, Cawa Chi Shin, Cawa Ca Bun, Cawa Cun, Cawa Sha Tapen, Cawa San Antone. [As of yet, local translators have not agreed on conventional spellings for these names.]

The song that I sang for you all, I learned it at the same hill cave. A man a long time ago was taken into the hill cave, named Seea god, close to Bom hill. That man, when he was young, he was taken into that hill and he is still living. We spoke to each other. He encouraged me to do my job. He said that if I face difficulties, let me not fear. Let me not fear the song that he taught me. It is not written in any song book, none at all. So, I advise you to keep all my advice in your heart. Don't forget the song. Someday I will be dead. A bad-minded person will kill me but I am not afraid of anything. My life is laid for it already. This is my twenty-sixth village visit already. I am sure that I have more to go until my time ends."

[Juan's closing song] "Long ago in the day of the old-time people, they honored their work in the name of their corn food. The father and the mother are the leaders. They are honored by the people. Tomorrow they will be planting their milpa [field]. They advise their children to be obedient. They burn their incense three times a day: morning, noon, and evening. Young and old, we all give thanks and call the names of the thirteen hill gods. The young generation now, they are losing the honor of the old time people. We are abandoning our beliefs. The years of burnt offerings—your father and mother are rejecting it. And now, the birds, and insects are destroying our crops."

THE SIGNIFICANCE OF JUAN'S TESTIMONY

The Narrative Context

In spite of the different renderings, there appears to be little confusion among Toledo's Mayans regarding Juan's vision of waste, carelessness, and the need to return to traditional hunting and farming disciplines. However, the transcription of Juan's visionary testimony in the village of Dolores now provided an original baseline version against which Toledo educators, Thomas, and I could compare the prior two accounts and analyze Juan's narratives both in the context of the broader Mayan ethnogenesis, as well as in comparison to the local collection of hill spirit narratives. While a thorough analysis of the three versions would provide material enough for a separate study, a careful review indicates that the two secondhand versions are generally in agreement with the transcription of Juan's speech. A number of key variables might account for certain obvious discrepancies. The accounts of Thomas and Micala each attempt to record versions of Juan's talks that occurred at two different times and places and preceded the Dolores narration. While all three versions had their origins in the Kekchi language, different people translated each narrative into English. Last, both Thomas's and Micala's accounts were casual retellings that did not attempt to achieve verbatim accuracy.

A textual analysis, one that examines the "conventional signs" that Barbara Tedlock (1992) describes, demonstrates that each version begins with a journey. Juan (J) describes his journey as homeward bound, while in Thomas's version (T) the catechist is going hunting and in Micala's account (M) he is heading to a wedding ceremony. Each version introduces a young boy or child (M) who precipitates a rubbing (T, J) or closing of the eyes (M) that begins the visionary journey to the abode of a spirit "person" (J), also referred to as a "spirit chief" (T) or an old man (M). Juan narrates his travels throughout the "apartments" in the "hill cave" ["ground" (T), "big house" (M)].

The heart of Juan's message concerns the "corn wasted, thrown away," as well as the "abuse" and "careless" treatment of animals. The other two accounts invert the concerns, placing the "wounded, suffering animals" (T) and the "wounded gibnut" and "injured big snakes" (M) before the wasted corn, grains, and "prepared food" (T). Juan tells his listeners that the hill spirit demands that they must use their corn and animals "wisely" and "not destroy or waste it." Furthermore, they should "share it with the one who does not have." He goes on to quote the biblical adage, "Ask and you shall receive." Juan's catechetical training again manifests itself as he cites Leviticus. Thomas's version demands that listeners "must return to the old rituals," and Micala describes the injunction to "hunt with care in the old ways and not ruin the animals."

A key addition to Juan's longer account is the vision within the vision of a traditional hunter who, after offering ritual prayers, is rewarded with a deer by the hill spirit. Juan provides his listeners with this inside view of the simple and efficient exchange of ritual devotion for needed nourishment. Juan names the hill spirit as *Torio Shan* and goes on to alert his audience to his all-encompassing mission, that he is "told to preach the message all over the world." It is clear from his frequent border crossings that Juan does not believe in the limitations of political boundaries. "All over the world" would seem to indicate the pan-Mayan diaspora, if not the broader world beyond Mesoamerica. Though the story is fundamentally a Mayan story, Juan's biblical references indicate his catechetical training as well as the pervasive syncretic relationship between the beliefs of the old Maya and Christianity. Since Juan still embraces his role as a catechist, it appears that he is promoting the ability to act in a manner that Redfield and Villa Rojas suggest is "ceremonially bilingual" in "two equally good modes of religious expression" (1934, 124).

As Tedlock has placed Juan's vision in the context of the regional validation of Mayan traditionalism, so too the local collection of Mayan narratives indicates that Juan's success in Toledo is due to a cultural resonance based on a long local tradition of hill god visions that continues to be renewed until the present date. A number of local narratives, collected in 1993 by Princeton University's Stephanie

Fryberger and Thomas Teul, and graciously contributed to *Stories in the Air*, a collection of Toledo Mayan stories, describe visionary encounters with hill spirits. In each narrative, the hill spirit offers help or enlightenment to a visitor in exchange for the performance of special duties. While these other accounts relate to infidelity, ceremonial dances, and the violation of sacred space, they all provide local narrative documentation in reference to Tedlock's description of "culture pattern dreams" (B. Tedlock 1992, 468). These narratives demonstrate that Juan's vision, while perhaps the most significant current account, is part of a rich collection of contemporary Toledo oral narratives that sustain and renew an enduring Mayan corpus of beliefs.

Juan's Testimony Language and Identity

In the years following independence, Mayan leaders, government personnel, and foreign assistance agencies have increasingly promoted adult and community education in Toledo's hinterland. On his visits to Belize, Juan enters this informal infrastructure and routinely delivers his message in a church or community building, the focal points of contemporary Mayan discourse. Assuming his catechetical posture, he testifies to the entire community, depending on "converted" adults to spread his message among family members, neighbors, and children.

Inspired by Juan's fervor and his messages of ritual renewal and sustainability, Mayans and others have taken it upon themselves to broadcast this moral code of living in balance with the earth. While languages often create boundaries between people, T.M.C.C. members and educators have spread Juan's message beyond traditional ethnic borders by translating his visionary account into English and Mopan. Juan and his followers apparently consider this visionary message to be of such critical importance that they are willing to risk the alterations that can occur in translation in order to reach their rain forest audience and beyond. In fact, since Juan has permitted and encouraged the audiotaping of his testimonials, interested villagers can refer to the original Kekchi version for inspiration and to check the authenticity and equivalence of the translations.

Juan's message, both in Kekchi and in translation, has the potential to enter Kekchi discourse at a number of sites, including the village council, church, school, community meetings, market-bus rides, and casual conversation. A hallmark of Juan's testimony is his use of powerful words and concepts that link modern residents to the ancient identity and traditions of the "old Maya." These words and concepts have the potential to enter community discourse as an incipient generative vocabulary and act as seeds of further cultural renewal. Modern literacy programs that have attempted to integrate reading with "reading the world" (Freire 1970), that is, providing a critical and empowering outlook on readers' surroundings, have made use of generative vocabularies. These key words of analysis and power offer significant linguistic and pedagogical potential for reflection, instruction, articulation, and enhanced community consciousness regarding peoples' social, physical, and political environment.

As each narrative version of Juan's experience indicates, he is employing just such a generative vocabulary (e.g., mission, hill spirit, waste, carelessness, abuse, scarcity), and his followers are making their best efforts to translate his message into English for expanded community discussion in the wake of his testimonial visits. Juan announces that he is on a "mission"; he is a messenger and an "example." Could this be a case of Kekchi Mayan signification, an appropriation of the Catholic proselytizing "mission" to indicate the hill god's enlistment of this catechist?

Juan's visionary journey to the abode of the Mountain-Valley returns his listeners and readers to the physical and spiritual locus of cultural renewal and care of the earth. The hill spirit, also known by names such as Mountain-and-Valley God (Colby and Colby 1981), *dueño de cero* (Oakes 1951), *Totilme'iletik* (Fabrega and Silver 1973), and Earth Lords (B. Tedlock 1992) throughout other parts of the Mayan world, is the most significant spiritual reference in this particular complex of visionary narratives.

> A key symbol of pan-Mayan ethnic identity is the sacred earth. In several Mayan languages the earth is known by a term that literally translates into English as "Mountain-Valley." The earth appears frequently within Mayan myths, dreams, and visions referring both to the physical features of the landscape, including mountains, hills, volcanoes, valleys, caves, lakes, and springs, as well as spiritual beings who inhabit this sacred geography, guarding the forest and controlling the weather. (B. Tedlock 1992, 454)

A litany of critical terms is contained in the different narrative versions as some modern farmers are accused of being responsible for waste, pain, carelessness, wounding, maiming, abuse, scarcity, damage, hurt, destruction, and hatred. Juan weaves together an indictment against those who would abuse and damage the community, as well as the land and living things. The narrative's hill spirit leaves no doubt that such behavior will result in scarcity, pain, and destruction.

While Juan's cautionary vocabulary is explicit and threatening, he is equally clear about what people must do to return to the "old ways." Hunters and farmers must return to the "old rituals," praying, using game and grain "wisely," asking "permission" of the hill spirits, and acting with "honor" and obedience. At the very end of his talk, Juan sings a song that specifically outlines the path that people must follow. They must "burn their incense three times a day," "give thanks and call the names of the thirteen hill gods," and present "burnt offerings." The rich diction of Juan's narrative echoes translations of stories from the old Maya. These are the words and concepts that Mayan leaders in the T.M.C.C. are articulating as they promote a return to ritual farming and hunting, while at the same time investigating modern innovations, such as sustainable logging operations. These words and concepts offer students their own indigenous, generative vocabulary that they may use to discuss both cultural renewal and cooperative, sensitive adaptation to modern times. These essential words and concepts offer the promise of good crops, abundant games, arable land, and community. Since it is beyond the scope of my study to describe the widespread impact of Juan's testimony, I will now discuss the impact of his narrative in the context of Toledo's schools.

JUAN'S TESTIMONY IN AN EDUCATIONAL CONTEXT

Juan began testifying about his vision at a time when the Toledo education system was beginning to evolve its literacy programs to consider a dual language approach that accommodates the goals of nation-building and ethnic cultural renewal. In addition to discussing Juan's speeches, a number of Mayan leaders and educators have encouraged the textualization of Juan's speech in English as a means of reaching those Kekchi who are not literate in their language. Specifically, the English translation is included in *Stories in the Air*, a school text that, when widely distributed, can potentially place Juan's visionary account before every secondary school student and adult reader in Toledo.

The translation of Juan's testimony into English presents key insights into the evolving nature of language and identity for Toledo's Kekchi Maya. Since independence, many Kekchi parents, teachers, and leaders have identified themselves not only as Kekchi but as Belizeans. Most Kekchi have embraced their new country since it offers political stability, a healthy standard of living, essential human services, land rights to those who farm its bush, and a safe haven from Guatemala's state terrorism. Most Toledo Mayans recognize that to be a Belizean, capable of fully functioning in their newly independent state, it is necessary to learn English, the language that is required in schools and provides the best opportunity for entry into a wider labor pool, national discourse, and the larger English-speaking world. While many adult Mayans, particularly elders and those women who remain close to their homes, are marginally fluent in English, virtually all adults encourage the younger generation to learn English.

For those Kekchi who are not literate in their Mayan tongue, education in English, particularly utilizing the district texts, is providing a vehicle that is capable of complementing Kekchi efforts to instill a broader understanding of their own cultural heritage. The Toledo readers inform students about certain aspects of Kekchi history, traditions, and spirituality, as well as reinforcing and validating these beliefs. Ten years of school observations and teacher testimony indicate that stories such as Juan's visionary account often spark classroom discussion and debate regarding similar stories. Likewise, when students are assigned to collect oral stories and folkways from relatives, this material adds to the growing body of Toledo oral lore that is the foundation of the textbook program and provides a significant contribution to the T.M.C.C. archives. Mayan students report that they often first hear a story in Kekchi or Mopan and then they must seek family help with translation. In this way, such school assignments further encourage the use and learning of ethnic first language, as well as familial sharing. This home-school connection demonstrates once again how the potent vision of Juan the Catechist is one of the forces that drives Kekchi cultural renewal.

Though the impact of Juan's moral teachings has been discussed in previous sections, it is worthwhile to consider the views of Toledo educators who have actually worked with these stories. In an interview with the author, District Education Officer Fabian Cayetano offers this reflection on the educational and moral potential of stories such as Juan's testimony for all the students in Toledo. Fluent in Kekchi, Cayetano is a Garifuna, a community whose members also believe in protectors or owners of the earth and sea.

J. Kelly: The stories of the hill spirit, the Mountain-Valley—when stories like these go into a textbook, how do you see a story like this enhancing a child's identity as a Kekchi?

FC: Some beautiful things happen, Jerry. One, the Kekchi firmly believes that everything has an owner. He also believes that he's owned—he has an owner as well. The trees have an owner . . . the rivers, the fish, the animals, the mountains, the land, the precious corn. They all have owners.

The Kekchi spiritual relationship with his god, or with the owner of the mountains and the animals—it's not one of a distant relationship. It is a relationship whereby I can *communicate* with this owner, confident that he will respond to my request by giving me a piece of meat, a piece of fish, a curassow, a peccary. Before I even leave my hut, the shelter and comfort of my house, let me pray, let me ask, let me trust with the faith and sincerity that I request also.

Two things turn out there. The spirituality of the Kekchi is integrated with the life of this person. It's not a catechism, written thing, where this is what you do on Sunday. *No!* This man lives his spirituality, practically integrated into his life.

There is also the respect for the sanctity of life. We don't go shooting all the peccaries. We look for the good sized ones. We shoot three, we know you can only bring three back. We're not going there to pleasure hunt. (laughs) We only want for our meat.

Then there's the sharing. The head hunter could have said, "OK, I claim all, I give you a piece, I give you a piece. To hell with you. The rest is mine." (laughs)

No! The head hunter says, "Cut up everything—what we will sell, what we will share, how we will share the money that we get."

So. Concrete sharing, actually is the experience there. The child sees sharing concretized—in the hunterman's life. The reading strengthens the sharing attitude. It reinforces the sharing attitude. Better yet, if the class teacher could grasp this story and bring out the spirituality of the prayers, of the asking in faith, and the thankfulness, gratitude—the world needs much more of gratitude nowadays.

Cayetano reiterates one of Juan's key messages, that true caring for the earth and living things must be accomplished in community. The ideal set before Belizean children is not merely some antilittering campaign or a passing call for moral rearmament. Rather, Juan's vision is at the root of Kekchi identity and spirituality, a communal identity in harmony with each other and the earth. Cayetano himself demonstrates in his commentary how moral values are routinely transmitted in narrative form when he makes his own brief reference to the small hunting party.

Louis Cucul is a Kekchi native of Aguacate village; as teacher and principal of that village's elementary school, he has used the district readers for a number of years. A co-editor of *Stories in the Air*, Louis is a strong advocate of the use of indigenous narratives for cultural renewal. In a 1994 conversation, he acts as both the medium and the message in offering his reflections on the visionary narrative of Juan the Catechist:

I hope to write another story, a true story about a catechist and avoiding the waste of things we already have, precious things like food. I know that you know the story by way of Micala and I want to do some work on that one. I got all the information from my grandfather who went to listen to this man in Kekchi at Dolores or Crique Sarco. He told my family the story of Juan and the hill cave.

These stories, in some way or other, should be put in text. It takes a lot of work, typing and proofreading and so on. Maybe other cultures will be interested in getting them published. That story is supposed to be spread around.

Three people from our village went to hear this story and they returned and alerted people to it. They had to come up with some type of offering or sacrifice. That's why I really have it in mind to work on these stories for the textbooks.

I'm sure that these stories will help and we have to stress to people that these stories are true stories. We need to make people aware because much of the new generation doesn't go by our ancestors. I think that traditional stories will really help.

Clearly educators such as Cayetano and Cucul have moved considerably beyond the British lecture hall model that many Toledo teachers were originally exposed to in their youth. Both men view education as an experience that has the potential to involve students in the active engendering of moral values. The various pedagogical processes involved in the textbook project, including interviewing, writing, taping, transcribing, and reading, serve to validate not only traditional stories but also the ecological bush wisdom (Scollon and Scollon 1981) that Toledo's Kekchi, Mopan, and Garifuna have garnered and used for generations. Just as Juan's account of the hill spirit provokes student interest when it is read, discussed, and written about in class, so too these emergent teachings fuel family and community discussion, potentially bringing the cultural renewal process full circle.

The spread of Juan's visionary narrative occasions a final optimistic consideration. Although Belize basically offers the world a history of interethnic peace, its citizens still must contend with a legacy of competition and rivalries that were fostered by the colonial system. Juan's story, along with many other indigenous narratives that document each ethnic group's heritage and contemporary life-ways, serve to validate and illuminate in print peoples' histories that of necessity often had to remain hidden during the colonial era. Today the widespread use of English and Creole functions to allow Belizeans from all ethnic groups to work toward the caring and tolerant community that is at the heart of Juan's testimony.

ACKNOWLEDGMENTS

I am indebted to Thomas Teul for his friendship, trust, and guidance. Thomas died tragically in 1995. My thanks to Dean Scott, my co-worker and fellow traveler, for his fine map of southern Belize.

NOTES

1. Members of this Mayan group in Belize most commonly refer to themselves as "Kekchi." The official Guatemalan spelling *Q'eqchi* is used most often in the wider Mayan world and scholarly literature.

2. While there is no universal accord regarding varieties of Creole, Hancock's description of Belizean Creole English in the context of 100 pidgins and Creoles is both useful and apt.

3. Superimposing the route indicated by the title of Roy Cayetano's paper, "A Report on a Tour of Toledo Villages on the Trail from Blue Creek to Aguacate by Way of Crique Sarco," over the maps of the Toledo District offers some indication of the scope and remoteness of the Toledo educational enterprise.

4. In her 1992 conclusion to the revised edition of *Time and the Highland Maya*, Barbara Tedlock indicated that in 1991 she was doing research on visionary narratives in southern Belize. In 1993, I sent her the three versions of Juan's narrative. She was kind enough to respond, informing me that Juan's visionary narrative "closely resembles a Kekchi myth collected by Jon Schackt nearly twenty years ago." I am indebted to her kindness and scholarship in the shaping of my analytical framework for assessing the significance and meaning of Juan's narrative.

5. The Belize New Hampshire Teacher Program was created by staff members of the University of New Hampshire's Live, Learn and Teach Program. For ten years veteran teachers from New England have visited Toledo schools to confer and collaborate with Belizean teachers.

6. Nature's Way Guest House, a gathering place for backpackers, ecotourists, and researchers, is located in Punta Gorda. William (Chet) Schmidt and his wife, Damien, provide lodgings and assistance to many Toledo visitors. Nature's Way also houses the office of the Toledo Ecotourism Association (T.E.A.), a Mayan cooperative that sponsors guest houses in remote Garifuna and Mayan villages.

7. Thomas and I edited a preliminary version of Juan's story for the textbook program. In accord with the district textbook protocol, we transcribed Juan's story using correct English spelling, while retaining the narrator's syntax. Textbook transcribers routinely correct severe grammatical errors that might reflect negatively on the narrator, as well as presenting inaccurate models for student readers. Regional errors, such as the commonplace reversal of gendered pronouns, are also corrected.

Members of the T.M.C.C. preferred a translation of Juan's testimony that preserved some of the poetic quality of the original Kekchi. Although I presented examples of ethnopoetic formats (Swann 1992; D. Tedlock 1993), the T.M.C.C. opted to go with what they knew best, the paragraph style.

REFERENCES

Basso, Ellen B. 1992. "The Implications of a Progressive Theory of Dreaming." In Barbara Tedlock, ed., *Dreaming: Anthropological and Psychological Interpretations*. Sante Fe, N.M.: School of American Research Press.

Berkey, Curtis. 1995. "Mayas of Belize and Conservation." *Cultural Survival* 19(2): 13–16.

Bierhorst, John. 1990. *The Mythology of Mexico and Central America*. New York: Morrow.

Canby, Peter. 1992. *Heart of the Sky: Travels Among the Maya*. New York: Harper Collins.

Cayetano, E. Roy. 1984. *A Report on a Tour of Toledo Villages on the Trail from Blue Creek to Aguacate via Crique Sarco*. A report submitted to Belize Ministry of Education.

Chapman, Anne. 1978, 1992. *Masters of Animals: Oral Traditions of the Tolupan Indians, Honduras*. Philadelphia: Gordon and Breach.

Clifford, James, and George E. Marcus, eds. 1986. *Writing Culture: The Poetics and Politics of Ethnography*. Berkeley: University of California Press.

Colby, Benjamin N., and Lore M. Colby. 1981. *The Daykeeper: The Life and Discourse of an Ixil Diviner*. Cambridge, Mass.: Harvard University Press.

Fabian, Johannes. 1986. *Language and Colonial Power*. Berkeley: University of California Press.

Fabrega, Horacio, Jr., and Daniel B. Silver. 1973. *Illness and Shamanistic Curing in Zincatan*. Stanford, Calif.: Stanford University Press.

Farris, Nancy M. 1984. *Maya Society Under Colonial Rule: The Collective Enterprise of Survival*. Princeton, N.J.: Princeton University Press.

Freire, Paulo. 1970. *Pedagogy of the Oppressed*. New York: Herder and Herder.

———. 1973. *Education for Critical Consciousness*. New York: Continuum.

Freire, Paulo, and Donaldo Macedo. 1987. *Literacy: Reading the Word and the World*. South Hadley, Mass.: Bergin and Garvey Publishers.

Goody, Jack. 1976. *The Domestication of the Savage Mind*. Cambridge: Cambridge University Press.

Halliday, M.A.K. 1987. "Language and the Order of Nature." In Nigel Fabb, Derek Attridge, Alan Durrant, & Colin MacCabe, eds., *The Linguistics of Writing*. New York: Methuen, 135–55.

Hancock, I.F. 1971. "A Survey of Pidgins and Creoles of the World." In D. Hymes, ed., *Pidginization and Creolization of Languages*. Cambridge: Cambridge University Press, 509–23.

Kozol, Jonathan. 1978. A New Look at the Literacy Campaign in Cuba. *Harvard Educational Review* 48(3): 341–77.

Le Page, R. B., and Andre Tabouret-Keller. 1985. *Acts of Identity: Creole-Based Approaches to Language and Ethnicity*. Cambridge: Cambridge University Press.

Lofty, John S. 1992. *Time to Write: The Influence of Time and Culture on Learning to Write*. Albany: State University of New York Press.

Marcus, George E. 1986. "Contemporary Problems of Ethnography in the Modern World System." In James Clifford and George E. Marcus, ed., *Writing Culture: The Poetics and Politics of Ethnography*. Berkeley: University of California Press.

McLaughlin, Daniel. 1992. *When Literacy Empowers: Navajo Language in Print*. Albuquerque: University of New Mexico Press.

Menchu, Rigoberta. 1984. *I, Rigoberta Menchu: An Indian Woman in Guatemala*. Ed. Elizabeth Burgos-Debray. London: Verso.

Miller Valerie. 1985. *Between Struggle and Hope: The Nicaraguan Literacy Campaign*. Boulder, Colo.: Westview Press.

Nelson, Richard K. 1983. *Make Prayers to the Raven: A Koyukon View of the Northern Forest*. Chicago: University of Chicago Press.

Ngũgĩ wa Thiong'o. 1986. *Decolonizing the Mind: The Politics of Language in African Literature*. Portsmouth, N.H.: Heinemann.

Oakes, Maud. 1951. *The Two Crosses of Todos Santos: Survivals of Mayan Religious Ritual*. Princeton, N.J.: Princeton University Press.

Ong, Walter J. 1982. *Orality and Literacy*. London: Routledge.

Perera, Victor. 1993. *Unfinished Conquest: The Guatemalan Tragedy*. Berkeley: University of California Press.

Redfield, Robert, and Alfonso Villa Rojas. 1934. *Chan Kom. A Maya Village*. Washington: Carnegie Institution of Washington.

Rosaldo, Renato. 1989. *Culture and Truth: The Remaking of Social Analysis*. Boston: Beacon Press.

Said, Edward W. 1993. *Culture and Imperialism*. New York: Alfred A. Knopf.

Scollon, Ron, and Suzanne B. K. Scollon. 1981. *Narrative, Literacy and Face in Interethnic Communication*. Norwood, N.J.: Ablex Publishing Company.

Stoll, David. 1993. *Between Two Armies in the Ixil Towns of Guatemala*. New York: Columbia University Press.

Street, Brian V., ed. 1993. *Cross-Cultural Approaches to Literacy*. Cambridge: Cambridge University Press.

Swann, Brian. 1992. *On the Translation of Native American Literatures*. Washington: Smithsonian Institution Press.

Taylor, Kenneth Iain. 1990. "Why Supernatural Eels Matter." In Suzanne Head and Robert Heinzman, eds., *Lessons of the Rainforest*. San Francisco: Sierra Club Books, 184–96.

Tedlock, Barbara. 1982. *Time and the Highland Maya*. Albuquerque: University of New Mexico Press.

———. 1992. "The Role of Dreams and Visionary Narratives in Mayan Cultural Survival." *Ethos* 20(4): 453–76.

Tedlock, Dennis. 1993. *Breath on the Mirror*. San Francisco: Harper San Francisco.

Tyler, Stephen A. 1986. "Post-Modern Ethnography: From Document of the Occult to Occult Document." In James Clifford and George E. Marcus, eds., *Writing Culture: The Poetics and Politics of Ethnography*. Berkeley: University of California Press.

Williams, Raymond. 1977. *Marxism and Literature*. New York: Oxford University Press.

5

"We Don't Speak Catalan Because We Are Marginalized": Ethnic and Class Meanings of Language in Barcelona

Kathryn A. Woolard

The equation of language and ethnic identity is a tenet of Western tradition that, from origins in the European Romantic era, has come to be a commonsense assumption around much of the world. Social science has recognized that this linkage is historically specific rather than natural or essential. But as noted by Collins (this volume), the way in which the link is forged, maintained, or restructured in actual communities is not particularly well understood. Collins questions and examines the process by which language comes to figure so centrally in group feeling. I will consider here the process of restructuring this link as it occurs in Catalonia, Spain.

In politically autonomous Catalonia, attempts have been made to attenuate or redefine a particular kind of linkage already established between language and ethnic identity. However, these attempts reveal the complex imbrication of various social identities that has become the focus of social analysis in recent years. Ethnicity, gender, class, and national identity are increasingly understood to be mutually constitutive (e.g., Frankenberg 1993; Streicker 1995). Moreover, not just ethnicity but other group identities such as social class and gender are well known to be routinely indexed through variable uses of language. Therefore, if the significance of language choice shifts on one identitive dimension in response to policy decisions, other dimensions of social identity may become more salient. New, unintended sociolonguistic meanings may become entrenched.

In an effort to extend public uses of Catalan, official language policy in Catalonia over the last one and a half decades has moved toward neutralizing some of the ethnic connotations of the language and making it a civic language more than an ethnic one. Such policies reduce the ethnic signaling value of Catalan, in order to make it publicly available to people of varying degrees of identification with the Catalan nationalist project.

These language policies have indeed gone some way toward reducing the ethnic closure of Catalan. But the social meaning of the language has not been dissipated so much as reorganized. In this chapter I argue that as ethnic distinctions in the use of Catalan fade under official policies and as Catalan becomes a public, civic language, unintended class distinctions have come into sharper relief and are taking up the surplus of sociolinguistic meaning.[1]

MINORITY LANGUAGE MAINTENANCE
AND GROWTH

Catalonia is now a politically autonomous community in the northeast corner of Spain, with the cosmopolitan city of Barcelona at its political, social, and economic center. Catalan is the distinctive Romance language spoken in Catalonia (and neighboring areas). During centuries of subordination to Castilian (as the Spanish language is known in Spain) and decades of state repression under the Franco dictatorship, the Catalan language survived as a lively, much-used vernacular. For example, in a survey taken at the time new policies were established in 1983, 93 percent of speakers born in Catalonia of parents born in Catalonia claimed Catalan as their principal language (Dirección General de Política Lingüística 1984).

Catalan owes its survival rate, striking for a minoritized language, in large part to its status as a defining criterion of a prestigious ethnic identity associated with relatively high social-class standing. Traditionally, to be Catalan is to speak Catalan, and to speak Catalan is to claim to be Catalan. As a Catalan demographer was quoted as saying, "A Catalan is a person [gentleman] who speaks Catalan" (García 1991).[2] Conversely, use of Catalan was traditionally interpreted as a claim to *be* Catalan, rather than as just a signal of acquired linguistic proficiency and/or desire to communicate.

This pattern of minority language survival, while unusual in its extent and tenacity, conforms to a frequent observation in the sociology of language. A key role in symbolizing ethnic identity and defining community membership has often been found to contribute to the maintenance of minority and nonstandard languages as valued resources in local social networks (e.g., Gal 1979; Labov 1972; Milroy 1980).

However, the sociolinguistic literature suggests that dominant languages are not ideologically linked to ethnic identity in the same way that minoritized languages are. One explanation that has been given for the traditional assimilative power of English in American society is that this society and language were mainly ideologized as "nonethnic" in character. Joshua Fishman noted that "American nationalism was primarily non-ethnic or supra-ethnic in comparison to the nationalisms of most of Europe . . . it did not obviously clash with or demand the betrayal of immigrant *ethnic* values" (1965, 149). "Just as there is hardly any ethnic foundation to American nationalism, so there is no special language awareness in the use of English" (1966, 29–30). I stress that it is an ideology, not a fact, of ethnic neutrality that Fishman singles out. He argues that this American ideology of language promotes the acceptance of English as a seemingly neutral language of upward mobility. Such a disarming appearance leads rapidly to bilingualism and then, ironically, to language shift.

In a more critical mode, the French sociologist Pierre Bourdieu (1982) has made a similar point. In his view, a language like French succeeds in becoming a dominant language that displaces other competitors because institutions such as schools purvey it as a universalistic attribute of authority. Quite the opposite of being construed as an ethnic, particularistic property, the dominant language variety is dissociated from its social roots. Under the persuasive power of schools and media, people come to misrecognize the social basis of the language's power over them and endorse its authority. The ties of the particular form of speech to particular social groups is obscured by these apparently universalistic institutions.

Whether we accept the more benign or the more critical vision of the role of public ideology in extending the domain of a language, both views argue that a close and explicit ideological linkage of language to an ascriptive ethnic identity is not characteristic of languages that succeed in establishing dominance over others, like English and French. The rare threatened minority language that survives and makes a bid to become a principal public language may be in a paradoxical position, then. Ethnic signaling value, a quality that can contribute to survival under conditions of subordination, may be a limiting factor when acquisition and use by a larger population become a goal.

LANGUAGE NORMALIZATION
IN AUTONOMOUS CATALONIA

Catalan is such a rare threatened but upwardly mobile language. In post-Franco Spain, Catalonia is politically autonomous and officially bilingual. Although Catalan never fell out of use in informal and intimate arenas during periods of subordination and repression, it was long excluded from official institutions and formal public uses. Since political autonomy was reestablished in 1980, Catalan language planners have campaigned for linguistic "normalization." This term is ambiguous and encompasses varying long- and short-term sociolinguistic goals. In the first stages of language policy making, the need was to make Catalan a language considered appropriate and used in all domains of social activity, formal and informal, official and intimate, oral and literate. In the Catalanist conceptual schema, "normal" languages that haven't been artificially suppressed through political means fill this entire spectrum of communicative functions. In the long term, the goal of most language planners is for Catalan to become the unmarked ("normal") medium of general communication in the community, a role long held by Castilian. Ideally, Castilian is to be used not for primary public communication within Catalonia (although there is increasing recognition that it will probably always be a significant home language), but for relations with foreigners and with the rest of Spain.

The attainment of such a long-range goal depends not only on successfully recapturing official, public, and mass-mediated domains of language use for Catalan, but also on extending it to a large population of Castilian speakers. The high level of language maintenance among autochthonous Catalans (whom I'll call simply "Catalans," in keeping with traditional local usage) is not enough to support the full catalanization of regional institutions. In the twentieth century, particularly in the 1960s, Catalonia received very large numbers of Castilian-speaking immigrants, the majority from southern Spain. These immigrants and their children and grandchildren (usually called "Castilians") form at least half the population of the metropolitan area of Barcelona. Particularly significant to the process of sociolinguistic change examined in this chapter is the fact that these Castilian speakers are heavily concentrated in the working class and are especially numerous among unskilled workers. Native Catalans, on the other hand, are more concentrated in the middle and upper classes, thus endowing the Catalan identity with much of its prestige and desirability.

Because of their demographic weight, recruiting Castilians as second-language speakers of Catalan is an important component of language planning. This recruitment is particularly challenging in that it must be accomplished in large part through voluntary means, since the Spanish Constitution sets implicit limits on the extent to which use of Catalan can be officially mandated. Knowledge of Castilian is incumbent on all Spanish citizens, and its use is constitutionally guaranteed. Use of the other languages of Spain in their appropriate communities is established in the Constitution only as a right, not an obligation.

During the Franco years, the ethnic symbolism of the Catalan language helped not only in native speaker maintenance, but also in recruiting some immigrant speakers who were socially and psychologically positioned for a change in ethnic identity. By acquiring and using Catalan as a habitual language, they abandoned a view of themselves as Castilians and established a claim to Catalan identity. But such ethnolinguistic conversions were relatively few. In the 1983 survey cited earlier, 87 percent of those aged 15–20 years had been born in Catalonia, but only 43 percent of them claimed to speak Catalan frequently.

My research at the start of autonomy in 1979-80 suggested an explanation for this pattern: the language-ethnicity symbolic link was hindering the acquisition of Catalan by more people than it encouraged. Because of the success of castilianizing language policy during the Franco years, virtually all Catalans were bilingual in Catalan and Castilian. An etiquette of language choice led the majority of Catalans to switch to Castilian when addressing native speakers of Castilian, even when it was apparent that the Castilian understood, and in some cases even spoke, Catalan. This automatic switch was conceived of as politeness, but it had the effect of an ethnic boundary–maintaining mechanism.

An experimental measure I used to study language attitudes among young people confirmed the social significance of this etiquette. The experiment used the well-known "matched-guise" design (Lambert et al. 1960; see Woolard 1989 for a full account).[3] In that study, the use of Catalan earned speakers higher status evaluations than did the use of Castilian, regardless of the ethnolinguistic origins of the speaker or the listener. However, on measures of solidarity, only Catalan listeners valued the speaking of Catalan very highly, and only for *native* Catalan speakers. The speaking of Catalan won no increase in solidary feeling from Catalan listeners when the speaker was a native Castilian-speaker (and, presumably, identifiable as such by accent clues). Also important, Castilian listeners significantly penalized their fellow Castilians for the use of Catalan. The matched-guise test suggested that Castilian speakers had little to gain in their personal relations with Catalans by attempting to speak Catalan, while they had much to lose in solidarity from co-members of their own ethnolinguistic group.

In my reading of the experimental results, ethnographic evidence, and the survey data I have cited, a successful strategy for extending Catalan to nonnative speakers might capitalize on the existing prestige of Catalan, but it ultimately would depend on attenuating the ethnic symbolism. It would be necessary to create a perception of Catalan as a more neutral "public voice," rather than a distinctive ethnic voice, in order to create not simply institutional access but also social and emotional access to the language for nonnative speakers.

In the years following autonomy and that initial research, Catalonia developed a number of new language policies. A campaign was launched in 1981 with the slogan "Catalan is everybody's," signaling the goal of extending identification with Catalan to those not usually ethnically identified as Catalan. A "Law of Linguistic Normalization" was passed in 1983, establishing a legal frame for official and public use of Catalan. A fully Catalan-medium television channel was initiated in that same year. But most important, catalanization of the schools began in earnest in 1983, with progressively greater requirements in the ensuing years for teaching of and in Catalan at all levels. Catalonia looks to the school as one of the main vehicles for catalanization of the whole society (Tuson 1985).

Did linguistic policy changes lead to a restructuring of the language-identity link that might encourage the use of Catalan by new sectors of the population? A repetition of the language attitudes experiment in 1987 suggests that they did. The results for the status measure were unsurprisingly similar to those of 1980, with Catalan enhancing a speaker's perceived intelligence and effectiveness. But solidarity ratings were no longer patterned according to the speaker's linguistic origins. Catalan listeners generalized their preference for hearing Catalan to the two native speakers of Castilian in the sample. In 1980, these speakers' use of Catalan did not win them increased solidarity ratings from Catalan listeners. But in 1987 it did. Moreover, the statistically significant preference among Castilian listeners in 1980 for the Castilian guise of these same speakers was gone in 1987. Castilian-speaking listeners no longer penalize second-language speakers of Catalan with significantly reduced feelings of solidarity (see Woolard and Gahng 1990 for a fuller discussion).

It appears, then, that the bond between Catalan ethnic identity and the Catalan language has been attenuated. The speaking of Catalan now matters more than the identity or origin of the speaker. If policy changes have indeed made possible such changes in attitudes as suggested by the experiment, are they being translated into changes in language *use*?

CHANGES IN LANGUAGE USE: SCHOOLS AND YOUNG PEOPLE

Most sources tell us that educational linguistic policy has been very successful in increasing knowledge of Catalan (e.g., CIDC 1987). However, the little research that has been done and the many opinions that have been expressed are generally negative about increases in the actual use of Catalan by nonnative speakers.

For example, one team of teacher-researchers comments:

We are seeing an evident improvement in the knowledge of Catalan among our students. . . . However, this improvement in knowledge of Catalan contrasts with a reality that we also experience daily in the schoolyards, in the corridors, in classes and cantinas of the schools where we work. . . . we become aware that we are training Catalan-writing students, and that only rarely are they transformed into effective Catalan speakers. (Erill et al. 1986, 1)[4]

It is important to ask what the commentators might have in mind when they write of "effective Catalan speakers." Tuson (1985) gives a somewhat more positive evaluation of sociolinguistic change, because she is more attentive to differing norms of language use for different communicative activities. Tuson found that changes in the explicit language norms for formal purposes *did* affect primary school students' actual linguistic behavior in formal school contexts (1985, 208–9). But, on the other hand, she found the traditional norm of accommodation to Castilian operating at the informal level.

To pursue the notoriously difficult question of actual language use, I turned to ethnographic observation in Barcelona area schools. Some of the teachers of Catalan whom I met, particularly those who worked in schools where the overwhelming majority of students were of Castilian-speaking background, despaired of any success for their efforts to teach students Catalan. "They never speak it," several told me, confirming the observations of Erill et al (1992). Don't the students speak Catalan in class? I would ask, pursuing the meaning of "never." Ah, well yes, students speak Catalan in class, to the Catalan teacher, "because they have to." But in the halls, among the students themselves, one hears only Castilian, teachers told me sadly. They measured their success—or lack thereof—by the standard of everyday language choice, strikingly echoing the view expressed by Erill and his colleagues.

Underlying this evaluation of the situation were unexpressed assumptions about the goal of Catalan instruction. The goal of educational linguistic policy as given explicitly in official documents (Arenas i Sampera 1987) is that by the end of primary school, every student be able to understand, speak, and write both official languages. But many teachers implicitly assume the goal of their own teaching efforts to be that of "normalization": to make Catalan the language normally used by their students in daily relations.

Although this goal was indeed shared by many language planners, pedagogic strategies (particularly for secondary school) were generally not designed to achieve that goal (and there is reason to doubt that pedagogy alone could ever do so). The emphasis of the secondary curriculum was on grammatical analysis and prescriptive written forms. Nothing in that curriculum acknowledged that they were teaching Catalan not only to nonnative speakers, but to non-speakers in many cases. The overt recognition of existing ethnolinguistic differences that a special curriculum would demand was usually avoided in official spheres. From its earliest days, the post-Franco Catalan government steadfastly rejected any characterization of Catalonia as consisting of "two communities" and eschewed policies that grouped the populace around the linguistic criterion.

Public language policies were moving to diminish the ethnic significance of the Catalan language. School policies, rightly or wrongly, had shied from acknowledging any differentiation of students on the basis of language. Yet in their classroom practice, some teachers unwittingly worked against this trend toward ethnolinguistic neutralization. They expected their students to be motivated to use Catalan through the emotional and political symbolism that had led the teachers themselves to their own profession. A large proportion of teachers of Catalan were, quite understandably, ardent Catalan nationalists. They had chosen to teach Catalan because of their love for the language as a symbol of their identity and nation. Such Catalanists still hoped their students would rise to the defense of Catalan, a sincere motive for the teachers but not an appealing one for young Castilians, particularly since Catalan is not so obviously oppressed under conditions of political autonomy.

In the most concentrated Castilian-speaking communities on the working-class periphery of Barcelona, particularly in vocational schools, the teachers were quite justified in their despair. In those schools, there were still large groups of students even among the youngest classes who appeared basically untouched by linguistic normalization and Catalan teaching. Conversation not only in the halls, but even in Catalan class was dominated by Castilian, a Castilian heavily tinged with the accents of Andalusia even though the great majority of students had been born in Catalonia.

Not all schools, however, presented the same picture. In public secondary schools around the metropolitan area, where students were of more mixed linguistic background, considerably more second-language use of Catalan could be heard. I spent several months attending classes with and observing a first-year group in a public high school in the metropolitan area. This school was known for its Catalan orientation but offered mixed-language instruction to a student body in which working-class Castilian speakers were heavily represented.

The class I observed was a group of 21 girls and 15 boys from a variety of neighborhoods, who took all their classes together. All but one of them was born in the Barcelona area, though more than a third of their parents were not. About one-third of the class had Castilian as their mother tongue, and the rest were of Catalan-speaking origins. Most of them were 14 years old, and this was the late winter and spring of their first year in high school.[5]

I found varying responses to catalanization among the thirteen native Castilian speakers in the group. Six students of Castilian language origin spoke Catalan fluently and frequently, and an equal number never or almost never used it, especially among peers. Boys and girls were equally represented among users and non-users of Catalan.[6]

Two boys, Rafael and Víctor, had taken on a primarily Catalan identity, deliberately changing over to Catalan language habits in the summer before beginning their studies at this school. These two used Catalan habitually in all their relations with each other and with Catalans, and preferentially with bilingual Castilians. Rafael chose the moment for his linguistic transformation deliberately, since the change from primary to secondary school offered him an opportunity to make the change in language choice convincingly. In the summer before beginning high school, Rafael made an agreement with Víctor, who was changing schools with him, that they would speak only Catalan. "Between ourselves, because we knew each other since we were little, since nursery school, we always spoke in Castilian, and now we always speak in Catalan," Rafael explained.[7]

Indeed, I found that Rafael and Víctor used Catalan together at all times, even in murmured exchanges as lab partners in science class. So successful was the transformation that some of Rafael's classmates did not realize he was not a native Catalan speaker until it was mentioned in a class discussion I conducted on the topic.

At the other end of the spectrum, there were a number of boys and girls in the class who retained strong and self-consciously monolingual "Castilian" and "Spanish" identities, although they were all born in Barcelona. These included a close-knit group of four girls (Elena, Rosario, Adela, and Margarita). "I'm Catalan, I ought to say so," admitted Elena, meaning she had been born in Catalonia. But she claimed to feel only Castilian and Spanish. Some of these girls recalled insulting epithets aimed at them. Some belonged to Andalusian cultural clubs and flamenco dance groups. All were vocal fans of the "Real Madrid" soccer team, an effective way of signaling Castilian identification in a region where support of the Barcelona soccer team has long been an expression of catalanism.

All of these girls had acquired some competence in Catalan, and I heard all but one of them use it effectively in classroom exchanges. However, they spoke it only while doing classroom work, and then they used it with any consistency only in Catalan class. Catalan-speaking teachers frequently switched to Castilian to address these girls directly and to give them individualized instruction. To all of their peers and most other Catalan-speaking teachers, these girls generally spoke in

Castilian. Tellingly, Rosario and Elena initiated and sustained conversations in Catalan with me and with an Andalusian-origin teacher who taught his class in fluent but accented Catalan. That is, they chose to use Catalan when the interlocutor not only stood outside the peer group but also, like them, did not use that language as a badge of Catalan ethnic identity.

These two types of response to the ethnolinguistic challenge faced by Castilian speakers were similar to patterns I had seen in 1980. Both complete catalanization on the one hand and a reactive consolidation of a Castilian identity on the other reproduced a long-standing ethnolinguistic dichotomy. Each of these responses was signaled by predominantly monolingual behavior in key domains.

However, a new response I had not seen much of before was displayed by a third subgroup in the class, three second-generation immigrant girls (Marta, Josefina, and Laura). These were fluent Catalan speakers who used that language consistently with Catalan-speaking teachers, outsiders like myself, and Catalan-dominant peers. Their Catalan-speaking peers usually addressed them in Catalan, and teachers who switched to Castilian to speak to Elena and her group addressed these girls in Catalan. Nonetheless, Marta and company openly maintained their primary identity as Castilian speakers, publicly speaking Castilian to each other, unlike Rafael and Víctor. Marta and her friends switched back and forth between Catalan and Castilian as they worked on their science lab assignments, in ways that neither the native Catalan speakers in the class nor the catalanized Rafael and Víctor did. While they claimed to feel more "Catalan" than "Castilian," this group of girls appeared to be welding a new bilingual identity that had not been available to Castilian language-origin students of their age in 1980, and they were making it work socially.

The differences in patterns of linguistic adaptation are not idiosyncratic. Use of Catalan as a second language in this group was clearly conditioned by social class. Put most baldly, middle-class students used Catalan, and working-class students did not. The boys and girls who learned and frequently used Catalan, whether as a habitual language or a fluent second choice, all lived in the more central, middle-class areas of their town identified as Catalan neighborhoods. Rafael's father was a bank controller and his mother a school teacher, while Víctor's father held a managerial position in telecommunications. Another boy's parents were an accountant and a graphic artist. Marta and Josefina's fathers, immigrants from Andalusia themselves, were small businessmen, the owner-operators of a textile workshop.

In contrast, the Castilian-identified girls and boys who did not use Catalan with peers were almost all children of manual laborers. Elena and Margarita's fathers were factory workers, and Margarita's mother was a worker in the so-called second economy, putting in part-time hours in a factory run in a private garage. Rosario's father was a gardener, and her mother worked the night shift in a public residential institution. Adela's father was an unemployed construction worker. Castilian-identified boys included children of construction workers. Taxi driver was the most elevated and socially ambiguous occupation in the lot. All of these students lived in Castilian-dominant working-class neighborhoods on the periphery of the city.

Among students of Castilian origin within a single classroom, then, the more peripheral the neighborhood and the more marginal the family's economic status, the less likely they were to use the Catalan language informally, especially in peer relations. Literally, the more central the neighborhood and the more economically privileged the family, the more likely these young Castilian speakers were to use Catalan as an active social resource as well as to identify with Catalans.[8]

The Catalan language has of course long had class connotations in Barcelona, but this relationship was traditionally indirect, mediated by ethnic origins. Traditionally it owed to the language's nearly exclusive association with autochthonous Catalans, who were concentrated in the upper socioeconomic strata. What I saw in this classroom was a new pattern, in which social class was also systematically related to the use of Catalan as a *second* language. A kind of unintended "class cleansing" of language affiliation seemed to be taking place, straightening any blurry lines where the fairly redundant cleavages of language, class, and ethnicity had not been perfect before.

For this group of students, social class was more directly indexed by Catalan: Catalan was a discursive tool mastered and used by middle classes, regardless of their ascriptive ethnicity. As Catalan had become more a necessity for getting work done in formal institutions and public spheres and for success in school, it was also a resource acquired and used by middle-class Castilian speakers. That such use of Catalan could be detached from traditional Catalan ethnic identity was shown by the girls who claimed a bilingual identity through their public switches in language choice.

As middle classes had become identified with Catalan resources, Castilian identity became residual among these young people, identified more than ever by *not* speaking Catalan and with working and/or lower classes. Considerable evidence emerged in interviews with these students that showed that many thought about Catalans and Castilians in terms of class differences.[9] As some of the quotes below make explicit, Castilian identity is tied to poverty and lower-class status; and from lower status, Catalan interviewees sometimes move to a discussion of class-cultural stereotypes of vulgarity, rudeness, and loudness. However, Castilian-origin and Castilian-identified kids also mentioned economic and class-cultural differences, albeit in a different tone. I quote here a number of different students (most but not all Catalans) to show the strength, consistency, and tenor of these notions.

Eva: "If they're badly dressed and all, then they seem more, more Castilian, no?"

Victòria: "It seems like Castilians have, have less money, or they have less social standing. I don't know, with the way they dress, too. I find them ruder. They do their own thing, they shout on the streets."

Rafael (CS origin): "Man, normally Castilians are less cultured, or they're more from the [working-class] barrios."

Angels: "Castilian, I consider ruder, more coarse. More bumpkin. The, the, those girls [Margarita and her friends], I mean always, I don't know, they have, they're cruder, they say more swear words."

Josefina (CS origin): "I think that Catalans are more I don't know, more refined we could say."

Rosa: "Margarita and the others, you notice it [that they are Castilian] by their coarse way of talking."

Gabriela: "Castilians are cruder, more vulgar."

Mirella: "When I think of Castilians, I think of the cleaning lady at our house, or the employees my father has at the factory, and, sure, with the people in our classroom maybe there wouldn't be so much differences, but I picture Castilians with a lot of paint [make-up] on, in a style, Catalan people wear make-up too, but only to give color. But more Castilian people go more in a style, a lot of color here [on cheeks], heavily painted eyes and lips, more in that style, you know? . . . Castilians shout a lot."[10]

Rosario (CS): "Here, those who live better are Catalans, because they've been here a long time and they have the better jobs, which is natural, and the others are immigrants who've had to do the jobs that are somehow hard, no? . . . If you go to a good restaurant, and maybe you'll find a lot of Catalans there; there'll be some Castilians too. But if you go to one of those bars that puts out *tapas* and all that, there you'll find a lot of Castilians. [Here at school] we have a good time on the playground saying stupid things and we laugh a lot. But with them I never see that."

The vulgar connotations of Castilian and Castilians are evident in many of these quotes, and these connotations are clearly traceable in this discourse to the class-belonging of these languages in this city.

HOW CLASS MEANINGS OF LANGUAGE
ARE CONSOLIDATED

How do different patterns of language use develop for students at the same school who share a Castilian-language background but differ in their social-class identity? Three connections can be singled out:

1. Class constrains residence, and neighbors influence linguistic repertoire. The users of Catalan in my study all lived in the more central and middle-class areas of their city, identified as dominantly Catalan neighborhoods. The non-users lived in Castilian-dominant working-class neighborhoods on the periphery of the city. These differences in residence created different early opportunities to interact with Catalan speakers informally and as equals.

2. Class worked both directly and through residence to determine the kind of elementary school that was accessible to the child, and the quality of the school affected exposure to Catalan. These children did not begin school in immersion programs. Most of them reported that they first spoke Catalan in classroom activities, not in play with peers, and most began to produce the language actively only when they encountered Catalan teachers who insisted on it. For many among the middle class, but not the working class, full Catalan-medium instruction began in the second cycle of elementary school. The particular elementary schools of the middle-class students in this group offered more subjects in Catalan in earlier grades, had more teachers who were native speakers and likely to use and insist on Catalan with students, and had more native Catalan-speaking students.

   School-based mastery of Catalan certainly does not entail or automatically enable use of Catalan with peers. But it does create linguistic capital on which learners can build new habits when the social opportunity arises. Kids from working-class neighborhoods had a much weaker school-based mastery of Catalan. With all the will in the world to be recognized as a Catalan speaker, Josep, the Castilian-identified student who was taking his first steps into Catalan use, did not have the linguistic resources that Rafael and Victor did to effect this transformation.

3. Since schooling is the principal vehicle for exposure to and acquisition of Catalan for those from Castilian-dominant neighborhoods, the language takes on the connotations of the officially sanctioned institution. As the students view school, so they see Catalan.

In contemporary Western societies, social class is generally positively correlated with school achievement. Even more to the point, attitudes toward schooling also correlate with class. Resistance to school values and practices seems to run higher among working-class than middle-class kids in Barcelona just as it does in the English schools that Paul Willis classically described (1977). Resistance to Catalan as a school-based language accompanied this.

None of the non-users of Catalan in this group was considered by teachers to be doing well in school, and most were viewed as "disastrous" students. By spring quarter, most of them were failing five or more subjects out of ten, and teachers spoke of many of them as weak students, as cheating, or as mistaking school achievement as a matter of appearance and classroom bravado. (Adela dropped out before the year was over.) In contrast, only two speakers of Catalan, among both native speakers and the second-language users, were doing poorly (and significantly, these two were closely allied with Castilian friends).[11] Middling and high-achieving students used Catalan; low achievers and reluctant students did not. Alienated from school, poor students were further alienated from the Catalan language they associated with school.

In a number of ways, then, middle-class students are better positioned than working-class students to appropriate Catalan as a social resource.[12] Students in another school not only confirmed these class linkages of the languages but also offered a social analysis of the meaning of language choice. I visited a university preparation Catalan class in one of the poorest, most overwhelmingly Castilian zones within the city of Barcelona proper. In this neighborhood, the university-bound student was a rarity, as was the Catalan speaker. On the day of my visit the teacher led the class in a discussion of diglossia and normalization. Characterizing Castilian as the high-prestige language in Catalonia, she asserted that bilingualism was abnormal and that bilingual schooling was impossible. She asserted that the speaking of Catalan signified identity, stating that the decision to use the language reflected whether one feels Catalan or Spanish. The teacher no doubt spoke from personal experience. I knew that she was a "converted" native Castilian speaker herself, although I had been cautioned that she was uncomfortable discussing this fact even with friends. This teacher never mentioned her own linguistic transformation to her students, and it was not used as a resource in encouraging students toward similar behavior.

A girl spoke out to object to the teacher's construction of language choice as a matter of identity. She argued that this view created problems for students like her. She did not want to be forced to choose one identity or the other, but rather to maintain both. She rejected her teacher's position as denying her that possibility.

Other students joined in rejecting the teacher's psychologically oriented, ethnicity-stressing vision of the meaning of language behavior in contemporary Catalonia. They had their own more sociological analysis of the difficulties of language choice. For them, speaking Catalan was not about *who* you were ethnically, but *where* you were admitted in society. "We don't speak Catalan because we are socially marginalized" (*marginats*), they asserted matter-of-factly. With this sociological label, these teenagers summarized their own spatialized, interlocking experience of class and ethnicity in a de facto segregated neighborhood, segregated largely by economic forces. These students expected and planned to use Catalan when they got to the university, because there they would be among Catalan speakers. (I found their apparent faith in the ease and automatic nature of such a situated change in language practices poignant.) Their argument meant, though, that the majority of their young neighbors who would never experience university life were equally unlikely to find a use for the Catalan language.

CONCLUSION

In the past decade Catalanist language policies and increased public use of Catalan have weakened the ascriptive ethnic equation of the Catalan language with the autochthonous population. The experimental measure of language attitudes suggests that new public language allocations were changing the symbolic value of Catalan and its ideological links to ethnic identity. Classroom ethnography indicates that although some Castilian-speaking students were still motivated to use—or not to use—Catalan by the forces of ethnic identification, others have been affected by the change in symbolic values, learning and using Catalan fluently for varying purposes. In institutional settings or social groups where these young people think of Catalan as a "normal" mode of public discourse rather than as a private ethnic marker, they are able to use Catalan with fewer social obstacles and less ambivalence than that which hindered second-language speakers in the past. Some are even able to forge a new ethnolinguistic identity and a new allocation of the bilingual repertoire that challenge the traditional dichotomy of Catalans and Castilians.

However, these are mostly children of the middle and upper-middle classes who can feel most at home in the public spheres that have become Catalan-speaking over the last decade. Social class differences organize life so that working-class speakers may feel themselves to be marginal to these important communicative domains.

As the Catalan language has become more of a necessity for getting work done in formal institutions and public spheres and for high achievement in institutions like schools, it has also become a social resource more predictably acquired and used by middle-class Castilian speakers, whose interests are most often identified with these institutions. Now Catalan has higher class connotations not just because native Catalan speakers tend to be from the higher classes, but because middle and upper-middle class individuals from non-native ethnolinguistic backgrounds also tend to have good control of and make more extensive use of Catalan. With faint but growing echoes of the process Bourdieu described for French, the class meaning of the Catalan language is becoming accentuated as the ethnic symbolism recedes.

ACKNOWLEDGMENTS

Some of the material presented here was published in a chapter entitled "Linkages of Language and Ethnic Identity: Changes in Barcelona, 1980–1987," in James Dow, ed., *Language and Ethnicity; Focusschrift in Honor of Joshua A. Fishman on the Occasion of His 65th Birthday, Vol. II*, Amsterdam/Philadelphia: John Benjamins, 1991, 61–81. It appears here by permission of John Benjamins.

Because of delays in publication, this chapter should not be taken as a report on current language practices and politics in Catalonia. It is based on research only through the beginning of the 1990s.

I am grateful to the Social Science Research Council, the Comité Conjunto Hispano-Norteamericano, the Fulbright Program, the Spencer Foundation, the Wenner-Gren Foundation, and the University of Wisconsin Graduate School Research Foundation for funding the two periods of field research on which this report is based. The opinions and conclusions presented here are mine alone and do not reflect the positions of these organizations.

Tae-Joong Gahng carried out the statistical analysis of the 1987 experiment briefly discussed here. Many thanks to him and to the speakers, students, teachers, and colleagues in Barcelona who made this research possible, as well as to the many colleagues who have commented on this work as it has evolved over the years.

NOTES

1. Gendered meanings of the languages are also developing, but the complexity of these puts them beyond the scope of this paper. For discussions of gender, see Pujolar i Cos (1997) and Woolard (1997).

Outside observers, working from Bourdieu's (1982) theory of misrecognition and the symbolic violence of class privilege, might suggest that this language-class nexus is not an unintended outcome at all. That is, official language movements are often analyzed as not really being about language at all, but are seen as means to obtain or protect economic privilege. Language requirements are often a way for an ethnic group to monopolize jobs. I do not believe this analysis applies to the Catalan case. Catalans have long had more privileged economic positions than the average Castilian speaker in Barcelona and had experienced no decline or threat of decline at the time of autonomy. They did not need to devise new rules to protect their access to jobs or privilege, and I see no evidence that nationalist linguistic programs veiled such an intent. What was visible was a fair amount of sensitivity and discomfort about the class implications of language.

2. *"Un catalán es un señor que habla catalán."* This comment was attributed to the sociologist Anna Cabré. It is unlikely that any gender or social status connotations were intended by the choice of *"señor,"* although "gentle" social standing is indeed typically associated with this socially prestigious language, as is indicated in this chapter.

3. The matched guise technique was developed by Wallace Lambert and colleagues in the late 1950s and early 1960s for research on language attitudes in Montreal. In this kind of experiment in bilingual communities, listeners hear an audiotape recording of several speakers reading the same text, some in one language, some in translation to the other language. Listeners are unaware that they are actually hearing each speaker twice, once in each language. As they listen, they are asked to give their evaluation of each voice on a series of personal traits. Typically and in this case, the personal traits cluster into a "power" or "status" dimension—likability, attractiveness, sense of humor, and so on. Since only the language "guise" varies, while speaker and referential context and style of the text are held constant, any difference in the ratings of the two guises of a given speaker is arguably attributable to attitudes, perhaps covert, toward the languages.

4. "Venim observant una evident millora en el coneixement del catalá per part dels alumnes que ens arriben, la qual cosa sembla tenir relació directa amb l'augment de cursos fets de llengua catalana a E.G.B. Aquesta millora en el coneixement del català contrasta amb una realitat que també palpem quotidianament als patis, als passadissos, a les classes i a les cantines dels instituts on treballem: la llengua que més sovint se sent parla als alumnes entre ells no és pas el català. Arribem a prendre consciència d'estar formant ciutadans catalanoescrivents, i que rarament es transformen en catalanoparlants efectius."

5. I spent a little over three months visiting this group several times a week, attending classes and going on field trips with them, observing and noting their interactions and language choices. I tape-recorded them working in small groups, and got a number of them to tape conversations at home and with friends outside of school. I talked informally with their teachers and sat in on the teachers' meeting in which each student was evaluated and grades were given. Finally, I did a somewhat formal interview, lasting from 45 minutes to close to 2 hours, with all but one of the 36 students.

All student names used here are pseudonyms. As I have used a different system of pseudonyms here than in some previous publications, readers may have difficulty matching individuals in my different accounts.

6. There is a real but not straightforward link between gender and language patterns in this group. Girls and boys are found in both the Catalan-using and the more resistant groups, but there are differences in the social patterns of use. These complex patterns are analyzed in Woolard (1997).

7. "Entre nosaltres com que ens coneixiem des de molt petits des de parvuls, sempre parlavem en castellà i ara sempre ens parlem en català."

8. In this sense the case study group is representative of the general school population of the city. This pattern was confirmed in a recent analysis of a

large-scale survey of young people taken in the same city the year before my
research (Erill et al. 1992).

9. My question asked if there were differences between "Catalan speakers"
and "Castilian speakers," but students uniformly responded in terms of
"Catalans" and "Castilians." I should stress that at least half of the kids were
reluctant to describe ethnic differences. Of those who did, many would then
deny that such differences were found among their classmates. As Boix Fuster
(1993) has pointed out, students prefer to think of relations with classmates as
interpersonal, not interethnic, and they "flee from conflict," as Erill and associates (1986, 1992) put it.

10.

Eva: si va mal vestit i així, doncs ja sembla més..més castellà, no?

Victòria: Sembla que els castellans tinguin, tinguin menys diners.., o tinguin
mm més baixa categoria. No sé..amb la forma de vestir també,..trobo que son
més maleducats,..van molt a la seva, (speaking rapidly) criden pel carrer...

Angels: Castellà, jo considero mes brusc, no sé més basto (smiling voice). Més
pagesot (laughs). La, la, aquelles, vull dir, sempre, no sé ten, son més bastos,
diuen més renecs, més paraulotes.

Josefina: Penso que els catalans són més més no sé més fins podriem dir..

Rafael: Home, normalment els castellans, tenen menys cultura,..

Rosa: La Margarita i les altres, se'ls hi nota per la forma de parlar bastes...

Gabriela: castellans més bastos, més vulgars.

Mirella: ...quan penso en gent castellà, penso en la senyora que ve a fer feines
a casa, amb els empleats que té el meu pare a la fàbrica, que vale, si penses
amb la gent de la classe potser no tindria tanta diferència i tants blocs tant
diferenciats, però clar com m'imagino que van molt pintades, molt en plan,
no sé que la genta catalana va més, amb maquillatge però per donar color
només. En canvi la gent més castellana doncs va més en plan, aquí molt
coloret, ulls molt pintats i uns llavis, més en plan així, no? [Later in interview
not recorded] "Castellans son molt de cridar."

11. This is not to say that Catalans never do poorly in school. In fact, two
Catalan students in this group had failed so many of their subjects the past year
that they were held back—a position that ironically established them as class
leaders, looked up to by others. They were now doing well.

12. The reputation of this school for a Catalan atmosphere would bias the
sample, in favor of those who are positive toward Catalan. Students antagonistic
to Catalan were unlikely to elect to go there, but that ought to be as true of the
working class as of the middle class.

REFERENCES

Arenas i Sampera, Joaquim. 1987. *Catalunya, escola i llengua*. Barcelona: La Llar
     del Llibre.
Boix Fuster, Emili. 1993. *Triar no es trair: Identitat i llengua en els joves de Barcelona*.
     Barcelona: Edicions 62.
Bourdieu, Pierre. 1982. *Ce que parler veut dire*. Paris: Fayard.
CIDC. 1987. *Padrons municipals d'habitants de Catalunya, 1986: Cens lingüístic*.
     Barcelona: Consorci d'Informació i Documentació de Catalunya.
Direcció General de Política Lingüística. 1984. *Les expectatives d'ús, actituds i
     necessitats lingüístiques entre la població adulta de l'aglomeració urbana
     barcelonina*. Barcelona: Departament de Cultura de la Generalitat de
     Catalunya.

Erill i Pinyot, Gustau, Jaume Farras i Farras, and Ferran Marcos i Moral. 1986. "Ús i actituds devant de la llengua catalana dels estudiants de secundaria. Sabadell, 1985-86." Paper presented to the II Congress of the Catalan Language, Lleida (6 May).

Erill i Pinyot, Gustau, et al. 1992. *Ús del català entre els joves a Sabadell*. Barcelona: Generalitat de Catalunya, Departament de Cultura.

Fishman, Joshua. 1965. "The Status and Prospects of Bilingualism in the United States." *Modern Language Journal* 49: 143–55.

Fishman, Joshua. 1966. *Language Loyalty in the United States*. The Hague: Mouton.

Frankenberg, Ruth. 1993. *White Women, Race Matters: The Social Construction of Whiteness*. Minneapolis: University of Minnesota Press.

Gal, Susan. 1979. *Language Shift*. New York: Academic Press.

García, Fernando. 1991. "Cataluña está amenazada por la falta de inmigración extranjera." *La Vanguardia* (August 8): 18.

Labov, William. 1972. *Sociolinguistic Patterns*. Philadelphia: University of Pennsylvania.

Lambert, W. E., R. C. Hodgson, R. C. Gardner, and S. Fillenbaum. 1960. "Evaluational Reactions to Spoken Languages." *Journal of Abnormal and Social Psychology* 60: 44–51.

Milroy, Lesley. 1980. *Language and Social Networks*. Oxford: Basil Blackwell.

Pujolar i Cos, Joan. 1977. "Masculinities in a Multilingual Setting." In Sally Johnson and Ulrike H. Meinhof, eds., *Language and Masculinity*. Oxford: Blackwell Publishers, 86–106.

Streicker, Joel. 1995. "Policing Boundaries: Race, Class, and Gender in Cartagena, Colombia." *American Ethnologist* 22(1): 54–74.

Tuson, Amparo. 1985. *Language, Community and School in Barcelona*. Berkeley: Unpublished Ph.D. dissertation, University of California.

Willis, Paul. 1977. *Learning to Labour*. Westmead, England: Saxon House.

Woolard, Kathryn A. 1986. "The Politics of Language Status Planning: 'Normalization' in Catalonia." In Nancy Schweda-Nicholson, ed., *Language in the International Perspective*. Norwood, N.J.: Ablex, 91–102.

———. 1989. *Double Talk: Bilingualism and the Politics of Ethnicity in Catalonia*. Stanford: Stanford University Press.

———. 1991. "Linkages of Language and Ethnic Identity: Changes in Barcelona, 1980–1987." In J. Dow, ed., *Language and Ethnicity: Focusschrift in Honor of Joshua A. Fishman on the Occasion of His 65th Birthday*. Vol. II. Amsterdam/Philadelphia: John Benjamins, 61–81.

———. 1997. "Between Friends: Gender, Peer Group Structure, and Bilingualism in Urban Catalonia." *Language in Society* 26(4): 533–60.

Woolard, Kathryn A., and Tae-Joong Gahng. 1990. "Changing Language Policies and Attitudes in Autonomous Catalonia." *Language in Society* 19: 311–30.

6

The Politics of Representation: Class and Identity in Cochabamba, Bolivia

María L. Lagos

Tata Trinico, an 84-year-old *campesino* (peasant), who has a light complexion and green eyes, was, in 1985, one of the wealthiest men in Tiraque, a province in the highlands of Cochabamba, Bolivia. He owned some one hundred hectares of land and, along with his extended family, he was a moneylender and a merchant. He also owned trucks and established sharecropping agreements with numerous peasant households. Yet, in spite of his wealth, he was not accepted as a social equal by the *vecinos* (townsfolk), who considered him an "Indian" campesino.

In rural Bolivia, as in many other parts of Latin America, it matters whether one is defined by others as an "Indian" or "white" because such definitions locate the individual within a hierarchical classificatory scheme in which some groups are accorded dominant status over others. These definitions, which are underlain by implicit or explicit, real or imagined differences, have consequences in the lives of people but in practice, social and ethnic boundaries are not fixed in an all-pervasive and impenetrable mold because diacritic markers of difference are extremely ambiguous and are contested in discourse and daily life.

This paper is about social and cultural constructions of class and ethnic identity in rural Cochabamba. It examines the ways in which situated social agents simultaneously reproduce and transform dominant discourses of personhood as they attempt to make sense of and shape a changing social reality in which old, local markers of class and ethnic difference have become so ambiguous as to risk rendering them practically meaningless. In this process, the meanings of key discursive categories have been contested and new criteria for difference have been invented. What has not changed, however, is the fact that definitions of self and others continue to rest on imputed "racial" distinctions between "whites" and "Indians" and on the contrasting images associated with "whiteness" and "Indianness"; the first connotes superiority, modernity, and urban life and the second inferiority, backwardness, and the countryside.[1] By focusing on the shifting and situational meanings of two keywords—"indio" (Indian) and "campesino" (peasant), the discursive categories used in opposition to "white" that pervade representations of self and others in Bolivia—I will seek to demonstrate that, in order to understand the politics of representation, we need to relate discourse to ongoing social transformations. Whereas the discourse that debases "Indians" and the countryside emerged with conquest, the meanings of its keywords have been contested and have certainly changed through time as people position themselves in both cultural and social struggles.

That domination entails not only force but also the incorporation or the internalization of dominant discourses or "ways of seeing the world" (Williams 1977) has been recently addressed by numerous scholars who use and elaborate the Gramscian concept of hegemony or Foucauldian notions of discourse. In a recent study, Keesing (1992) argues that hegemonic forms of domination are not only incorporated and subverted by subordinate groups, but also impose limitations as to what is politically feasible, even as to what can be thought and done. In examining the processes of domination, accommodation, and resistance in the Solomon Islands, Keesing shows that Kwaio discourse has incorporated the categories and semiology of colonial rule and white supremacy. The important point of his analysis is that rather than just being mirror images or parodies of the structures and language of political domination, subordinate understandings of dominant categories constitute the weapons through which the Kwaio seek to engage with power on its own turf. The Kwaio adopt this "language" precisely to maintain a certain degree of autonomy outside of dominant control. This example, as well as many from other colonial situations, serve as necessary reminders that, within contexts of unequal power relations, subjects are not autonomous and that agency is not voluntaristic action, as recent studies seem to suggest (cf. Ortner 1984; Sahlins 1985), but are delimited by both social and cultural constraints (Asad 1993; Wolf 1994). By focusing on "indio" and "campesino" as keywords that can be both potentially exclusionary or inclusionary, this essay seeks to illuminate the "dialectic of ideology and counterideology" (Keesing

1992, 225ff). Paying attention to discursive forms of domination and the ways in which they are simultaneously reproduced, elaborated, negated, and transformed helps us to understand how dominant cultural constructs not only inform (or dis-inform) regional representations of personhood, but also shape shifting intra- and interclass alliances and oppositions that may sustain power and domination or challenge them in unexpected ways.

The area under investigation encompasses the central valleys and the eastern highlands of Cochabamba.[2] Long known as among the most important granaries in the Andes, the central valleys have attracted settlers and displaced people since pre-Inka times, when highland Aymara polities, situated to the west of the valleys, set up colonies on them. In the fourteenth century, after the Inka conquest of the valleys, the state redistributed the lands among different ethnic groups, established large state farms for the production of maize, and replaced some of the population with Quechua-speaking groups transferred from other parts of the empire (Larson 1988). The Spanish conquest further fragmented the social ties between those settled in the valleys and their highland nuclei, intensifying, at the same time, the spatial movement of peoples. These factors also facilitated the early expansion of haciendas to the point that by the eighteenth century no Indian communities existed in the central valleys and much of the surrounding highlands, having been replaced by haciendas populated with landless Indians and mestizos. By the eighteenth century too the region was the most mestizo of Upper Peru (later Bolivia). Furthermore, the historical record, from the mid-nineteenth century to the revolution of 1952, reveals a constant process of hacienda fragmentation and accumulation of land in which emergent families replaced old ones; of dispossession and movement of the laboring poor through the region's haciendas and coca plantations; to rural towns and to more distant mining camps and cities to work sometimes as wage laborers, petty traders, muleteers, artisans, hacienda tenants, or sharecroppers. In this process, some individuals and families remained poor all their lives, others were able to purchase small plots of land and become *piqueros* (landowning peasants) or to buy the necessary materials and tools to establish themselves as artisans; in yet other instances, some accumulated wealth. As family fortunes rose and fell, so did the families' ethnic status (Lagos 1994).

If the boundary between "Indians" and "non-Indians," in Latin America, as Eric Wolf wrote (1986, 327), "has never been static, but rather an arena contested by people on both sides of the labor reserve and internal colony," cultural and social boundaries have been particularly fluid in Cochabamba since colonial times. Certainly, the spatial and the social movement of peoples have both contributed to the ambiguities in the representation of self and others; but in order to understand these movements and shifting representations of differ-ence, it is first necessary to examine both in relation to power and hegemonic forms of domination of the Andes.

THE MAKING OF A MODERN HEGEMONIC DISCOURSE

Spanish colonialism, a violent process in which the city became the locus of power and "civilized" life, subjugated the indigenous pop-ulation and placed it under the subordinate colonial category of "Indian" (Bonfil Batalla 1972).[3] But whereas the unequal relationship between city and countryside and between "white" and "Indian" have certainly perdured, conceptions about "Indians" and their place in society have changed through time. The discourse that debases "Indians" and the countryside has not been a transhistorical, mono-lithic one; rather, it has been produced, reproduced, challenged, and modified in ongoing intra- and interclass struggles and debates. Indeed, since early colonial times, different members of dominant society have held diverse views regarding the elusive category "In-dian" they had themselves created and argued about the nature of these human beings, about the best means to "civilize" them and wrest them from Satanic influences, and about the place Indians and individuals of "mixed blood" should be accorded in society. Most important, the violent and everyday forms of resistance through which subordinate groups have constantly challenged exploitation and dom-ination simultaneously have certainly influenced dominant perspec-tives and policies affecting them. As a result of these actions, the colonial state, which had initially sought to order Europeans and Indians into two distinct "republics," was soon faced with a growing number of individuals who left their villages of origin and settled in mining centers, towns, and haciendas. By breaking their ties with their villages of origin, they avoided tribute exactions and forced labor drafts. In so doing, they also ceased being "Indians" and "passed" into ambiguous categories or "castes" such as mestizos and cholos. This massive movement of people challenged the colonial state, which was confronted with reduced revenues and with too many people who could no longer be incorporated into the protocols of village inspection and who thus remained outside of the state's direct control.

If tribute had been the most important social relation distinguishing Indians from non-Indians under colonial rule, its abolition after inde-pendence in the nineteenth century raised new dilemmas regarding the definition of "Indians" and created what has come to be known as the

"Indian problem."[4] As Warman indicates (1970, 19), "Since the triumph of liberalism [and the end of formal segregation] the Indian became an abstraction. The Indian, a colonial creature, evaporated; it was necessary to reinvent it." It was then, he argues, that the "Indian" became an object of anthropological preoccupation. No longer a fiscal category, it is not surprising that the concept "Indian" was shaped by prevailing Social Darwinian notions of race and positivist ideas of progress (cf. Demelas 1981; Grieshaber 1985). Since then, "objective" definitions of "Indians" usually refer to individuals and groups who live in the countryside, speak a "backward" native language, dress in exotic ways, and have traditional, unchanging cultures.[5] But "Indian" also connotes characteristic and essential personality traits that people seemingly inherit and preserve for many generations, traits that may lie dormant, but that can reemerge in unexpected, often violent ways (cf. Taussig 1987). Such perspectives also shaped what dominant groups and the state considered to be the central aspect of the "Indian problem": what to do with the traditional, ignorant, pagan, unruly "Indians," who by their mere presence and apparent unwillingness to modernize weighed down the possibilities for economic development and modernization. The introduction to the Bolivian population census of 1900 clearly reflects this view:

> In a short time . . . we will have the indigenous race if not erased completely from national life, will be at least reduced to its minimal expression. . . . If this could be a benefit . . . considering that if there has been a retarding cause in our civilization it is owed to the indigenous race, essentially refractory to all innovation and to all progress, since it has refused and tenaciously refuses other customs that have not been transmitted by tradition from their remote ancestors. (cited in Grieshaber 1985, 55)

Several explanations and solutions were advanced to understand and solve this problem, ranging from expectations that the "inferior race" would necessarily die out or that it could be replaced by or whitened with European immigrants, to *indigenista* policies seeking to educate and integrate Indians to modern society.[6]

In the making of this dominant discourse, other, more subterranean voices offered other explanations of the "Indian problem" and proposed radical, albeit different, solutions (cf. Mariategui 1971). This alternative perspective posited that the problem was neither cultural nor racial, but rather a social one: "Indians" were in fact a social class of exploited tenants, sharecroppers, and peasants. By subsuming "Indians" under the category of peasants, proponents of this perspective argued that the solution to the problem rested on structural transformations. The underlying assumption of all of these solutions was, of course, that "Indians" and everything that was associated with them had to be eliminated, improved, or denied for the Latin American countries to become modern nation-states.

Because of these debates and the ways in which these have been shaped by opposing ideologies and by diverse forms of resistance on the part of subordinate groups, "Indian" is not, nor has it ever been, an innocent term. It is, rather, a charged sign of contradictory, contested meanings (cf. Vološinov 1973). For some, to be an "Indian" has been central to the counterhegemonic discourse and actions of subordinate groups in the Americas and a banner for political mobilization. For others, the word elicits negative images and feelings, which are reinforced by fear of an essentialized "Other." It is then not surprising that within the parameters set by this discourse "indio" (Indian) is also a pejorative term.

Unlike the colonial category "Indian," "campesino" has a shorter history. It began to be widely used in official and public discourses after the implementation of agrarian reforms in the Andean countries to refer to those who live in the countryside, substituting a modern term for the colonial construct "indio." In Bolivia, for instance, the government of the National Revolution of 1952 signed one of the most radical agrarian reform decrees in Latin America on August 2, 1953, the day that used to commemorate the Dia del Indio (Day of the Indian).[7]

Like "Indian," "campesino" carries contradictory meanings held by different people with diverse objectives. To many of those directly involved in militant actions before and after the revolution, the term denotes empowerment. To some of the ideologues responsible for the drafting of the reform laws, the term was associated with expectations that private property of land would turn "Indians" into entrepreneurial farmers who, in the pursuit of profit, would shed their traditional, backward cultural practices. To others, "campesino" is just a new word to refer to "Indians," implying that a change in words has not altered their essential nature, as statements I heard many times in Bolivia clearly demonstrate: *Los campesinos son mentirosos, mañudos y egoistas. No se les puede confiar*" (Peasants are liars, untrustworthy, and selfish. They should not be trusted), "*Estos laris de mierda has roto esto*" (These shitty *laris* [terms used in the area to refer to highland campesinos who are considered the most backward and traditional ones] have broken this), "*Cómo puede trabajar con esos salvajes y analfabetos?*" (How can you work with those savages and illiterates?). In sum, campesinos are depicted as ignorant, dirty, illiterate, untrustworthy beings because, as a city resident told me, at any time, "*Se les puede salir el indio*" (They can reveal the Indian within). Furthermore, as a discursive construct, "campesino" glosses over class distinctions. Importantly, therefore, its meaning varies in specific situations and for different audiences. We will return to this difference in the meanings of "campesino"—as a discursive construct or as a social relation—when we analyze the notion of "campesinidad" (of being campesino) and the ways in which it is contested in discourse and daily practices.

While a modern civilizational discourse emerged, not surprisingly, in the city and among "white" dominant groups, what is important for the purposes of this chapter is how those who live in rural towns and villages and whom urbanites tend to portray as "Indians," "cholos" (a term now used to portray upwardly mobile "Indian" parvenus), or "campesinos," reproduce, modify, or challenge this discourse as situated social agents.

THE REPRODUCTION OF AND CHALLENGES TO A DOMINANT DISCOURSE

In a region where the majority of the population lacked direct access to land before the implementation of the agrarian reform of 1953, ethnic definitions tended to correspond to class distinctions. Ownership of land, especially of large haciendas, was probably the most important criterion for white status, followed by residence in the city of Cochabamba, where most hacendados lived. The ethnic status of owners of small haciendas or small plots of land, who lived in rural towns or villages, was not so clear-cut because they were not members of an "aristocratic" class of hacendados or *"gente de apellido"* (people with an old and prestigious surname) or because they were, in local parlance, *"agricultores"* and *"costureras"* (male and female landowning peasants). Thus, some were white, others were mestizo, but none were Indian. All others, most of whom did not own land or owned minimal amounts of land, were mestizo and, a very few, Indian. These were the artisans, petty traders, muleteers, and tenants and sharecroppers settled on haciendas. In sum, wealth and place of residence, independent of phenotypic traits, were key criteria for ethnic categorizations. Cultural practices and class markers such as forms of address (i.e., *don/doña*), dress, manners, family background, and social ties based on marriage and friendship were additional criteria for difference. Being a town resident, a *vecino*, also conveyed superior status largely because of its association with the city and the special connotation this term had in early colonial times, when it defined people who owned a house in town, could bear arms, and formed part of armed militias (Molinié-Fioravanti 1982, 136).

Language, or rather the ability to speak fluent Spanish, also symbolized an association with the city and modernity. In contrast, Quechua, a native language spoken by a large percentage of the population in Cochabamba, has always been associated with "Indianness." As Albó (1974, 224) puts it, "Both Quechua and Spanish are markers . . . of great efficacy for social discrimination because, as labels, they symbolize the social classification of the speaker in any situation." In practice, however, and with the possible exception of wealthy men who lived in the city, few were fluent speakers of Spanish. Apparently, even wealthy city women spoke little or no Spanish (Grieshaber 1985). They, as well as their husbands, spoke Quechua, possibly because they were often raised by monolingual Quechua-speaking servants. Furthermore, both languages have incorporated a number of words and grammatical constructions from one another. This is a phenomenon that has now intensified, along with increasing bilingualism,[8] leading some to claim that what people actually speak in the countryside of Cochabamba today is "quechuañol" (Cideti n.d., 7).

Many of the markers for cultural and social difference became particularly ambiguous after the National Revolution of 1952. One of the reasons for this ambiguity is that land is no longer controlled by a small group of hacendados. On the contrary, most of the households of former hacienda tenants and sharecroppers became owners of the lands they worked.[9] Second, the processes of social differentiation, which had already existed before agrarian reform, intensified after the dissolution of the hacendado class and the departure of wealthy merchants from the town, leading to the formation of a new rural merchant class, composed of both wealthy villagers and townsfolk. Unlike their predecessors, the power of the nouveau riche lies not in their political control over land, but in the establishment of intimate relations of work and exchange with poor households: animal shares contracts, sharecropping agreements, advanced sales and money loans, barter and market exchanges, and transport of crops and manure at exorbitant fares (Lagos 1994). Third, the lives of vecinos and villagers intricately intertwine, for they enter into long-term production and exchange relations and establish shifting political alliances. What is more important, however, is that both wealthy and poor share similar origins and many cultural practices and beliefs, as evidenced by the generalized use of Quechua and, increasingly, Spanish; a reliance on reciprocity and fictive kinship to expand personal networks; and celebration of similar life-cycle and religious rituals such as the worship of Pacha Mama (Mother Earth), Christ, the saints, and virgins; and so on. But this does not mean, of course, that culture is shared in a homogeneous way. Rather it means that, while Tiraqueños share a common cultural language, the meanings that they assign to the same concepts, relationships, and practices, such as "white," "indio," "campesino," sharecropping, reciprocity, ritual, and so on, may be different. In other words, there is no intrinsic meaning in the cultural categories and practices themselves, making any agreement as to what their meanings might be, or what would be the appropriate language to use in particular situations, or the correct ways to celebrate rituals all subjects of debate and, often, conflict. Moreover, even if a certain consensus is achieved, this does not mean that it will be a long-lasting agreement (cf. Lagos 1993; Smith 1989). These debates of daily life are crucial for understanding the politics of difference, that is, the ways in which people define themselves and others in specific situations and contexts and how their forms of representation reproduce, modify, or challenge a hegemonic discourse of difference.

Being Native to the Town

Seldom do people in Tiraque and in the central valleys of Cochabamba publicly indicate that they are "white," "mestizo," or "Indian"; rather, they identify themselves by their place of origin, which, depending on the context, could be "la estancia" (highland village) or "el pueblo" (the town). When more specificity is required, people name a village, town, region, province, or department (cf. Abercrombie 1991; Albó 1980). During my three years of fieldwork. I met only one campesino who publicly acknowledged being an "Indian," which he did by having embroidered "Indio Libre" (Free Indian) on his *coraza* (a short poncho). Otherwise, and within a context in which difference is emphasized, villagers use *"noqayku"* (the exclusive Quechua form for "us") to distinguish themselves from *"paykuna"* ("they" in Quechua) or vecinos.[10] Similarly, it was only in the privacy of their homes that vecinos sought to validate their white ancestry by telling me that their ancestors were hacendados or had been born in the city, moving to Tiraque many generations back, unlike other vecinos whom they considered to be "cholos" because, they claimed, their ancestors had been Indian or mestizo. The point is that Tiraqueños rarely make public claims of white or Indian ancestry for themselves or others. Only in moments of conflict or in the midst of heated discussions are the terms "indio" or "cholo" hurled against others with the intent to insult them. On these occasions, the negative images and feelings associated with dominant perceptions of inferior races indicate that the subject of the verbal attack is behaving like an Indian or cholo. As insults, then, these terms connote essences rather than phenotypic traits. When people wanted to insult me, for instance, they usually called me *"gringa,"*[11] but in one of my stays in the city of Cochabamba, a man called me "India arrogante" (arrogant Indian), to which I replied: *"Prefiero ser india que chola como usted"* (I'd rather be an Indian than a cholo like you).

Hegemonic representations of race permeate Tiraqueños' definitions of self and others, even if these are not usually openly stated in public. Vecinos in particular actively reproduced dominant discursive constructs of difference; for this, they relied on the elusive contrast between the "civilized," "white" town and the surrounding "backward," "Indian" countryside. This was not always easy to do because, as we have seen, old criteria for difference lost their effectiveness, and vecinos had to elaborate old markers and invent new ones to assert their superior position within a hierarchical classificatory scheme. But the social and cultural divide between vecinos and villagers is not so clearly defined as vecinos may wish it to be because class, gender, and other distinctions divide and unit vecinos and villagers in ways that cannot be reduced to ideological "ethnic" differences. Similarly, the distance between town and village is not neatly demarcated in space. Vecinos often go to the villages to oversee the sowing and harvest of the crops they plant in sharecropping agreements with villagers, to exchange goods, to visit their fictive kin, or to participate in a ritual celebration. Villagers also go often to town to attend mass and meetings of the Central Campesina (the provincial organization of campesino unions) and the Irrigation Committee, to run errands, to relax in *chicherías* (locales to sell chicha, or corn beer), to visit their vecino fictive kin, and to participate in civic parades and other formal festivities. Some villagers have moved to town, some even buying houses around the main square (the most prestigious place in the town), an action that most vecinos resent because they feel their town has been invaded by "indios."

In the face of these intimate connections between town and villages, vecinos continuously try to distance themselves from villagers in many ways: by not marrying them (only a very few, poor vecinos do so), by not inviting them to their life-cycle rituals and to the town's religious festivities, and by excluding them from the dances and meals that follow civic celebrations in town, even though villagers are asked to contribute with food. As villagers often say, "*Como siempre, los del pueblo nos marginan*" ("As always, townspeople marginalize us"). In face-to-face, everyday encounters, vecinos make use of distinct forms of address to mark this distance: they always address adult villagers by their first names or, if they do not know them, they address them as "*hombrecito*" or "*mujercita*" (little man or little woman), even if they are older than themselves, and they use the familiar form of address, "*tu*," if they are speaking Spanish. In contrast, villagers always address vecinos by adding "*don*" or "*doña*" to their first names.

In addition to these subtle and not so subtle practices, townsfolk have recently redefined one of the criteria for being a vecino: being native to the town. This right is not based on residence, as it used to be, but on birth, thus effectively excluding villagers who live in the town from privileges only accorded to vecinos. Such privileges include the right to get involved in the town's affairs, to occupy public office, and to be "white." This unwritten exclusionary rule is also extended to non-campesino outsiders or "foreigners," such as priests and nuns, school-teachers, government and non-governmental officials, especially when vecinos perceive them as meddling too much in the town's affairs. After a man from Potosí, who was married to a Tiraqueña and a town resident, was elected president of the town's Civil Committee, some vecinos tried to nullify the election because, they said, "He is an upstart [advenedizo]. What are people from other towns going to think when Tiraque elects a foreigner to occupy a position of authority? As if there were no people here!"

The conflict between Padre Esteban, a Spanish priest, and vecinos will serve to illustrate how "being native to the town" can be deployed in specific situations. Padre Esteban's fourteen-year residence in the town was punctuated by his recurrent conflicts with vecinos, neither missing any opportunity to let the other know their mutual dislike. A follower of the tenets of liberation theology, the priest took the church to the villagers, actively engaging them in small-group discussions of the Bible and celebrating baptisms, marriages, and mass in the villages. He also embarked in a campaign to dissuade people, villagers in particular, to stop patronizing the chicherías in town. He did not waste any opportunity to let vecinos know that he did not agree with many of the things they did, such as drinking, conspicuous consumption, as displayed, for example, in the town's celebration of the patron saint, their arrogance toward villagers, and so on. Vecinos did not like any of this. They criticized the priest for spending too much time in the countryside at the expense of the town and for "wanting to rule the town," as many told me, a right he did not have because he was a "stranger," a "foreigner." Behind his back, many people accused him of being a kharisiri[12] (a very serious charge indeed), a communist, a spy; some even questioned whether he was a Catholic. The vecinos' grievances and accusations were summarized by one of them:

> [He is] a communist and an evangelical because this priest says mass even in the corral for donkeys and pigs [en el corral de los burros y de los chanchos] and, because of him the town is now silent [ha quedado silencio], our chicherías and stores do not sell; we cannot even sell candles now. (Cideti n.d., 43)

But this was not all. Padre Esteban also changed the liturgy, substituting Spanish or Quechua for Latin, simplifying the altar and the vestments he used to perform ritual. This he did even though vecinos had told him many times that they preferred the pomp and circumstance of old. If they disliked these changes, they could hardly tolerate the fact that the priest said one of the two Sunday masses in Quechua. One Saturday, the wife of a truck owner went to see Padre Esteban to ask him to give the Quechua mass in Spanish, because the next day was her husband's birthday and they wanted to attend mass as part of the celebration with their friends. The priest told her that too many campesinos attended that mass precisely because it was in Quechua and he would probably say it in Quechua. And this he did. But soon after mass started, the trucker's wife interrupted the priest and told him that he should say it in Spanish, to which the priest replied: "If you can understand the Bible and explain the passage I will read in Spanish, I will then switch to Spanish." After he read the passage extremely fast, the woman said: "I cannot understand it because you read it too fast." She left the church crying, accompanied by her husband and friends, all of whom were furious for having been humiliated in front of villagers in their own church and town.

This event raises a number of issues worth noting. First, it illuminates the paradoxes underlying a debate over the appropriateness of using Quechua—the language of "indios"—in a Western religious ritual. This was obviously unacceptable to vecinos who, even though they are fluent speakers of Quechua, are particularly concerned with the context in which either Spanish or Quechua should be used. Second, it points to one of the principal causes underlying the animosities that existed between the priest and vecinos. In his unorthodox practices, the priest recurrently crossed the ideological divide so carefully crafted by veci-nos to maintain their distance from the countryside and the "indios" living in it. Finally, this conflict also underscores the ways in which vecinos desperately sought to reproduce a hegemonic discourse of difference in a new, changing social context. For all practical purposes within this changing social field difference did not quite exist between vecinos and villagers, as if they were two distinct ethnic or status groups. As we have seen, they share more commonalities than differ-ences. Precisely because of this, vecinos constantly tried to recreate and reinvent difference in involuted ways in order to reassert their superior status. As I have sought to demonstrate elsewhere (Lagos 1994), the final paradox is that whereas vecinos reproduce and elaborate domi-nant forms of racial difference, which debase the countryside and "Indians," these forms of representation are meaningful only insofar as the audience is regionally based. This is because, within a larger context that includes the city, both vecinos and villagers are associated with the countryside and thus depicted as "cholos" or "indios." And this, more than anything else, is probably the main reason vecinos reproduce a dominant discourse of difference based on "white" and urban notions of supremacy.

Being a Campesino

As we have seen, the category "campesino" was imposed on the rural population by the state after the revolution of 1952. The revolutionary government also imposed the *sindicato agrario* (agrarian union) on the former hacienda tenants, sharecroppers, and landowning peasants as a basic precondition for them to make legal land claims and to regulate every aspect of social life within the village. While in other parts of Bolivia the union was superimposed on already existing villages and forms of governance or acted as a parallel form of village organization, in the central valleys of Cochabamba and Tiraque the union became the nucleus around which communities were re-created and functioned as the only form of political organization within the village.

We also saw that "campesino" carries different and contrasting meanings, which mask class differences and reinforce the division between town and villages, as well as subjective distinctions stemming from it. Ambiguous in its meaning because of the many ways in which the concept can be interpreted and used in specific instances, what makes "campesino" different from "indio" is that what it means to be a campesino is contested and negotiated in public, thus pointing to the inherently political and gendered nature of this keyword. What I argue is that "campesino," as a discursive construct, and campesino organizations, as loci of political practice, constitute the main links between Tiraqueños and the state as well as other institutions of civil society, which have simultaneously influenced and defined both political discourse and practices in Bolivia. Indeed, since the revolution the state and political parties have sought to influence the course of Bolivian history by attempting to control campesino organizations, particularly those encompassing higher levels of organization than the village union, such as the subcentral, central, federation, and confederation of peasants.[13] Simultaneously, subordinate groups have often mobilized under the "campesino" banner to challenge state policies and practices. Thus, an analysis of the ways in which "campesino" is used in different contexts will serve to illuminate not only the politics of representation, but also the politics of accommodation and confrontation.

The campesino union is a predominantly male organization, affiliating all the adult men who own land or crops in a village. In some villages, however, single or widowed women who own land can be full members of the union. Modelled after labor unions, a secretary general and 12 other positions comprise the leadership of the union, ideally elected among all members on a rotational basis. Meetings usually take place every two weeks on Sundays to discuss matters of concern to village members. Everyone has the right to speak and vote, except for women who attend these meetings to represent their absent husbands (a right that is however accorded to their adolescent sons), and decisions are reached by consensus. There are, of course, numerous conflicts over land and water, theft, religious and political affiliation, wealth, gender, and personal animosities that punctuate village and intervillage life. But what is not contested is being a campesino, since everyone takes it for granted that if someone lives in the village and owns land or crops, he or she is a campesino. This is, however, the restrictive, village-based meaning of "campesino."

Within a context larger than rural villages, "campesino" is not only a descriptive category to identify those who live in villages and to depict them, from the perspective of vecinos, as "Indians" with a new name, but a more politically charged discursive category with contradictory purposes: to establish broad alliances or to build a following in factional disputes. In either case, to create unity out of real or perceived heterogeneity is not an easy task and requires a broader, more explicitly stated definition of "campesino" than the one used within the context of the village. Thus, the inclusive definition of "campesino" relies on criteria that can incorporate both villagers and vecinos. Within a regional context, then, to be a campesino is to have access to land, to have the ability to speak Quechua, and to drive the ox-drawn plow (a male activity par excellence), attributes that most vecinos (some of whom are also members of campesino unions) share with villagers. These are public, openly stated notions of "campesinidad," through which diverse actors identify themselves as campesinos, even though these representations of self may be challenged by others (cf. Lagos 1994). In these debates, which become particularly salient in regional politicking, language and characteristic speech forms take on a particular significance. Unlike the conflict over the use of Quechua in church, Quechua is the predominant language of campesino politics. In fact, it is one of the most important criteria for inclusion in the generalized peasant category. Failure to speak it fluently automatically disqualifies an individual to claim campesino identity, as the conflict over the control of the Casa del Campesino (the headquarters of the Departmental Federation of Peasants) in the city of Cochabamba illustrates.

In 1982, at the height of intense repression by a military government, the building was forcibly taken over and retaken by opposing campesino factions. In one of these takeovers, staged by the "leftist" faction, a young man urged others to take further actions that seemed quite imprudent at the time. While most of those present did not consider these suggestions viable, they did not think much of them until the young man began to take notes, just at the precise moment when others were identifying themselves, giving their names and that of their villages. This apparently innocent act aroused suspicions. Distrusting the young man, several men questioned his identity. At first, the man answered that he was a provincial campesino delegate, then he said he was a representative of the Central Confederation of Labor. But, when he failed to produce credentials validating membership in these organizations, he said he was a student. None of these positions disqualified him as a campesino, but he failed to pass a crucial test for campesino identity when he did not speak Quechua in spite of constant urgings that he do so. This was the ultimate proof that he was definitely not a campesino, and he was asked to leave the meeting.

Although a crucial marker of a broadly defined campesino identity, always used by both vecinos and villagers in the political arena, the Quechua they speak differs from colloquial Quechua. Indeed, speakers borrow more than usual from Spanish, making the language characteristically redundant and repetitive. The following examples illustrate this: *aswan experiencia* (more [Quechua] experience [Spanish]), *chakipi rijkani hasta Ucureñakama* (I used to walk to Ucureña). The last example shows the use of the same preposition—to—in both Spanish (hasta) and in Quechua (kama). Speeches are also punctuated by the frequent repetition of a number of Quechua and/or Spanish asseverative words, such as *ajina* (a Quechua form with which the speaker indicates previous knowledge of a fact) or *evidentemente* (Spanish for "evidently"). Another characteristic of political speeches is that speakers use a number of figures of speech and chichés to convey political affiliation (i.e., *compañeros* [comrades] or *hermanos* [brothers]) and to distinguish themselves and their audience from others. Village leaders, for instance, often use *noqayku* (the exclusive Quechua form for "us") when their message is specifically directed to villagers. Alternatively, if they want to address both vecinos and villagers they use *nonqanchej* (the inclusive Quechua form for "us").

Quechua and political rhetoric, as manifested in public speeches, serves then to distinguish leaders from nonleaders and villagers from vecinos, and simultaneously to unite them as campesinos. Yet these political representations of self and others, as campesinos, are nevertheless ambiguous because the concept glosses over class differences but does not erase them. While most Tiraqueños, both vecinos and villagers, speak Quechua and know how to plow, some are not peasants but members of a dominant class. Everybody knows this because in Tiraque no one can lead an anonymous life, just as everyone is aware of the vecinos' claims to racial superiority and of their efforts to distance themselves from villages.

But it is precisely because of the ambiguity of the concept "campesino" and the political purpose it carries that what it involves to be a campesino is contested in public debates and simultaneously used as an idiom of an "imagined" class to build broad alliances, including vecino and villager, poor and wealthy, "white" and "Indian"

Tiraqueños. By representing themselves as "campesinos" in a way that enables them to transcend factional oppositions, ethnic subjectivities, and class contradictions, they are able to translate heterogeneity into unity. This allows them to engage in collective actions against the state and global forces that affect, in one way or another, the livelihood of all.[14] In choosing "campesino" rather than "Indian," as a form of collective representation in these struggles, Tiraqueños put aside pervasive dominant images that relate the countryside with Indianness and engage directly with power by relying on a "modern" official discourse and on campesino organizations, both of which were, paradoxically, imposed on the rural population by the state.

It is in mobilizations such as these, as well as in a wide range of practices pertaining to campesino unions, where the connections between the practice and rhetoric of the politics of accommodation and confrontation best manifest themselves, as the following examples illustrate. For a village or higher-level union organization to be recognized, for instance, requires a number of symbols: a national flag and emblem, a union banner, a stamp, in addition to the "traditional" *pututu* (horn) to call union meetings and to mobilize people for political action. Campesinos also conduct union meetings with strict formality: they follow an agenda; everyone who wishes to speak has to request *la palabra* ("the word"); and when new leaders are elected, they have to take an oath of office, using words similar to those pronounced by the president of Bolivia. Furthermore, every time union members make decisions, such as establishing a cooperative or taking over vacant lands, the event is always marked by formal speeches, the national anthem and flag, Spanish-written documents, and, if possible, by the presence of civic and church authorities.

CONCLUSION

By relying on a number of symbols and practices of nation and modernity, campesinos no doubt seek to legitimize their actions. In doing so, however, they do not, as some would argue, mimic power; rather, they speak the very language that they consider important for challenging the state regarding what they probably perceive as the most pressing issues affecting their lives. They thus represent themselves as an imagined class of rural producers or as citizens rather than as imagined ethnic groups.

This is not to deny that for Tiraqueños ethnic differences are important. As we have seen, vecinos in particular spend a considerable amount of time and creativity reproducing and modifying a hegemonic and essentialist discourse that associates Indianness with the countryside and whiteness with the urban setting. But whereas these subjective representations of personhood are effective means for social exclusion among people who share similar origins, but who are divided by class distinctions irrespective of place of residence, self-definitions that are based on putative ethnic differences are only meaningful within the region. Within a wider context, both vecinos and villagers are perceived as "Indians," or worse, as "cholos."

Why Tiraqueños reproduce a dominant discourse of racial difference rather than challenge it, as highly differentiated ethnic groups have done in western Bolivia and in other parts of Latin America, is an important question that may generate different responses. Whatever the "correct" answer might be, the fact that Tiraqueños have sought to challenge power by relying on an idiom of class and citizenship instead of race underscores a recurrent problem in anthropology: the relationship between class and ethnicity. In addressing this issue, most scholars now accept that these are not static categories and that social actors have multiple, conflicting identities. But there has been a tendency to conflate discourse with social relations at the expense of the social practices and transformations that shape the very discourse that gives meaning to changing social relations. The challenge for us is to analyze dominant discourses of personhood and the ways in which they are constantly reproduced, subverted, and elaborated in ongoing debates of daily life and to situate them within ongoing processes of social transformation.

ACKNOWLEDGMENTS

The fieldwork on which this article is based was carried out from January 1982 through January 1985 and in short summer return visits. I would like to thank the Fulbright Foundation, the Inter-American Foundation, and the Research Foundation of the City University of New York for funding this research. I am also grateful to Richard Blot for his helpful suggestions to improve earlier versions of this chapter.

NOTES

1. For an excellent analysis of dominant images of the countryside in English literature, see Williams (1973) and Roseberry (1989) for a study of images of the peasant in Venezuela.

2. I conducted field and archival research (1982–85) in the Valle Alto and in the province of Tiraque, located on the highlands east of the central valleys of Cochabamba. The province extends through the Cordillera of Cochabamba and divides into three zones: the yungas or steep subtropical valleys where coca is produced, the mountains, and a high valley, overlooking the Valle Alto, where

potatoes, barley, fava beans, and other crops are grown. The town of Tiraque is situated on the valley, sixty kilometers from the city of Cochabamba on the Cochabamba to Santa Cruz highway, and fifty-eight villages are dispersed in the mountains and valleys.

3. While Bonfil Batalla was one of the first anthropologists to refer to colonial categories, it is only more recently that anthropologists have been concerned with such categories.

4. In some countries, like Bolivia and Peru, tribute was soon reinstated to remain the most important source of government revenue until the incorporation of these countries into the global structure of capitalism in the late nineteenth century and the consolidation of the liberal state, when tribute was finally abolished.

5. A comparison between the 1990 and 1950 population censuses in Bolivia reflects how the change in the definition of "Indians" from a fiscal to a cultural category led to a considerable increase in the number of Indians in Cochabamba (Grieshaber 1985).

6. *Indigenismo* refers to a movement, first developed in Mexico and other Latin American countries, but quite late in Bolivia, seeking to improve the social conditions and cultures of Indians. It was also a national project to create modern nation-states with a homogeneous national culture.

7. This was not the first time that an agrarian reform was implemented in Bolivia. After independence in 1825, and particularly in 1866 and 1874, several decrees sought to privatize communal lands with the justification that private ownership of land was an important means to modernize the nation-state.

8. According to a recent study, 72 percent of the population in Tiraque province are bilingual speakers, although the proportion is higher in the town than in the countryside, and even higher among men that women (Cideti, n.d., vol. 3:7–11).

9. The rural poor (tenants, sharecroppers, landowning peasants, and artisans) of the central valleys and surrounding highlands of Cochabamba played a crucial role in the years following the revolution and during the implementation of agrarian reform. Organized in armed militias, they seized hacienda lands, animals, and crops; terrorized hacendados, most of whom abandoned their properties; and became de facto owners of the lands.

10. Unlike Cochabambinos, Aymara-speaking groups refer to themselves as *jaqi* (person) in contrast to *q'ara* (naked) or white (Albó 1980).

11. In Bolivia, *gringa* means foreigner. The term can also be used to signify light skin or hair and it is applied to both people and animals. In its diminutive form, *gringuita* is a form of endearment; similarly, *cholita*, the diminutive of *chola*, is a non-insulting form to address women who wear *polleras* (broad, gathered skirts). *Cholita* also connotes "Indian" in its female manifestation but without carrying the stigma usually associated with the concept.

12. *Kharisiris* (Aymara for "the one who cuts or beheads") are beings who wander in the countryside looking for unsuspecting victims in order to extract fat from their bodies. There are many versions about the uses made of the fat: Some claim that it is processed into oil for baptisms; others assert that the fat is sold to soap factories. Foreigners are often accused of being kharisiris. But when people are pressed to confirm the charges, no one claims that they actually saw them because those who encounter kharisiris usually die; accusations are based on statements such as "people say so" (cf. Ansión 1989).

13. In every administrative district, a Subcentral or Central Campesina represents all the village unions in its district; in turn, the former constitute the

Departmental Federation of Peasants (Federación Sindical de Campesinos) and these form the National Confederation of Peasants.

14. Nowadays, these forms of mobilization include road blockades, marches, hunger strikes, and market boycotts.

REFERENCES

Abercrombie, Thomas. 1991. "To Be Indian, to Be Bolivian: 'Ethnic' and 'National' Discourses of Identity." In G. Urban and J. Sherzer, eds., *Nation-State and Indians in Latin America*. Austin: University of Texas Press.

Albó, Xavier. 1974. *Los mil rostros del Quechua*. Lima: Instituto de Estudios Peruanos.

————. 1980. *Khitipxtansa: Quiénes somos?* La Paz: Centro de Investigación Promoción del Campesinado.

Ansión, Juan. 1989. *Pishtacos: De verdugos a sacaojos*. Lima: Tarea, Asociación de Publicaciones Educativas.

Asad, Talal. 1993. *Genealogies of Religion: Discipline and Reasons of Power in Christianity and Islam*. Baltimore: Johns Hopkins University Press.

Bonfil Batalla, Guillermo. 1972. "El concepto de indio en América: Una categoría de la situación colonial." *Anales de Antropologia* 9: 1–22.

Cideti (Comité Interinstitucional para el Desarrollo de Tiraque). n.d. Diagnóstico socioeconómico de la microregión Tiraque. Vols. 1 and 3. Unpublished manuscript.

Demelas, Marie Daniele. 1981. "Darwinismo a la criolla: El Darwinismo social en Bolivia, 1880–1910." *Historia Boliviana* 7(2): 55–82.

Grieshaber, Erwin P. 1985. "Fluctuaciones en la definición del indio: Comparación de los censos de 1900 y 1950." *Historia Boliviana* 5(1–2): 45–84.

Keesing, Roger M. 1992. *Custom and Confrontation: The Kwaio Struggle for Cultural Autonomy*. Chicago: University of Chicago Press.

Lagos, Maria L. 1993. "'We Have to Learn to Ask': Hegemony, Diverse Experiences, and Antagonistic Meanings in Bolivia." *American Ethnologist* 20(1): 52–71.

————. 1994. *Autonomy and Power: The Dynamics of Class and Culture in Rural Bolivia*. Philadelphia: University of Pennsylvania Press.

Larson, Brooke. 1988. *Colonialism and Agrarian Transformation in Bolivia*. Princeton: Princeton University Press.

Mariategui, Jose D. 1971. *Seven Interpretive Essays on Peruvian Reality*. Austin: University of Texas Press.

Molinié-Fioravanti, Antoinette. 1982. *La Vallée Sacrée des Andes*. Paris: Societé d'Ethnographie. Travaux de l'Institute Français des Etudes Andines.

Ortner, Sherry. 1984. "Theory in Anthropology Since the Sixties." *Comparative Studies in Society and History* 26(1).

Roseberry, William. 1989. *Anthropologies and Histories: Essays in Culture, History, and Political Economy*. New Brunswick, N.J., and London: Rutgers University Press.

Sahlins, Marshall. 1985. *Islands of History*, Chicago: University of Chicago Press.

Smith, Gavin. 1989. *Livelihood and Resistance: Peasants and the Politics of Land in Peru*. Berkeley: University of California Press.

Taussig, Michael. 1987. *Shamanism, Colonialism, and the Wild Man: A Study in Terror and Healing*. Chicago: University of Chicago Press.

Vološinov, V. N. 1973. *Marxism and the Philosophy of Language*. New York: Academic Press.

Warman, Arturo. 1970. "Todos Santos y Todos Difuntos." In A. Warman, M. Nolasco Armas, G. Bonfil, M. Olivera de Vasquez, and E. Valencia, eds., *De eso que llaman la antropologia mexicana*. Mexico: Editorial Nuestro Tiempo, pp. 9–58.

Williams, Raymond. 1973. *The Country and the City*. New York: Oxford University Press.

———. 1977. *Marxism and Literature*. London: Oxford University Press.

Wolf, Eric R. 1986. "The Vicissitudes of the Closed Corporate Peasant Community." *American Ethnologist* 13(2): 325–29.

———. 1994. "Perilous Ideas: Race, Culture, People." *Current Anthropology* 35(1): 1–12.

7

The Narrative Construction of E'ñapa Ethnicity

María Eugenia Villalón

A growing anthropological literature on ethnicity, nationalism, and ethnogenesis documents the dynamic, processual, and creative nature of collective self-representations. The present chapter develops that perspective, focusing on two E'ñapa accounts of how Indians and non-Indians first arose in this world and how the power differential between them came about.[1]

Although these two accounts can be read simply as "origin myths," I argue here that they are more fruitfully understood as communicative occurrences that produce and reproduce ethnicity in E'ñapa society. As we examine the formal linguistic and semantic features of the narratives, we see how the E'ñapa Indians of Venezuela formulate, imagine, and transmit ethnic differences through narrative discourse. We also note how these processes embed in history and building upon culturally specific symbolic dichotomies developed and inscribed in the colonial encounter. Before describing these processes dealing with ethnic differentiation in and through discourse, however, some background ethnographic, historical, and theoretical information seems in order. The next few paragraphs address that need, briefly describing who the E'ñapa are and what collective experiences underpin the imagery of the ethnic self and Other they elaborate in their narratives. Following that,

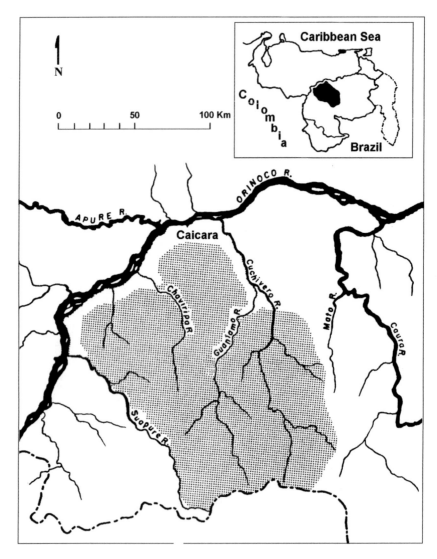

Figure 7.1. Territorio E'ñapa

I suggest an analytical framework to deal with the concept of ethnicity before presenting and analyzing the two stories.

ABOUT THE E'ÑAPA

The Carib-speaking E'ñapa, also known as Panare, number approximately 2,500 persons nucleated in some 48 villages in Bolívar State,

Venezuela. With the exception of one community located in the Amazonas State, all are found between the Cuchivero and Suapure rivers, which flow into the southern shores of the Middle Orinoco River (see Figure 7.1). The E'ñapa are horticulturists, growing sweet manioc and sweet potatoes as staples. They also hunt, fish, and gather wild foods and forest products. Although some communities are much more isolated than others, nowaday most E'ñapa interact regularly with tourists and surrounding *criollos* (non-Indian Venezuelans), to whom they sell handicrafts, produce from their plots, and forest products like wild honey. Occasionally some E'ñapa work on a contract basis for local *criollos*.

E'ñapa villages are kin-based and typically accommodate a few related extended families. These families used to share communal houses until very recent times. Besides parents, young children, and perhaps one or two related adults, the extended family commonly includes adult unmarried sons and daughters, as well as young married daughters with their spouses. This group constitutes the basic unit of production and socialization among the E'ñapa. There is strong preference for cross-cousin marriage and the newly married man is expected to provide a period of bride service to his father-in-law. Village life is conducted by the elders, led by a headman if there is one. Very frequently a prominent shaman, a magico-religious and ritual specialist, doubles as headman and political leader. Among the most important ceremonial activities, accompanied by singing, dancing, and huge amounts of manioc beer, are funerals for the recently departed and male initiation rites. Although E'ñapa communities and families enjoy substantial autonomy, and there is no formal sociopolitical organization or authority beyond them, several villages may comprise a loose regional network within which marriage alliances are preferentially structured, shamanic service provided, ceremonial life shared, and goods exchanged (Villalón 1984).

Until the last thirty years, in the sparsely populated Venezuelan hinterlands, the E'ñapa lived in peaceful equilibrium with their *criollo* neighbors, establishing in some cases fictive kinship bonds with local *compadres* (Dumont 1978, 49–65). Beginning in the mid-1960s, however, this balanced coexistence progressively eroded as three related events unfolded: (1) the Guaniamo River diamond rush; (2) *La Conquista del Sur* (the Conquest of the South), a national investment and expansion plan designed to develop the isolated and economically backward southern territories; and (3) the construction of roads from Caicara del Orinoco to Puerto Ayacucho and San Juan de Manapiare to the South, which, like a pitchfork, cut deeply into E'ñapa lands. As a result, the Indians lost a considerable portion of their territory and were forced to compete for diminishing resources with swelling waves of newcomers.

State-sponsored activity by foreign Catholic and Protestant New Tribes missionaries engaging in evangelization, coupled with the socioeconomic and cultural changes initiated by newcomers, created additional pressures. Yet, in spite of them, the E'ñapa have kept, to a remarkable degree, control of their own social dynamics and boundaries. They have done so mostly by exercising a variety of resistance strategies conferring upon them an "invisibility" that so far has worked to their advantage, promoting cultural survival. For instance, in contrast to other Venezuelan Indian groups such as the Ye'kwana, Pemon, or Kari'ña, the E'ñapa refuse involvement in "development" schemes and shun the path of *mestizaje* through intermarriage with *criollos*. Similarly, the E'ñapa eschew political activism, resisting the organizational and leadership transformations it entails. To this day they do not participate in Indian movements or organizations and have not established a collective bargaining relationship with the State. Another weapon the E'ñapa deploy to preserve their livelihood and spatial integrity is restrained, sporadic, and focused violence (Villalón 1992). Occasionally cutting down fences, burning *criollo* huts, or killing (and eating) herd animals constitute practices that seek to restore some symmetry in the relationships with the dominant society, emulating the nature of political power the State exercises over the Indians. Taken together, E'ñapa resistance strategies articulate a set of defiant cultural practices that spring from and strengthen the E'ñapa sense of selfhood and cultural uniqueness. These sentiments, however, coexist with marked ambivalence towards the dominant *criollo*, for while the E'ñapa resent their economic and technological supremacy, as well as their patronizing and discriminatory practices, they also harbor a tinge of admiration for the material abundance *criollos* enjoy. Overall, this complex and somewhat contradictory set of predicaments frames the business of keeping distances and marking ethnic boundaries among the E'ñapa. It constitutes the contemporary backdrop to the ethnic sentiments and images in-narrated in the stories examined later.

THINKING ETHNICITY

In keeping with the ideas expressed in the opening paragraph, and moving away from the reification and "primordialism" that tainted earlier approaches (Comaroff and Comaroff 1992; McKay 1982), ethnicity may be conceived as a historically rooted *process*, inscribing in culture *relations* between social selves and Others, formalized and transmitted in and through *discourse*. Emphasizing the situated, processual, relational, and discursive nature of ethnicity leads us to think of it as an evolved outcome of particular historical conditions, and also as a process primarily concerned with the cultural production of conceptions of peoplehood (Fox 1990, 3–4) manifested and reproduced (although not exclusively) in discourse. As such, ethnicity involves the production, establishment, and transmission of interrelated public, collective identities that particularize and stereotype social groupings. It is simultaneously a mode of social classification (i.e., a way of articulating differential groupings) and a mode of "inventing" selves and Others focusing on perceived differences. Given that communication is essential to the process of producing and establishing this type of claim, ethnicity can be succinctly characterized "as a type of social process in which notions of cultural differences are communicated" (Eriksen 1991, 128). Furthermore, as already implied, that process is essentially a dichotomous, oppositional, and reactive one (Thomas 1992, 213), objectifying a constructed cleavage between "us" and "them" (see also Comaroff and Comaroff 1992). Finally, even though the production of public collective selves might be related to race, nationality, or class distinctions, the chief distinguishing feature of ethnicity is that it engenders categories of collective selfhood based on common predicaments and shared perceptions of cultural uniqueness. Before discovering how these intertwine in the two stories we will be examining, however, a few introductory remarks on E'ñapa narrativity will be useful.

E'ñapa waramaipu

Our two stories are examples of an unlabeled style of narration included in a broad semantic field known as E'ñapa waramaipu, "E'ñapa language" or "speech." Because no single English term identifies adequately the type of narration involved, I have translated the native term as *inherited narrative*. By this expression I mean a marked speech style, distinguished by its formal and semantic features, learned and received from others, to which the E'ñapa attach special value (Villalón 1992, 6). The label "inherited narrative" thus highlights a particular style of narration, rather than a body of narrative content. It also steers clear of such fuzzy terms as "oral tradition," "oral literature," or "myth," which not only deify dynamic discursive phenomena, but also imply an epistemological grid alien to E'ñapa thought.

Tellings of E'ñapa waramaipu are artistic performances. Most take place in a serene ambiance, usually at dawn or at night, when the people are resting cozily in their hammocks around the hearth. All that is needed to trigger a performance is a good storyteller and someone willing to hear him or her. The event need not be overtly dialogic, in the sense of requiring a formalized interlocutor, but the narrator must be able to monitor audience involvement even in the dark. Female performers tend to be discreet and aim their tale at the immediate family circle. Experienced and esteemed male narrators, on the other hand, may enthrall an entire communal house or summer camp. Another occasion when one may hear *E'ñapa waramaipu* is during the concluding phases of ceremonial festivities, which mark the transition to the secular order of things and to normal life. These phases complete days of ritual drinking, singing, and dancing; and amidst the collective euphoria that ensues one may spot a group enjoying *E'ñapa waramaipu*. Thus, every E'ñapa normally socialized knows about the stories and probably has heard them dozens of times throughout his or her lifetime. Acquiring the skills to become a good storyteller, however, requires more than repeated listening and mnemonic ability. It demands mastery of rhetorical structures and metalinguistic codes, superior linguistic competence, and verbal creativity, in addition to interest, dedication, and practice. Master narrators, not surprisingly, command a lot of respect and authority among the E'ñapa.

NATIVE WRITER AND ANTHROPOLOGIST

Like many other E'ñapa, To:se', the young man who in 1974 wrote the stories presented here, heard *E'ñapa waramaipu* throughout his childhood and early adolescence mostly from his father and uncle. Both of them were shamans and headmen of repute. In 1974 To:se' was the only E'ñapa who wrote in his native language. He had learned on his own, applying the Spanish writing skills he was acquiring in school and borrowing a Ye'kwana[2] alphabet he had seen elsewhere. While To:se' was growing up in the Warei savana, he and two other boys were brought to Ciudad Bolívar by the bishop, who hoped two of them would enter the seminary upon completing their education, and a third would eventually replace his aging chauffeur. Much to the bishop's dismay, none of these plans materialized, but To:se' managed in time to complete his elementary schooling in Cumaná and take a teaching post among his people. The years spent in the coastal town of Cumaná were very trying for the young To:se', who endured *criollo* discrimination, economic hardships, and the patronizing practices of the bishop's retinue. In those years To:se' returned regularly to Ciudad Bolívar during school breaks, and it was then and there, lodged at our home, that he wrote the narrative corpus from which come the two stories we will soon read. The decision to write rather than narrate them was his, but the project was conceived by my partner Henry Corradini. As To:se' wrote his stories, we transcribed and translated them with his aid. In the course of these working sessions To:se' shared with us his considerable knowledge of E'ñapa culture, indispensable for a full understanding of the deeply contextualized *E'ñapa waramaipu*. But he particularly loved to muse upon, contrast and compare, the practices and noesis reflected in the narratives with his experiences in the *criollo* world. These discussions provided him with some emotional relief, while they enriched considerably our perspective on Indian-*criollo* relations, of which, of course, we were part. In retrospect I may mention that the long chain of recontextualizations involved as the *E'ñapa waramaipu* passed from To:se''s head to a handwritten notebook, then to a typewriter, (much) later to a computer, and eventually to a chapter in this book meant that, contrary to what we thought at the time, we were not strictly "recording" or "preserving" *E'ñapa waramaipu*, but recreating it as well. Then, as now, To:se' and we may anchor a piece of the present in the narratives, drawing new meanings and interpretations from them as our knowledge and experience broaden. The discussion that follows should be seen in this light, for although the interpretations are my own, they draw upon many years of shared dialogues with To:se', Corradini, and the texts themselves. This is not intended as a disclaimer, but rather as an acknowledgment of the multiple voices that resonate in the *E'ñapa waramaipu* and of the contingent nature of texts themselves (cf. Hanks 1989).[3]

FRAMES AND THEMES

The discursive style identified as *E'ñapa waramaipu* characterizes diverse stories. A substantial number of them comprise one major cycle that begins with the emergence of mankind and ends in modern times. Three temporal frames structure chronologically the cycle's unfolding events. The first frame is labeled *Mare:waka wiciña' E'ñapaya*, "when Mare:waka [the culture hero] lived among the E'ñapa"; the second, *E'ñapa we'ca'kë në'na'*, "when animals were human"; and the third, *E'ñapa wësɨnëpë pake'* "formerly [when] the E'ñapa fought [with each other]"; or *E'ñapa (n) tonpɨ wësɨnën pake'* "formerly [when] the ancestors were fighting [each other]." Each temporal frame, in turn, corresponds to an open sequence accommodating a number of tales: (1) the emergence of mankind from the primordial mountain, (2) a series of metamorphoses, which spawned the different animal species, and (3) a period of internal warfare. Two types of past, furthermore, embed the narrative sequences: *pakeputu*, the remote past, and *pake'*, a more recent or verifiable past.[4] The first two narrative sequences and temporal frames overlap partially in the span covered by *pakeputu*, since all events unfolding therein took place in Mare:waka's time. His presence amid the E'ñapa is one of the semantic markers identifying the remote past. On the other hand, the stories comprising the third sequence, which in-narrates a traumatic period of E'ñapa warfare, unfold exclusively in the recent past. The accounts I present here are cast in the remote past and are representative of sequences 1 and 2, respectively.

E'ñapa and *Criollos*: The Confrontation

The remainder of this chapter will be devoted to the idea that the accounts of To:se' exemplify a narrative practice that produces and reproduces ethnicity in E'ñapa society, primarily through the elaboration of culturally specific symbolic dichotomies inscribed in the colonial encounter. These dichotomies are developed narratively through the manipulation of contrastive linguistic forms and tropes, suggesting that E'ñapa self-representations are strongly oppositional and reactive (Thomas 1992, 213; see also Friedman 1992, 842–46; Urla 1993, 830, 837). My analysis seems to support Thomas's claim (1992, 214) that reactive objectification is a fundamental and ubiquitous cultural process facilitating reciprocal differentiation. I propose that the colonial encounter provided a totalizing experience in the midst of which, and against which, the E'ñapa reimagined themselves as a new unity distinct from that other conflated category comprised by Spanish and *criollo* invaders. That is, in the face of a sharply and irrevocably changed reality, the E'ñapa repositioned themselves in it, defining a new public collective identity.

This collective identity is approximately two hundred years old. The E'ñapa encountered the white colonizer in the eighteenth century, when the Spanish troops finally overcame Carib resistance and crossed the Orinoco River to pursue the occupation of its southern shores. From that period at the earliest must derive the semantic kernel of the inherited narratives presented here, for both objectify the collective self and Other in terms of a fundamental dichotomy: "we" (Indians) and "they" (non-Indians or *criollos*). These categories are coded lexically as *E'ñapa* and *tato'*. The latter is, unquestionably, the most significant Other the E'ñapa recognize—so significant, in fact, that they have always been there, part and parcel of the beginnings of man and society. As such, the emergence of *criollos* along with the E'ñapa in Mare:waka's time constitutes a narrative procedure that "updates" history and naturalizes a major historical event, leaving native cosmogony intact and fully in force (cf. Gossen intra; Vansina 1985, 119).

A NOTE ON TRANSCRIPTION AND PRESENTATION

Interpreting *E'ñapa waramaipu* will be eased if the reader bears in mind the following points. The E'ñapa sounds are transcribed according to the International Phonetic Alphabet with these few exceptions: /c/ stands for an alveolo-palatal voiceless affricate, akin to the English "ch"; /tʸ/ for an alveolo-palatal voiceless stop; /'/ for a glottal stop, and /ñ/ for an alveolo-palatal nasal, similar to the Spanish "ñ". The English translation follows closely the original text; hence it is more literal than "literary." Capitals are avoided, and the few punctuation marks employed signal prosodic contours and voice switches. The text layout is meaningful and designed to "translate" visually the rhetorical structure of the E'ñapa waramaipu. Indentation and spacing, for instance, distinguish formal, hierarchical, narrative segments such as "stagings," "acts," or "episodes." These, in turn, are built upon lines (set off by pauses, intonational contours, and/or syntactic criteria), which constitute the fundamental structural unit in this type of discourse. Other non-hierarchical rhetorical components like lexico-semantic parallelisms, lexical markers, or cronotopes, together with the various hierarchical units, shape the formal structure of the E'ñapa waramaipu. They all interact actively in the production of narrative meaning and aesthetic appeal (cf. Villalón [1992] for a fuller discussion).

THE EMERGENCE

1   *e'ñapa wapatakanya' arawaya*
     the E'ñapa emerged from [Mount] Arawa

2   *arawayawo we'ca'kë e'ñapa pake'*
     within [Mount] Arawa existed the E'ñapa long ago

3   *yu:tën mare:waka e'ñapa wë'yaka*
     Mare:waka goes towards the abode of the E'ñapa

4   *arawayawa*
     within [Mount] Arawa

5   *yɨmuku:kañe mare:waka na:ta'*
     Mare:waka opens up the entrance

6   *arawæ na:tan*
     [Mount] Arawa's entrance

7   —*ata:nkapë'të animonton paken!*—
     —you all come forth first!—

8   *kañe mare:waka e'ñapa uya*
     says Mare:waka to the E'ñapa

9   *yo:patakan e'ñapa atawan we'ke'*
     not all the E'ñapa come forth

10   *asa' apo'*
     two men

11   *asa'kë winkɨ'*
     also two women

12   *asa'nan'*
     four

13   *yu:tën mare:waka tato' yɨwë'*
     Mare:waka goes towards the *criollos'* abode

14   *na:tan muku:ka*
     to open its entrance

15   *yu:tën mare:waka tata' ye:*
     Mare:waka goes towards the *criollos'* den

16   *muku:ka ta'ta*
     opens the cave

17   *yɨmuku:kañe mare:waka tato'*
     Mare:waka releases the *criollos*

18   —*apataka animoton!*—
     —get out you all!—

19   *kañe mare:waka tato' uya*
     says Mare:waka to the *criollos*

20   *yo:patakan tato' atawan*
     all the *criollos* come forth

21   *yu:cin mare:waka aya:pe e'ke' e'ñapa uya*
     Mare:waka is unhappy with the E'ñapa

22   *ku:re e'ke' e'ñapa wicinpë*
     they are too few

23   —*kai' mici animonton atawan apataka: 'ka?*—
     —why didn't you all come out?—

24   *ya'ka:pañe mare:waka*
     asks Mare:waka

25   —*apataka:'kama nicanton!*—
     —they didn't come out!—

26   *kañe e'ñapa*
     say the E'ñapa

27   *yo:sa:pësɨn mare:waka marana i'kɨtɨ*
     Mare:waka begins to chop copaiba wood

28   *yama:nëse'ña e'ñapa:pe*
     to shape E'ñapa

29   *yawa'kɨtɨñe mare:waka marana asa'nan'*
     Mare:waka chops four pieces of copaiba

30   *ipet*ʸ*akase:i'pe ku:re*
      and then cleaves them in many pieces

31   *yama:nëñe mare:waka marana e'ñapa:pe*
      Mare:waka shapes the copaiba like E'ñapa

32   *yu:simɨnkan mare:waka marana ma:nëñe e'ñapa:pe*
      Mare:waka finishes shaping the copaiba like E'ñapa

33   *yo:sa:pësɨn tɨna ma:në arawæ pianpë*
      begins to create rivers at the foot of [Mount] Arawa

34   *kamo:nton e'ñapa tinaipe*
      so they the E'ñapa would have water

35   *e'ñapa ma:nëpo:mën*
      once the E'ñapa were created

36   *yu:cin mare:waka ku:re mon arawæ wë'ya*
      Mare:waka stayed long there by [Mount] Arawa

37   *e'ñapaya*
      with the E'ñapa

38   *e'ke' tato' mon arawæ wë'ya*
      there were no *criollos* there by [Mount] Arawa

39   *yu:të'pë nansa'*
      they had gone far away

40   *yɨ:wënta:'taman mare:waka yo:ramæipu e'ñapa uya*
      Mare:waka manifests himself addressing the E'ñapa

41   —*në:'pe oci't*ʸ*ë'pɨma amën?*—
      —what do you want to be?—

42   *ya'kapopë'ñe mare:waka*
      asks Mare:waka

43   —*ko:tape i:'kë amën!*—
      —red howler monkey be you!—

44   *kañe mare:waka ko:ta uya*
      says Mare:waka to the red howler monkey

45   —*caca' amën!*—
      —[and] you hoatzin!—

46   *kañe mare:waka caca' kuya*
      says Mare:waka to the hoatzin

47   *ice'tɨñe mare:waka ku:re atawan në'na'*
      thus Mare:waka named many all the animals

48   *yo:sama:nën atawan ice't*ʸ*ësa' në'na'pe*
      all the named ones turned animals

49   *yu:cin ice'tʸësa'pɨ' asama:në'ka*
      but the unnamed ones were not transfigured

50   *e'ñapa pi:nkën*
      they were inherently E'ñapa

51   *aso'ma'ka në'na'pe*
      did not turn into animals

52   *yu:cin arawaya e'ñapa we'tʸa:ñe në'na' e'ke'*
      when the E'ñapa lived within [Mount] Arawa there were no
      animals

53   *e'ñapa we'ca'kë në'na'.*
      the animals were E'ñapa.

Here, in the broadest sense, the E'ñapa craft a way of thinking and talking about *criollos* and about themselves. The narrative describes and frames a new social reality and its collective actors primarily in quantitative terms, foregrounding a numerical difference as one enduring and central distinguishing feature of new emerging ethnic identities. Notice that the story in-narrates and thematizes the colonial encounter and its antagonisms in terms of contrasting quantities: only two E'ñapa couples obeyed Mare:waka's original mandate to issue forth,[5] while all *criollos* complied, surfaced, and henceforth reproduced inordinately. It is this initial and crucial difference in conduct that leads to the formation of two populations radically different in size (and eventually in power) as new and opposed social categories.

Insofar as contrasting magnitudes help define those categories, they also objectify the Other and subjectivize the self, relocating it in a larger, more complex social map. This quantitative mode of categorizing people and behavior, furthermore, both naturalizes and transcendentalizes a particular historical outcome, because it forges an alternative truth and embeds the enduring experience of domination, minority status, and demographic insignificance, in comprehensible cosmological terms. These processes, in turn, validate native epistemology and contemporary ethnic boundaries.

In sum, the numerical argument developed in and through the emergence discourse provides a conceptual/narrative grid for the formulation of new social knowledge and the interpretation of a conflictual/contested reality. In this sense, E'ñapa discourse incorporates and exploits the issue of numbers much as Western modern societies employ statistics as a "technology of truth production" (Urla 1993, 819). Urla argues that the practice of counting people and property, once primarily an instrument of the State, has become a question of immediate consequence to the distribution of economic and political power and to the experience of everyday life in modern stratified societies (819). "In the hands of the socially or politically disenfranchised, numbers may also be a language of social contestation, a way ethnic groups, women, and minorities can make themselves visible [and] articulate their 'differences' from the dominant society" (818). Certainly this seems the case among the E'ñapa. But the "Emergence" text also shows that assessing and comparing magnitudes to advance differentiating claims is not strictly a Western modern predicament, nor is it confined to contemporary hierarchical nation-states, as Urla argues. The "politics of numbers"—counting and gauging size—is indeed a mode of social categorization, but one neither exclusively "Western" or "modern," nor restricted to stratified state societies. Rather, it seems more a human predicament, a widespread societal practice for the crafting of public collective identities in contested situations.

Beyond that, the E'ñapa's numerical argument implicitly attributes moral depravity to the white adversary, because in the native cultural context *criollo* proliferation is accounted for in terms of their perceived sexual incontinence. Hence, contrary to what might be expected, the Indians' initial failure to surface completely and the enduring demographic scarcity resulting thereof do not signal an ontogenic weakness, but superior morality and sociality that contrast with the whites' moral inferiority. The reasoning goes as follows: While the E'ñapa admire large families, which confer prestige and sociopolitical ascendancy, they also believe that successive pregnancies should be delayed until the preceding child is entirely weaned (approximately three or four years). The fathering of many children is therefore more feasible among polygamous males. However, since it is commonly known that polygyny is not an accepted practice among *criollos*, the E'ñapa attribute their large numbers to their failure to space children properly. The vast numerical advantage of the *criollo* rests, therefore, on reprehensible sexual conduct evinced by unrestrained ("animal-like") serial siring. As we will see shortly, imbuing the *criollos* with animal-like traits is a salient rhetorical device in E'ñapa discourse for substantiating emerging social polarizations.

A third point worthy of note is the "Emergence" text's handling of time and locale, which further elaborates the primordial divide between E'ñapa and *tato'*. As the story as a whole predicates, and as lines 36–39 emphasize, all the cultural hero's deeds while at Mount Arawa[6] aimed at improving E'ñapa life and culture. This was the sole object of his efforts and concerns. The whites, contrariwise, disappeared from the site soon after creation and went on to occupy alien and remote spaces:

36   Mare:waka stayed long there by [Mount] Arawa

37   with the E'ñapa

38   there were no *criollos* there by [Mount] Arawa

39   they had gone far away.

In these lines the E'ñapa explicitly appropriate Mare:waka's time and place, adding physical (chronological and spatial) distance to the ontogenic and moral divide predicated more generally between Indians and whites. In defining particular time and space settings as the E'ñapa's own, these appropriations demarcate historical, chronological, and spatial domains that exclude and differentiate the Other in subtle ways at times. Note, for instance, that in contrast to the E'ñapa, who dwelled inside Mount Arawa "long ago," *criollo* place and time of emergence remain imprecise throughout the narrative. Whereas Mare:waka implants the E'ñapa in a specific place, time and chain of events, the *tato'* disappear immediately and forever from undefined creation grounds. Put more bluntly, E'ñapa and *tato'* shared (and share) nothing save an instant of Mare:waka's attention (however cursory for the whites) and a fleeting original proximity, neither of which deserves elaboration. In this way the narrative inextricably links topography with emerging identities, positing Mount Arawa as a "lived" place for the E'ñapa—a spatialized experience that literally "grounds" their collective identity and sets them apart from all Others. In the process, claims to a unique history materialize, bolstering ethnic differentiation. Mount Arawa, as the site of Mare:waka's extraordinary agency, is a unique social landscape. It embodies E'ñapa culture and constitutes the foundation of E'ñapa autochthony. Seen from another angle, the spatialization of history and ethnicity achieved in "The Emergence" advances a power claim through exclusion of whites from privileged domains. Altogether, these meanings encoded in the account show that places (and time) "are not simply settings for social action, nor . . . mere reflections of society," but rather "politicized, culturally relative, [and] historically specific . . . constructions" (Rodman 1992, 652, 641).

Having reached this point, let us next pay some attention to the more significant formal linguistic features present in "The Emergence." This gives us a broadened perspective on the ways ethnic differences are imagined and communicated in E'ñapa narratives. Later, a closer look at the interaction between meaning and form furnishes a more detailed understanding of how ethnic boundaries are enacted through reactive objectification and stereotypic categorization. For a start, let's turn our attention to lines 13–16 of the "Emergence" account:

13   *yu:tën mare:waka tato' yɨwë'*
        Mare:waka goes towards the *criollos'* abode

14   *na:tan muku:ka*
        to open its entrance

15   *yu:tën mare:waka tata' ye:*
        Mare:waka goes towards the *criollos'* den

16   *muku:ka ta'ta*
        opens the cave

The word *yiwë'* in line 13 is a possessed form of *wë'*, meaning "home" or "abode." This form implies a human subject or at least one with a high degree of animacy. It contrasts with *ye:* which normally denotes an animal's lair or den, a meaning derived from the word's most general sense of "container." Thus the shift from *tato' yiwë'* in line 13 to *tata' ye:* in line 15, both characterizing the *criollos'* place of confinement, effectively signals an ontological degradation assigning *criollos* animal-like attributes. The demotion is then openly formulated in line 16, which unequivocally defines the whites' chthonian dwelling as just a hole or a "cave." Once the demotion of the Other is established by differentiating the nature of the original abodes, the narrative ratifies and legitimizes this downgrading, adjusting Mare:waka's linguistic behavior. We need now to compare lines 7 and 18, which convey his commands for emergence:

7   —*ata:nkapë'të animonton paken!*—
        —you all come forth first!—

18   —*apataka animonton!*—
        —get out you all!—

When Mare:waka addresses the E'ñapa (line 7), he chooses a respectful verbal exhortative, *ata:nkapë'të*; but when he addresses the *criollos* (line 18), he modifies conspicuously his speech, employing a plain imperative, *apataka*. This shift is highly significant for the E'ñapa because the use of imperative verbal forms is considered impolite and is therefore avoided among adults, especially in non-intimate contexts. For this reason plain imperatives are usually restricted to interaction with social unlikes such as children, subordinates, and pets and are employed with care lest offense be taken. Given these sociolinguistic norms, the shift from an exhortative to an imperative form when vocalizing orders or demands immediately communicates a status difference, placing the addressee in a socially inferior slot. Thus, by modifying the linguistic shape of his two commands, Mare:waka communicates contrasting social and affective meanings that publicly ratify and sanction the primordial divide between E'ñapa and *criollos*, as well as the latter's social and moral inferiority. In a few lines, then, lexical and semantic elements, verbal morphology, and implicit sociolingustic norms all come together to construct an enduring negative representation of the intrusive Other. Last, it is worth noting that Mare:waka's rude order to the *tato'* inside Mount Arawa parodies the latter's often-contemptuous speech towards Indians in everyday life. In the narrative world of the E'ñapa, the power relationship manifested in and through discourse is exactly the reverse of the one that normally holds among Indians and *criollos*, between whom language and power invariably coalesce to confirm the former's subordinate status.

RED HOWLERS AND HOATZINS, AN EMBLEMATIC DICHOTOMY

The production of the negative stereotype is continued in the last part of the plot (lines 40–47), where Mare:waka speaks again, transfiguring some E'ñapa into animals. Let us pay close attention to the species named in those lines, for the choices made are motivated and highly significant. That is, the species featured in the narrative combine several analogic paths in the production of metaphors that incorporate both the perceived characteristics of the animals as well as the signification of their differences. The red howler, with which the E'ñapa identify strongly, is the biggest primate in the area and the most humanlike. It has a yellowish-reddish fur that the E'ñapa associate with the color of their skin, enhanced by the use of the red annato dye. These monkeys have a distinctive social organization and follow the oldest male, which directs the orchestrations of the troop and enjoys the privilege of solo howling (Cabrera and Yepes 1960, 107). The behavioral norms of the howlers are especially noticed by the E'ñapa, who deem them analogous to their own ceremonial behavior, in which a shaman or leader executes the solos and directs the chorus of participants. In addition, the howlers exhibit a composed demeanor, move with grace and dignity, and do not accept captivity (Emmons 1990, 124–25; Gremone, Cervigón, Gorzula, Medina, and Novoa n.d., 35). The E'ñapa value strongly these physical and behavioral qualities, which are incorporated into their own ideas of comportment and conduct. In contrast, they despise the hoatzins' cacophonous song, awkward flight, and foul smell (Gremone, Cervigón, Gorzula, Medina, and Novoa n.d., 94–95; Phelps and de Schauensee 1979, 121). It is fairly clear, then, that the howler and the hoatzin predicate metaphorically contrasting cultural values and images. The qualities attributed to each, which "mark" them culturally, "become potential key elements in activating cognitive schema in specific contexts" (Isbell 1985, 298). For this reason I believe that the full cultural significance of the lexical choices manifest in "The Emergence" lies beyond the metaphoric, metonymic, and synesthetic relationships predicated in this particular account. Specifically, the perceived *contrast* between the two species appears most relevant, since the formulation of the antonym partially explains the lexical choices and the meaning of the tropes. The labels "red howler" and "hoatzin" encode two tropes deliberately opposed in the narrative, just as E'ñapa and *criollos* are opposed by nature and circumstance. Seen from another angle, the particular species selected and contrasted suggest that human/animal metaphors in E'ñapa inherited narrative may predicate patterns of social interaction between different groups and types of persons, as Urton (1985, 4) has suggested for South American oral literature in general.

OF MONKEYS AND *CRIOLLOS*

The ideations and communicative forms described are further developed in the following story To:se' wrote in Ciudad Bolívar in 1974. He titled it *Om Arakon*, The Cicada and the Squirrel/Capuchin Monkey.[7] In this story Squirrel Monkey disobeys a shaman's injunction, opening up his sacred pouch and letting the enclosed helper cicadas escape. As punishment, Squirrel Monkey is metamorphosed into a *criollo*.

Om Arakon

1	*yamaikañe e'ñapa pian yi'kamawæ'*
	an E'ñapa shaman hangs up his pouch
2	*i:ye yɨwanpë*
	on a tree trunk
3	*tʸamokaintʸa:ñe*
	while [others] work
4	*kanowa' kata:ñe*
	carving out a trough
5	*o' ce:*
	container for the manioc beer
6	*ku:ri ci'ce e'ñapa*
	there were many E'ñapa
7	*i'yan kën om icen*
	shaman is master of cicadas
8	*në'na' icen*
	master of animals
9	*pinkë icen*
	master of peccaries
10	*yu:wë:pɨn kën arakon*
	Squirrel Monkey comes
11	*kanowa' kañe e'ñapa wë'yaka*

where the E'ñapa are carving out the trough

12   *yupupu'kañe kën arakon*
    Squirrel Monkey lets them out [the cicadas]

13   *om icen kamawayawo*
    from the master of cicadas' pouch

14   *t^ye:yawo*
    from their own container

15   —*co:ñe amën?*
    —what are you looking for?

16   *në:' ci'ñe amën?*
    what do you want?

17   *yu'kamawæ' kuyupupu'ka amë!*—
    don't open my pouch!—

18   *kañe kën om icen*
    says master of cicadas

19   *yaciña'kañe kën arakon kent^yasan*
    Squirrel Monkey pokes into it pertinaciously

20   *asawantaka'ka kënpë*
    ignoring him

21   *yo:patakan kën om*
    the cicadas fly out

22   *yo:sa:mën ka'kë*
    go way up

23   —*yu' kamawæ' kayaciña'ka wa'kë:të!*—
    —I said not to poke into my pouch!—

24   *kañe om icen*
    says master of cicadas

25   *yo:so'napɨn arakonpë*
    gets mad at Squirrel Monkey

26   —*maaa! ya'pi'!*—
    —hell! you'll see!—

27   *kañe e'ñapa pian*
    says the E'ñapa shaman

28   *kano' mo:sakanpan*
    calling forth the rain

29   *arakon pu'mañepe*
    to beat against Squirrel Monkey

30   *yu:wé:pɨn mën kano' kën arakonpain'*

the rain falls all over Squirrel Monkey

31   *arakon pu'mañe yi'punpë*
      beating against Squirrel Monkey's head

32   *i'wet^yapasa' e't^ya:ñe*
      as he squats cringed

33   *yupucukuyatan arakon i'pun*
      bluing Squirrel Monkey's head

34   *yo:so'man arakon mënpa*
      at that moment Squirrel Monkey metamorphoses

35   *waso'masa'kë arakon tatape*
      Squirrel Monkey was metamorphosed into a *criollo*.

Although at first sight this story can be construed as a gibe and as an alternative origin myth of *criollos*, I think it is far more, artfully elaborating certain tropes in order to formulate and communicate a negative ethnic stereotype. In the paragraphs that follow we will see how the story utilizes specific narrative conventions to associate squirrel monkeys (*arakon*) with *criollos*, and in this fashion satirizes and mocks the most significant Other.

That association is effectively wrought due to the fact that the E'ñapa hold a negative image of *arakon*. This monkey represents for them the cultural antithesis of the admired and emblematic red howler. In contrast to the latter, the squirrel monkey is brownish or ash-colored. A casketlike dark spot covers his crown and descends like sideburns, while his nose is blackish, resembling the mustache and beard of *criollos*, which the E'ñapa lack. His behavior also contrasts markedly with that of the dignified howler. *Arakon* is a noisy and rambunctious animal, steals food in the gardens, masturbates in public, and is easily tamed. These perceived contrasts in physiognomy and behavior, culturally reinterpreted, have been polarized and encoded ideologically in the dichotomy red howler/squirrel-capuchin monkey. This opposition predicates in relation to other significant bipolarities already described, like the contrastive pair E'ñapa/*criollos* and the analogous one red howler/E'ñapa, both formulated in "The Emergence." Now *Om Arakon* consolidates a tropic identification between squirrel monkeys and *criollos*, attributing to the latter the focal negative traits compacted in the animal's adverse cultural image. For example, the E'ñapa associated the easily domesticated squirrel monkey's behavior with the servile conduct observed in certain *criollo* groups like soldiers, servants, and peons. Similarly, the E'ñapa perceive *criollos* as loquacious and strident. Their behavior is judged voluble and their gestures exaggerated. In short, *Om Arakon* elaborates the self-differentiating discourse formulated in the "Emergence" narrative, encoding and conveying a social definition of the Other that amounts to an ethnic antithesis of the E'ñapa. That antithesis is structured by means of a tropic movement that posits the squirrel monkey as the cultural antithesis of the red howler. In other words, the dichotomy red howler/squirrel monkey present in E'ñapa cultural imagery predicates metaphorically the E'ñapa/*criollos* dichotomy formulated in "The Emergence." Both dichotomies, in turn, build upon and signify in relation to the symbolic identification between squirrel monkey/*criollos* and red howler/E'ñapa thematized and elaborated in the inherited narrative. Once more we see how E'ñapa narrators manipulate linguistic form and tropes, linking together referential and poetic meanings (cf. Ohnuki-Tierney 1990, 96) in order to articulate opposing conceptions of self and Other.

CONCLUDING REMARKS

Throughout these pages we have focused on the ways notions of peoplehood and distinctiveness are formulated, imagined, and communicated in *E'ñapa waramaipu*. Although much more could be said about To:se''s narratives, I hope to have shown that they display a rhetorical organization of cultural images that may be understood as an analogic synthesis of ethnic reactive oppositions. If, as Eriksen (1991, 129) argues, the act of communicating and articulating cultural differences is a fundamental aspect of ethnicity, then these narratives, achieving just that, constitute discursive instances that communicate and reproduce ethnic configurations. However, "The Emergence" and *Om Arakon* are far more than verbal manipulations of symbols that produce and convey social uniqueness. All along I called attention to the multiple ways in which they *en-act*, legitimize, and naturalize ethnic boundaries. The narratives, then, lie at the heart of E'ñapa politics of self-representation. In deploying such devices as numerical argumentation, artful manipulation of synesthetic tropes, and parody, they help construct differentiating collective representations of personhood that defy the invasive and homogenizing procedures of *criollo* society. Hence, the narratives are one form of resistance, providing a "private hidden transcript" (Colburn 1989; Scott 1989) for understanding, approaching, and managing ethnic encounters in ways that challenge the dominant script. Needless to say, neither the ethnic polarizations nor their enactment could be adequately understood outside the discourse that articulates them.

NOTES

1. This chapter rests on several years of shared work with the E'ñapa, with our main E'ñapa collaborator, To:se', and with Henry E. Corradini. Without their

patient and willing collaboration, I could not have written it. The paper is a revised, expanded version of earlier presentations made at the 31st Conference on American Indian Languages, American Anthropological Association Annual Meeting, San Francisco, December 1992, and at the 48th International Congress of Americanists, Uppsala, July 1994. Those presentations were made possible, in part, by travel grants from the Consejo Nacional de Investigaciones Científicas y Tecnológicas (CONICIT) (1992), the Vice-rectorate of the Universidad Central de Venezuela, and the Consejo de Disarrollo Científico y Humanístico (CDCH) of that same institution (1994). The 48th International Congress of Americanists likewise partially funded my trip to Sweden. I gratefully acknowledge their support. I also wish to thank Charles Briggs for his continued encouragement, and all participants in the seminar Discourse and Power: An Interdisciplinary Perspective, Universidad Central de Venezuela, 1995, for their comments on the E'ñapa texts. The editor of this volume, Richard Blot, carefully reviewed my drafts offering very helpful commentaries. Last, my colleague Lourdes Giordani located and sent me very useful sources, an invaluable aid to the likes of me working in the Third World. To all my sincere thanks.

2. Ye'kwana is another Carib language spoken in Venezuela.

3. For a fuller discussion of the themes addressed in this paragraph, see Villalón (1992).

4. The recognition of *pakeputu* and *pake'* as external, temporal frames of reference for inherited narratives should not be confused with their actual use in storytelling, where the handling of the terms is quite fluid and context-sensitive.

5. In other versions of the story, two E'ñapa (i.e., one couple) emerge.

6. Mount Arawa is a complex and polysemous concept in E'ñapa thought, being simultaneously a "real" topographic landmark located in the Upper Cuchivero River, an instance of spatialized history, and the E'ñapa's *locus amoenus*, imagined as a translucent dome. It still harbors those that were unwilling to surface.

7. The term *arakon* includes the capuchin monkey (*Cebus sp.*) and the squirrel monkey (*Saimiri sp.*), two closely related species that live in association. According to Eisenberg (1989, 249) *Cebus* is probably the focal species. Although I translate the term mostly as "squirrel monkey," it should be borne in mind that the native designation may also include the capuchin monkey.

REFERENCES

Cabrera, Angel, and José Yepes. 1960. *Mamíferos Sud Americanos*. Buenos Aires: Ediar S.A. Editores.

Colburn, Forrest D. 1989. "Introduction." In Forrest D. Colburn, ed., *Everyday Forms of Peasant Resistance*. New York: M. E. Sharpe, ix–xv.

Comaroff, John, and Jean Comaroff. 1992. *Ethnography and the Historical Imagination*. Boulder, Colo.: Westview Press.

Dumont, Jean-Paul. 1978. *The Headman and I. Ambiguity and Ambivalence in the Fieldworking Experience*. The Texas Pan American Series. Austin: University of Texas Press.

Eisenberg, John F. 1989. *Mammals of the Neotropics: The Northern Neotropics*. Vol. 1, *Panama, Colombia, Venezuela, Guyana, Suriname, French Guiana*. Chicago: University of Chicago Press.

Emmons, Louise H. 1990. *Neotropical Rainforest Mammals: A Field Guide*. Ill. François Feer. Chicago: University of Chicago Press.

Eriksen, Thomas Hylland. 1991. "The Cultural Contexts of Ethnic Differences." *Man*, n.s., 26(1): 127–44.

Fox, Richard G. 1990. "Introduction." In Richard G. Fox, ed., *Nationalist Ideologies and the Production of National Culture*. American Ethnological Society Monograph Series, No. 2, James L. Watson, ed. Washington: American Anthropological Association, 1–14.

Friedman, Jonathan. 1992. "The Past in the Future: History and the Politics of Identity." *American Anthropologist* 94(4): 837–59.

Gremone, Carlos, Fernando Cervigón, Stefan Gorzula, Glenda Medina, and Daniel Novoa. n.d. *Fauna de Venezuela: Vertebrados*. Caracas: Editorial Biosfera.

Hanks, William F. 1989. "Text and Textuality." *Annual Review of Anthropology*, ed. Bernard J. Siegel, Alan R. Beals, and Stephen A. Tyler, 18: 95–127. Palo Alto, Calif.: Annual Reviews.

Isbell, Billie Jean. 1985. "The Metaphoric Process: 'From Culture to Nature and Back Again.'" In Gary Urton, ed., *Animal Myths and Metaphors in South America*. Salt Lake City: University of Utah Press, 285–313.

McKay, James. 1982. "An Exploratory Synthesis of Primordial and Mobilizationist Approaches to Ethnic Phenomena." *Ethnic and Racial Studies* 5(4): 395–420.

Ohnuki-Tierney, Emiko. 1990. "Monkey as Metaphor? Transformations of a Polytropic Symbol in Japanese Culture." *Man*, n.s., 25(1): 89–107.

Phelps, William H., Jr. and Rodolphe Meyer de Schauensee. 1979. *Una guía de las aves de Venezuela*. Caracas: Gráficas Armitano, C.A.

Rodman, Margaret C. 1992. "Empowering Place: Multilocality and Multivocality." *American Anthropologist* 94(3): 640–56.

Scott, James C. 1989. "Everyday Forms of Resistance." In Forrest D. Colburn, ed., *Everyday Forms of Peasant Resistance*. New York: M. E. Sharpe, 3–33.

Thomas, Nicholas. 1992. "The Inversion of Tradition." *American Ethnologist* 19(2): 213–32.

Urla, Jacquelina. 1993. "Cultural Politics in an Age of Statistics: Numbers, Nations and the Making of Basque Identity." *American Ethnologist* 20(4): 818–43.

Urton, Gary. 1985. "Introduction." In Gary Urton, ed., *Animal Myths and Metaphors in South America*. Salt Lake City: University of Utah Press, 3–11.

Vansina, Jan. 1985. *Oral Tradition as History*. Madison: University of Wisconsin Press.

Villalón, María Eugenia. 1984. "Network Organization in E'ñapa Society: A First Approximation." *Antropológica* 59–62: 57–71.

———. 1992. "Forma, significado y política de la narrativa heredada e'ñapa. Un análisis etnopoético." Ph.D. dissertation. Caracas: Instituto Venezolano de Investigaciones Científicas.

8

Ebonics, Language, and Power

Michael H. Long

> Modern education not only corrupts the heart of our youth by the
> rigid slavery to which it condemns them, it also undermines their
> reason by the unintelligible jargon with which they are over-
> whelmed in the first instance, and the little attention that is given to
> accommodating their pursuits to their capacities in the second.
>
> William Godwin, An Account of the
Seminary (1783), p. 31

The current furor and confusion over the role of "Ebonics" in education
is but a recent skirmish in a long-running struggle. The controversy is
not new, not confined to "Black English" or to English in general, not
confined to education, and certainly not confined to the United States.
It surfaces in North America and around the world time and time again.
On all five continents, coercive power relationships between socioeconomic elites wielding state power and oppressed groups wielding little
or none find linguistic reflexes. The elites speak the "official" state
language or the "standard" variety of a language—in the present case,
"Standard English" (SE)—which they made official or standard; the
oppressed groups (not necessarily minorities, as in the present case) are
decreed by the same elites to speak a less acceptable or unacceptable
language or a socially stigmatized variety of the same language, like
"Black English." Very real objective linguistic differences thus provide
yet another excuse for discrimination in many areas of public life,
including education, so-called criminal justice systems, employment,
media access, and even labor unions. The public policy decisions that
result from these periodic convulsions, often enshrined in statute and
case law, concern linguistic human rights, and they have wide-ranging
social consequences for hundreds of millions of people. The rhetorical

barrage surrounding the present struggle serves to confuse the real issue or to ensure that they are not discussed at all, which benefits only one side in the status quo.

For these reasons and because the role of language in education is but one of several examples of the critical nexus of language and state power, the Ebonics issue is a vital one for working people everywhere. The radical right in the United States recognize its importance and are all over the mass media, using it to push their own domestic agenda, i.e., a relentless attack on the burgeoning U.S. underclass, spiced with obvious racism, one manifestation of which is the defunding of public education. Symptomatic of the level of confusion, misinformation, and disinformation, at least one supposedly radical left group, the (Trotsky-ite) International Socialist Organization (ISO) (U.S. equivalent of the British SWP), has unwittingly aligned itself, albeit for different reasons, with radical conservative demagogues like Rush Limbaugh, Mike Royko, William Raspberry, and George Will; the ISO opposes attention to Ebonics because it sees such attention as an irrelevant distraction from the "real issues" in U.S. education—racism and lack of funding (see, e.g., the editorial and letters section of the January 3 and 17 issues, respectively, of the ISO's paper, *Socialist Worker*). Perhaps in reaction to the 300-year denial to African-Americans of access to literacy, educa-tion, and socioeconomic status typically associated with command of SE, usually well-meaning liberals like Kweisi Mfume, Maya Angelou ("incensed"), Jesse Jackson ("ungrammatical English"), and Ellen Goodman ("legitimizing slang") have come out with reactionary, ill-in-formed public pronouncements. Some familiarity with the basic lin-guistic concepts involved and with research findings on (in this case, educational) solutions is required for an informed and appropriately targeted response and also in order to initiate a long-overdue discussion of libertarian approaches to language education and language in education.

EBONICS

Ebonics is a term coined by Robert Williams at a 1973 conference, the proceedings of which, edited by Williams, were published two years later as *Ebonics: The True Language of Black Folks*. He defined it as

> the linguistic and paralinguistic features which on a concentric continuum represent the communicative competence of the West African, Caribbean, and United States idioms, patois, argots, idiolects, and social forces of black people. . . . Ebonics derives its form from ebony (black) and phonics (sound, the study of sound) and refers to the study of the language of black people in all its cultural uniqueness. (1975, vi)

The *Journal of Black Studies* devoted a special issue (Tolliver-Weddington 1979) to Ebonics. Other terms more often employed by linguists are "Black English," "Black English Vernacular" (BEV), and "African-American Vernacular English" (AAVE). The term AAVE is used here, except when citing those who refer to "Ebonics."

The other terms more accurately reflect the fact that we are concerned not just with the sounds, or pronunciation, of "Black English" such as final-consonant deletion (*they see him* for "they seed him"), final consonant cluster reduction (*mos* for "most") or 'th'/'f' substitution (*wif* for "with"), but with its grammar (morphology and syntax), meaning (lexicon and semantics), and use (discourse and pragmatics) as well. With considerable variation both within and across speakers, common morpho-syntactic differences between AAVE and SE, for example, involve subject-verb agreement (*She like, They like*), copula deletion (*They feels as though they even*), past-time reference (*He done seen him*), negative inversion (*Don't nobody see*), and double (sometimes even triple) negatives (*I ain't never doin that no more*) (see, e.g., Fasold 1972; Labov 1972; Wolfram 1969). There is nothing inferior (or superior) about any of these constructions. If some varieties of AAVE can give expression to an idea about time much earlier than the time of speaking by use of a nifty auxiliary: "I *bin* read that book," whereas most "white" varieties have to use a clumsier adverbial construction, "I read that book *a long time ago*," to say the same thing (example courtesy of Ralph Fasold), it is not that AAVE is better or the white varieties worse, just that they are different.

The fact that most AAVE speakers are intelligible to speakers of other varieties most of the time, and vice versa, does not alter the fact that some differences do nevertheless cause communication breakdowns and that those can occur without speaker or hearer, e.g., teacher and student, understanding either that or why they have occurred. The late Charlene ("Charlie") Sato (1989) showed, moreover, that the degree of difference and its import for instruction often go unrecognized, affecting both comprehension and classroom participation in hidden ways. For example, many an SE-speaking immigrant in Hawai'i has interpreted Hawai'i Creole English (HCE) *neva*, in I *neva see him*, as SE "never," instead of what it really means, i.e., "didn't," in "I didn't see him," *neva* functioning as a past-time marker in HCE. Similarly, the African-American child who writes *I be fighting*, which is true, only to have a white SE-speaking teacher correct it to *I am fighting*, which is false, for example (courtesy of Ralph Fasold), is frustrated and confused, and his teacher is blissfully unaware of the fact (or the facts).

Dialect differences can also often lead to differential participation in classroom interaction, as Sato (1989) showed, that in turn being interpreted by some teachers as a sign of low academic ability or an "attitude" problem. To cite but one example, in a study of a first-grade classroom in Berkeley, Michaels (1981) described how a Caucasian teacher's own tightly organized "topic-centered" style, in which thematic development is accomplished through lexical cohesion, the linear ordering of events, and so on, matched that of the white students in her class, but failed to accommodate during the same lesson to her African-American students' "topic-associating" presentational style, with its series of segments or episodes that are implicitly linked in highlighting some person or theme. Familiar prosodic (intonational) features of the white children's speech, for instance, made it easy for the teacher to time her comments and questions appropriately for them, allowing her to provide successful linguistic scaffolding. Conversely, she appeared to misread stress-placement and vowel-lengthening cues in the black children's speech, resulting in her disrupting rather than supporting and elaborating on their presentations. (For additional examples of often unrecognized comprehension problems and clashes in interactional style arising from dialect differences in education, see Sato 1989.)

Numerous linguistic studies of AAVE over the years have documented its richness, expressiveness, and communicative adequacy (see, e.g., Labov 1969, 1995). Like any other natural human language or language variety, AAVE is systematic and rule-governed, its rules sometimes less complex than those of SE, sometimes more so. To illustrate the greater complexity (example courtesy of Ralph Fasold), AAVE offers three tenses (*He thinking about it, He be thinking about,* and *He think about it*) for two in SE in the same domain (*He is thinking about it* and *He thinks about it*), allowing more precision. Those rules and the varieties are, again, not better or worse, just different. AAVE is not a separate language, however (as the original Oakland, California, School Board resolution unfortunately implied, allowing opponents another opening for their attacks), just a variety of English. While there are no hard-and-fast rules, the usual criterion for distinguishing separate languages from separate varieties of the same language (including geographically based, ethnically based, or social class–based dialects) is mutual intelligibility. If 80 percent or more of what speaker A says is comprehensible to speaker B, they are usually held to speak different varieties of the same language, not different languages (although there are exceptions; Danish, Norwegian, and Swedish, for example, are much closer than this, yet are referred to as separate languages). Which of two or more varieties of a language is considered the prestige variety is not a linguistic issue, but a sociolinguistic one, that is, a function of the prestige of its speakers. In the often quoted words of the linguist Max Weinreich, "A language is a dialect with an army and a navy."

The stigmatization of AAVE reflects not its linguistic qualities, but negative attitudes towards AAVE speakers. For example, it so happens that a number of features of AAVE are also common in several varieties of American English spoken by some whites in southern states, such as Arkansas, Georgia, Alabama, Mississippi, and the Carolinas, yet they are not considered problematic when produced by the likes of such fine moral guardians as Bill Clinton, Jimmy Carter, Howell Hefflin, Strom Thurmond, or Jesse Helms. Similarly, some varieties of "standard British English" are just as different from "standard American English" in pronunciation and vocabulary (although not in major systems like verb structure) as "standard American English" is from AAVE, sometimes more so, yet they rarely elicit the same hostility. For example, most British speakers say *lift, boot,* and *holiday* for American *elevator, trunk,* and *vacation; Have you got the time?* for *Do you have the time?*; and *Have you seen today's paper?* for *Did you see today's paper?* Yet many Americans still hold what they wrongly think of as (homogenous) "British English" in high esteem, higher even than they hold their own variety, in some cases. These and numerous other examples that could be cited from around the world show clearly that positive or negative evaluations are not linguistically based; the "problem" with "non-standard" varieties lies in the ears and prejudices of the hearers, not the mouths and minds of their speakers. It would be a mistake, however, to dismiss negative attitudes towards AAVE as simply one more manifestation of racism. While much of the criticism and many of the critics may well be racially motivated, the same stigmatization is often performed by speakers of a "standard" language or dialect at the expense of speakers of a "non-standard" one who are members of the same ethnic group. Obvious examples include speakers of "standard" British English and "Cockney" English or of "restricted" and "elaborated" codes in the United Kingdom (see later discussion), "standard" American English and Appalachian English, "high" and "low" German, and "standard" French and Quebecois or Cajun French. Power is at least roughly distributed along racial lines in many societies, including the United States, and in turn with linguistic differences, but it is the *power* to discriminate along racial, linguistic, or any other lines that is the real issue.

Even "standard" English varies considerably with geography, ethnicity, social class, and other factors, as well as over time. Compare, for instance, what is considered SE by elites in New York, California, and Alabama, or in India, Australia, Singapore, and Nigeria, or in London, Liverpool, and Edinburgh. It quickly becomes apparent that the ruling classes (of different ethnic backgrounds) in English-speaking countries around the world all have their own peculiar local notions of SE, which always happen to coincide with the way they and their friends speak, and which they proceed to exploit as one more means of discriminating against those who speak differently. In fact, if anything approaching a universal "standard" variety exists at all, it is found only in the written form of English or any other language. Discriminating against people for the way they speak is even more unwarranted than might be obvious to any rational person, for nobody speaks either "English" or "Standard English"; everyone speaks a variety of English, and SE speakers speak but one variety of SE.

The same relationship between language and the power to discriminate determines which variety gets to be called standard and which non-standard. The fact that the answer can change over time as the locus of power changes, even within the ruling elites, again belies the notion that there is anything inherently superior or inferior about any one variety. This is true at both the national and international level. It used to be a virtual requirement in the U.K., for example, for BBC radio and television news readers and reporters to speak "standard" British English—something close to the "plum in the mouth" accent of Edward Heath and Margaret Thatcher that is pervasive on the Tory Party benches to this day. With the election of the Labour Party's Harold Wilson, the first British Prime Minister to speak with a (northern) regional accent, however, a much wider range of regional (and to a lesser extent, social class–based) accents soon became "acceptable" and perfectly adequate to do the same jobs. British TV and radio today boast accents from most parts of England, Scotland, Wales, and Northern Ireland. Internationally, with the shift in the locus of English-speaking world power from the U.K. to the United States, the model of English favored for the teaching of English as a foreign language in most countries in Asia and Latin America has shifted from British to American, too. If and when a non–English-speaking country or regional alliance comes to replace the United States as the dominant world power, English itself will eventually give way. By the end of the 21st century, it may be Mandarin Chinese that everyone is learning—not because Chinese is superior to English, any more than English is superior now. It is simply, again, a question of power.

LANGUAGE AND IDENTITY

AAVE is the variety of American English, itself taking several distinct forms, that is spoken by many, but by no means all, African Americans, particularly, but not only, in the inner cities, as well as by a few other groups, such as some southeast Asian refugees who grew up in African-American neigborhoods. AAVE is usually identified with the race and ethnicity of its speakers, but many African-Americans, especially members of the black middle classes, seldom experience it as children; others do so but choose not to speak it, or do so only rarely and only in certain settings in which they consider its use appropriate. AAVE is better seen as not simply a matter of race, therefore, but of social class and to some degree of age, for it tends to be especially strong and salient among the young urban poor. Among black youth, linguists have found evidence of AAVE's increasing divergence from "standard" (i.e., currently mostly white, middle-class) spoken American English, especially in its pronunciation and intonation, apparently as a marker of group solidarity and resistance (see, e.g., Bailey 1987, 1993; Bailey and Maynor 1989; Labov and Harris 1986).

The same trend was reported by Sato (1991) among adolescents in Hawai'i. Most Hawaiian children, like (this time) the majority of people who grow up in the Hawaiian Islands, especially those from working-class backgrounds and educated in public schools, are speakers of another "non-standard" (albeit, this time, majority) variety, Hawai'i Creole English (HCE), often referred to locally as "Pidgin." Paralleling disputes over AAVE, the status of HCE in Hawai'i's classrooms has also been the subject of a long, continuing struggle (see Sato 1985). HCE is currently experiencing something of an upswing through the increasing productivity of fine local poets, novelists, dramatists, and lyricists like Joe Balaz, Eric Chock, Rodney Morales, Wai-Tek Him, and Lois-Ann Yamanaka, many published through Bamboo Ridge Press, who write at least partly in HCE, often about the everyday lives of local working-class families. HCE's persistence and vibrancy, along with increasingly positive attitudes to it among its speakers, especially Hawaiian youth, seems to reflect its perceived desirability as a marker of "local" identity and resistance to economic and social oppression, including in recent years, resistance to comical attempts by Hawai'i's educational bureaucrats and politicians to eradicate HCE from the schools. Most "locals," that is, those born and raised in the islands, experience discrimination every day at the hands of (this time) the minority of "standard" English-speakers, most of whom are *haole* (outsiders, typically Caucasians). It is the *haole*, together with Japanese corporations, who dominate the grossly exploitative tourist industry, which accounts for about 35 percent of all jobs and wealth in the fiftieth state. With Sato our most articulate and expert spokesperson, a coalition of applied linguists, linguists, and graduate students from the University of Hawai'i, public school teachers and children, local artists, and several Wobblies, among others, helped organize strong, at least partly successful community-based resistance to the state legislature's and Hawai'i Board of Education's assault on HCE in 1987, as well as (ultimately unsuccessfully) for a major court case the same year (*Kahakua et al. v. Hallgren*), which involved accent discrimination against HCE speakers in the workplace (see Sato 1991 for an account of both struggles).

To sum up so far, AAVE, like HCE and like language everywhere, is a conscious part of people's identity. To attack a language or language variety by discriminating against it in education, as by forcing students to be educated through someone else's language or language variety, is to attack its speakers. It is an effective way of breaking down resistance and of rendering communities and cultures more vulnerable to state control. As the current rapid spread of English as a vehicle for international capitalism worldwise illustrates, the spread of an "official" language or "standard" language variety increases the influence of its existing speakers and facilitates absorption of new ones into an English-speaking (especially, now, U.S. capitalist) worldview. Linguistic dependency quickly translates into political, economic, and cultural dependency, or as Pennycook (1995) puts it, "English in the world" quickly becomes "the world in English."

Governments know all this. It is no accident that, as part of the fascist dictatorship's brutal suppression of the Basques after 1939, Franco made it illegal to speak Basque and an imprisonable offense to teach it; or that the indigenous Hawaiian language (now being revived through school immersion programs) was suppressed by the plantation owners and missionaries to the point of extinction; or that the same politicians, for example, Dole and Gingrich, and forces behind current movements to make English the (only) offricial language of the United States are those on the wrong side of every other struggle for social justice; or that Israel obliges Arabic-speaking university students to take their classes and exams in Hebrew (despite Arabic being an official language in Israel), or that the United States, Britain, France, Germany, and now Japan consider it so important to spend so much (of other people's) time and money on teaching their national languages overseas. When then Vice-President Dan Quayle, not renowed for his own language abilities, made a speech urging thousands of young Americans to join the Peace Corps to go and teach English to the newly "liberated" citizens of Hungary, Rumania, and elsewhere in Eastern Europe, was it because of a sudden interest in foreign language learning on his part?

What is true of languages is true of language varieties. Governments and elites understand the gatekeeping opportunities afforded them by support of a "standard" variety as a requirement for access to power. The fact that discrimination against speakers of other languages and of non-standard dialects is often carried out by people of the same race, upper-class against working-class and/or regional dialect-speaking white children in Germany and the U.K., for example, shows that the issue is fundamentally one of power, not race. While power imbalances are often strongly correlated with racial differences, as in the present U.S. case, it would be a mistake to dismiss the attack on Ebonics as simply another manifestation of racism, as some have done, and to lose sight of the important linguistic issues in the process. Racism and underfunding may be more important overall than language issues in public education in the United States, but as explained earlier, there is ample independent evidence of the importance of linguistic discrimination in education for African-American and many white children, too. Hence, the addition of linguistic discrimination—or what has been termed "linguicism" (Phillipson 1992; Skutnabb-Kangas, Phillipson, and Rannut 1995; Tollefson 1995)—to racism, sexism, and the long list of other forms of oppression experienced by working people may be acceptable to politicians, corporations, right-wing ideologues, media barons, some prominent liberals, and other representatives of state power, but it is surely unacceptable to those who value individual freedom and diversity of all kinds, including linguistic diversity, and who oppose any manifestation of state coercion. Gratifyingly, as shown by the cases of Hawai'i (where HCE is still very much under siege, nonetheless) and several African-American communities in the United States, among others, it is increasingly unacceptable to a growing number of working people themselves.

THE OAKLAND SCHOOL BOARD RESOLUTION

According to a January 15, 1997, article in *Education Week*, approximately 53 percent of the 52,300 K-12 student population in the Oakland, California, school district is black, and 47 percent is Asian or Latino. There are very few white students. A plurality of the teaching staff is white, the next largest group black. Oakland teachers had not had a raise in five years; in February 1996 they went on a two-month strike over pay and conditions, especially class size, black and white teachers standing shoulder to shoulder on the picket lines. They won a partial victory over wages, but little else. The schools themselves, like public schools almost everywhere in the United States, are underfunded and rundown. Student test scores are low and getting worse; of the 28,000 black students, 71 percent are in special education classes and 64 percent have been held back a grade; on a four-point scale, their collective grade point average is a meager 1.8.

Against this background, on December 18th, 1996, the seven-member Oakland School Board unanimously adopted a resolution recognizing Ebonics as a legitimate "genetically based" (sic) "language" (sic) spoken by many of its African-American students and proposing to seek state and federal funds in order to mount additional training programs. (Some programs, costing $200,000 a year in state and federal funding, were already in effect for 3,000 students in the district). Their purpose was not, as has often been asserted, to "teach Ebonics" (which the students already know, after all), but initially to accept student participantion in Ebonics, while pointing out differences between

Ebonics and SE to the children, as the resolution clearly stated "for the combined purposes of maintaining the legitimacy and richness of such language . . . and to facilitate [African-American students'] acquisition and mastery of English-language skills." Like the successful five-year Ebonics program in the Dallas public schools, recently shut down because of funding cuts, the Oakland resolution's first objective was to help sensitize teachers to linguistic differences between AAVE and Standard English (SE). On a par with programs designed to help immigrants who speak a different language to learn English, the second aim was to help AAVE speakers learn SE and to do so without denigrating or (as if this were possible by fiat) eradicating the home (AAVE) variety. The third goal was to begin instruction in reading, math, and so on in AAVE, on the usually unchallenged pedagogic principle of starting where the students are and then gradually making the transition to SE. Subsequent public comments by School Board members suggested that the resolution was an honest, well-intentioned (not to mention, for the most part scientifically supportable) attempt to do something tangible to help a large group of underachieving students in their care.

A few voices were raised publicly in support of the general thrust, at least, of the Board's proposal during the weeks that followed, including that of the country's preeminent professional association for linguists, the Linguistics Society of America (LSA), which at the end of its annual conference, fortuitously meeting in Chicago early in January 1997, issued a formal resolution broadly supportive of the Oakland initiative. The LSA resolution stressed AAVE's well-documented rule-governed systematicity, appending a list of nearly 30 scientific books on the subject, noted that the distinction between "language" and "dialect" is usually made more on social and political than linguistic grounds, and termed recent public characterizations of Ebonics as "slang," "mutant," "lazy," "defective," "ungrammatical," and "broken English" as "incorrect and demeaning." The resolution further noted evidence from Sweden, the United States, and other countries to the effect that pedagogical approaches which recognize the legitimacy of non-standard varieties of a language help their speakers learn the standard variety and concluded that "the Oakland School Board's decision to recognize the vernacular of African-American students in teaching them Standard English is linguistically and pedagogically sound." A resolution to expand language programs for African-American students was introduced in January by a member of the Los Angeles School Board, the second largest in the United States.

Supporters, however, were simply overwhelmed by an immediate and intense barrage of angry, often blatantly racist, sometimes close to hysterical, criticism from all sides. Different interest groups singled out different aspects of the resolution, parts of which really were open to criticism because they were linguistically uninformed or poorly communicated. With hardly a pause for breath, let alone unwanted debate or hearings on the real issue, and obviously relieved at the easy "out" the resolution allowed his agency, U.S. Department of Education Secretary Richard W. Riley quickly issued a statement saying USDOE would certainly not be funding any education programs for AAVE speakers or their teachers, since, contrary to what the Oakland resolution had stated, Ebonics was not a "separate language"—about which, since Ebonics is simply one variety of English, the USDOE was right. Others reacted negatively to the idea that Ebonics, or any other "language," was "genetically based," and in this, too (see later discussion), they were right, while managing to avoid the real issue.

For numerous right-wing commentators with their usual surfeit of air-time in the mainstream media—often their own regular newspaper columns and whole TV shows—a common approach was simply to assert that support for Ebonics was an unfounded, minority, "liberal" position, just one more dangerous example of divisive "Afrocentrism," and then quickly to lose the original language-in-education issue amidst a melange of baseless, sweeping charges about "European" civilization and "white" history and culture being under threat in the curriculum. Aristotle was Greek and white, for instance, but how many students learned that at school? an irate George Will demanded to know, within minutes of the start of an ABC Television Current Affairs "debate" supposedly on Ebonics. To make matters worse, the ideologues' task was facilitated by the shield provided them in the form of the strong condemnations of the Oakland resolution issued by prominent black liberals, notably Maya Angelou, who had credibility as the current U.S. poet laureate. Such pronouncements on the issue were given exceptionally good media coverage. For instance, perhaps because of his increasingly more reactionary political stances on a number of issues in recent years, the Reverend Jesse Jackson is often sought out and presented by mainstream journalists as if he were an official spokesperson for all African-Americans; meanwhile, more radical (although often equally reactionary) African-American leaders with large followings, such as the Reverend Louis Farrakhan, are marginalized.

The scent of blood in their nostrils, politicians in Massachusetts and Virginia introduced bills to prohibit the teaching of Ebonics in public schools (something the Oakland resolution had not suggested) and to make "Standard English" Virginia's official language; a Republican congressman from New York, Peter King, introduced a bill to prohibit the use of federal funds to support "any program that is based on the premise that 'ebonics' is a legitimate language." It is no coincidence that King is an activist in another currently hot area of state encroachment

on linguistic human rights in the United States, the heavily corporate-
funded "English-only" movement, in which he is one of many federal
politicians backing legislation to make English the official language of
government and to abolish bilingual education programs. This initiative, were it successful, would severely damage the educational life
chances of hundreds of thousands, if not millions, of already disadvantaged immigrant children who are speakers or would-be speakers of
English as a second language, just as the current lack of equivalent
programs for AAVE speakers damages the educational life chances of
many African-Americans, Latinos, and other speakers of SE as a second
dialect. These groups of second-language and second-dialect speakers
are heavily overrepresented among low-skilled workers. Unluckily for
them, they constitute a sector that, outside of some service industries,
is increasingly irrelevant to business (hence, government) interests
following corporate flight to alternative supplies of more easily exploited and far cheaper labor in the third world. This makes the strong
legislative and corporate support for such measures as "English-only"
and their lack of support for language in education programs understandable but no less reprehensible.

Faced with the media onslaught, on January 15 the Oakland School
Board unanimously adopted a somewhat modified version of their
original resolution. While continuing to maintain (falsely) that Ebonics
is not a dialect of English and stating (arguably correctly) that some
linguistic features of Ebonics (although probably only a few lexical
items) have their origins in West African and Niger-Congo languages,
references to Ebonics as "genetically based" were removed. The earlier
call to have children educated in their "primary language," Ebonics,
was also modified to clarify the intention of the original resolution, that
education should begin where children were linguistically—an uncon-
troversial proposition in any other aspect of education—and to move
them toward SE over time.

As should be obvious by now, however, the details and fate of the
Oakland resolutions are not the real issue. If the Oakland initiative is
stymied and eventually goes away, as seems likely, the critical role of
language and of language varieties in education will not. It is useful,
therefore, to continue the debate a little further here in the hope that
our own response can be that much better informed whenever and
wherever the language police strike next, as well as to stimulate long-
overdue discussion among those more seriously interested in libertarian approaches to both language education and language in education.
The remainder of this chapter is intended as no more than a brief
preliminary contribution to that discussion. It addresses the issues from
an admittedly reactive, defensive stance, situated in the current sociopolitical context that faces education workers now. A fuller, more con-

structive, and more interesting treatment will need to presuppose highly complex future societies—like those most of us live in today, but societies organized on egalitarian lines, where individual freedom will be cherished, where linguistic oppression, and even linguistic genocide, will no longer be issues to be confronted, but where the role of language in education will always be important since, as Marshall (1986, 40) put it, "freedom is the basis of education and education is the basis of freedom." A useful place to start, given the critical relevance of each to the current debate, is with a sketch of, first, the relationship between genetics and the environment in language and language learning, and, second, educational options for "unofficial" or "non-standard" language or dialect school-age populations.

NATURE AND NURTURE IN LANGUAGE

In sharp contrast to neobehaviorist views of language learning, which were largely demolished by Chomsky's devastating review of B. F. Skinner's *Verbal Behavior* (Chomsky 1959), most modern theorists—not least, Chomsky himself—posit a critical role for biology in language acquisition, and a much less important one for the linguistic environment. Such views are broadly consistent with several widely observed phenomena. (1) While a few complex grammatical constructions can remain problematic into the early teens, normal children have developed sufficient knowledge of the grammar, lexicon, and sound system of whichever language(s) they hear around them to carry on conversations with ease by age five. This is an astonishing feat, although one that often goes unremarked upon for being the norm. Children accomplish it at an age when most of them still have trouble with far simpler psychomotor and cognitive tasks, like tying their shoelaces, kicking a soccer ball, doing simple addition, or drawing a plan of their house. (2) All normal children are successful, and at roughly the same age, regardless of substantial differences in IQ that affect their achievement on other nonlinguistic tasks and despite substantial variation in home linguistic environment, child-rearing patterns, cultural setting, and (at least surface) structural differences in the languages being learned. (3) Even some severely mentally retarded children, such as Turner's Syndrome cases, manage relatively normal morphology and syntax. (4) Despite having been successful with language learning as children, which principles of transfer of training would indicate should help them with similar tasks later, people trying to learn new languages as adults often do very poorly, even when—like many immigrants—they are motivated, intelligent, and have plenty of opportunity. In fact, recent research findings suggest that mastery of foreign or second languages at the same level as native speakers of those languages appears to require that first exposure to the L2 occur before age six if a perfect accent is ever to be hoped for, and by the mid-teens for native-like morphology and syntax (for review, see Long 1990, 1993).

Observations like these combine to suggest the existence of a powerful, innate human learning capacity—one that dissociation data like those on Turner's children suggest is language-specific (i.e., separate from general learning abilities) and "modular" and one that is biologically programmed to operate optimally on a maturational schedule within the bounds of one or more so-called "critical periods." Chomsky (1988, 173–74) put it this way: "Acquisition of language is something that happens to you; it's not something that you do. Language learning is something like undergoing puberty. You don't learn to do it; you don't do it because you see other people doing it; you are designed to do it at a certain time."

It is clear that every child, whatever his or her ethnic or social class origins, is born with the same innate capacity to learn whichever language(s) he or she is exposed to, to do so at a very young age, and to do so remarkably fast. There is some evidence that children first exposed to a second dialect of a language after age six, like those first attempting second-language acquisition after that age, are unable to master the new variety to native-like standards, with the prognosis deteriorating markedly for those first exposed as teenagers and with morpho-syntax also problematic for starters older than the mid-teens (see, e.g., Chambers 1992). If second dialect acquisition really is subject to the same putative maturational constraints that seem to affect second-language acquisition, the linguistic flexibility routinely demanded of ethnolinguistic minority schoolchildren is even more discriminatory than previously thought. Requiring a radical change of accent by adults for certain kinds of employment could be demanding the biologically impossible and so constitute a violation of civil rights law in some countries, although, of course, one that few courts are likely to recognize, whatever the merits, for fear of the socioeconomic consequences of offering legal protection for the linguistic rights of people other than those whom judicial systems primarily serve to protect.

This much is due to nature. Which language(s) or language varieties are learned during this period, conversely, is determined by nurture, that is, the linguistic environment. In other words, the ability and timetable for acquiring language are genetically based, not the languages themselves. Caucasian or African-American children born to English-speaking parents in Chicago will learn whatever varieties of English they hear spoken around them, principally those of their parents, other caretakers, and age peers. A child of whatever ethnicity born to a linguistically mixed couple can learn both languages (say English and Spanish) if both are used with him or her sufficiently, although overwhelming exposure to one of them outside the home often leads to that language being "dominant," or to the child's ability in it being stronger. Any of those children whose family suddenly moves early enough to an environment where another language is spoken will learn that second or third language (say German or Japanese) instead of, or in addition to, English and/or Spanish, given sufficient exposure. The genetic inheritance for language acquisition is equal and universal, regardless of the social-class origins or ethnicity of the child and regardless of the language or language variety in the environment.

On the basis of such facts as well as the discovery of a more controversial set of putative structural universals in human languages (the "Universal Grammar") and the alleged impossibility of accomplishing a task as complex as language acquisition so quickly and only by listening to the input, Chomsky has been prominent in arguing, further and very influentially, that what is innate is not just the language-learning capacity, but the capacity plus substantive knowledge of those universal grammatical principles and of the restricted ways in which languages may vary. Children are born already knowing the properties of human language, from this perspective; they are successful so uniformly and so quickly because all they have to do is to "tune in" to the particular language or languages—English, Spanish, Farsi, Arabic—being used around them, the basic properties of which they already "know" at some level, register the particular ways those principles are realized in the language they are hearing, and master its vocabulary and pragmatics, plus the discourse conventions and cultural norms of its speakers by observing the behavior of those around them: language socialization. Children do not "learn" their native language, from this perspective; rather, it "unfolds." Language learning is even more heavily a function of nature, in this view, with nurture and the environment (linguistic input) again simply determining which particular languages are learned. There are several rival linguistic theories and accounts of child language acquisition, of course, but successive formulations of Chomsky's position have now constituted a highly influential theory of grammar for over 30 years.

Language acquisition is thus a product of both nature and nurture. Every child comes into the world innately equipped to learn one or more languages. Members of any particular ethnic group are not genetically programmed to speak a particular language or language variety but rather whichever one(s) they are exposed to early enough. An important corollary of this for the Ebonics debate is that every language or language variety is a reflection of the same human capacity, and as such, inevitably of equal communicative potential. This is the case regardless of any differences two languages or varieties of a language may exhibit at any one point in time in such areas as their "technical" vocabulary for discussing the colors of tropical foliage, personal computers, or Sumo wrestling and of course regardless of their current social prestige.

EDUCATIONAL OPTIONS

If all but a few severely mentally abnormal children are genetically endowed with the same (species-specific) capacity for language learning, it follows that the particular language, such as English, or variety of a language, such as AAVE, that they end up speaking must have the same inherent communicative potential and, at some deep level, the same fundamental linguistic properties as any other, notwithstanding differences among them on the surface and at any one point in time. There is no justification for equating "non-standard" with "substandard," therefore, no justification for assessing children's intellectual ability from the way they speak, and no scientific basis to the idea that linguistic differences are genetically based or indicative of different scholastic potential.

The same fundamental linguistic qualities and communicative potential notwithstanding, it is clear that languages and language varieties can differ in potential and prestige at any one time (Hymes 1992). While that is due to the power and prestige of those who speak them, not to any inherent superiority of the systems themselves, the fact remains that in a hierarchically organized society, access not only to power but also to freedom and control over people's own lives can often depend at least in part on language. Linguistic differences serve ruling elites as one more gatekeeping mechanism by which to deny access to power. Accent, speech style, or command of a prestige language variety can determine success or failure in employment (Sato 1991), guilt or innocence in court (Eades 1992, 1994), and—of primary concern in the Ebonics debate—self-esteem and achievement in school.

The importance of home-to-school language switch has long been documented in numerous countries. The vast majority of children throughout the world enter primary school with at least some degree of mismatch between what they have grown used to linguistically by listening to their caretakers and playmates in and around the home and the language of schooling. In many parts of Africa, Asia, and Latin America, children have to learn a new language if they want any formal education at all, and sometimes a third language in order to continue on to secondary or tertiary education. The fact that some of those children succeed both in mastering the language(s) required and in completing their education does not make the task less of an imposition;

nor does it compensate for the vast number of others who fail at both or do less well because of the extra linguistic burden with which they are confronted.

Where varietal disjunctions are concerned, the British sociologist of language Basil Bernstein (1971 and elsewhere) drew widespread attention to the educational impact of differences between what he described as the "restricted code" spoken by most working-class British children on entry to school, itself a function, he said, of the traditional "positional" structure of most British working-class families ("No more ice-cream because I said so"), on the one hand, and on the other, the "elaborated code" (no more ice-cream because if you eat more now, you won't want your dinner later") spoken by most middle-class children, which was the language of teachers and of schooling. It was largely that linguistic difference, he claimed, that accounted for the staggering and tragic, persistent educational failure of working-class children, including their frequent failure even to complete secondary education. While subsequent studies showed that the codes themselves may not be linguistically more or less complex than one another, few linguists or educators have challenged Bernstein's basic claim about the importance of the disjunction itself. Rather, applied linguists have described the impact of analogous cases in public education around the world (see, e.g., Malcolm 1994, on Aboriginal English in Australian schools; McGroarty 1991 on ethnolinguistic minority dialects in the United States; and Sato 1985, 1989 on HCE in Hawai'i). In all such settings, several alternatives exist for educators. While particular local situations often require unique solutions, some general principles and broad options can be distinguished.

With varying degrees of subtlety, the usual solution favored by states everywhere is *submersion* in the official language or prestige "standard" dialect as soon as children enter school. This favors the children of parents who speak the language or dialect concerned, disfavors those who do not, and increases the likelihood of linguistic, political, and cultural *assimilation* of groups, such as immigrants or racial blocks, that if left linguistically intact, might eventually threaten the hegemony of current elites. Submersion programs should not be confused with the widely successful *immersion* programs, like French immersion for English-speaking Canadians, in which children who speak the dominant national language, English, receive all or part of their curriculum delivered through the other official, but minority, language, French (their L2), and, as evaluation studies show, typically graduate with a good command of French (comparable to native speakers in listening and reading, less good in speaking and writing), with no adverse effects on their achievement in other subjects. In immersion, all students start as a linguistically and educationally homogeneous group, usually as beginners, making it possible for teachers to adapt their (L2 French) speech appropriately and keep content instruction comprehensible. In submersion, on the other hand, non–English-speaking or limited–English-speaking children are thrown in with English-speaking children in English-medium classrooms. The speech they hear around them is initially incomprehensible because it is addressed primarily to children who already speak English, making it difficult for the non-native speakers to learn either the language or the subject matter being taught through it. Submersion programs are also known as "sink or swim." Countless immigrant and other linguistic minority children sink (see, e.g., Schinke-Llano 1983). These are the programs favored by the "English-only" movements.

Slightly less obviously coercive are various kinds of *transition* models, which allow use of the home language or dialect in the early stages, but quickly introduce the official language or standard variety, and move children from one to the other, such that the home language or dialect is replaced by the new one, a process known as *subtractive bilingualism* (adding the second language, but losing the first). In theory, for example, "transitional" or "early-exit" bilingual education programs in some parts of the United States allow classroom use of Spanish for some subjects, while gradually introducing English for others, from the first one to three years of school, after which Spanish is dropped. In practice, studies show, Spanish, the most widely spoken minority language in the United States, rarely is used or survives even that long in such programs. The fate of less well supported languages is even worse.

Much more respectful of linguistic rights, as well as of students' identities and cultural backgrounds, are models that seek to add the second language or dialect while validating and preserving the first, so-called *maintenance* bilingual programs. Examples include what are known in the United States as "late-exit" bilingual education programs, which, in theory, allow classroom use of Spanish (or some other L1) for up to the first six years of schooling, while gradually introducing English in selected subjects, before transitioning to English. These programs aim to maintain the students' first language and add the second, in *additive bilingualism*, graduating bilinguals, not monolingual L2 English speakers. Continuation of Hawai'ian for the first six years of the fledgling Hawai'ian immersion programs was recently approved after intense pressure and not a little direct action on the part of parents and hawaiian activists and their supporters. In practice, unfortunately, true maintenance programs are extremely rare, as it seems there is a vast difference between rhetoric and practice when it comes to school boards digging up the money, curriculum materials, and personnel to implement true six-year maintenance bilingual education.

Evaluation research in this area has been scant and often of poor quality, but a five-year, three-way comparative study (Ramirez 1992; Ramirez et al. 1991) of (1) early-exit and (2) late-exit Spanish bilingual programs and (3) programs for Spanish-speakers that were English-medium from the outset, at 27 sites around the United States found fairly consistent positive relationships between the length of time classroom Spanish use continued and children's eventual attainment in other subjects, including reading, math, and the L2, English. The Ramirez and associates study and others suggest that bilingual education can work quite well, yet it is precisely bilingual programs, and especially maintenance bilingual programs—which have hardly ever been given a chance to show what they can do—that are under attack from the "English-only" forces and the likes of Gingrich, Dole, and Buchanan, as part of the more general onslaught on immigrants, ethnolinguistic minorities, and public education in the United States and elsewhere. A parallel attack has occurred in Australia. The widely admired, well-informed, and socially progressive Australian Language Policy (LoBianco 1987), which championed (indigenous) Aboriginal and (immigrant) heritage language rights and supported multilingualism and multiculturalism, was gutted and—with the surprising exception of continued support, in theory, at least, for Aboriginal languages—replaced by something approaching an "English-only" policy when it was rewritten in 1991 by a team of federal bureaucrats. The bureaucrats, it should be noted by those still seduced by "labor parties" (an oxymoron), were working commissioned directly by the Minister of Education of the ALP (Australian Labour Party) Hawke/Keating regime, not the right-wing Howard (Liberal Party) government, which simply finished the job.

A general methodological principle, noted earlier, that is apparent in the relatively successful immersion and bilingual programs is that a good teacher or educational program starts where the students are. This is not questioned in the case of subject matter instruction. Few people would suggest trying to teach the tennis serve before the forehand, multiplication before addition, or cardiac surgery before anatomy. The same principle applies with language. There is a vast body of literature documenting the way caretakers (typically parents and elder siblings) adapt their speech and/or conversation to the current linguistic abilities of children acquiring their first language and then, while conversing with them at their level and thereby making *what* they say comprehensible, simultaneously provide them with models of *how* to say it in an increasingly native-like, adult manner. The same phenomena have repeatedly been observed in child and adult second-language acquisition (for review, see Long 1996). In other words, if given the opportunity, people of all ages use their innate language-acquisition capacity to learn languages by using what they know so far to try to communicate, and in the process learn a little more. As Hatch (1978, 404) put it, "language learning evolves *out of* learning how to carry on conversations."

Starting where the students are is essentially what the Oakland resolution proposed. Quite apart from the preceding rationale, there is a fair amount of evidence (although not as much or as good evidence as one would like) of the effectiveness of the same principles applied to education through a second dialect. Simpkins and Simpkins (1981), for example, compared reading gains by 530 AAVE-speaking children, grades 7 through 12, in 21 classes in five parts of the United States using Houghton-Mifflin's three-stage *Bridge* reading program (see Labov 1995 for a useful critique of these and other reading materials) with gains by AAVE students in six classes using traditional SE materials in remedial reading classes. The treatment group first learned to read using a text written in AAVE, then a transitional reader, and finally an SE reader. The average gain in reading scores for students in the bridge program was 6.2 months for the four months of instruction. The control group students gained only 1.6 months in the same period. It should be noted, however, that there were several methodological problems with the study, which unfortunately was suspended after four months, because of objections from some African-American community members, among other things, to the use of different curricula for black and white children.

After reviewing work by Boggs, Watson-Gegeo, Speidel, and others documenting a wide variety of dialect-based problems in the classroom, Sato (1989) went on to describe several programs, such as those in the Kamehameha [Schools] Early Education Program (KEEP), that have been used with children in Hawai'i and elsewhere to address both comprehension and classroom participation problems arising from both dialect differences and differences in teachers' and students' interactional styles. The latter involve such phenomena as culturally based differences in the significance of pauses and silence in talk, notions of "precision" and "relevance," an orientation toward trusted peers rather than adult authority figures, a preference for cooperation rather than competition, the function and interpretation of various kinds of questions, and the perceived appropriateness of various kinds of responses (e.g., "direct" or "indirect") to those questions. These and many other linguistic differences affect comprehension, participation patterns, and learning in classrooms, but are important far beyond classrooms. Eades (1992, 1994, and elsewhere), for example, has shown how these differences have cost Aboriginal defendants dearly in Australian courts on more than one occasion.

The problems, Sato argued, must first be recognized and understood. They can then be addressed successfully at a variety of levels, both inside and outside the classroom. What is called for, however, she wrote,

> is not simply consciousness-raising, that is, informing teachers about sociolinguistic diversity. . . . The bureaucracy of the school system itself should be analyzed. . . . Working in organizations such as teachers' unions and parent-teacher associations can also lead to a more sympathetic treatment of minority schooling issues. A recent controversy in Hawai'i over the State Board of Education's proposed "English Only" policy [see Sato 1991] illustrates how effective collective action by teachers, students, parents and researchers can be against reactionary views toward sociolinguistic diversity. (Sato 1989, 276–77)

Overall, where educational outcomes turn partly on differences in varieties of a language, Sato advocated models where children's home variety, such as HCE or AAVE, is validated and preserved, while a second—usually "standard"—variety is added, to graduate students who command two or, in practice, a range of speech levels and styles and whose attainment in content areas will not have been impeded by instruction that was delivered from the outset through a variety that was initially unfamiliar to them. If additive bilingualism, as in the case of French immersion programs in Canada, is a worthy linguistic and educational goal for the children of dominant language groups, why not this approach for the children of Oakland, Hawai'i, and elsewhere? Sato's recommendations eight years ago are just as apt today:

> It has been argued that understanding of the political context of teaching SESD [standard English as a second dialect] and greater familiarity with differences in varieties and the classroom experiences of minority students are necessary for both policy making and pedagogy. The "nonstandard" approach to the teaching of SESD advocated here takes as fundamental (a) the social and linguistic integrity of minority varieties of English and, therefore, (b) the need to design sociolinguistically appropriate pedagogy for speakers of such varieties. Rather than remediation of students' language and replacement of minority varieties with "proper" English, the teaching of SESD may prove more successful if systematically practiced as *additive bidialectalism*. (Sato 1989, 276–77, emphasis added)

A BROADER DEBATE

As indicated earlier, the preceding discussion is not only preliminary, but has been conducted within the stifling constraints entailed in the continued existence of imperialist nation-states, whether monopoly capitalist or authoritarian socialist. Many current problems with language in education around the world are epiphenomena, nasty by-products of such things as the need of states everywhere for "national unity" (i.e., acceptance of the status quo, or their legitimacy), one manifestation of which is a fear of linguistic diversity among their own (or increasingly, the world's) peoples. The useful gatekeeping function of official languages and standard dialects for those wielding state power, likewise, has already been noted. Hierarchical power structures, centralized authority, and state control over (compulsory) education systems are among the mechanisms that make state-mandated violations of students' and teachers' identities and language rights possible in the first place. State coercion, often in the form of punishment and "failure" at school, and ultimately involving brute force and imprisonment in some countries, is what sanctions discriminatory language policies. Likewise, some proposed solutions advocated within the same restricted terms of reference are equally clearly illusory. Struggles to force governments, or even the United Nations, to recognize linguistic human *rights*, for instance, as the Israeli, Australian, and many other far worse cases show, are really no more than struggles for just as easily revokable temporary *licenses*, and simultaneously serve to legitimize states as the arbiters in such matters, when it is governments that are often the problem, not the solution.

What is needed among those seriously interested in language issues, in education, and in areas where the two intersect, is a far broader debate than has been initiated here. For example, what are the generally accepted principles, assuming such principles exist, that underlie libertarian educational theory and practice? There is a rich anarchist intellectual tradition in education, found, among many other places, in the writings and practice of Godwin, Tolstoy, Bakunin, Morris, Fourier, Michel, Faure, Robin, Kropotkin, Ferre y Guardia, Puig Elias, Cohen, Goldman, Holt, Illich, Duane, and Ward. Is that tradition adequate for tomorrow's complex multilingual, multicultural societies, industrial or otherwise, or are areas of it, at least, in need of updating? What are the lessons to be learned from practical implementations of anarchist ideas about education in different countries, some of which have been described and analyzed in a number of valuable recent books and articles (see, e.g., Avrich 1980; Shotton 1993; Smith 1983; Spring 1975; Ward 1995; Wright 1989; and articles in *The Raven* Nos. 10 and 16, and in *Lib Ed*)? In sum, would most problems of linguistic human rights, in education and elsewhere, simply disappear with the advent of voluntary communities, *l'éducation integrale*, a radically learner-centered educational symbiosis of mental and manual work, voluntary schooling, informal education, control of their workplaces by education workers (including students) and their industrial unions, and other promises of anarchism and anarcho-syndicalism, or might there still be at least a few problems in paradise?

REFERENCES

Avrich, P. 1980. *The Modern School Movement: Anarchism and Education in the United States*. Princeton, N.J.: Princeton University Press.

Bailey, G. (1987). "Decreolization?" *Language and Society* 16: 449–73.

———. 1993. "A Perspective on African-American English." In D. Preston, ed., *American Dialect Research*. Philadelphia: John Benjamins, 287–318.

Bailey, G., and N. Maynor. 1989. "The Divergence Controversy." *American Speech* 64: 12–39.

Bernstein, B. 1971. *Class, Codes and Control*. London: Routledge and Kegan Paul.

Chambers, J. K. 1992. "Dialect Acquisition." *Language* 68(4): 673–98.

Chomsky, N. 1959. "Review of *Verbal Behavior* by B. F. Skinner." *Language* 35: 26–58.

———. 1988. *Language and Problems of Knowledge: The Managua Lectures*. Cambridge, Mass.: MIT Press.

Eades, D. 1992. *Aboriginal English and the Law*. Brisbane: Queensland Law Society.

———. 1994. "A Case of Communicative Clash: Aboriginal English and the Legal System." In J. Gibbons, ed., *Language and the Law*. London: Longman, 234–64.

Fasold, R. 1972. *Tense Marking in Black English*. Arlington, Va.: Center for Applied Linguistics.

Hatch, E. M. 1978. "Discourse Analysis and Second Language Acquisition." In E. M. Hatch, ed., *Second Language Acquistion: A Book of Readings*. Rowley, Mass.: Newbury House, 401–35.

Hymes, D. 1992. "Inequality in Language: Taking for Granted." *Working Papers in Educational Linguistics* (University of Pennsylvania) 8(1): 1–30.

Labov, W. 1969. "The Logic of Non-standard English." *Georgetown Monographs on Language and Linguistics* 22. Washington: Georgetown University, Center for Applied Linguistics.

———. 1972. *Language in the Inner City*. Philadelphia: University of Pennsylvania Press.

———. 1995. "Can Reading Failure Be Reversed? A Linguistic Approach to the Question." In V. Gadsden and D. Wagner, eds., *Literacy among African-American Youth*. Cresskill, N.J.: Hampton Press.

Labov, W., and W. A. Harris. 1986. "De Facto Segregation of Black and White Vernaculars." In D. Sankoff, ed., *Diversity and Diachrony*. Philadelphia: John Benjamins, 45–58.

LoBianco, J. 1987. *National Policy on Languages*. Canberra: Australian Government Publishing Service.

Long, M. H. 1990. "Maturational Constraints on Language Development." *Studies in Second Language Acquistion* 12(3): 251–85.

———. 1993. "Second Language Acquisition as a Function of Age: Substantive Findings and Methodological Issues." In K. Hyltenstam and A. Viberg, eds., *Progression and Regression in Language*. Cambridge: Cambridge University Press, 196–221.

———. 1996. "The Role of the Linguistic Environment in Second Language Acquisition." In W. C. Ritchie and T. K. Bhatia, eds., *Handbook of Second Language Acquisition*. New York: Academic Press, 413–68.

Luke, A., A. W. McHoul, and J. L. Mey. 1990. "On the Limits of Language Planning: Class, State and Power. In R. Baldauf and A. Luke, eds., *Language Planning and Education*. Clevedon, U.K.: Multilingual Matters, 25–44.

Malcolm, I. G. 1994. "Aboriginal English Inside and Outside the Classroom." *Australian Review of Applied Linguistics* 17(1).

Marshall, P., ed., 1986. *The Anarchist Writings of William Godwin*. London: Freedom Press.

McGroarty, M. 1991. "English Instruction for Linguistic Minority Groups: Different Structures, Different Styles." In M. Celce-Murcia, ed., *Teaching English as a Second or Foreign Language*, 2d ed. Cambridge, Mass.: Newbury House–Harper and Row, 372–85.

Michaels, S. 1981. "'Sharing Time': Children's Narrative Style and Differential Access to Literacy." *Language in Society* 10: 423–42.

Pennycook, A. 1995. "English in the World/The World in English." In J. W. Tollefson, ed., *Power and Inequality in Language Education*. Cambridge: Cambridge University Press, 34–58.

Phillipson, R. 1992. *Linguistic Imperialism*. Oxford: Oxford University Press.

Ramirez, J. D. 1992. "Executive Summary" [special issue]. *Bilingual Research Journal* 16(1–2).

Ramirez, J. D., S. D. Yuen, and D. R. Ramey. 1991. *Executive Summary Final Report: Longitudinal Study of Structured English Immersion Strategy, Early-exit and Late-exit Transitional Bilingual Education Programs for Language-minority Children*. San Mateo, Calif.: Aguirre International.

Sato, C. J. 1985. "Linguistic Inequality in Hawai'i: The Post-Creole Dilemma." In N. Wolfson and J. Manes, eds., *Language of Inequality*. Berlin: Mouton, 255–72.

———. 1989. "A Non-standard Approach to Standard English." *TESOL Quarterly* 23(2): 259–82.

———. 1991. "Language Attitudes and Sociolinguistic Variation in Hawai'i." In J. Cheshire, ed., *English Around the World: Sociolinguistic Perspectives*. Cambridge: Cambridge University Press, 647–63.

Schinke-Llano, L. 1983. "Foreigner Talk in Content Classrooms." In H. W. Seliger and M. H. Long, eds., *Classroom-oriented Research in Second Language Acquisition*. Rowley, Mass.: Newbury House, 146–64.

Shotton, J. 1993. *No Master High or Law: Libertarian Education and Schooling 1890–1990*. Bristol: Libertarian Education.

Simpkins, G., and C. Simpkins, 1981. "Cross-cultural Approach to Curriculum Development." In G. Smitherman, ed., *Black English and the Education of Black Children and Youth*. Proceedings of the National Invitational Symposium on the King Decision. Detroit: Center for Black Studies, Wayne State University, 212–40.

Skutnabb-Kangas, T., R. Phillipson, and M. Rannut, eds. 1995. *Linguistic Human Rights: Overcoming Linguistic Discrimination*. Berlin: Mouton de Gruyter.

Smith, M. P. 1983. *The Libertarians and Education*. London: Allen & Unwin.

Spring, J. 1985. *A Primer of Libertarian Education*. New York: Free Life Editions.

Tollefson, J. W., ed. 1995. *Power and Inequality in Language Education*. Cambridge: Cambridge University Press.

Tolliver-Weddington, G. 1979. "Ebonics (Black English): Implications for Education." *Journal of Black Studies* (Special Issue) 9(4).

Ward, C. 1995. *Talking Schools*. London: Freedom Press.

Williams, R. L. ed., 1975. *Ebonics: The True Language of Black Folks*. St. Louis: Institute of Black Studies.

Wolfram, W. 1969. *A Sociolinguistic Description of Detroit Negro Speech*. Arlington, Va.: Center for Applied Linguistics.

Wright, N. 1989. *Assessing Radical Education: A Critical Review of the Radical Movement in English Schooling, 1960–1980*. Milton Keynes: Open University Press.

9

Containing Language Difference: Advertising in *Hispanic* Magazine

Bonnie Urciuoli

INTRODUCTION: SAFE AND UNSAFE DIFFERENCE

The past decade has seen intense public discussion of multiculturalism in the United States. Discourses about difference overlap and sometimes conflict, leaving no one model of multiculturalism. However, what most such discourses have in common is a tendency to treat the "cultures" that are "multi" as a set of containers, each equated with a category of personal identity. In this model, a person labelled as Hispanic-American or Asian-American or African American is perceived as an embodiment of his or her culture. The differences among cultures are tucked into carefully demarcated social spaces, and those social spaces are outlined in ways peculiarly suited to American self-definition. Within these spaces, language difference is rationalized and justified in ways that fit a general cultural vision of how to be a good American.

A particularly interesting case of such cultural processing is the construction of the Hispanic in the United States. The referent for "Hispanic" is ambiguous: it implies Spanish-affiliated origins in the Western Hemisphere, which has both linguistic and postcolonial overtones. "Hispanic" also has race overtones in that distinctions are commonly made between black, white, and Hispanic. In some contexts the race overtones are conflated with class: "the Hispanic underclass." At the same it has become one of the key categories deployed in constructing the United States as a "multicultural" nation.

The connection made in U.S. public consciousness between "Hispanic" and the Spanish language gets sticky in public venues, especially public education. Language differences are often portrayed as a danger to the harmony of the nation. It is therefore interesting to see how a major media enterprise aimed specifically at a Hispanic audience handles language difference and makes it safe for public consumption. In its reporting and advertising, *Hispanic* magazine constructs and projects a vision of how to be Hispanic in ways coherent with being a good American citizen. Any connection between origin difference and working-class status is recast in terms of individual social mobility. Above all, the Spanish language is used in carefully selected ways.

I have written elsewhere (Urciuoli 1994) about racial, ethnic, and class dimensions of the ideology of citizenship in the United States. The ideal U.S. citizen epitomizes hard work, the will to better oneself, the desire to achieve, the ability to produce. Ideally, these qualities indicate control over oneself and one's destiny. Ideally, one's nation of origin provides the moral wherewithal (as "family solidarity" or "work ethic" or "belief in education") to enhance that control and move one along the path of good citizenship. If origin differences stand in the way of that control, they must be cast off. Within this moral frame, differences in how one is named or looks or sounds are somewhat minimized. Everyone is imagined to be the same in the ways that are definingly American, and differences are safely contained. Outside this frame, origin differences are far more likely to be read as signs of potential disruption. This is especially true of language which, in the United States, is regarded as something individuals can and should control.

This moral frame is made clear in the personal character requirements for naturalized citizenship: "good moral character, understanding of and attachment to the fundamental principles of the Constitution of the United States, ability to read, write and speak English" (U.S. Code 1952). These requirements have changed little since 1795. By contrast, racial and national origin constraints on eligibility first began to change with the ratification of the Fourteenth and Fifteenth Amendments in 1868 and 1870. Not only did former slaves become citizens, so did anyone born in the United States (except for, e.g., children of diplomats). This automatically made the children of immigrants citizens. At the same time, starting with the Asian exclusions of the 1880s, Congress began setting limits on immigration and naturalization, culminating in the passage of the National Origins Quota Act of 1924. The results of these policies corresponded to the degree of racialization: southern and eastern Europeans were far more limited than northern and western Europeans; Japanese and Chinese were excluded altogether.

As a result, a two-tiered system of citizenship came into being. The ideal citizen was of English origin. Racial distinctions (which were generally conflated with nation and region in the nineteenth and early twentieth century) began with distance from England (particularly south and east); even Germans and Scandinavians were racially marked with respect to the English. In effect, the racial polarity of white versus black that had always characterized U.S. perceptions of citizenship (see Shklar 1991) was complicated by racial markedness along the lines of national origin ("Italian") or geographic area ("Oriental"). This type of scaling is evident in much of the sociological and immigration policy writing of 1910–1930. The Dillingham Commission Report on Immigration presents a fairly restrained example (United States Immigration Commission 1911), while Madison Grant's writings such as *The Passing of the Great Race* presents a rhetorically vivid picture that resonated with U.S. public consciousness during World War I and the 1920s (Grant 1916).

By the 1950s, descendants of European immigrants were far less racialized than they had been in the 1920s. As Italians, Poles, and Jews came to be seen as less problematically white, the racialization of people from Asia, Latin America, and the Caribbean stood out even more sharply. With growing labor migration from Mexico to the Southwest and from Puerto Rico to the Northeast, Puerto Ricans and Mexicans were increasingly targeted as the antithesis of good citizenship. This is seen in the 1964 Congressional testimony concerning the lifting of immigration restrictions (legislation that was passed in 1965) where frequent references were made to, for example, the "avalanche of Puerto Ricans and other Caribbeans which have inundated the Atlantic seaboard" (U.S. House of Representatives 1964, 689). People of Latin American origin were, and often still are, typified as undigested, non-assimilating lumps, the antithesis of the good citizen as self-motivated, class-mobile producer who assimilates culturally and linguistically (see Chock 1991, 1994, on perceptions of Latin undocumented aliens in Congressional testimony). The clearly expressed willingness to assimilate linguistically emerges as an important pledge of good faith toward social mobility, and thus an absolute requirement of good citizenship.

LANGUAGE DIFFERENCE AS CULTURAL DANGER

Speaking a language other than English is seen as a particularly disruptive form of difference. English has long been seen as the key to class mobility. Silverstein (1987) describes the referentialist linguistic ideology that pervades public discussion of language in the United States: words have absolute, context-free meanings, pronunciations have pure and universal forms. In this ideology, anyone in the United States can learn to speak English clearly and correctly, without contamination from other sources or systems.[1] Unequivocally correct word meanings and sentence forms are supposed to be recoverable from authorized sources like *Webster's* or the *Oxford English Dictionary* and are freely accessible to everyone through public schooling. Given this ideology, it is no surprise that heated arguments have emerged about the dangers of unrestrained linguistic diversity, nor that English Language Amendments have been proposed.[2]

The various forms of English Language Amendments typically begin by stating: "The English language shall be the official language of the United States." The English-only versions call for prohibition of languages other than English by local, state, or federal government. This would mean that no publicly funded information or service would be available in any language except English, except for transitional bilingual education, foreign language instruction, or emergency information. The rationale for this, as expressed by the amendments' sponsors and supporters, is that English is the medium through which all Americans or potential Americans (i.e., immigrants) would share a clarity of understanding that transcends any social circumstance, facilitates class mobility, and enhances democratic participation.

In this ideology, schools have a civic duty to teach students the common language. As Senator Walter Huddleston (D-Kentucky 1973–85) put it, the "misdirected policy of bilingualism" kept children "languishing . . . in a state of prolonged confusion, suspended between two worlds and not understanding what is expected of them" (Crawford 1992, 115). Secretary of Education Edward Bennett (1985–88) put it in these terms: "To be a citizen is to share in something common—common principles, common memories, and a common language in which to discuss our common affairs" (Crawford 1992, 358). This "common language . . . [of] our political, economic and social life" (359) is packaged and certified in public education. According to Bennett, teaching in the students' original language cheats them of this opportunity and is unjustifiable, even in the name of cultural pride. Bennett cites Ronald Reagan's assertion that bilingual programs are useful insofar as they make scholarly skills, democratic participation, and social progress in the American mainstream more, not less, accessible.

The same model of idealized, certified packaging applies to all foreign languages. Senator Hayakawa (R-California 1977–83), an avid English-only supporter, enthusiastically described how his son and daughter had learned Spanish, French, and Japanese in ways that, as he put it, paid off in a general appreciation of the affiliated national cultures and in a better job for his son. He opposed the "usurpation" of English by the "ethnic chauvinism" of the (specifically) Hispanic leadership, whose aim was not an "enriched communication" built on a shared English base but "a foreign language within our borders" (Crawford 1992, 94–100).

The idea that unbounded language difference is a form of pollution developed in the context of European colonial history, along with the idea, as argued in Anderson (1983), that languages come in packages to match nation-state boundaries. Linguists studying code-switching and other language contact phenomena have extensively demonstrated the complex regularities that govern bi- and multilingual behavior. Yet there remains a sharp sense that bilingualism, especially among working-class immigrants, leads to disorder and pollution; see for example Walsh's (1991) study of teachers' attitudes toward bilingual Puerto Rican students in the Boston school system and the internalization of such attitudes by students. Such majority attitudes toward language difference are in many ways analogous to attitudes toward race difference. When people talk about origin differences as the antithesis to or lack of whiteness, they perceive origin as racially marked, the sign of an underclass that threatens the nation. When people talk about foreign languages as the denial of English, they talk about them as threats to the integrity of the nation. When origin differences are seen as another way to embody the class-mobile idea of Americanness (ideals originally white), they are transformed into ethnicity and become acceptable. When foreign languages provide the means to secure a job or signal upwardly mobile ethnic solidarity, they are acceptable. Foreign language courses in high schools and college are justified as useful. Bilingual programs garner more public support when the native language is used to make the transition to English and not maintained for its own sake. Foreign language in public places is most acceptable when packaged in artistic performance; when overheard on the street or in a store, it can draw malicious remarks from passers-by. Thus, insofar as Spanish is identified with foreign-accented "Spanglish"-speaking immigrants who want bilingual education and ballots, Spanish is likely to be regarded by media, educators, and legislators as an intrusive language of social disorder that obstructs proper mobility: the language of a raced "underclass" people. Insofar as Spanish is taught by properly certified teachers, contained in "transitional" bilingual programs, or used emblematically in largely English discourse, it becomes relatively acceptable as the language of the ethnicized Hispanic-American.

While English-only sentiment has targeted many immigrant groups, Spanish-speakers have been its primary target. The existence of Spanish and English in the United States is conventionally presented in zero-sum terms, the one existing at the expense of the other (Zentella 1988). In polls of public attitudes toward Official English legislation, questions are framed to suggest that English, the language of progress and democracy, is endangered by irrational demands of special-interest groups (Zentella 1990). The wording of ballot initiatives is similarly framed (Woolard 1989). Spanish-speakers successful in business, especially Cubans in Florida, are seen as somehow cheating the system by not using English as the route to prosperity (Castro, Haun, and Roca 1990). How then does a general-interest magazine that describes itself as "for and about Hispanics" deploy Spanish in ways compatible with the magazine's theme of class mobility?

SPANISH IN *HISPANIC*

Hispanic is the only general interest English-language magazine for a U.S. Hispanic audience. It covers news, finances, sports, political representation, education, arts, and entertainment. Established in 1988, it targets a young, upwardly mobile readership. According to a survey by the Simmons Market Research Bureau (1991) 69.2 percent of readers are 18–44 years old; 63.2 percent were born in the United States; 75.7 percent attended or graduated from college; 72.7 percent have "white collar" jobs. The average household income of readers is $56,000; 70–90 percent travel, own one or more cars, use or have major credit cards; 87.9 percent prefer to read English. There are 225,000 subscribers. As its editorials consistently state, the magazine's goal is the unity, growth, and prosperity of the U.S. Hispanic community.

Flores (1993) talks about a Latin community in terms of a Latino imaginary, a construction of a sense of an imagined shared Latin experience that is both a reactive and constructive response to a history of geopolitical conditions. By this definition, *Hispanic* is one of many possible Latino imaginaries, but it is also specifically constructed to work within the U.S. imaginary, focused on good citizenship.[3] This can readily be seen in the way the magazine's regular and special features are laid out. Regular departments include: From The Editor, Letters, This Month (political, art, and entertainment events involving or affecting Hispanics), Careers, Money, Travel, Business, Reviews, and Hispanic Calendar. Feature articles cover hot social issues, features on famous Hispanics, politics, the arts, national cultures of Latin countries, business reports, career opportunities, sports, and entertainment. All are in English.

The feature stories and editorials make it clear that the magazine's principal mission is to publicize the venues available to young Hispanics, especially those just out of college, for career advancement in major corporations. Business- and career-related features in the four issues examined here (December 1993 through April 1994) cover topics like how to buy computers, the hundred U.S. companies providing maximum career opportunities to Hispanics, advice for women facing sexual harassment at work, a profile of Hispanic labor leader Dennis Rivera, career opportunities for Hispanics in the federal government, and a profile of Hispanic computer executive Larry Cabrinety. The messages engendered in these features are reinforced by the sizeable number and range of advertisements for recruitment and social consciousness, far outnumbering the consumption-oriented advertising. Features not directly about business reinforce the class mobility emphasis from other angles. Stories on the Hispanic family adapting to changing social situations and on Hispanic students studying abroad highlight the importance of looking to and planning for the future. Features on sensible shopping for Christmas, skiing in the Rocky Mountains, and an upscale Salvadoran restaurant in Washington, D.C., highlight a sense of rational, sensible enjoyment. These messages are reinforced by the consumption advertising: one enjoys oneself in a sensible manner. Messages about cultural heritage are framed by endorsement from major corporations: Budweiser, Miller Brewing, Philip Morris.

Recruitment advertising, which targets social mobility through work, makes up the highest proportion of advertising in the magazine, as can readily be seen in Appendices 9.1 and 9.2. Magazines like *Time* or *Newsweek* run a far higher proportion of consumer advertising.[4] So too does *Ebony*, the magazine to which *Hispanic* is most comparable. *Ebony's* reporting and advertising address an African-American readership, and many of its advertisements and features focus on issues related to class mobility, minority recruitment, and cultural consciousness. But where such ads and features predominate in *Hispanic*, they make up a significantly smaller proportion of *Ebony's* total range of offerings. *Ebony* carries a far larger proportion of consumer ads, and nearly all its ads carry some clear index that they address an African-American readership, generally through the models in the photographs. By contrast, a fairly high proportion of ads in *Hispanic* carry no clear index of their intended readership. Most of the consumer ads in *Ebony*, like most consumer ads in *Hispanic* and indeed most consumer ads in U.S. general interest magazines, highlight the sensible nature of their products. However, some genres of advertising, most notably makeup, perfume, and liquor ads, focus instead on the luxurious or romantic/sexual nature of the product. These ads turn up far more frequently in *Ebony* than in *Hispanic*.[5]

The sparing but strategic use of Spanish made by *Hispanic's* advertising should be examined across the full range of advertising in the magazine. To this end, I examined four issues of *Hispanic*: December 1993 (84 pages, 45 ads), January-February 1994 (double issue of 132 pages, 75 ads), March 1994 (80 pages, 46 ads), and April 1994 (88 pages, 47 ads). The advertising falls into the following general categories:

CONSUMPTION of goods, services, or entertainment. Goods include autos, food and drink, clothing, and electronic goods. Advertising for goods stresses enjoyment and luxury or sensible and rational use value; many stress both. Services include banking, insurance, financing and credit, housing, travel. Service advertising generally stressed how much sense it makes for the consumer to use these services.

RECRUITMENT for business and career opportunities. Some recruitment advertising stressed the opportunities themselves, other advertising led off with discussion of the company's general sense of social consciousness. As long as the advertising led into a recruitment message, I kept it separate from the next category.

SOCIAL CONSCIOUSNESS advertising gives examples of social/cultural sensitivity or social action on the part of a major corporation (e.g., R.J. Reynolds or Anheuser Busch) or organization (the U.S. Army) without overtly recruiting.

SOCIAL CONSCIENCE advertising represents organizations that exist to address social problems (e.g., Save the Children).

CONTESTS, COMPETITIONS, FESTIVALS, and SEMINARS, many cosponsored by *Hispanic*. Examples: Teacher of the Year; art competition; sales career seminar.

The advertising may or may not explicitly target a Latin-origin audience by means of an index, a physical or linguistic sign linking it to such a readership.[6]

NO EXPLICIT INDEX. Nothing in the advertisement itself indicates its audience. The consumer ads might appear in any magazine; the minority recruitment advertisements target no specific minority.

NON-LINGUISTIC BUT CLEARLY LATIN-ORIGIN INDEXES. The advertising uses photos and drawings of people whose hair, skin, and faces suggest Latin origin, often with Spanish names. Sometimes ads refer to locales in Latin America.

EMBLEMATIC LINGUISTIC INDEXES. The advertising uses a word or phrase of Spanish to signal Hispanic identity or solidarity, sometimes with non-linguistic Latin-origin indexes.

ALL SPANISH. All or nearly all text is in Spanish.

Using these categories, the advertising in these four issues of *Hispanic* can be sorted to show the ads using Spanish indexes in contrast to those that do not. The number in parentheses indicates the total number of items in each category. Appendix 9.1 provides a complete list of advertisers. Appendix 9.2 shows how advertising from each of these categories was deployed in a given month. The figures confirm, on a month-by-month basis, the general trends noted hereafter.

NO EXPLICIT INDEX (81 ads):
Consumption of goods:
    Sensible (11): mid-range autos, trucks, electronics
    Enjoyable (2): luxury autos, cigarettes
    Sensible/enjoyable (6): mid-range autos, appliances, clothing
Consumption of services (10): financial, insurance, health
Recruitment/opportunity (37): corporations, federal agencies, military
Social consciousness (13): corporations
Social conscience (2)

NON-LINGUISTIC BUT CLEARLY LATIN-ORIGIN INDEXES (55 ads):
Indexes are specified in parentheses. The most frequent such index was models' physiognomy, meaning that the ad used dark-haired, often dark-skinned models with faces likely to be seen as Latin.
Consumption of goods:
    Sensible (4): auto, electronics
    Sensible/enjoyable (3): clothing, mid-range auto, food
    Culturally conscious media/entertainment (3)
Consumption of services (6): educational, travel, housing
Recruitment/opportunity (16): corporations, federal agencies, military
Social consciousness (15): corporations
Culturally conscious competitions, etc. (8): sponsored by corporations, often cosponsored with *Hispanic*.

EMBLEMATIC LINGUISTIC INDEXES (11 ads):
Consumption of goods:
    Sensible/enjoyable (1): mid-range autos
    Enjoyable (4): clothing, food, entertainment
    Culturally conscious (2): calendar, booklet
Consumption of services (1): financial
Recruitment/opportunity (2): corporation, military
Social/cultural consciousness (1): corporation

ALL SPANISH (13):
Consumption of goods:
    Enjoyable (8): liquor, beer, cigarettes, food, mid-range auto, clothing, cameras
    Sensible (1): toothpaste
    Sensible/Enjoyable (1): beer

Contest (1)
Consumption of services (1): financial
Recruitment/opportunity (1): corporation

Corporate advertisers do not use Spanish to guide people up the class-mobility ladder. Of the 81 ads with no explicit index of Latin identity, 50 feature corporations recruiting or advertising their social/cultural consciousness. Of the 55 ads with non-linguistic indexes of Latin identity, 39 feature corporations recruiting, being socially/culturally conscious, or sponsoring cultural events and competitions. Of the 11 ads using emblematic Spanish indexes, 3 feature corporations recruiting or being socially/culturally conscious. Of the 13 ads entirely in Spanish, one features corporate recruitment. The one exception is the Avon Corporation, whose ad is aimed explicitly at women, most likely women in the home.

The largest proportion of advertising in *Hispanic* has no explicit Latin index. The ads that do use Latin indexes mostly use visual indexes—and carefully contained visual indexes at that. When Spanish is used in an ad it is more often than not used without strong visual indexes, as if the most acceptable image of a Hispanic person in advertising is one that does not carry too many Latin-origin signs. (Appendix 9.1 tells which emblematic Spanish ads also use visual Latin indexes.) Most advertising that uses Spanish is consumption-oriented and generally stresses the enjoyable over the rational. It is interesting that Spanish is not heavily featured in advertisements for culturally conscious items or events.

In the December 1993 issue, 36.2 percent of the ads feature no Latin index, as well as 53.3 percent of the ads in the January-February and March 1994 issues and 41.3 percent in the April issue.[7] When these ads present products, they generally do so as rational consumer choices. For example, most car and truck advertising was for mid-range products (Ford, Chevy, Buick, Chrysler/Dodge, etc.), stressing dependability, engineering, economy, and safety, sometimes linking those qualities to good styling and a comfortable ride. The only exception is cigarette advertising, which has little to offer except style and pleasure. The services advertised are mainly financial (investment or insurance) and for that very reason oriented toward rationality and mobility. These are all ads that appear in mainstream magazines. Recruitment advertising is by its nature aimed at a minority audience but a considerable proportion of recruitment ads do not specify a Hispanic audience.

In the December 1993 issue, 29.8 percent of the ads feature non-linguistic Latin-origin indexes, as do 33.3 percent of the ads in the January-February and March 1994 issues and 47.8 percent of the ads in the April issue.[8]

Again, products are advertised as primarily sensible or as sensible and enjoyable. A sizeable proportion of these ads are also aimed at corporate or military recruitment or at corporations presenting themselves as socially conscious. In short, the proportion of ads addressing sensible consumption or social mobility under a corporate or deal aegis is about the same for ads that do not carry Latin indexes and for those that do. It is instructive at this point to examine the semiotic structure of a couple of these ads.

An ad may be thought of as a communicative event in Hymes's (1974) sense: the advertiser is the sender or addressor, the reader is the addressee, the item advertised is the message topic, and the advertising design and copy make up the message form. From a speech act perspective, advertising is directive insofar as it attempts to move the addressee to some kind of action (i.e., buying something or taking the course of action featured in the ad). This makes it important to understand the way in which the advertiser construes the addressee's cultural person: in what ways does the advertiser construe the addressee as Hispanic? Advertising is expressive insofar as it reflects the advertiser's image of itself: how do megacorporations portray themselves? Advertising is referential insofar as it provides information about the subject of the ad, the product, service, or recruitment opportunity. Advertising is stylistic/poetic insofar as it focuses on the form of the presentation itself, the words and images in the copy. In the two categories of ads so far described, the reader is addressed as a rational decision maker and a modest, sensible consumer, the advertiser expresses an image of itself as civic-minded and helpful, the product is referenced as practical (either for personal use or for its mobility potential), and the aesthetic is deployed in support of the rational rather than as form for form's sake: a poetics of the sensible, so to speak. This is especially noticeable in auto ads, which deploy what amounts to a technology of poetics.

In non-linguistic Latin indexed ads (and in some of those using emblematic Spanish), these communicative elements are deployed to suggest addressees who "look" Hispanic in carefully controlled ways, but who dress, think, and act in ways that move people into the U.S. middle class. The American Dream figures prominently in these ads, a phrase directly invoked in Housing and Urban Development ads for low-interest homeowning or U.S. Army/Hispanic Serving Institution ads calling for businesses to help students in Hispanic Serving Institutions complete their education and "fulfill their American Dream." Ads for the Chrysler-Dodge-Plymouth minivan (Figure 9.1) and for ITT both deploy Latin indexes framed by messages about planning for the future. Both use images of children, an image commonly featured in Latin-origin index ads. These construct an addressee with family feelings and

While other car companies have been busy copying our minivans, we've engineered the MINIVANS of the future.

Dodge Caravan

Plymouth Voyager

In 1984, we invented the minivan. Since then, we introduced the first available integrated child safety seats and the first driver's minivan air bag.* We added available anti-lock brakes and a child guard lock on the sliding door. For 1994, we added a front passenger air bag* and made the child safety seat recline.

So, while everyone else tried to imitate the DODGE CARAVAN and PLYMOUTH VOYAGER, Chrysler Corporation's engineers made them even safer by meeting the 1998 passenger cars safety standards.** That's why our minivans are the best-selling ever.

THE MINIVAN COMPANY

*Always wear your seat belt for a fully effective air bag. **Excludes sunscreen glass and Caravan C/V model. For more information, please call 1-800-576-MINIVAN.

Figure 9.1

concerns that one must be practical about and express the corporate advertiser's sense of itself as personal and caring. They also include in the ads' referential content a sense of children as embodiments of hope for the future, and planning for the future is a key theme in all *Hispanic* advertising. The minivan ad's Latin index consists of a dark-haired boy and girl. Standing against a backdrop of planets, they wear space suits and the boy carries a helmet displaying the Chrysler logo, technopoetic-ally enhancing the references to the minivan's reputation for safety and good engineering, the minivans of the future. The ad for ITT financial services features a photo of the regional manger for San Juan (Puerto Rico) and the six boys on the basketball team she coaches. The text describes how the regional manager and the ITT company itself both understand the importance of helping people. Whereas the minivan ad has one visual index, the ITT ad has several: the manager's name and photo, the boys on the team, and the locale itself, aesthetically enhanced by the palm tree and water in the background. Again, concern for children—their future, their success—is the core element in the pro-jected Hispanic identity. The visual indexes are presented as part of that concern; they are also framed by the ad's references to sound financial planning. The key difference between the two ads is that the minivan ad uses imaginary children and the ITT ad uses a photo of a real employee and real children to express the corporation's social/cultural consciousness. As the information in Appendix 9.1 suggests, recruit-ment and social consciousness ads commonly use pictures of real peo-ple to express that sense, suggesting the corporations' groundedness in the real world.

A much smaller proportion of ads features Spanish. In the December 1993 issue 19.1 percent of the ads feature emblematic Spanish, but only 6.7 percent of the ads in the January-February 1994 issue, 8.9 percent of ads in the March issue, and 2.2 percent of the ads in the April issue.[9] The semiotic structure of recruiting ads with emblematic Spanish is much like those with non-linguistic Latin indexes. For example, AT&T has two ads that feature Latin and black students in high school science labs. One has no Spanish text, the other has the word *Visión* superimposed at top. Both deploy images of children in a high-tech setting to convey the importance of getting educated, invoking the same "look to the future" message as the ITT and minivan ads. In the same vein, the Air Force recruitment ad features a pilot giving a thumbs-up gesture in the cockpit of his plane, with *Adelante* (forward) across the top of the ad and text describing how the Air Force can move one forward and up, closing with the words "Aim High! ¡Hoy! [today]." In both ads, the choice of Spanish text is stylistic rather than referential, reinforcing the impact of the visual Latin indexes.

Once emblematic Spanish is introduced into copy for product ads, shifts in the construction of the addressee become evident. An increasing proportion of ads emphasize enjoying the product and the proportion of recruitment and cultural consciousness ads decreases altogether. The function of Spanish remains stylistic rather than referential, as may be seen in ads for Honda and for Stetson hats. Both encourage a sense of stylishness. The English text in the Honda ad emphasizes style ("elegance, power and self-assurance") and sense (safety and good engineering), closing with ¡*Algo grande está pasando!* (something big is happening!), which reinforces the style angle. The Stetson ad shows only a picture of the hat and the sloan "it's not just a hat . . . it's a Stetson" in Spanish and English, drawing on the idea of Stetson quality and style as standing in a class by itself. Its link to Hispanic identity is established not by any other Latin index in the ad but by an adjacent page of text and pictures announcing the Tejano Music Awards sponsored by Stetson.

Spanish text also appears emblematically in cultural consciousness oriented advertising. The Hispanic Writers' Calendar, cosponsored by the Hispanic Association of Colleges and Universities and the Miller Brewing Company, uses bilingual text (i.e., the same text in Spanish and English) on the calendar, which is pictured in the ad, but the ad copy itself is all in English. Budweiser's "Living Legacy" ad (Figure 9.2) features Spanish in the name of the musical styles in which the featured musician specialized and in the name of the school he founded. Both ads related Spanish text to art as accomplishment and to productive careers. Both stress planning for the future: calendars are used to plan future endeavors; the music school, "looking to the future," passes on music to new generations. This ad piles up Latin indexes in the way that the ITT ad does, the whole framed by a message about rational planning. It should also be noted that the addressors are major corporations (brewing companies in fact) that focus on themselves as champions of Hispanic cultural achievement.

A relatively small proportion of ads features Spanish-only text: 14.9 percent in the December 1993 issue, 6.7 percent in the January-February 1994 issue, 4.4 percent in the March issue, and 8.7 percent in the April issue.[10] These ads are mostly oriented toward consumption, generally pleasurable consumption. Of particular interest here are the ads for Johnnie Walker (Figure 9.3) and Miller (Figure 9.4). Both layer visual and linguistic indexes in ways that contrast strikingly with any other product ad. Both are vividly sexual.

The Johnnie Walker ad features a hand stroking the strings of a black guitar with gold trim, a guitar whose outline suggests a stylized female figure. The untranslated and not-entirely-translatable text, *Bolero para el palador* (*bolero* for the palate) plays on the reader's awareness of the meaning of *bolero*. Here we see a sharp contrast between referential and poetic. In the Budweiser ad featured in Figure 9.3, *bomba y plena* are referred to as objectifications of Puerto Rican culture and as career accomplishments of the featured musician; there is no sense of how they feel to people who do them. In the Johnnie Walker ad, the copy focuses

Figure 9.2.

Bolero para el paladar.

Antes, después y siempre. Etiqueta Negra.

Figure 9.3.

only on the feeling evoked by the idea of the bolero, a highly sexualized form of musical expression. The poetic function dominates here, with a focus on form for form's sake in both language and visual image: the curve of the guitar, the phonetic repetition of /r/ and /l/, the metaphor *bolero para el paladar*, the lack of reference to product information, the

Figure 9.4.

syntactic parallelism (triple adverb) in *Antes, después y siempre* (now, later, and always), the phrase *Etiqueta negra,* the translation of "'Black Label" (the name of the whiskey), which in Spanish carries the sense of a formal "black tie" affair. These layered indexes assume a reader who knows how to interpret them. By contrast, the far less sexualized Johnnie Walker Black Label ad in *Time* for December 13, 1993, features a liquor bottle inside a paperweight showing a festive winter scene with text referring to the appropriateness of serving the product at holiday gatherings.

The Miller ad, with its black-and-gold-dressed models and its use of *de etiqueta negra,* invokes a similar reading. The phrase *La Más Fria* (the coldest one—feminine) is sexualized, frequently occurring in *bolero* lyrics that play on the notion of cold women (such as the dark-eyed, dark-haired women in the ad sitting on beer coolers).[11] By contrast, the English versions of the ad use the phrases "Get out of the old, get into the cold" and "In case of extreme heat, break open." The sexualization of the Johnnie Walker and Miller ads is quite specifically Latin, drawing on specifically Spanish semantics and affiliated cultural knowledge. These are the only two advertisers that do so. The ads use language and images to play on a sense of Latin identity that stands at odds with the general framework of carefully contained rationality that shapes most of the magazine's advertising and features. At the same time, their very infrequency may be part of that framing, as if to say to the reader, "We know this is part of you but not too big or uncontrolled a part."

Other all-Spanish ads show some degree of sexualization or invoke images of sparkle, through not with the same suggestive language. There are two ads for Sears clothing with a Christmas theme in the December 1993 issue. One shows an elegantly posed dark-haired woman in a black-and-gold dress and the text *Inolvidable* (unforgettable), adding that the dresses will shine at holiday parties and bring out one's best—and they are on sale. The other, for children's clothing, also invokes visions of sparkle with the text *Esta navidad no solo el arbolito brillara* (this Christmas it isn't only the tree that will shine); it associates Spanish with domestic celebration and family affection. The same issue has an all-Spanish Kodak ad focusing on images of family and memory. The text is a translation of the English-language version of the ad (make this Christmas one you'll always remember), again making a connection between Spanish and domestic affection.

The other ads with all-Spanish text are Winston cigarettes, Goya foods, Kerns Mango Nectar, Budweiser beer (all featuring products to enjoy, the Budweiser ad also focussing on safe, controlled drinking), Colgate toothpaste (which focuses on family concerns by featuring a smiling child), and World Cup Soccer Scratch-and-Win tickets. There is one all-Spanish ad for a big-ticket item, the Toyota Camry. This uses the sentence *Aquí tiene su merecido* (Here you have your just desserts) to play up the sense of luxury and elegance, in addition to the technopoetics of a powerful engine and well-designed safety features.

Throughout these ads, the addressee emerges as someone who feels, remembers, loves family, likes to have fun, likes to look good, all qualities associated with the use of Spanish. These are also qualities that might, if not carefully contained, be associated with a highly raced perception of Hispanics as out-of-control emotional sensualists. So these qualities are sparingly invoked and surrounded by images of smart, rational, class-mobile consumers. Two advertisers run all-Spanish ads that specifically reinforce the idea of class mobility: First Union National Bank and Avon. Running a picture of a family group or a father and baby, First Union sells the idea of security, for example, *La seguridad es importante. La suya. La de nosotros.* (Security is important. Yours. Ours). The copy goes on to assure customers that First Union has been in business for over 86 years with no annual losses. In sharp contrast to the Spanish text in the Johnnie Walker and Miller ads, the ad copy emphasizes the referential, providing specific information, and thus addressing the potential consumer as an informed decision maker. There are no visual indexes of Latin identity in the ad; language itself is apparently enough.

Avon's recruitment ad, the last all-Spanish ad in these four issues, deploys other Latin indexes, that is, names and photos of three women in U.S. Latin locales (New York, Florida, California). The text of the ad is sharply directive: *¿Cuánto quieres ganar? . . . Depende de Ti* (How much do you want to earn? It depends on you) and referential (stating the hours and income each woman earned and explaining how the reader could take advantage of this opportunity). The ad's use of Spanish is geared to the gender of the addressee and her likely status as a housewife and mother who needs to organize her work schedule around home and family concerns. The Avon ad is the only ad in the four issues examined here that suggests an addressee who might not read English. At the same time, the information it provides and the assumptions it projects about the addressee imply that there need be no language barrier to economic independence.

CONCLUSION

It is no accident that Spanish is used so sparingly in *Hispanic*. The magazine provides a blueprint for acceptable ethnic diversity: One may be different in any way that does not impede achievement. An ethnic personal style works if it accents a business look. Spanish names and origin indexes work if they show where one came from and how far one came. Spanish text is generally used stylistically (rather than referentially) to enhance the vision of a class-mobile Hispanic persona with carefully contained invocations of domestic concern, pleasure, and sexuality. There is little layering of linguistic and visual indexes, as if either suffices to invoke a sense of Hispanic identity but both together might spin out of control, moving away from a vision of ethnic achievement and toward an older vision of racial stereotype.

The use of Spanish in the magazine responds to the same principles that shape attitudes toward language in the United States generally, especially the idea that uncontrolled language difference is a form of pollution. For example, when media and politicians talk about a Spanish-speaking underclass, they view Hispanics in highly racialized terms. When Spanish is seen as a challenge to public spaces assumed to be the rightful domain of English alone, as in education or balloting, racialized assumptions about Hispanics are compounded by assumptions about unwarranted group separatism that is seen as a danger to the United States as nation-state. Such public responses to Spanish-speaking people replay U.S. attitudes toward language difference that have been around since immigration from non–English-speaking countries came to be seen as a threat well over a century ago. Most groups have responded in about the only way that ethnic groups can respond to get public respect: They find ways to portray their differences as contributions, not threats, to the nation-state. This is an old principle for coming to be seen as a good ethnic citizen, and it is the principle behind the editorial and advertising policies in *Hispanic* magazine.

NOTES

1. See Urciuoli (1998) for discussion of New York Puerto Rican bilinguals' perceptions of this ideology and its effect on their experience of language.

2. Sixteen ELAs proposed between 1981 and 1990 (Crawford 1992, 112).

3. The vision of a Hispanic community proffered by Alfredo Estrada, the editor of *Hispanic*, may not be the one Flores prefers, but it does work according to Flores's definition. The problem lies in the way people in the United States, including Flores and Estrada, talk about community in terms of an assumed consensus without addressing the particular forms of social action resulting in such consensus or conflicts that may be masked by apparent consensus (see Varenne 1986). Hence there is a range of ideas as to what constitutes a community, all based on the assumption of shared experience but without specifying how, historically, that sense of sharedness is grounded and where it might not be shared.

4. For example, *Time* magazine for December 13, 1993, ran 100 pages with 53 partial- or full-page ads. All but three of these ads were consumption-oriented, mostly products (only six were for financial or insurance services). The stress in product advertising ran heavily to upscale, sensible consumption of cars, watches, computer hardware and software, and electronics. There were three liquor ads.

5. The December 1993 issue of *Ebony*, 142 pages, carried 71 partial- or full-page ads. These included 3 ads for cigarettes, 9 for clothing, 4 for pharmaceuticals, 8 for liquor and beer, 9 for cars, 6 for food, and 14 for cosmetics and hair/skin care products. *Hispanic* runs a far lower proportion of clothing, car, or liquor ads, few cigarette and food ads, and no cosmetics ads. The same issue of *Ebony* had five social-consciousness ads and one recruitment ad. The number of recruitment ads in the January 1994 issue increased to seven, as did the number of social consciousness ads, five of which were commemorations of Dr. Martin Luther King's birthday by American Airlines, Delta, Coca-Cola, Dupont, and McDonald's. In short, some of the same type of advertising appears in both magazines, but the proportions are markedly different.

6. An index is a sign of coexistence or causality. A Spanish name, dark skin, dark hair, or Spanish language may all be read as coexistential with or even "caused" by being Hispanic.

7. Decimals rounded off to nearest tenth.

8. The non-linguistic Latin-indexed ads cited here appeared in the following issues: Housing and Urban Development (1-2/94); Army/Hispanic Serving Institutions (12/93, 1-2/94, 3/94, 4/94); Chrysler-Dodge-Plymouth minivan (12/93, 1-2/94); ITT (12/93, 1-2/94); AT&T (1-2/94).

9. The ads with emblematic Spanish cited here appeared in the following issues: AT&T (12/93); USAF (12/93; 1-2/94); Honda (12/93, 1-2/94, 3/94); Stetson (3/94); Hispanic Writers' Calendar (12/93, 1-2/93, 3/93; Budweiser Living Legacy (12/93).

10. The all-Spanish ads cited here appeared in the following issues: Johnnie Walker (12/93, 3/94); Miller (12/93, 4/94); Sears (12/93); Kodak (12/93); Colgate (1-2/94); Budweiser (1-2/94); Goya (12/93, 4/94); Kerns (4/94); Winston (12/93); Toyota Camry (1-2/94); World Cup Soccer (4/94); First Union National Bank (1-2/94, 3/94); Ávon (12/93, 1-2/94).

11. Thanks to Marvette Pérez for pointing out the culture-specific aspects of bolero invoked in the Johnnie Walker and Miller ads.

REFERENCES

Anderson, Benedict. 1983. *Imagined Communities*. London: Verso.

Castro, M., M. Haun, and A. Roca. 1990. "The Official English Movement in Florida." In K. L. Adams and D. T. Brink, eds. *Perspectives on Official English: The Campaign for English as the Official Language in the USA*. Berlin: Mouton de Gruyter, 151–60.

Chock, Phyllis Pease. 1991. "'Illegal Aliens' and 'Opportunity': Myth-Making in Congressional Testimony." *American Ethnologist* 18: 279–94.

——. 1994. "Porous Borders: Retelling America in the Illegal Alien Crisis." *Political and Legal Anthropology Review* 17(2): 45–50.

Crawford, James, ed. 1992. *Language Loyalties: A Source Book on the Official English Controversy*. Chicago: University of Chicago Press.

Flores, Juan. 1993. "The Latino Imaginary: Dimensions of Community and Identity." Ms.

Grant, Madison. 1916. *The Passing of the Great Race; or, The Racial Basis of European History*. New York: Charles Scribner's Sons.

Hymes, Dell. 1974. *Foundations in Sociolinguistics: An Ethnographic Approach*. Philadelphia: University of Pennsylvania Press.

Shklar, Judith. 1991. *American Citizenship: The Quest for Inclusion*. Cambridge, Mass.: Harvard University Press.

Silverstein, Michael. 1987. *Monoglot "Standard" in America*. Working Papers and Proceedings of the Center for Psychosocial Studies No. 13. Chicago: Center for Psychosocial Studies.

Simmons Market Research Bureau, Inc. 1991. *Hispanic* Subscriber Study.

United States Code. 1952. *Aliens and Nationality: Immigration and Nationality Administration*. Title 8, Pt. 1443b.

United States Congress, House of Representatives. 1964. Immigration. Hearings before the Subcommittee No. 1 on HR7700 and 55 Identical Bills to Amend the Immigration and Nationality Act and for Other Purposes of the Committee on the Judiciary, 88th Cong., 2nd sess.

United States Immigration Commission. 1911. *Reports of the Immigration Commission*. Washington, D.C.: Government Printing Office.

Urciuoli, Bonnie. 1994. "Acceptable Difference: The Cultural Evolution of the Model Ethnic American Citizen." *Political and Legal Anthropology Review* 17(2): 16–34.

———. 1998. *Exposing Prejudice: Puerto Rican Experiences of Race, Class, and Language*. Boulder, Colo.: Westview.

Varenne, Hervé. 1986. "Drop in Anytime." In H. Varenne, ed., *Symbolizing America*. Lincoln: University of Nebraska Press, 209–28.

Walsh, Catherine. 1991. *Pedagogy and the Struggle for Voice: Issues of Language, Power and Schooling for Puerto Ricans*. New York: Bergin and Garvey.

Woolard, Katherine. 1989. "Sentences in the Language Prison: The Rhetorical Structuring of an American Language Policy Debate." *American Ethnologist* 16: 268–78.

Zentella, Ana Celia. 1988. "Language Politics in the U.S.A.: The English-only Movement." In B.J. Craige, ed., *Literature, Language and Politics in the 80's*. Athens: University of Georgia, 39–53.

———. 1990. "Who Supports Official English and Why?: The Influence of Social Variables and Questionnaire Methodology." In K. L. Adams and D. T. Brink, eds., *Perspectives on Official English: The Campaign for English as the Official Language in the USA*. Berlin: Mouton de Gruyter, 161–77.

APPENDIX 9.1

Complete list of advertising appearing in *Hispanic* from December 1993 through April 1994: Most of these are full-page ads; a few of the recruitment ads are partial-page ads appearing near the end of the magazine.

NO EXPLICIT INDEX:

Consumption of goods:

Sensible: Ford, Neon auto, Buick, GM, Chevy trucks, Toyota financing, Digital printers, Pentax cameras, Metropolitan Life booklet "Healthful Eating: A Family Affair," SPRINT. (There was also a small ad for a self-help tape entitled "Lose Your Accent." This item nicely illustrates the idea that linguistic difference is likely to be perceived as disorder and must be controlled if one is to be mobile.)

Enjoyable: Marlboro

Sensible/enjoyable: Cadillac Seville, Mercury, Ford Taurus, Chevy, Pontiac, GE appliances, J.C. Penney budget accessories

Consumption of services:
  Nations Bank, Discover, Chase Manhattan, U.S. Savings Bonds, Metropolitan Life, AFLAC insurance, State Farm, Aetna, American Physical Therapy Association, Ryder Trucks
Recruitment/opportunity:
  U.S. Department of the Interior, U.S. Department of Justice, U.S. Dept. of Commerce, Patent Office, U.S. Army, U.S. Army ROTC, Coast Guard, Air National Guard, Lockheed, Boeing, Diamond Shamrock (petroleum), JP Morgan, Morgan-Stanley (financial services), CIT (lending), Dunn & Bradstreet, Union Bank, Long Beach Bank, Resolution Trust Corp., FDIC, Chubb Insurance, New York Life, Kraft General Foods, Honda, MCI, Federal Express, UPS, Metro-North Railway, Dallas Fire Dept, Toys R Us, Nordstroms, Matsushita (electronics), Monsanto (chemicals), Chili's Restaurants, Allied Signal Aerospace, Rustoleum, John Deere, Gillette
Social consciousness:
  General Motors, Hoechst Celenese, Northern Telcom, WMX Technologies, MCI, Xerox, Nations Bank, Time-Warner, NIH, Anheuser-Busch, American Federation of Teachers and Chrysler Corp., Waste Management, Inc.
Social conscience:
  Save the Children, Department of Education

NON-LINGUISTIC BUT CLEARLY LATIN-ORIGIN INDEXES:
Indexes are specified in parentheses. The most frequent such index was models' physiognomy, meaning that the ad used dark-haired, often dark-skinned models with faces likely to be seen as Latin.
Consumption of goods:
  Sensible: Chrysler/Dodge Minivan; AT&T business telecommunications; Chevy Trucks (all models' physiognomy); IBM (name of employee).
  Sensible/enjoyable: J.C. Penney accessories; Dodge Intrepid (both models' physiognomy), Goya (name and type of products)
  Culturally conscious media/entertainment: *Hispanic Magazine Guide to Hispanic Excellence*; Latino U.S.A. on National Public Radio, Tejano Music Awards
Consumption of services:
  GMAC Smartlease; HUD (both models' physiognomy); World Travel Associates Ltd. (names of owners); Savannah College of Art and Design (name of contact person); United Airlines (Latin American map); Travel in Mexico
Recruitment/opportunity:
  Latino Elected and Appointed Officials Education Fund and Shell Oil; HEB Groceries; Toyota (both models' physiognomy); Coca-Cola (models' physiognomies, references in text); Nuskin; Dean Writter;

Rockwell; American Airlines; U.S. Army; Pitney Bowes; GE; Pruduential; West Point; U.S. Secret Service (all names/photos of featured employees or recruitees); Lockheed (references to Mayans), Prudential Philip Morris Companies (sketches of employees)

Social consciousness:

U.S. West telecommunications; Southwestern Bell; AT&T (all models' physiognomy); Pepsico (picture of Paul Rodriguez with two Hispanic executives; names/photos of employees and beneficiaries); Budweiser (saluting Dominican baseball); GM (names/photos of employees); Sara Lee (name/photo of recipient); R.J. Reynolds (photo in urban locale, models' physiognomies); Mobil (pictures, references in text); World Cup Soccer 1994 and its sponsoring businesses (soccer motif); ITT (locale and name/photo of featured manager); Philip Morris assisting in publication of volume *Hispanic Presense in the United States*; U.S. Army and Hispanic Serving Institutions (names/photos of beneficiaries); Anheuser-Busch Hispanic Scholarship Fund; Nissan (references in text, models' physiognomies)

Culturally conscious competitions, etc.:

J.C. Penney Hispanic Designers Model Search; Nestlé/*Hispanic* 1994 Teacher of the Year; Hispanic All-Star Sweepstakes; Hispanic Sales Career Seminar; 7-11/*Hispanic* Scholarship; *Hispanic*/Sathers Candy Art Contest; *Hispanic*/Miller Brewing Co. Short Story Contest; Chicago Latino Film Festival

EMBLEMATIC LINGUISTIC INDEXES (I have also specified where these use non-linguistic indexes; note that most do not):

Consumption of goods:

Sensible/enjoyable: Honda

Enjoyable: Stetson, Columbia House Music; Pepsi; MTC Mexican restaurant chain

Culturally conscious: Miller Beer Hispanic Writers' Calendar; 7-11 brochure/exhibit on Hispanic Role Models

Consumption of services:

Bank of America

Recruitment/opportunity:

AT&T (models' physiognomy); U.S. Air Force

Social/cultural consciousness:

Budweiser salutes Rafael Cepeda musician/"Living Legacy" (who) created the *Escuela de Bomba y Plena*

ALL SPANISH:

Consumption of goods:

Enjoyable: Johnnie Walker; Miller (models' physiognomy); Winston; Goya; Kerns Mango Nectar; Toyota Camry; Sears (models' physiognomies); Kodak

  Sensible: Colgate
  Sensible/Enjoyable: Budweiser
Consumption of services:
  First Union Bank
Recruitment/opportunity:
  Avon (names/photos of distributors)
Contest:
  World Cup Soccer Scratch and Win Tickets

APPENDIX 9.2

Advertising appearing in *Hispanic* in each month from December 1993 through April 1994.

December 1993. 47 ads

NO EXPLICIT INDEX: 17 ads
  Consumption of goods: 6 (3 sensible; 3 sensible/enjoyable)

  Consumption of services: 3

  Recruitment/opportunity: 6

  Social consciousness: 1

  Social conscience: 1

NON-LINGUISTIC BUT CLEARLY LATIN-ORIGIN INDEXES: 14 ads
  Consumption of goods: 3 (1 sensible; 2 sensible/enjoyable)

  Consumption of services: 3

  Recruitment/opportunity: 3

  Social consciousness: 5

EMBLEMATIC LINGUISTIC INDEXES: 9 ads
  Consumption of goods: 5 (3 enjoyable; 1 sensible/enjoyable; 1 enter-
    tainment; 1 cultural consciousness)

  Recruitment/opportunity: 2

  Social consciousness: 1

ALL SPANISH: 7 ads
  Consumption of goods: 6 (all enjoyable)

  Recruitment/opportunity: 1

January-February 1994. 75 ads

NO EXPLICIT INDEX: 40 ads
  Consumption of goods: 7 (1 enjoyable; 6 sensible/enjoyable)

  Consumption of services: 6

Recruitment/opportunity: 19

Social consciousness: 6

Social conscience: 2

NON-LINGUISTIC BUT CLEARLY LATIN-ORIGIN INDEXES: 25 ads
Consumption of goods: 2 (both sensible)

Consumption of services: 5

Recruitment/opportunity: 9

Social consciousness: 8

Culturally conscious competition: 1

EMBLEMATIC LINGUISTIC INDEXES: 5 ads
Consumption of goods: 3 (1 enjoyable; 1 sensible/enjoyable; 1 culturally conscious)

Recruitment/opportunity: 1

Social consciousness: 1

ALL SPANISH: 5 ads
Consumption of goods: 3 (1 enjoyable; 1 sensible; 1 enjoyable/sensible)

Consumption of services: 1

Recruitment/opportunity: 1

March 1994. 45 ads

NO EXPLICIT INDEX: 24 ads
Consumption of goods: 6 (2 sensible; 4 sensible/enjoyable)

Consumption of services: 2

Recruitment/opportunity: 14

Social conscience: 2

NON-LINGUISTIC BUT CLEARLY LATIN-ORIGIN INDEXES: 15 ads
Consumption of goods: 1 sensible/enjoyable

Consumption of services: 1

    travel: 1

    entertainment: 1

Recruitment/opportunity: 6

Social consciousness: 3

Culturally conscious competition: 2

EMBLEMATIC LINGUISTIC INDEXES: 4 ads
Consumption of goods: 4 (2 enjoyable; 1 sensible/enjoyable; 1 culturally conscious)

ALL SPANISH: 2 ads

    Consumption of goods: 1 enjoyable

    Consumption of services: 1

    April 1994. 46 ads

NO EXPLICIT INDEX: 19 ads

    Consumption of goods: 7 (3 sensible; 4 sensible/enjoyable)

    Consumption of services: 5

    Recruitment/opportunity: 5

    Social conscience: 5

NON-LINGUISTIC BUT CLEARLY LATIN-ORIGIN INDEXES: 22 ads

    Consumption of goods: 1 (sensible/enjoyable)

    Consumption of services: 1

    Culturally oriented media: 2

    Recruitment/opportunity: 7

    Social consciousness: 5

    Culturally conscious competitions: 6

EMBLEMATIC LINGUISTIC INDEXES: 1 ad

    Consumption of services: 1

ALL SPANISH: 4 ads

    Consumption of goods: 3 (enjoyable)

    Contest: 1

10

The Other Tongue, the Other Voice: Language and Gender in the French Caribbean[1]

Ellen M. Schnepel

LANGUAGE AND GENDER: AN OVERVIEW

With the 1980s there has been an increasing linkage of two distinct approaches to the study of culture, the symbolist and materialist schools. A recognition of the symbolic and linguistic aspects of power, domination, and global political economy has entered the anthropological debate (Gal 1989a, 345).[2] As part of this emerging concern with language and power, a new interest in language-and-gender studies has been developing quite distinct from earlier work on this topic.

During the first half of the twentieth century linguistic work relevant to issues of "women's speech" (Chamberlain 1912; Jespersen 1922; Sapir 1929; Haas 1944; Flannery 1946; Pittman 1948)[3] focused on two areas of research: ethnographic studies of "tribal" languages in which men and women spoke totally different languages, or at least different dialects;[4] and secondly, the issue of language change, e.g., the reported cases of the loss of male/female distinctions in language.[5] In these studies focusing on linguistic structure, men's language was always taken as the norm, and women's language as deviating from that norm (Conklin 1974).

Beginning in the 1970s, the study of the relationship between language and gender was generalized to all languages, not just those languages distinguished by so-called "women's speech." New approaches and methodologies to the problematic were proposed and framed within a feminist perspective. These changes were due to several related factors: first, sociolinguistic field research at the time was conducted primarily by men (among others in the U.S., Labov, Shuy, Wolfram, Riley, Gumperz, Hymes, Fasold, Stewart); and secondly, informants were predominantly, if not exclusively, male since male speech was considered the norm or representative of *both* sexes. Labov even claimed that "males are the chief exemplars of vernacular culture" (Labov et al. 1968, 41), and in his inner-city studies of language, he focused specifically on male adolescent peer groups.[6] When male speech was not studied exclusively, the speech of mixed groups was the subject, but never women by themselves.

The infusion of a feminist discourse to language (Lakoff 1973, 1974; Kramarae 1982; Thorne and Henley, eds. 1975; Thorne, Kramarare, and Henley, eds. 1983; Martin 1987; Philips et al., eds. 1987; Gal 1989b) prompted studies to focus specifically on gender-marking conventions in language—the various ways in which languages set women apart but also how women set themselves apart through language behavior distinct from the male norm—in domestic relations, at work, in the courtroom, and so on. These studies reveal that to understand the differential use of language by gender, one must acknowledge the social differentiation of the sexes, the structure of male dominance in society, and the gender division of labor in the household as well as the workplace (Rosaldo and Lamphere, eds. 1974). Thus, gender must be analyzed not in isolation but in relation to other social variables, such as class, age, social network, education, occupation, race, or ethnicity.

LANGUAGE AND GENDER IN THE CARIBBEAN: A FIELD OF STUDY

Given the importance of gender display in the Caribbean and the cultural significance of talk, one would think that gender would be an important component of language and performance studies in the region, particularly with the emerging interest in creoles and lesser known language varieties. Yet the results of our attempt to document interest in language and gender in the Caribbean are disappointing. There is Douglas Taylor's early work (1951) on the language of the Black Caribs in British Honduras (present-day Belize), in which he discusses sex-based differences in this language,[7] and studies of language shift among Amerindian groups due to changing relations of gender and labor as these communities become more integrated into the global economy (see Wright 1986).

Within creole studies hierarchical relations in talk or the foundations of inequality in speakers have been discussed in terms of racial, cultural or class domination but rarely by examining gender relations.[8] Even in Caribbean cultures and maroon societies where gender roles are more clearly stratified (e.g., S. Price 1983, 1984, on the Saramaka), scholars of language do not show a compelling interest in gender as an issue. This omission—with a few notable exceptions for the Anglophone Caribbean (Wilson 1969, 1973; Abrahams 1970, 1983; Reisman 1970, and more recently Yelvington 1989)—contrasts markedly with the numerous studies of Afro-American speech genres (e.g., riddling, joking, swearing, storytelling, gossip) or the verbal dueling among black speakers in urban areas of the U.S. (e.g., "the dozens," "sounding," "signifying," rapping, ritual insults), which may involve distinctions according to the sex of the speakers or their audience.

Whereas scholars of language have frequently focused on ethnicity to handle many language issues, we find the concept of ethnicity (cf. Barth 1969) to be insufficient in and of itself to deal with the problematic of language and power in the French Caribbean. Racial and ethnic boundaries there are fluid, forming a kind of continuum in a society which is increasingly characterized by French-Creole bilingualism. Furthermore, the semantic duality of the term *créole* renders the concept of ethnicity somewhat ambiguous for our purposes. While *créole* refers to a linguistic phenomenon shared by *all* Antilleans, it is also used to categorize the local black/mulatto/white population of Afro-European descent. In terms of social classification, it therefore excludes certain ethnic minorities in the French islands: for example, the East Indian, Syro-Lebanese, or Chinese communities, who, as more recent immigrants to the region, have been acculturated to the Creole language. Thus, to *be* "créole," and to *speak* "créole" do not merge neatly.

As creole studies in the Caribbean turn increasingly to glottopolitical issues,[9] we find gender functions as one of the more salient indices by which to examine the language-and-power relation and that it provides a much richer and more profitable approach than that of ethnicity alone. This chapter focuses on differential relations between the sexes towards language in the French *départements* of Guadeloupe and Martinique where grassroots movements exist to change the role and status of the local French-based Creoles.

Our concern here is with the complex relation between language behavior and ideology: in particular, the transmission and penetration of ideas about language and the manner in which these ideas are used and manipulated in everyday life to reinforce and reproduce systems of inequality, such as gender, class, and culture. Using anthropological data as well as evidence from sociolinguistic research in the region, we shall trace how gender distinctions in language ideologies are linked to language practice and language policy, including informal, non-governmental efforts at creole language planning.

SOCIOHISTORICAL BACKGROUND
TO GUADELOUPE AND MARTINIQUE

Under French domination since 1635, Guadeloupe and Martinique share the major currents in Caribbean history—European conquest, eradication of the indigenous Amerindian population, colonization, introduction of African slaves, development of a plantation economy based on sugar, and mercantilist expansion. These classic sugar colonies gave rise to highly stratified societies resting on three ethnic components: African slave labor, which by the end of the 17th century had surpassed the Europeans in number; a mixed-race group constituting an intermediate social stratum eager for knowledge and power; and the white creoles (known as *Békés* in Martinique and *blancs pays* in Guadeloupe). This group played the role of landed aristocrats, and following the abolition of slavery in the French islands in 1848, established themselves as a modern mercantile bourgeoisie. Within this configuration, "race" (color) and class correlated closely.

Due to somewhat divergent island histories, the intermediate group, referred to as *gens de couleur*, is numerically more important in Martinique where it exercises an influential social, economic, and political role. In Guadeloupe, this middle stratum has been much more precarious, in large part due to the devastating social and economic consequences of the French Revolution during which the white creole planters in Guadeloupe were almost totally eliminated or fled to other islands in the West Indies. This precipitated a crisis in capital which resulted in the massive introduction of metropolitan and Martinican financial interests during the course of the 19th century (Lasserre 1961, 288). To this day in Guadeloupe, non-local interests control not only the sugar industry but also the import-export, banking, and tourist industries. In addition, with these social transformations, racial mixing has occurred much less frequently in Guadeloupe than in Martinique. As a result, the development of a middle class (composed essentially of the professional classes of doctors, lawyers, pharmacists) is a relatively recent phenomenon in Guadeloupe (Beaudoux-Kovats and Benoist 1972).

With the passage of the assimilationist law on March 19, 1946, these French colonies (along with French Guiana on the northeastern coast of South America and Réunion in the Indian Ocean) were transformed into "Départements d'Outre-Mer" (DOM), subject to the same administrative law and, theoretically, the same rights and privileges as *départements* in the metropole. Political assimilation was not, however, an abrupt or unexpected modification of colonial status but rather the logical culmination of a century-long process of progressive incorporation of these territories into metropolitan France. The 1946 law merely accelerated this movement and contributed to the expansion of French institutions (the national educational system, social services, political organizations, communication and transportation networks) to the new DOM.

Departmentalization ushered in an era of widespread social changes, among them the installation of a highly centralized governmental infrastructure. This was accompanied by a visible influx of metropolitan French (or *métros*) to the Antilles who filled positions as upper-level administrators, civil servants, technocrats, and cadres in the enlarged police and military forces. In spite of land reform, attempts to diversify the economy, and other large-scale economic transformations—e.g., the decline of the sugar industry and agriculture, urbanization, and expansion of the tertiary sector—Guadeloupe more than Martinique has retained its rural character, and 14 percent of its active working population is employed in the primary sector (INSEE 1988, 9). Nonetheless, these economic changes precipitated the exodus of country people to the city. Today, one-fourth of the Guadeloupean population lives in the urban centers of Pointe-à-Pitre/Raizet and Basse-Terre; in Martinique, the more modern of the two islands, close to one-third of the population of 360,000 (according to census figures in 1990) lives in the region of the capital, Fort-de-France. In addition, beginning in the 1960s, one has witnessed large-scale migration to France of Antilleans of all social strata in search of education, jobs, and training. These migratory flows have created new inter-ethnic tensions on both sides of the Atlantic.

A decade after the implementation of political assimilation, many Antilleans who had originally supported the change in political status had become disillusioned with the policy. Rather than leading to full social and economic equality, political integration had brought about increased economic and commercial dependency on the metropole and a progressive loss of cultural autonomy. With the fading of cultural distinctions, new demands for group identity and local control began to be expressed. In Martinique, a movement for autonomy arose in the late 1950s, led by Aimé Césaire and his newly created party, the Parti Progressiste Martiniquais (PPM). In Guadeloupe, discontent was manifested more vocally through an independence movement which emerged in the 1960s with the formation of the group GONG (Groupe d'Organisation Nationale de la Guadeloupe), and this movement has undergone significant changes over the last two decades. As a result of these parallel anti-colonialist movements, promoted by workers', peasants, as well as teachers' unions, and by leftist and far-left political

parties, the right by default has become the defender of departmentalization and assimilation. Since the election in May 1981 of the Socialist
candidate, François Mitterrand, as President of France a policy of de-
centralization or regionalization has been increasingly pursued.

Earlier in this article we spoke of the discontinuities in the socioeconomic histories of Guadeloupe and Martinique. Similarly the islands
have followed two very different courses of action since 1981. Prudence
and calm have ensued in Martinique where Césaire announced a mor-
atorium on the status issue while PPM leaders expressed the need to
address workers' economic and social demands instead of focusing on
the struggle for national liberation. With no leader of the dimension of
Césaire nor any part of the force of the PPM, a climate of revolutionary
violence has characterized Guadeloupe (Canneval 1989). Calling for an
armed struggle, militant *indépendantistes* embarked on a period of ter-
rorist attacks and bombings in a strategy to destabilize an already
weakened economy. The sector most affected was the tourist industry,
which to this day has not fully recovered. In 1989, amnesty was granted
to the leaders of ARC (Alliance Révolutionnaire Caraïbe), and a certain
calm has returned to Guadeloupe.

Today local protests over the status question have lost much of their
popular appeal as new concerns are being registered with respect to
European integration and its consequences for the French Antilles.

THE SOCIAL CONTEXT OF LANGUAGE
IN THE FRENCH ANTILLES: TRADITIONAL
AND EMERGING ATTITUDES

Since colonization in the 17th century, two languages have co-existed
in the French Antilles: French, the language of the original *colons* and
now the official code of schools, government, courts, and church; and
a local vernacular, French-lexicon Creole, which originated during the
slavery era. Creole developed in the colonial plantation society and is
now the vehicle of local traditions and culture. French and Creole
operate in somewhat complementary ways; therefore, certain researchers have characterized the situation as that of diglossia (cf. Ferguson
1959; Fishman 1967, 1972b).[10] These two languages are acquired in
different social contexts: Creole in the home, French in the school. They
are associated with distinct social classes, although no social stratum
uses one or the other language exclusively. They are differentially
evaluated. French is held in high prestige: its power equated with that
of its speakers. Originally it was the appanage of the ruling class. Later
it expanded to the local elites, and it now includes the middle strata.
Until quite recently, Creole was considered to be a deformed variety of

French, a stigmatized *patois* associated with slave culture and lack of education, and the index of an inferior social status. At one and the same time, the two languages reflect and reinforce local systems of stratification and inequality.

Language patterns differ in the two islands. A decade after the implementation of the law on departmentalization, an ethnologist asserted that community life in Guadeloupe had retained much more of its African heritage and cultural influences than in Martinique (Leiris 1955). In spite of French hegemony and sociocultural transformations over the course of 45 years, the vitality of Creole is evident in Guadeloupe and its survival is not threatened to the same degree as is the case in Martinique. The distribution of Creole as well as its usage by diverse social strata across a wide range of contexts contrast sharply with existing language norms in Martinique where the French language and culture have penetrated island life and mores more deeply, widely, and perhaps one could say, successfully.

Today nationalist movements on both islands are revaluating Creole, transforming it into a cause and symbol of Antillean cultural and linguistic identity. The defense of Creole has been waged on several fronts: graphic (through the elaboration of a writing system for Creole), literary (through the production of texts in a variety of genres), and pedagogical (through popularization of the phonetic script and an attempt to introduce Creole in the school system). At the same time, Creole has been "unleashed" in new oral domains, such as the broadcast media, political discourse, and more relaxed patterns of usage.

Yet with the simultaneous currents of increased penetration of the French language (i.e., top-down) and renewed usage of Creole (i.e., bottom-up), there has never been any systematic survey in either island to determine the proportion of monolingual Creole speakers, the percentage of bilinguals, the nature of linguistic variation,[11] or even the rates of literacy[12] (evaluated, of course, only in terms of French). In fact, numerical figures for the degree of bilingualism or monolingualism in each island are manipulated to serve various political agendas. Assimilationists, on the one hand, stress the essentially bilingual nature of the society; nationalists, on the other hand, exaggerate the number of people whose French competence and comprehension are poor.

Even with the cultural awakening and a new frame of reference which associates Creole with solidarity and local values, linguistic ambivalence persists. The following quotation from a Guadeloupean newspaper in 1944 would today be received with humor by some and agreement by others.

[. . .] Vers la fin du siécle dernier, le français était la langue des bourgeois, des gens distingués par leur richesse ou leur haute position sociale. Il était le pendant du piano, du carosse, du pince-nez à chaînette d'or et autres attributs d'une bourgeoisie fastueuse et opulente. Il était la langue d'une classe. Les gens pauvres devaient se complaire dans l'humilité et n'osaient montrer les oreilles en pratiquant une langue qu'ils n'avaient pas la possibilité d'apprendre convenablement. Aujourd'hui, grâce à la diffusion de l'instruction qui en assure la vulgarisation, il est devenu tout simplement la langue des gens polis, de tous ceux qui montrent de la correction dans les manières et le langage. [. . .]

Le créole, patois vague et sans souplesse, doit sa vitalité à deux facteurs essentiels: 1) à l'emprise de l'habitude qui conduit trop de nos lettrés à en user immodérément au mépris de toute dignité; 2) à l'ignorance, pour nos illettrés, d'idiomes plus "nobles." Il en résulte que le créole prime le français dans un pays pourtant bien français de coeur et d'aspirations.

Il n'en reste pas moins vrai que le créole est en plus d'un point frappé de stérilité. A cause de l'insuffisance de son vacabulaire, de la sécheresse de ses vocables, son usage se limite à l'expression de la connaissance vulgaire. Il est incapable de traduire, avec leurs variétés, les acquisitions de la science moderne, ce terme pris dans son sens générale. Il ne peut suffire qu'aux ignorants. Sa syntaxe, instable et imprécise, varie avec les colonies où il est usité, voire avec les parties d'une même colonie. [. . .][13]

HOW THE LINGUISTIC DUALITY PLAYS OUT ON THE LOCAL SCENE

During research undertaken in 1981 and 1982 (Schnepel 1982) in Guadeloupe in St. François, an agricultural and fishing community in the process of transforming to a tourist economy, we administered a survey questionnaire on language attitudes and behavior to a sample of 30 individuals, selected to reflect the diversity of the population in gender, age, class, and ethnicity. A direct interview followed the inquiry. Among those questioned, there was almost total agreement that courting is more appropriate in French, though use of Creole by the couple afterwards is more socially approved. On the other hand, Creole was widely acclaimed by both women and men of all ages and classes to be the preferable language for jokes and humor, the code more suitable for the expression of anger and the language of choice for insults. Nonetheless there were gender taboos in language. Respectable women were not to use certain expressions. In Creole, the most extreme form of insult is a phrase *kouni a manman-w*[14] ("your mother's vagina") or *kyou a manman-w* ("your mother's behind" or "your mother's ass"), which strikes at the very strong attachment of a man to his mother and points to the fact that any aspersion of one's mother in the West Indies is an equally serious insult (see Wilson 1969, 135). Such sexual taboos abound and are an important tool in maintaining social structures.

Further questioning and observation of language practice revealed that among the middle strata, the women tended to *under-report* their use of Creole while women in the lower strata *over-reported* their use of French in the household (Schnepel 1982). The men of varying social class backgrounds, however, were much less self-conscious in admitting their use of Creole, singling out the importance of speaking it with childhood friends and in community settings. These accounts seemed to replicate Trudgill's (1972) findings in Norwich, England, which revealed that women of working and middle-class backgrounds exhibited speech forms closer to the standard and, in fact, over-reported their use of prestige forms. In contrast, men from these same status groups not only used more "lower-class" speech forms, but attached a positive value (referred to as "covert prestige") to often stigmatized speech features which were associated with membership in the working class. Thus, in order to signal their masculinity and sound more "macho," men tended to identify with lower-status groups by imitating their speech, while women of all class backgrounds (except the lowest) were known to reproduce the speech of the dominant group or "hypercorrect" towards the standard. Trudgill's explanation for this difference between the sexes in linguistic behavior, which he labelled linguistic insecurity, was that women try to compensate for their subordination by signaling status linguistically. When lacking occupational status, women more than men rely on symbols of status, such as correct and prestigious speech.

Certain feminists have contested Trudgill's analysis. Aebischer (1985) questions on what basis Trudgill establishes the equation: hypercorrection = linguistic insecurity. She offers an alternate explanation. Instead of being a sign of linguistic insecurity, she states that hypercorrection is the manifestation of "hyperadaptation" in the sense that Kafka gives to it in *The Trial*, in qualifying the behavior of a foreign person.

> Having perfectly internalized the cultural norms of a society which one wishes to integrate and in which one seeks acceptance, this person not only adheres to it but accentuates it (Aebischer 1985, 42, author's translation).

According to her, hypercorrection among certain women is a subjective phenomenon of hyperadaptation (*ibid.*). In our opinion, this linguistic behavior can be linked to the identification or emulation of the individual with a culture—whether his/her own or that of the Other.

Was there then in the French Antilles a subtle gender distinction in who identifies more closely with Creole and who uses it more frequently? Or were the self-reported accounts of language usage by

Guadeloupean women merely indications of the penetration of the dominant ideology which conflicted with real language practice (see Woolard 1985)? As scholars of the relationship of language attitudes to behavior point out:

> The declarations of those questioned about their behavior, whether this be linguistic or other, are called representations. In other words, what people believe they are doing or saying is the expression of their ideology. [. . .] this ideology influences in a certain way their real behavior, but it cannot be said that the two are entirely interrelated (Kremnitz 1983, 118–19, author's translation).

When we later questioned people in St. François about who spoke "un bon créole," or who were the most widely respected *conteurs* (storytellers) in Creole,[15] invariably the names given were those of older men not women, even though several people spoke fondly of the role of their grandmothers in transmitting oral traditions. One notable exception was an 80-year-old woman, a cobbler in the neighboring town who was also a performer (guitarist/singer).[16] At our first meeting, she was dressed in pants and along with her male friends, we spent the afternoon drinking rum and dancing to music on an old phonograph in her home. Later that same day, when we returned to St. François, local men were amused by our afternoon foray and remarked in Creole: *"ka fè zanmi"* (which signifies in French, "she's a lesbian"). The issue here is certainly not sexual orientation but rather local representations of what constitutes proper behavior befitting a woman. Other examples in Creole abound. For example, the Creole expression *on mal-fanm* (placing the male marker before the noun for "woman") means literally a 'male-woman.' The phrase refers to a strong-willed woman and has a pejorative significance, implying that the woman doesn't know her place.[17] This is just one example of how language sets women apart as a group.

> Language is an arbitrary system of signs and symbols which serves to categorize the world in some socially agreed upon fashion. Speakers of the same language share, as their common heritage, the same set of linguistic categories. Among the most frequent categorizations is the designation of sex. [. . .] When women become a special group each time they are referred to, the speakers of a sex-marking language come to think of them *as* a special group, differing in many more ways from men than by sex alone (Conklin 1974, 51).[18]

GENDER AS A FACTOR IN LANGUAGE EVALUATION

But let us pursue the issue of the linguistic subordination of Creole and the over-evaluation of French by women. Madeleine Saint-Pierre

(1972, 257-58), in a study of language usage in the community of Trinité in Martinique, found that women generally are more inclined to avoid Creole than are men, and she questioned if this is because women speak more often than men to young children to whom they have the responsibility of giving the very best. Other scholars also allude to the tendency of women to speak more often in French when they meet in the city whereas men will speak together more easily in Creole (André 1987, 64). While this division, masculine-Creole/feminine-French, is certainly not rigid, it clearly operates.

A recent study by the sociolinguist Christian March (1989, 1990) examined what languages mothers use when addressing their children, to determine whether there exists a linguistic subordination more accentuated among mothers and, if so, to attempt to explain it. This research was conducted at a women's center serving 439 mothers in Lamentin, the second largest commune in Martinique. The sample comprised 34 women (90% from economically disadvantaged backgrounds and 10% from the middle strata), all mothers with children under the age of six. The sample was divided into two age groups: 17–25 (n = 16) and 26–39 (n = 18); and distinguished between single mothers (n = 20) and those living as a couple (n = 14).

March administered a questionnaire on language usage and analyzed responses as reflections of ideologized representations. The women reported a low frequency of Creole use and a high frequency of French use in a variety of situations when speaking with their children, *except in situations when they were angry*. Two-thirds of the mothers questioned (64.71%) reported that they rarely used the vernacular with their child, whereas the same percentage used Creole when angry with the child (March 1990, 56–57). When the mothers were questioned if the fathers used Creole with the child, according to the responses of the mothers, the majority of fathers (67.65%) spoke Creole "rarely" (44.12%) or "never" (23.53%) with the child, but used French "always" or "often" with them (March 1990, 59). While it is important here to distinguish between self-reported language usage and actual behavior and to interrogate the fathers themselves, March believed that the mothers who were questioned "used" the fathers as an example of representative authority (March 1989, 59). The fathers thus served as a confirmation of the mothers' representation of reality and their value system.

Additional questions about the mothers' language usage with other members of the household or with visitors revealed a greater usage of Creole, except when speaking with other children not their own, in which case French was used (88% of the mothers questioned). March concluded that the high valuation of French in exchanges with children was due to social pressures on mothers as the chief socializing agent in the family, particularly in female-headed households. Likewise it was due to the reality that success and social mobility passed through the French educational system where instruction was in the French language. Speaking French to their children was a maternal strategy to prepare the child for the eventuality of attending school in the belief that the child would experience fewer problems, such as linguistic interference from Creole.

Other ideologized representations of language emerge when the gender and age of children are examined. Our own survey in 1981-82 (mentioned earlier) pointed out that adults' attitudes towards their children's language behavior differed according to the sex of the child. Middle-class informants, from francophone households, mentioned it was more acceptable for a little boy to speak Creole than for a little girl. For example, the son often had the liberty to speak Creole with his father or other male visitors, but the same behavior was denied the daughter who was to maintain "politeness" (i.e., speaking French). Furthermore, swearing in Creole was the marker of being *"on ti-mal,"* part of the cult of masculinity, which was associated with positive evaluation and produced amused reactions among adults: *ou ka senti on nonm a prézan* ('you are a man now') (André 1985, 53).

Among young children in creolophone households, it is not uncommon to find little boys who know no French; and in francophone households, little girls who are unfamiliar with Creole. This pattern was confirmed by a retired primary school teacher who mentioned that in the days of single sex schools, she invariably used Creole in classroom instruction with her boys in Petit-Bourg, in Guadeloupe. Among metropolitan families, another aspect of gender-marking in language acquisition emerged, namely the greater accessibility of Creole to metropolitan boys than girls. For example, one 11-year-old son of a gendarme in St. François had picked up Creole rapidly from his Antillean school peers while a metropolitan girl of the same age whose parents managed a pastry shop in the town had little access to Creole as her Antillean girlfriends all spoke to her in French.[19]

To understand this solidarity of language-and-gender, one must grasp the particular complicity which ties Creole to the sexual (see André 1987). In a general way, Creole is connoted with being "common" (*vulgaire*), "dirty" (*malpropre*), or "badly brought up" (*malélivé* in Creole), while French is "respectable." If a man provokes or addresses a woman on the street, he does it in Creole. When he undertakes to court her, as we mentioned earlier, it is always in a polite fashion, keeping the sexual at a distance; and in order to set the sexual act apart, he expresses himself in French.

The two languages evoke the respective positions of the man and the woman in relation to sexuality: virility of the male versus modesty or reserve of the other.[20] Creole is not at a loss in vocabulary to exalt virility, but according to André, respectability can only be expressed through French.[21] The relationship between Creole and that which is sexual limits or circumscribes Creole's usage by a girl: a girl who speaks Creole, whatever she says, takes the chance of being "crude," of being chastised for cursing, and thus incurring shame.

LOCAL REPRESENTATIONS OF ORALITY AND LITERACY IN CREOLE

In the French Antilles, as the child enters secondary school, there is more acceptance of the use of Creole in the home. This mirrors changes in the life cycle of the child, with secondary school viewed as a rite of passage, a marker of a certain degree of maturity when the child is able to take on more individual responsibilities.

Although attitudes and norms towards the *oral* usage of Creole relax after the child enters secondary school, parents in Martinique and Guadeloupe are overwhelmingly hostile to Creole *literacy* classes in school.[22] The reality hardly merits their fears: in the early 1980s, in the French Antilles, only one secondary school in Capesterre Belle-Eau (Guadeloupe) offered supplementary Creole instruction through an experimental program to teach reading and writing. Of 840 eligible students, only 51 (6%) had enrolled voluntarily, with parental approval, in 1984-85, the second year of the official program.[23]

We were able to interview only a very small sample of mothers (just 15) who had children in the Creole classes. Two different discourses emerged. The lower-class mothers accepted the Creole literacy program on the basis that the classes would help their children distinguish between the two languages. Creole was accepted and viewed as a bridge to better mastery of French which would play a significant role in the child's later access to jobs and material resources. Mothers from the middle strata who were civil servants, teachers or administrators, and displayed a nationalist orientation, approved of the classes not due to some kind of compensatory explanation, as with mothers in the lower strata, but rather as a "right to cultural difference." This group of mothers, who considered themselves progressive, felt strongly about their children's need to recognize Antillean (Guadeloupean) culture and the Creole language as sources of enrichment and pride. This attitude was particularly strong among those civil servant parents who had just returned from years of residence in France.

Behind these distinct but complementary discourses, in our opinion, was the linguistic ambivalence of the two groups of mothers. On the one hand were economically disadvantaged mothers with limited French competence, who had been brought up in creolophone households. In the interview with us they often code-switched between Creole and French—but a French marked by "creolisms." On the other hand were upwardly mobile, politically conscious middle-class mothers who spoke a highly gallicized variety of Creole and whose education or residence abroad had alienated them from their native culture.

Within this very small sample of mothers, differential linguistic performances (i.e., creolized French of the lower strata and gallicized Creole of the middle strata) *related* indirectly to their favorable attitudes towards the Creole classes. However, each group's rationale was different: on the one hand, compensation, or the desire to master French; on the other, cultural pride, or the desire to master Creole. Ultimately these reasons were linked to the social class to which the mothers belonged. In each case, the mothers did not want their children to repeat their own personal, yet highly divergent, experiences with language: incomplete acquisition of French for those of the lower strata, and loss of the more popular or "authentic" form of Creole for those of the middle strata.

THE CREOLE MOVEMENT: LANGUAGE AND POWER IN THE ANTILLES

The debate and discourses surrounding the promotion of Creole in both Martinique and Guadeloupe are followed with interest only by a minority of people, primarily the intellectual elites with a nationalist orientation. The emergence of a new ideology founded on the revaluation of Creole is promoted by cultural and political militants (teachers, linguists, artists, performers, members of nationalist trade unions and political parties) who are, with a few exceptions, male. They are competent speakers of French who have become "re-creolized" after being alienated from their own local culture, either by growing up in families where Creole was forbidden to be spoken or through their years in France pursuing university studies. For the most part, the wives or female companions of the cultural militants do not share a commitment to the "Creole cause," and in a number of cases the spouses are metropolitan French.

One could extrapolate from the above observations and conclude that Antillean women are caught between competing ideologies: the dominant French ideology and an oppositional nationalist ideology, formulated, controlled and disseminated by a group of male "proto-elites" (Fishman 1972a). Bourdieu (1977) claims that the ability to impose a language (or language variety) as the legitimate form depends upon the authority of the speakers, the efficacy of their discourse, and their power to convince. The failure of the new pro-Creole discourse is related to the fact that the spokesmen do not have a credible, authentic

voice capable of convincing others—in particular, women and mothers—of the authority of their ideas.

Popular resistance to the new Creole ideology by parents, especially
women, is not founded on an intrinsic hostility to Creole, or
"Creolophobia," for Creole holds sentimental attachments for many
people.[24] The attitude which is most common along Antilleans, particularly the lower and working classes, is an urgent desire to master
French which does not necessarily imply hatred or scorn for Creole (see
Giraud 1985). In the "linguistic market" of the French Caribbean,
French and Creole occupy different niches, each with its own "value"
or "capital" in a system of local evaluation currently undergoing re-ex-
amination. French, however, dominates the market and is the norm
against which the prices of the other modes of expression are defined
(see Bourdieu 1977). In a sense women, who are mothers conscious of
their role as agents of cultural transmission to their children, are rejecting the "symbolic capital" of Creole on the linguistic market—defined
as the school, administration, workplace—where French is the language of social mobility, prestige, power and persuasion. In such a
context, the quest for group identity and linguistic rights conflicts with
basic material needs—such as education, jobs, and economic security—
especially when the vernacular language is equated with deprivation
from upward mobility for themselves and their children. In the choice
between economics and cultural nationalism, stomach wins out over
the heart.

On another level, popular resistance to Creole's promotion must be
understood within the changing meanings and uses of the vernacular
within the society. The special place of Creole in oral domains is not
challenged. In fact, it is currently in vogue, as shown in the widespread
popularity of Creole songs and *zouk* music (see Prudent 1989), performed by Antillean bands, such as Kassav'. These musicians and
singers are for the most part male, with the exception of the singer
Jocelyne Beroard. But there is opposition to the new "package" in which
Creole is being marketed which includes its written form and its new
role in literacy. For many people there already exists a written language,
French, with a well respected literary tradition and international status,
which functions quite well in its assigned task.[25]

Although the anti-assimilationist, nationalist ideology promotes the
notion that Creole is a language in its own right and the source of a
distinct Antillean identity, the activities of partisans of this avant-garde
movement are conceived very much in the image of French. The leaders
are, in fact, seeking to promote a traditional cultural form through
modern strategies, institutions, and forms. Their first priority was to
design a phonetic graphic system for the language, based on a scientific
coherence between sound and grapheme, in order to break with previ-

ous etymological spellings. The next step was to popularize the writing system through literacy campaigns and the production of literary works in Creole, with the eventual intent of introducing Creole instruction in the schools.

Between the intentions manifested and the realization of this project, there have been several obstacles. For one, very few experiments in literacy have been attempted, except for the work of Dany Bebel-Gisler and her staff at the school Bouadoubout in Lamentin, Guadeloupe. Secondly, while in theory the orthographic system was conceived for its simplicity and ability to unite the other Creole dialects of the Lesser Antilles, the reality proves otherwise. Aside from nationalist groups, the general populace finds the spelling inherently complex. If and when they write Creole, they do so in their own spontaneous fashion. Furthermore, no one has attempted an inquiry among the populace to determine which graphic system is preferred and along what criteria (for example, the "most Creole," the most readable, the most beautiful or aesthetically pleasing, etc.).[26] In addition, the variety of Creole promoted by certain intellectuals, which includes obscure neologisms and French-influenced discourse styles, is quite impenetrable to speakers of a more popular variety of Creole. This intellectualized Creole, based on the notion of "déviance maximale" with respect to French, appears much like a secret code, known and used only by the few who are initiated. Among them are included the university research group GEREC and the founding members of the Martinican monthly, *Grif-an-tè* (1977-1982), published exclusively in Creole. All of these individuals were men.

Within the nationalist debate, the women's question has been totally ignored. The protagonists have preferred to emphasize the language-and-politics issue, using it as a mask for a racialized discourse. They have not addressed the gender issue nor attempted to link the liberation of Antillean women—in social, economic, or political terms—with the national question. An anecdote may serve to illustrate this more clearly. On the occasion of a political rally in Capesterre Belle-Eau in November 1984, to raise funds for several Guadeloupean *indépendantiste* political prisoners who were on trial, Leila Casubie, a former political prisoner herself, was invited to speak. Addressing the Antillean audience in French, she apologized profusely for not speaking Creole, singling out her upbringing in France as the reason. Several weeks later, the anti-colonialist magazine, *Antilla Kréyòl*, published a letter in Creole from "Layla" (the Creole spelling of her name).[27] Was it a translation> Or was it composed by her male comrades? Hence, even her own voice had symbolically been appropriated and "dubbed" in Creole by militant nationalists.[28]

Critical questions surface concerning the relationship between gender and nationalism within the ideology of *créolité*. What is the image of the authentic Antillean, and does this include women as well as men? If women are not prominent leaders, portes-paroles, or even models for the movement, what role do they play in the elaboration and transmission of alternate ideas about language and culture, particularly for the next generation? Other questions also emerge. Who is constructing Antillean female identity, since for a long time women's existence has been confined and defined by men, colonizer as well as colonized? On what models is this identity based, on French or Antillean models? With language so intimately linked to identity, how traditionally do Martinicans and Guadeloupeans refer to, and compare, their masculinities and femininities; and how is this expressed linguistically? Finally, how is language being used to serve the cause of women?[29] We have certainly raised more issues here than we can answer without further empirical research.

CONCLUDING REMARKS

In returning to the title of this paper, "The Other Tongue, The Other Voice," the question remains whether women will find their own voice or create a new voice. Certainly more empirical research in the Caribbean is needed: for example, lexicographic studies of how Creoles and other lesser known language varieties set women apart; documentation of the variety of speech genres available to women (from gossip, ritual talk, and storytelling, to sexual banter); micro-level studies, rich in ethnographic description, of how women uniquely manipulate language, how they create new or different forms of resistance—or conversely collude with their oppressors—through their language choices; and how silence as well as verbal strategies can be powerful weapons for women. There is also a need for larger, more diversified sampling of the population in which gender is examined in relation to other variables, such as class, age, social network, ethnicity, and political or cultural orientation.

What we have presented here is more a stew than a banquet, neither totally raw nor fully cooked. In the years ahead, we can eagerly look forward to new research on "the-woman-of-words" in the West Indies as more attention is given to the important and complex issue of gender voices.

NOTES

1. This article was originally published in French in the Canadian journal, *Recherches Féministes*, vol. V, no. 1 (1992): 97–123, and was entitled "Une langue marginale, une voix féminine: langue et sexe dans les études créoles aux Antilles françaises." A shortened version of this article was originally presented at the

89th Annual Meetings of the American Anthropological Association in New Orleans in December 1990. Data was collected during two different periods of field research in the Antilles. A study of changing language attitudes towards Creole was conducted from May–August 1981 and December 1981–January 1982, in the town of St. François, Guadeloupe, funded by a Masters Learning Fellowship in Social Change from the Inter-American Foundation and a grant from the Latin American and Iberian Studies Institute at Columbia University. Doctoral research examining the politics of language in the Creole movement was undertaken during 18 months of fieldwork between July 1984 and June 1986. Residence was established in Capesterre Belle-Eau, Guadeloupe, and visits made to Martinique for comparative analysis. The project was supported by the Fulbright-Hays Doctoral Dissertation Research Abroad Program, the National Science Foundation (grant #BNS-8310440), and the Spencer Foundation.

2. Within the field of the "ethnography of speaking," for example, scholars of language are examining hierarchical relations in talk, the foundations of inequality in speakers, linguistic and symbolic aspects of political-economic processes, dominant and oppositional discourses, and the interrelationship of language and politics (cf. Bauman & Scherzer, eds. 1974; O'Barr & O'Barr, eds. 1976; Hymes 1980; Gumperz 1982). Sociolinguistic attention is being given to linguistic processes as diverse as multilingualism, pidginization and creolization, linguistic nationalism, standardization, and native language literacy, while linking these processes to the history of European colonialism and capitalist expansion.

3. See for example, Alexander F. Chamberlain, "Women's Languages," *American Anthropologist* 14 (1912): 579–581; Otto Jespersen, Chapter XIII, "The Woman," in *Language: Its Nature, Development and Origin* (Macmillan, 1922), 237–254; Edward Sapir, "Male and Female Forms of Speech in Yana," in St. W. J. Teeuwen, ed., *Donum Natalicium Schrijnen* (1929), reprinted in David C. Mandelbaum, ed., *Selected Writings of Edward Sapir in Language, Culture and Personality* (Berkeley, University of California Press, 1949), 206–212; Mary Haas, "Men's and Women's Speech in Koasati," in Dell Hymes, ed., *Language in Culture and Society: A Reader in Linguistics and Anthropoligy* (Harper & Rowe, 1964), 228–233; Regina Flannery, "Men's and Women's Speech in Gros Ventre," *International Journal of American Linguistics* 12 (1946): 133–135; and Richard S. Pittman, "Nahuatl Honorifics," *International Journal of American Linguistics* 14 (1948): 236–239.

4. The only cases of so-called "women's speech" to be studied extensively were those where women's and men's speech differed radically, e.g., Yana, Carib, Koasati, so that the distinctions in pronunciation, vocabulary, and grammar were hard to overlook.

5. Apparently gender differences are among the earliest fine points vulnerable to loss or merger due to language contact or the westernization of culture. In terms of natural linguistic change and reported language decay, the male forms have become generalized to the speakers, not the female ones (Conklin 1973, 1974).

6. Labov has since been taken to task by a number of people, including Nancy Conklin. She argues (1974) that women have their own vernacular, kinds of slang, and verbal rituals. It just awaits more empirical research. Certainly with the rise of female gangs in urban areas (for example, among Hispanic youth in East Los Angeles area), the documentation and analysis of female adolescent speech will provide an interesting cross-cultural comparison with Labov's inner-city work.

7. Early missionaries and chroniclers in the 17th and 18th centuries (e.g., Breton 1665, La Borde 1674, Labat 1742) laid claim to two different languages, male speech and female speech, along the Carib Indians. It was widely believed that the Caribs had killed off the male Arawaks and taken their women as hostages. The Arawakan women continued to speak their own language and to teach it to their children, while the boys at a later age would learn their father's language. Taylor (1977:26) is credited with pointing to the fact that these were not two separate languages but rather sex-based differences. Along with Rouse (1960), Taylor proposed that in the series of Carib invasions of pre-Colombian times, Carib men killed the Arawakan men, taking the Arawakan women as wives and eventually adopting their Arawakan language. This accounted for the different linguistic origin of male and female words in the language which are Carib and Arawakan in linguistic origin respectively. In accounting for these differences, some researchers have linked the variation to social and economic stratification in a culture where men and women live separately with little overlap in tasks. Although the gender-based division of labor is mirrored in the language, no firm statements can be made about the interaction of social and linguistic stratification in maintaining the sexual status quo (Conklin 1974: 53).

8. Sociolinguistic research in the field is still fairly limited. From an initial interest in "lower-class" or "rural" speech, researchers have expanded to look at residence (urban-rural, cf. Edwards 1977), social class (non-estate/estate workers, cf. Rickford 1979), and the issue of ethnic identity (cf. Le Page & Tabouret-Keller 1985). There is, as yet, little interest in gender as a compelling issue. For example, Bickerton's study of Guyanese creole in 1975 lists his informants in the appendix, divided quite representatively according to gender and ethnicity (Creole/East Indian); yet these social criteria never figure in distinguishing speech patterns or differential patterns of language acquisition and behavior. His focus continues to be a description of Guyanese grammar and his theory of the language bioprogram.

9. Research and development of creoles have evolved quite differently in the Anglophone area from the Francophone orbit where there are on-going efforts by native scholars and lay researchers to change the status and role of French Creoles. A variety of factors accounts for this difference. Among these are: status of each creole in the different contexts, historical relation of the creole to the official language, presence or absence of a linguistic continuum, degree of popular usage of the creole, speakers' attitudes towards language planification, presence of a native movement favoring the creole's promotion, local government's posture with respect to these efforts, political status of the territory or form of nationalism present.

10. Certain linguists question the applicability of diglossia to the Francophone Caribbean. To understand the arguments, it must be pointed out that Ferguson's classic model of diglossia (1959) has been widely circulated in the region, but Fishman's extension of the theory (1967, 1972b) is largely unfamiliar to local scholars. Prudent (1980: 100–104) argues, with respect to the French Antilles, that the presence of intermediary varieties of both Creole and French— referred to locally and within the literature as "créole francisé" and "français créolisé"—precludes a two-code system. Growing evidence in individual and collective discourse points to the presence of a continuum in which the intermediary varieties are now viewed as the pivotal arena for linguistic research and attention (cf. Prudent 1978, 1981). Furthermore, it must be taken into account that for a growing number of people in Martinique and Guadeloupe, especially among the elite and middle classes, French is becoming the first language

learned in the home, thus replacing Creole as the "native" variety. In addition, certain French Antillean children first learn Creole when associating with their school peers. Hence, the functional complementarity delineated by Ferguson is too restrictive in this case, and Fishman's extension of the theory to include "user-oriented" (as opposed to "use-oriented") diglossia may be more applicable here (cf. Britto 1986). For fuller comments on this issue, see Schnepel 1990: 70–71, 419–431.

11. An early study by Lefebvre (1976:91) reports the following about linguistic variation:

> As in the case with any situation of languages in contact, there is interference between the French and Creole varieties in Martinique. [. . .] there is variation in the Martinicans' speech. Neither a uniform variety of Creole, nor a uniform variety of French, is spoken by everyone. Geographical and social varieties of both French and Creole are spoken, those ranging from Creole (C_1) to Standard French (F_1) with intermediate varieties which I will refer to as creolized French (F_2) and gallicized Creole (C_2).

12. Literacy in the French Caribbean is considered relatively high for the region due to the fact that schooling is free and compulsory until the age of 16. However, no definition of literacy (or even "functional" literacy) has been proposed nor any standard to measure it. In the 1982 census for Guadeloupe, subjects were asked to respond to the question of whether they knew how to read and write. The results for the whole population of 327,002 inhabitants, representing all age groups, were the following:

	men	women	total population
responding "yes"	81%	83%	82%
responding "no"	19%	17%	18%

(Source: *Résultats du recensement de la population dans les départements d'outre-mer, 9 mars 1982: Guadeloupe*, INSEE: Basse-Terre, 1983, p. 59.)

It should be noted that of those persons responding "no," 40% (or a bit under 24,000) were from the age group of less than five years of age; hence they represented individuals who had not yet received formal education. This would mean, then, that the overall literacy figure for the island would be higher than 82%, if one included only those persons of school-age and older.

13. The English translation reads:

> [. . .] Towards the end of the last century, French was the language of the bourgeoisie, of people distinguished by their wealth or high social position. French was the pendant of the piano, of the coach, of the pince-nez with a gold chain, and other attributes of an ostentatious and affluent bourgeoisie. It was the language of a class. Poor folk were to take pleasure in humility and dared not to practice a language which they did not have the possibility of learning adequately. Today, owing to the spread of education which ensures the vernacularization of the language, French has become quite simply the language of polite company, of men and women who show proper correctness in conduct and speech.

> Creole, a vague patois without versatility, owes its vitality to two essential factors: 1) to the habit among too many of our educated people of using it immoderately to the scorn of all dignity; 2) to illiterates' ignorance of more

"noble" languages. This has resulted in Creole taking precedence over French in a country which is nevertheless very French in sentiment as well as aspirations.

It's all the more true that Creole is, above all, characterized by sterility. Due to its insufficient vocabulary, the paucity of its words, its usage is limited to the expression of common experiences. It is incapable of translating the varied knowledge of modern science, taken in its general sense. It suffices only for the ignorant. Its syntax, unstable and imprecise, varies with each colony where it is used, even in parts of the same colony. [. . .] (A Narfez, "La vulgarisation due français par l'école," in *La Tribune Syndicale et Laïque*, no. 23, 7th year, February 1944, p. 2).

14. The present editor (Blot) has challenged my renderings as too "clinical." He prefers the glosses "mother's cunt" and "mother's ass" as best capturing the intensity of the insults. I have chosen to retain my translations and cite my difficulty as a woman in using the word "cunt." I might also mention a related incident when an earlier version of this paper, along with an earlier version of Mentore's chapter in the present volume, was originally presented at the 89th Annual Meetings of the American Anthropological Association in a session on The Cultural Construction of Gender in the Caribbean. Whereas I had translated, even then, the Creole phrase with the word "vagina," Mentore in his paper used "cunt," provoking a reaction from the audience and a comment by the discussant who drew out attention to our different renditions of the Creole insult. This example raises once again the issue of the researcher's gender and how it may significantly affect the research process and result. It shows how we have yet to come to terms with some of the very issues we study. (Note that the spelling used for Creole in this text is the system elaborated in *Dictionnaire créole-français /Diksyonné Kréyòl-fwansé* (1984:7–10) by Poullet et al.)

15. While there is a good deal of talk about talk and it appears that one is constantly being judged by the way in which one talks or acts, to speak "good French" is evaluated on different terms from speaking "good Creole." For French, it is a question of using "correct" grammar and phonology, i.e., the inclusion of rounded vowels and metropolitan accents. For Creole, while it is felt by many people that the language has no grammar, vocabulary, or structure, speaking good Creole involves the incorporation of older expressions and the ability to tell stories with piquant phrases or plays on words to a captive audience.

16. In the era before every Antillean household had television, grandmothers often told stories to the children before bedtime or rocked infants to sleep by singing traditional lullabies. Many of these musical traditions are described in M-C Hazaël-Massieux's work, *Chansons des Antilles, Comptines, Formulettes* (Paris, CNRS, 1987). In light of the role of the family in transmitting oral traditions, it is surprising that no one had mentioned any older women to us. In retrospect, we believe the question could have been framed differently.

17. French creoles lack grammatical gender. As in many creoles, the sex of animate nouns can be indicated by juxtaposition of the Creole word for "male" or "female," systematically placed in front of the word to delimit the gender, a pattern found in many West African languages (Holm 1988: 86). The morpheme *fimèl-* is more frequent than *mal-*, indicating that the form designating the male variety is often the non-marked form (cf. M-J Cérol 1987: 108). However, *fimèl-* has not sufficiently lost its autonomous semantic character to be able to be classed as a prefix in word formation (Ludwig/Poullet 1989: 164). In other cases,

even when the gender of the noun is contained in the basic meaning of the word, the morpheme *mal-* may be added as emphasis to accentuate the more masculine or "macho" qualities of the individual (e.g., *on mal-boug*, 'a young fellow on whom one can count'; *on mal-nonm*, 'a real man'). Whereas the expression *on mal-fanm* is pejorative, that of *on mal-nonm* (as in the phrase "*On mal-nonm an tini la!*" which means "It's a man that I have here!") exalts the virility of the designated male person.

18. While the amount of gender-marking in a language may indicate how important the distinction between the sexes is for that particular culture, Conklin (1974: 51) maintains that "it is very difficult to assess the relationship between the structure of a language and the behavior, or the thinking, of its speakers."

19. Similarly French women complain that their Antillean boyfriends or husbands would not speak to them in Creole and they wondered how I had learned Creole when there were no formal classes offered. Not only had I learned Creole and spoke it regularly, but I came to learn how to manipulate it also to "neutralize" my gender status. With young men, who had been raised to court women using French, I found that by replying to their advances in Creole, and repeatedly in Creole while they tried to switch the conversation to French, my language choice frustrated their efforts, as no well respecting male would court a strange lady in Creole, especially a foreign female. With the older generation of men, particularly among the working or popular classes, my speaking Creole provoked a different response. It signaled that I had "frequented" the Creole milieu and therefore was open to their sexual advances. In this case, resorting to French signaled distance in the relationship, unless of course a different message was intended and then Creole would be maintained as the language of conversation.

20. This duality may call to mind the respect-reputation dichotomy proposed by Wilson (1969, 1973) or the categories of the "behaved" and the "rude" described by Abrahams (1983) in the local evaluation of behavior, particularly with respect to gender display.

21. In the vernacular, the only possible word associating the woman and sexuality is a word reserved for male usage—*koukoun*, which designates the female sexual organ and evokes a strong libidinal charge. The plethora of sexual terms in Creole has been noted by Ludwig and Poullet (1989), but unfortunately their lexical study did not try to unearth different terminology used by women as opposed to men for parts of the body. Of interest in Ludwig and Poullet's study would be the inclusion of gender as a factor in creativity in Creole, in addition to the variables of social class, age, and geographical zone.

22. The eventuality of classes in Creole became an issue once the Chancellor of Education in the Antilles, Bertóne Juminer, made the famous "Déclaration Louisiane" in May 1983 at an international conference of creole studies. In the speech delivered by a cultural attaché, the Chancellor spoke of introducing the Creole language and culture in schools in the Antilles and French Guiana. The announcement was in keeping with the 1982 laws for "regional languages and cultures" of the French Ministry of National Education. Reaction to the Creole announcement had the effect of a bomb, especially in more francophone Martinique where the bourgeoisie was outraged.

23. Of interest was the fact that two-thirds of the students in the supplementary Creole class were female students, with a plurality of East Indian girls. This trend was not related to a greater appreciation of local culture by young girls but rather pointed to the fact that they were generally stronger students, enjoyed school, and were enthusiastic about seeing their mother tongue written for the

first time. There was also less peer ridicule for a girl to stay after regular school hours to take the extra Creole class. Whereas the boys were expected to hang out with their peers, girls' behavior was more strictly circumscribed by school and home. In fact, the hour of Creole per week was viewed by many of the female students as an act of liberation, especially for those who didn't have the opportunity to speak Creole at home if their parents forbade its use.

24. Standard language varieties tend to be favorably evaluated along the status or power dimension, and non-standard varieties along the solidarity or friendship dimension (Rickford 1985: 151).

25. To fully understand popular reactions to written Creole, one really needs to look at the different meanings and kinds of literacy in Antillean society (see Street 1984). Women's literacy may differ from men's, children's from adult's, and domestic literacy from that of the workplace. But these issues remain beyond the present scope of this paper.

26. In a seminar on the Creole language held at the Fouillole campus in Pointe-à-Pitre, Guadeloupe, in July 1984, Marie-Christine and Guy Hazaël-Massieux, linguists at the Université de Provence, undertook an inquiry of the opinions of 20 participants on graphic choices for selected Creole words. While the responses were highly interesting (see G & M-C Hazaël-Massieux, *Le créole et la vie*, Pointe-à-Pitre, Conseil Local des Parents d'Eleves du Lycée Polyvalent de Baimbridge, 1984), the limited inquiry unfortunately did not attempt to monitor potential gender-based differences in spelling preferences for Creole words.

27. *Antilla Kréyòl*, no. 3, février 1985, page 10.

28. Such appropriation or imitation of the male-imposed standard was not confined to nationalist politics. While politics is deemed essentially a male domain and few women enter it successfully in the Antilles, female politicians do resort to the aggressive, even "vulgaire" political discourse of their male counterparts, as a tactic to gain credibility while destroying their opponents. The chief exemplar of this type of verbal strategy in Guadeloupe is Lucette Michaux-Chevry of the right-wing assimiliationist party, RPR (Rassemblement pour la République).

29. For example, we had the chance to attend several meetings, both local and departmental, of the Union des Femmes Guadeloupéennes (Union of Guadeloupean Women), an organization which is linked to the Guadeloupean Communist Party (PCG). The women have adopted traditional linguistic behavior towards French and Creole: they use Creole to express solidarity or for disseminating anecdotal information; French is the official language, used for formal addresses and official business. Linguistic behavior in other women's organizations, particularly feminist groups, needs to be observed and analyzed to see whether language is being used differently.

REFERENCES

Abrahams, Roger (1970). "Patterns of Performance in the British West Indies," in Norman E. Whitten, Jr., & John F. Szwed (eds.), *Afro-American Anthropology: Contemporary Perspectives*. New York: Free Press, 163–179.

—— (1983). *The Man-of-Words in the West Indies: Performance and the Emergence of Creole Culture*. Baltimore: The Johns Hopkins University Press.

André, Jacques (1985). "Le cog et la jarre: Le sexuel et le féminin dans les sociétés afro-caribéennes," *L'Homme* 96, XXV (4): 49–75.

—— (1987). *L'Inceste focal dans la famille noire antillaise*. Paris: Presses Universitaires de France.

Aebischer, Verena (1985). *Les femmes et la langage: Représentations sociales d'une différence*. Paris: Presses Universitaires de France.

Barth, Fredrik (1969). *Ethnic Groups and Boundaries: The Social Organization of Culture Difference*. London: Allen and Unwin.

Bauman, R. & J. Sherzer (eds.) (1974). *Explorations in the Ethnography of Speaking*. Cambridge: Cambridge University Press.

Beaudoux-Kovats, Edith & Jean Benoist (1972). "Les Blancs créoles de la Martinique," in J. Benoist (éd.), *L'Archipel inachevé: culture et société aux Antilles françaises*. Montréal: Presses de l'Université de Montréal.

Bickerton, Derek (1975). *Dynamics of a Creole System*. Cambridge: Cambridge University Press.

Bourdieu, Pierre (1977). "The Economics of Linguistic Exchanges," *Social Science Information* 16(6): 645–668.

Breton, Père Raymond (1665). *Father Raymond Breton's Observations of the Island Carib: A Compilation of Ethnographic Notes Taken from Breton's Carib-French Dictionary Published in 1665*. Trans. (1958) Marshall McKuskick and Pierre Verin. New Haven: HRAF.

Britto, Francis (1986). *Diglossia: A Study of the Theory with Application to Tamil*. Washington: Georgetown University Press.

Brown, P. (1980). "How and Why Are Women More Polite: Some Evidence from a Mayan Community," in S. McConnell-Ginet, R. Borker, N. Furman (eds.), *Women and Language in Literature and Society*. New York: Praeger.

Canneval, Jacques (1989). "La Guadeloupe en première ligne," *Autrement: Antilles, espoirs et déchirements de l'âme créole* 41: 67–73.

Cérol, Marie-Josée (1987). *Le créole guadeloupéen, un exemple de planification linguistique par défaut*. Thèse de troisième cycle, Université Paris III.

Cocklin, Nancy (1973). "Perspectives on the Dialects of Women." Paper presented at the American Dialect Society, Ann Arbor, Michigan, 1973.

—— (1974). "Toward a Feminist Analysis of Linguistic Behavior," *The University of Michigan Papers in Women's Studies* 1(1): 51–73.

Edwards, Walter (1977). *Sociolinguistic Behaviour in Rural and Urban Circumstances in Guyana*. Ph.D. Dissertation, University of York.

Ferguson, Charles (1959). "Diglossia," *Word* 15: 325–340.

Fishman, Joshua A. (1967). "Bilingualism with and without Diglossia; Diglossia with and without Bilingualism," *Journal of Social Issues* 23(2): 29–38.

—— (1972a). *Language and Nationalism: Two Integrative Essays*. Rowley, Mass.: Newbury House Publishers.

—— (1972b). *Sociolinguistics: A Brief Introduction*. Rowley, Mass.: Newbury House Publishers.

Gal, Susan (1989a). "Language and Political Economy," *Annual Review of Anthropology* 18: 347–67.

—— (1989b). "Between Speech and Silence: The Problematics of Research on Language and Gender," *IPrA Papers in Pragmatics* 3(1): 1–38.

Giraud, Michel (1985). "Les conflits de langues aux Antilles Françaises: fondements historiques et enjeux politiques," *Etudes Polémiques* 34: 45–65.

Gumperz, John (1982). *Language and Social Identity*. Cambridge: Cambridge University Press.

Holm, John (1988). *Pidgins and Creoles. Theory and Structure*, vol. 1. Cambridge: Cambridge University Press.

Hymes, Dell (1980). "Speech and Language: On the Origins of Inequality among Speakers," in D. Hymes (ed.), *Language in Education: Ethnolinguistic Essays*. Washington: Center for Applied Linguistics.

INSEE (1988). *Tableaux économiques régionaux: Guadeloupe*. Basse-Terre.

Kramarae, Cheris (1982). "Gender: How She Speaks," in Ellen Bouchard Ryan & Howard Giles (eds.), *Attitudes towards Language Variation: Social and Applied Contexts*. London: Edward Arnold.

Kremnitz, Georg (1983). *Français et créole: ce qu'en pensent les enseignants: le conflit linguistique à la Martinique*. Hamburg: Buske.

La Borde, R. P. de (1674). *Voyage qui contient une relation exacte de l'origine, moeurs, coutumes, religion, guerres et voyages des Caraïbes, sauvages des Isles Antilles de l'Amérique*. A. Liège, Belgium: chez P. van de Aa.

Labov, W., P. Cohen, C. Robins, & J. Lewis (1968). *A Study of the Non-Standard English of Negro and Puerto Rican Speakers in New York City*. Final Report, Cooperative Research Project 3288. 2 vols. Philadelphia: U.S. Regional Survey.

Lakoff, Robin (1973). "Language and Woman's Place," *Language in Society* 2: 45–79.

—— (1975). *Language and Woman's Place*. New York: Harper & Row.

Lasserre, Guy (1961). *La Guadeloupe: étude géographique*, 2 vols. Bordeaux: Union Française d'Impression.

Lefebvre, Claire (1976). "Discreteness and the Linguistic Continuum in Martinique," in Albert Valdman & Emile Snyder (eds.), *Identité culturelle et francophonie dans les Amériques*. Québec: Les Presses de l'Université Laval.

Leiris, Michel (1955). *Contacts de civilisations en Martinique et en Guadeloupe*. Paris: UNESCO.

Le Page, R. B., & André Tabouret-Keller (1985). *Acts of Identity: Creole-Based Approaches to Language and Ethnicity*. Cambridge: Cambridge University Press.

Ludwig, Ralph, & Hector Poullet (1989). "Approche d'un lexique scriptural—Kijan mo gwadloupéyan ka pitité?" in Ralph Ludwig (ed.), *Les créoles français entre l'oral et l'écrit*. Tübingen, Narr: 155–180.

March, Christian (1989). *Une autre approche épilinguistique de la question de la langue maternelle en Martinique. Une enquête chez les mères au centre PMI du Lamentin*. Mémoire de DEA en linguistique, Université de Rouen–Haute Normandie.

—— (1990). "L'attitude des mères martiniquaises dans le processus de minoration linguistique." *Nouvelle Revue des Antilles* 3: 53–63.

Martin, Emily (1987). *The Woman in the Body*. Boston: Beacon.

O'Barr, William M., & Jean F. O'Barr (eds.) (1976) *Language and Politics*. The Hague: Mouton.

Philips, Susan et al. (eds.) (1987). *Language, Gender and Sex in Comparative Perspective*. New York: Cambridge University Press.

Poullet, Hector, Sylviane Telchid, & Danièle Montbrand (1984). *Dictionnaire créole/français*. Fort-de-France: Hatier.

Price, Sally (1983). "Sexism and the Construction of Reality: An Afro-American Example." *American Ethnologist* 10(3): 460–476.

—— (1984). *Co-wives and Calabashes*. Ann Arbor: University of Michigan Press.

Prudent, Lambert-Félix (1978). "Diglossie ou continuum: quelques concepts problématiques de la créolistique moderne appliqués à l'Archipel Caraïbe." Communication du Colloque Théories et Pratiques de la Sociolinguistique, Université de Rouen, Haute-Normandie.

—— (1980). *Des Baragouins à la langue antillaise: Analyse historique et sociolinguistique du discours sur le créole*. Paris: Editions Caribéennes.

—— (1981). "Diglossie et interlecte." *Languages* 61 (mars): 13–38.

—— (1989). "La Pub, le Zouk et l'Album." *Autrement: Antilles, espoirs et déchirements de l'âme créole* 41: 209–216.

Reisman, Karl (1970). "Cultural and Linguistic Ambiguity in a West Indian Village," in Norman E. Whitten, Jr., & John F. Szwed (eds.), *Afro-American Anthropology: Contemporary Perspectives*. New York: The Free Press.

Rickford, John (1979). *Variation and Change in a Creole Continuum: Quantitative and Implicational Approaches*. Ph.D. Dissertation, University of Pennsylvania.

—— (1985). "Standard and Non-Standard Language Attitudes in a Creole Continuum," in Nessa Wolfson & Joan Manes (eds.), *Language of Inequality*. Berlin: Mouton.

Rosaldo, Michelle Zimbalist, & Louise Lamphere (eds.) (1974). *Woman, Culture, and Society*. Stanford: Stanford University Press.

Rouse, Irving (1960). "The Entry of Man into the West Indies," *Papers in Caribbean Anthropology*, no. 6.

Sainte-Pierre, Madeleine (1972). "Créole ou français? Les cheminements d'un choix linguistique," in Jean Benoist (ed.), *L'Archipel inachevé*. Montréal: Les Presses de l'Université de Montréal.

Schnepel, Ellen M. (1982). "Changing Attitudes Towards Creole in St. François, Guadeloupe, FWI." Report of a sociolinguistic investigation sponsored by the Inter-American Foundation.

—— (1990). *The Politics of Language in the French Caribbean: The Creole Movement on the Island of Guadeloupe*. Ph.D. Dissertation, Columbia University.

—— (1992). "Une langue marginale, une voix féminine: langue et sexe dans les études créoles aux Antilles françaises." *Recherches Féministes*, V (1): 97–123.

Street, Brian (1984). *Literacy in Theory and Practice*. Cambridge: Cambridge University Press.

Taylor, Douglas (1951). *The Black Carib of British Honduras*. Viking Fund Publications in Anthropology, no. 17. New York: Wenner-Gren Foundation for Anthropological Research.

—— (1958). "Use and Disuse of Languages in the West Indies." *Caribbean Quarterly* 5(1): 67–77.

—— (1977). *Languages of the West Indies*. Baltimore: The Johns Hopkins University Press.

Thorne, Barrie, & Nancy Henley (eds.) (1975). *Language and Sex: Difference and Dominance*. Rowley, Mass.: Newbury House.

Thorne, Barrie, Cheris Kramarae, & Nancy Henley (eds.) (1975). *Language, Gender, and Society*. Rowley, Mass.: Newbury House.

Trudgill, Peter (1972). "Sex, Covert Prestige and Linguistic Change in the Urban British English of Norwich," *Language in Society* 1: 179–195.

Wilson, Peter (1969). "Reputation and Respectability: A Suggestion for Caribbean Ethnology." *Man* 4(1): 70–84.

—— (1973). *Crab Antics: The Social Anthropology of English-Speaking Negro Societies of the Caribbean*. New Haven: Yale University Press.

Woolard, Kathryn (1985). "Language Variation and Cultural Hegemony: Toward an Integration of Sociolinguistic and Social Theory." *American Ethnologist* 12(4): 738–748.

Wright, Pamela (1986). *Language Shift and the Redefinition of Social Boundaries among the Carib of Belize*. Ph.D. Dissertation, City University of New York.

Yelvington, Kevin A. (1989). "Flirting as a Joking Relationship: Scenes from a Trinidadian Factory." Paper presented at the 14th Annual Conference of the Caribbean Studies Association, Barbados, May 1989.

11

Reclaiming Traditions, Remaking Community: Politics, Language, and Place among the Tolowa of Northwest California

James Collins

INTRODUCTION

It is a familiar argument that language figures centrally in group feeling, ethnic identity, and national loyalty. Less well understood is how language achieves such prominence—whether as an abstracted symbol of collective identity (in which "speaking English" means "being American"), a medium of practical interpersonal exchange, or the site and object of group activity. What follows is a case study of how efforts by the Tolowa of Northwest California to preserve their language connect with other aspects of their cultural and political life. It examines how language can be a site and object of group activity and how that activity goes together with other activities that are part of fashioning a collective identity in changing historical circumstances.

Although the analysis draws on insights and understandings gained from a decade of work on the Tolowa language, the bulk of fieldwork for this project was conducted in a four-week period in August 1991. It consisted of interviews with a range of Tolowa people, especially cultural and political activists, some work with historical materials, and attendance at various community events, for example, annual river-fishing and dances.

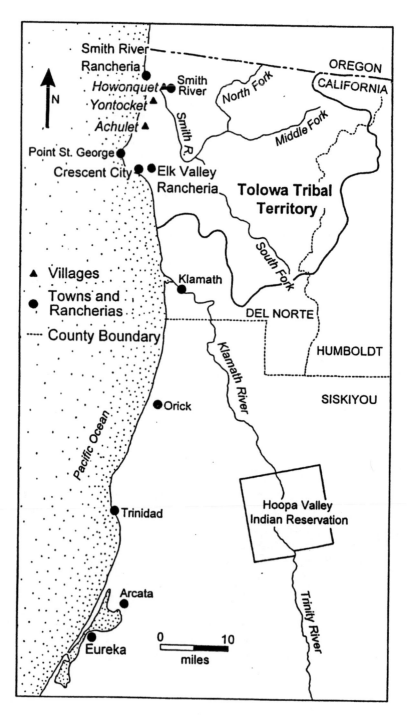

Figure 11.1.

My inquiry and analysis focus upon the relationship between the current circumstances of the Tolowa and their collective past. That relation between "tradition" and the present day is problematic, both for local people who must live with a keen sense of disjunction between their past and their present and for the anthropological analyst who is heir to a discipline that has sought the past by ignoring the present (Fabian 1983). The argument is organized in terms of themes that address both the present and the past as dimensions of language maintenance efforts, cultural practices such as dancing and fishing, and tribal government redefinition. Before taking up each theme, let me first provide some context for who the Tolowa were and are.

ETHNOGRAPHIC AND HISTORICAL CONTEXT

The Tolowa are an Athabaskan people numbering about 400–500 and living between Crescent City and Smith River, California. In many respects, they are similar to the surrounding white, rural working-class population—similar wagework, vehicles, clothing, musical preferences. But many Tolowa are dark-complected or at least identifiably "Indian," and hang together more with other Indians than whites; they have fishing rights, which they exercise and which put them in potential conflict with commercial or tourist fishermen (both non-Indian); they go to feather dances and salmon bakes; and some of them speak fully or know fragments of "Indian language," which academics and official types and now increasing numbers of local people call Tolowa and that is recognized as a language course in the local high school. They have a tribal council which is reorganizing itself and stipulating criteria for membership.

In aboriginal or pre-Contact times, the Tolowa probably numbered between 1,100 and 2,200, and they inhabited most of what is now Del Norte County (Gould 1978). Their neighbors were the Yurok, who lived along the Klamath River drainage, the Karuk, who lived inland in mountainous terrain, and the linguistically related Tututni and Hupa, the former living just north, in what is now Southwest Oregon, and the latter living south and inland, in what is now Humboldt County. According to the ethnographic record (Drucker 1937; DuBois 1936; Gould 1966, 1978), the Tolowa were a fishing, hunting, and gathering people who lived in six or seven major villages along the coastal plain between Smith River and Crescent City, Calif. They had a flat social structure in which exogamous, kin-based villages were the primary units of social organization and effective loyalty. Each village had a headman, a prominent and wealthy man, who held rights to village hunting, gathering, and fishing territories as well as to valued verbal lore and who possessed much dance regalia and other wealth. He was central negotiator and dispute settler. There was no other, larger unit of political organization or authority. Dancing and singing were important parts of a ceremonial life, which included naming ceremonies for the young, mourning ceremonies for the departed, shaman "training" for women, puberty rituals for girls, first-catch rituals for significant game and fish, and numerous purification rituals for those involved in illicit activities or a wealth quest.

The first recorded contact between Tolowa and whites occurred in 1828, in an encounter with the explorer Jedediah Smith (Gould 1966). Substantial contact, more accurately an onslaught, occurred after the 1850s, with the Klamath River gold rush and the subsequent development of fishing and timber industries in the area. The Tolowa suffered the same genocidal events and policies as many other native peoples in Oregon and Northern California in the latter half of the nineteenth century (see Norton 1979). By the turn of the century an original population of over a thousand was reduced to 121 on the government census (Gould 1978; Slagle 1987), from which it slowly rebounded to current figures. The consequences of massive dying and cultural disorientation have been emphasized in an anthropological literature which repeatedly announces the extinction or near extinction of Tolowa culture and language (Drucker, 1937; Gould, 1978).

For the Tolowa their past or tradition is thus an acute problem. It is both what they are, what sets them apart from a surrounding non-Indian society, and what they are not, for they have certainly changed since pre-Contact times. The very categories available for understanding tradition, identity, or group membership are problematic, for there is a highly indirect relation between the definitions of "tribe," "group," and "governing body" found in state and federal law, administrative rulings, and academic studies and the way that people actually live and are related to one another on the ground (Clifford 1988; Deloria and Lytle 1983). This is true of many Indian peoples, but particularly true of those in Northwest California.

This disjunction between legal-academic definition and Indian circumstance has various sources. One is that the legal-academic frameworks typically presume a degree of political integration or centralization not found in pre-white native California. There were Athabaskan-speaking folks living at various places in the Smith River drainage and the nearby coastal plain, from How-on-quet near the mouth of the Smith River to Crescent City along the coast, and inland well into the current Six Rivers National Forest. They shared a language, a significant set of cultural traditions and economic practices, and considerable genealogy. However, as noted earlier, the strongest, most pervasive form of social organization was an extended family village, not a drainage-wide political entity. These villages might be more closely related, in terms of practical daily contact, to nearby Yurok or Karuk settlements, rather than another Tolowa/Athabaskan village (Drucker 1937). That is to say, the effective social unit was a kin grouping, not a general tribal governing structure.

Another reason for the indirect relation between current Indian life and official definition is that the legal and bureaucratic rulings as well as the scholarly writings often overlook the historical processes that have complicated "tribal" tradition, genealogy, and membership. Military conquest resulted—as it usually does—in a great displacement of people. After Contact and the subsequent military subjugation, people from the Smith River area were driven to reservations as far north as Siletz, Oregon, and as far south as Hupa, California (Norton 1979; Slagle 1985, 1987). In addition, before the arrival of whites there was a great deal of exchange between diffferent peoples, including intergroup marriages (of Tolowa with Yurok, Karuk with Tolowa, and so forth), all of which produced an intermingling of peoples, tongues, and resources, making the pursuit of cultural or genealogical purity difficult, if not "untraditional."

Against this complex interplay of tradition and current circumstance, of official definitions and local realities, my original research into the relation between language renewal efforts and cultural dynamics emphasized two ideas. The first was cultural construction, that is, that in organizing and continuing various activities characteristic of "tradition," Tolowa folks were also remaking those traditions, because their lifeways had been severely disrupted by the onslaught of surrounding white society. The second was complex affiliation, that is, that in adopting different or overlapping categories of identity and belonging—such as "How-on-quet" (Smith River Rancheria) versus "Tolowa" versus just plain local "Indian"—people were evoking different visions of community and tradition and drawing upon different organizational resources. During the course of fieldwork, my thinking about these matters was both deepened and challenged, so that while the idea of culture as a construction is kept, continuities are also emphasized, and while the divisions in the community are addressed as frankly as possible, connections between different organizations, activities, and individuals are also emphasized.

Reworking Tradition: Improvising with the Past and Present

In many of my interviews and conversations with people involved in a range of cultural activities, a consistent theme was that "traditional" activities such as dance, fishing, and governance were continually changing, adapting older forms to new circumstances. This was true whether discussing the organization of a Rancheria Council or the conduct of a dance, whether discussing events in distant memory or events in recent view. The reasons for change and the timing of change differed for distinct activities, but the fact of change was unavoidable.

A traditional Nedash (Dance) was held at a homestead on the Smith River during the first weekend in August 1991, as it has been at this date and location for the last ten or so years. About 150 people attended the dinner held before and stayed on for the feather dances later that evening. A children's group and an adults' group in full dance regalia performed three sets, pounding their feet in line and in unison with chants, as separate dancers would spring out in front of the line, evoking the Deer or Hunter or Maiden and displaying both technique and costume. The Nedash began and ended with songs and prayers in the Tolowa language.

In discussing their participation or attendance at the dance, their own experience of dancing, and its meaning for their lives, a wide range of people talked about dancing as tradition: as part of childhood memories of family and community; as something emotional, some-times spiritual, but also something that was repressed or forbidden or allowed to "die out." These people also talked about change in dancing. Several commented on the songs not being the same as they used to be, and two men carried on a lively argument about changes in song—in their tempo, their lyrics, their use of primary and secondary singers. In that argument they compared such changes to changes in the nearby Brush Dance traditions as well as in the general Western Pow-Wow circuits of dance (see, for example, Jorgenson 1972). In their argument they revealed contrary tugs of the heart, for dance songs like "my grandfather used to sing," and for dance songs that changed because they were tailored by the individual singer, by his aptitudes and passions.

In addition to changes in songs, people also commented on the platforms upon which dancing occurred. Some felt that the lowered platform of the current dance site was different, not like the ground-level platforms they remembered. Others felt a platform must be low-ered, or certainly not above-ground, as some dances conducted in private houses in the 1920s and 1930s had been.

Still others commented on audience relations with dancers. One woman, who had herself danced and now had a daughter dancing, found that the "calling out"[1] of dancers by the audience, which had occurred to the great enjoyment of spectators, was "different," not something she remembered, something that made her feel a little strange. A few people commented on the lack of respectful reverence at dances, which they felt were spiritual events, and this comment fed into a wider, shifting discussion about dances in general (including Brush Dances and Pow-Wows) as social get-togethers, with associated joviality and good times, as well as serious spiritual events.

Like many other native people in California and other states, the Tolowa/Smith River Athabaskan people are in the process of reorganizing their collective identity in particular legal ways. They are establishing tribal membership rolls through the mechanism of the How-on-quet Indian Council.[2] This council, as a governing body, is itself judged from various angles. One council member sees it as nontraditional in that it uses formal democratic mechanisms of electoral representation (a chair and council members who are voted for in regular elections and who are bound by a written constitution and set of by-laws) as the source of its right to govern, rather than the strictly traditional authority of a "headman." A nonmember, who disagrees with some of its policies, sees the current council as "top-down" in its leadership. Unlike the Del Norte Indian Welfare Association, which was organized in the 1930s and served as a formal and informal governing body for Tolowa issues during several prior decades, the current Council is a representative body, not a direct membership organization. That is, whereas the DNIWA decided on issues at general membership meetings, the Council meets and establishes Rancheria policy, without continuous membership input or involvement. Some people spoken with saw the Council as unnecessarily narrow in its membership criteria, and they would cite the opinions of elders in arguing that this was not a proper, Indian way of viewing tribal membership. Conversely, yet another council member cited tradition, the views of his father and men of that generation, in arguing for a narrower definition of who should be allowed on tribal rolls.

The Council is thus a paradox. A body recognized by the United States government, it is in certain ways nontraditional. Yet it is also a key means through which Tolowa people will begin to reassert control over their collective affairs: stewardship of group land and economic initiative; health care provisions; and (re)claiming and (re)asserting rights to fishing resources. It is both an innovation and a way of struggling for self-determination as Indian people.

Language was a unifying feature of the Smith River dwelling people who have come to be known as "the Tolowa." Indeed, one of the impressive things about recent Tolowa history has been the consistent local effort, now extending over 24 years, to document, preserve, and transmit the traditional language. But it has been necessary to document, to preserve-in-writing, in order to transmit the language, because the speech community—the community of fluent, knowledgeable, regularly using speakers of the language—has been in drastic decline throughout the 1960s, 1970s, and 1980s. Although some people, more than the outsider would initially think, have an impressive knowledge of the language, apparently no one born since the 1930s has learned Tolowa as their first language, their mother tongue. English has been dominant in school, town, worksite, and home. In a process of self-denial familiar to many subjugated peoples, as well as many immigrant peoples, adults discouraged children from learning the Tolowa language because of their experience of prejudice against Indians and Indians ways, including Indian language.

The language program is thus also a paradox. The program has performed a massive and necessary task of documentation, but as Tolowa has changed from an oral tradition to a written language, its community of speakers and their range of uses of language have shrunk. As text replaces utterance something essential about the language is maintained: its sound structure, syntax, and vocabulary riches. Yet something has also changed; there are far fewer users, far fewer uses.

Closer Ties: Enduring Links Between Changing Activities

My original research proposal argued that there were basic divisions and tensions in local Indian life and tradition. It noted, for example, that there were different folks involved in the language program and the Tolowa Nation reacknowledgment efforts were different from those involved in the Rancheria Council(s), and that there were more and different Indian groups, and more women, involved in annual netfishing than were involved in the annual Nedash, which emphasized a more exclusive and consciously ceremonial "Tolowa" tradition.

There was and is some truth to these claims: distinct organizations and affiliations underpin cultural life, and differences and tensions exist. It is also true, however, that the differing cultural practices are closely interconnected. When one person was asked how she saw the relation between different cultural activities—dancing, having a language program, fishing, organizing a council—she replied, "[H]ow are they related? . . . I see them as all part of the same thing."

There are, for instance, historical connections as well as shared agendas between the Tolowa Language Program and the How-on-quet Council. As one council member noted, the Language Program serves as an example of Indian competence, of Indians taking control of their own circumstances, organizing and exerting themselves to maintain something important: their own linguistic traditions. When the Language Program first began, it survived because of the crucial support and participation of a number of recognized elders—fathers, uncles, and aunts of current council members, people who formed a core of now-deceased but clearly remembered community. Council members and language program members have had strong differences of opinion over the years, and questions continue to be raised about whether the language program materials have got the language "right." There is, however, also a widely voiced sentiment that "the Indian language," this linguistic tradition and resource that linguists call Tolowa, is somehow an important part of tradition. That understood collective past, tradition, is part of their identity in the present, and they want to carry it into the future, as word and deed.

There are also diverse connections between the language program and other cultural activities such as fishing or dancing. One language program veteran suggested that when engaged in traditional activities, you were more likely to use the language, and that using the language, having names for things and descriptions of actions, gave activities "a kind of resonance." A young girl, who was a dancer, wanted to take language classes because she "like[s] the language, like[s] the way it [the language] sounds" and, perhaps more pressingly, because "it's like everyone else knows it [the language] who dances." The person noted earlier, who saw differing activities as all part of same whole was a woman who had lived away from the Smith River area for more than a decade of young adulthood. When she had returned in the early 1970s, it had struck her how little the local Indians had, compared to other, better-organized Indian groups she had encountered around the country. She had quickly gotten involved in Rancheria-related educational and nutrition programs, and she was an early and forceful advocate of the language program, which all of her boys had attended for one or more years. Her boys and granddaughters all had or would take part in Nedash ceremonies, and the family insisted upon and acted upon their right to fish the rivers for salmon as well as the beaches for smelts. A local man, in young middle age, who had danced for over a decade, to "show respect for the Great Spirit . . . and to preserve our culture" was also a veteran of the language program. He had learned the language in various places—on the beach with elders or working with an uncle, in the language classes, and for a short period as a teacher. He viewed the language, like dancing, as part of a tradition to be preserved; not surprisingly, he insisted on his right, even where challenged by state or federal law, to fish and gather seafood.

BREAKS, DISORGANIZATION, AND REPRESSION

The preceding account of persisting, innovating traditions and of links between diverse cultural activities testifies to Tolowa persistence and tenacity. However, as with many other Indian groups in this country, Tolowa history of the last century-and-a-half has been brutal. There have been breaks in traditional practice, as well as innovation; there has been severe disorganization, as well as connection; and there has been both external and internal repression of Indian ways. It is to this that we now turn.

As noted earlier, a unifying feature of the pre-Contact Tolowa was their language, language in the sense both of grammar and vocabulary and of story traditions and ritual lore (Bommelyn and Humphey 1989; Collins 1992; Drucker 1937; Slagle 1987). This speech community has been endangered for several generations, making efforts at language documentation necessary. Although the community of speakers declined throughout the middle decades of this century, it was fluent, knowledgeable elders who joined together with those who were or would become accomplished speakers of Tolowa as a second language in order to begin a language program. This local effort to preserve the language has continued since the late 1960s, grappling initially with writing systems and formats for recording information and teaching, pushing for and gaining increasing recognition of their language program and its legitimacy in the local school district, and producing two editions of *Tolowa Language*, a combined dictionary, grammatical sketch, and cultural resource book (Bommelyn and Humphey 1989).

Alongside these laudable efforts, there have been problems. It is difficult to learn the traditional language in classroom settings, for it is a language quite different from English. The Unifon writing system is quite distinct from the English alphabet, which poses a barrier to many who would like to be able to consult *Tolowa Language* for reference questions. Although few have been able to learn the traditional language fluently in class, many have learned other language competencies: the traditional words to songs and prayers; the names for persons, places, and things; some useful conversational exchanges (*dasi[n]des* "have a seat"; *xəmtśi* "see you later"). But there is also a clear awareness, voiced by many older people and some not-so-old people, that the richness of vocabulary and conversational possibility that they associate with the speech of "the elders" is largely a thing of the past or a thing of books, preserved in print, but with few people able to speak in this way. That is, there is a question of what the Tolowa language will look like, or more precisely, sound like, in the mouths of its twenty-first-century speakers.

If the language program has been a site of significant effort at maintaining a shared linguistic tradition, the Rancheria Councils have been the focus of efforts at re-establishing and redefining shared political structures. The current Smith River Indian Council came into existence in the early 1980s after a legal battle reversed the Federal Termination Act implementation of the early 1960s (United States Congress 1953; Bureau of Indian Affairs 1961). The termination processes at Smith River profoundly affected the local Indian community. What had been a collective social group became an assembly of property owners, with clearer title to individual property and greater freedom to act with that property, but with loss of any collective claims to health and welfare services, to resource rights, and so forth. The Termination Act was itself just the latest in a series of federal and state efforts to break up Indian collectivities by turning them into individual citizens. The Allotment Act of the 1880s was an earlier effort; it reduced treaty-based rights to reservation land in exchange for homestead allotments of 80 acres per family (Spicer 1969, Document 14). In any case, as there has been a break in Tolowa forms of governance, let us briefly sketch a history of such political-leadership arrangements.

As far as can be told about the period prior to the 1850s and the arrival of whites, the political leaders of Tolowa groups were village headmen. As noted earlier, these were men who ruled by virtue of wisdom, wealth, family influence, and force of personality. They were not elected and did not rule with force of law, as we understand that in modern states, though their opinions had consequence, and they could mobilize violence and other sanctions when necessary. There is no evidence of councils of headmen or other *formal* mechanisms for coordinating the decisions of different village headmen (DuBois 1936). After military subjugation and during the reservation period, as well as during the landless period from the 1870s to the 1910s, if foodstuffs and other material support were provided for local Indians, whether from the government or private organizations, such supplies were typically distributed through the headmen and their families. That is, since before contact and up through the 1920s, headmen were the recognized form of government (Slagle 1985).

The first leadership organization that was established on formal-democratic principles (decisions by vote; elections; a constitution, by-laws, and officers, etc.) was the Del Norte Indian Welfare Association (DNIWA), established in 1936. Although it had Yurok and other Indian members, DNIWA was a predominantly Tolowa organization, both in terms of membership and leadership. For a 30-year period, from the mid-1930s to the 1960s, it represented Tolowa and other Indian peoples, providing a context for those people to discuss their situation and strategy, as well as many occasions for socializing, fun, and fundraising. It advocated for Indian rights at the county, state, and national level and provided an organizational means to secure modest group property and social welfare services (Slagle 1985).

The current Smith River Indian Council is not a direct lineal descendant of the DNIWA. As noted earlier, the mechanism of governing differs: the council governs by delegation, as an elected group making authoritative decisions, rather than from the direct membership vote or consensus used by the DNIWA. Members are different, of course. The

DNIWA activities began to diminish in the 1970s; the Council was not established until the early 1980s. Nonetheless, the Council does represent a Tolowa effort to reestablish and redefine what will be their form of collective leadership, of Indian government, in the 1990s.

This is being done in changed conditions. Personnel have changed, and the mission has also changed. The DNIWA advocated Indian rights and organized the distribution of service resources, but had no formal mandate to govern. The rancheria-specific How-on-Quet Community Association, founded early in the Termination process and ended with Termination's reversal in the 1980s, was a property-owners' organization. It looked after a water system and an Indian cemetery, but had little collective responsibility for anyone other than Rancheria property owners.

The current council has a larger responsibility, in particular, for a tribal membership that will be the most inclusive official (federal/state) definition of Tolowa/Smith River Athabaskan identity. Organizing after Termination and the consequences of Termination, the council is trying to come back, to reassert collective identity and governance, but it is coming back to a new place. There is less land than before, because much land was sold off subsequent to Termination; there are new understandings about resources to be negotiated, because local feelings about rights to fish, for example, are different in the 1990s than in the 1950s; and there are new senses of identity that will affect council policies and practices, because in the 1990s there is an emphasis on dual identity—being Indian and being American—rather than a felt need to lose the Indian in the American.

In addition to language and self-government, spiritual and cultural expression through dancing has also seen ruptures and breaks. As with other Native American peoples, and indeed with non-state native peoples throughout the world, Tolowa dancing was a central part of social gathering-together and spirit-expressing. It was a good time, it was art, and it was holy. Written documents from the 1860s onward record the existence of "Indian Dances" in the Smith River area, held as part of World Renewal ceremonies (Nedash) as well as for other occasions (Slagle 1985).[3] Various people today refer to the last great 10-Day Dance, held in 1910, as the Rancherias were being established and the village at Stundossun (Smith River Island, now eroded away) was being abandoned.

However, this expression of culture, spirituality, and social difference was often seen as threatening. Non-Indian governments at local, state, and federal levels saw dancing as unruly, perhaps a threat to public order. Christian churches often viewed dancing as irreligious or worse, non-Christian. In the last decade of the nineteenth century and the first two decades of the twentieth century, there are local press reports of various problems as Indian dances were combined with local (non-Indian) jigs and alcohol was a social stimulant, for good and bad. In the late 1920s, public dancing ended. Some claim that it was the result of a federal BIA regulation prohibiting Indian dances (Slagle 1985). Numerous local people claim, however, that it was the Christian churches, the Shaker, Four Square Gospel, Methodist, and other churches, that put a stop to dancing by forbidding it for their members. Perhaps it was both government and religion that pressured for an end to dancing. In any event, after the 1920s, dancing was a private and underground affair until the mid-1960s.

Many Tolowa adults, spanning a range of ages, remember dancing and singing as something occurring in the privacy of a home, or in small family-like gatherings. Small groups getting together for dancing and singing is something that occurred at Gushchu Hall (near Smith River) in the 1950s and early 1960s, for example, but there were few publicly held dances until the mid-1960s, when there began to be a more open and conscious reassertion of "Indian ways." In the late 1970s and continuing since then, there has been an annual World Renewal Nedash held each August at the Bommelyn place on the South Bank of the Smith (Nelechundun). These events are typically well-attended, though the numbers vary from year to year. In 1991 there were more than 150 people attending the Nedash, many Tolowa, various Yurok, Hupa, and Karuk folks, as well as a sizable minority of non-Indians, mostly in-laws but also onlookers and hangers-on, all gathered for an evening of food, talk, and several sets of traditional dancing by young people and adults.

Dancing is thus once again public, as cultural performance and spiritual observation. Like other dance traditions in the area, as well as the regional pow-wows, it is different from what it was 60 or 100 years ago. Songs are different, the relation with the audience has shifted, and there are more children involved and fewer adults. As with the language program and the council's efforts at self-government, dancing involves a remaking of older cultural forms that have been threatened or repressed; it is change and continuity.

ALWAYS A STRUGGLE

One striking thing about the cultural practices discussed, which are chief among the organized and visible aspects of current Indian life in the Smith River area, is that each practice has required a struggle, often prolonged and ongoing, in order to be maintained. Another way of putting this is that Tolowa community is made, not found, whether the issue is language maintenance, tribal governance, or resource rights. The language program began 24 years ago as a weekly extracurricular event held at the high school in Crescent City. That was the original meetingplace for the elders, other adults, and children interested in learning and preserving their linguistic heritage. Four years later, the language course was accepted for formal school credit. However, throughout the 1960s and 1970s, Tolowa parents and language teachers had to struggle with the school board in order to have Title VII monies allocated to that program and in order to maintain some control over course content and evaluation. Indeed, for the first 15 or so years of its existence, the language program received what funding it did through the Center for Community Development, affiliated with Humboldt State University. It was only in the mid-1980s that the language course was finally taken on as the financial responsibility of the local high school.[4]

The current Smith River Indian Council, in the process of completing a tribal constitution and membership enrollment procedure, is the result of an effort that began in the mid-1970s to reverse the Termination process. Termination hit the local community hard, dividing families and resulting in considerable loss of land through private sale. It was pressed for, with considerable force, by various government agencies, whatever the feelings of local Rancheria members in 1960. The effort to reverse the Termination began with a petition campaign to reconsider the facts of the action, initiated by a local man who is now a council member. Later, the Smith River group joined with other Indian groups in various Western states in the *Tillie Hardwick* case (*Tillie Hardwick et al. vs. United States of America* (Civ. No. 79-1710 SW. United States District Court, N.D. California)), and in 1983 the Termination Act was rescinded for the groups that were plaintiffs to the case. At each point in the case and the reversal process more generally, there has been pressure from the Bureau of Indian Affairs and other government agencies to restrict interpretation of who is Tolowa and what the exact nature of their special sovereignty will be. As the current council presses for clarification on resource rights (fishing or clam and mussel gathering) or land issues (access rights to beaches; the status of the lease of land that was the original "Reservation Ranch"), it will need to operate in official-legal arenas as well as in local contexts of social gatherings and informal meetings. In this respect, it will need to continue the legacy of DNIWA activism for Indian rights and welfare.

Fishing rights have been contested in this part of Northern California for over 30 years, and the disputes continue over who has a right to fish where. The situation on the Klamath has reached a temporary stability with the outcome of Senate Bill 2723 (the Hoopa-Yurok Settlement Act). Only those people enrolled in the Yurok tribe and with special buoy tags can fish, but that has been and will again be legally challenged by some of the Tolowa people excluded by Senate Bill 2723. Initial rights to fish the Klamath were won by challenging California Fish and Game, in a series of events, extending over a decade, that led to the *Raymond Mattz vs. Arnett* case (412 U.S. 481 (1973)). After a dispute and court case, people on the South Bank of the Smith River at Nelechundun won limited rights to fish in portions of the river. Various people also talk about a cat-and-mouse game currently going on between Tolowa fishermen and California Fish and Game officers, which may well lead to a legal case inquiring into Smith River/Tolowa rights to fish for salmon. As with tribal legal existence and language maintenance, resource rights are asserted, contested, and struggled over; they are never simply granted.

CONCLUSION

The preceding analysis explores how language preservation efforts relate to other aspects of contemporary Tolowa life, how they are part of that effort to reclaim and refashion the past that is a significant aspect of recent Tolowa history and that can be seen as the Tolowa contribution to the recent cultural renaissance in native Northwest California. Relations to the past are never simple, however, nor are questions of identity ever finally settled, for individuals or collectivities. This is particularly true for those traumatized aboriginal societies of North America that have survived into the latter part of the twentieth century.

Perhaps because they are a people who were nearly destroyed—by death and land loss in the nineteenth century, as well as by the Termination processes of the early 1960s—recent Tolowa history shows in sharp relief what social analysts have been arguing for nation-states and large-scale ethnic mobilizations. Tradition is always made as well as inherited (Hobsbawm and Ranger 1983), and print languages are primary modern instruments for construing community, as they archive a past and disseminate a linguistic present (Anderson 1983). In the Tolowa case, language provided a site for political efforts, as emerging civil rights concerns and enabling legislation and resources coincided with local concerns over the loss of "old stories." This led to new discursive forms and occasions (a printed language, distributed through books and taught in school) and it continued old, pre-Contact preoccupations with story lore and place names (both prominent in Tolowa Language Program publications). But language maintenance efforts must be seen as of a piece with other efforts at recuperating a sense and practice of collective life: reasserting a public right to dance and to fish, and turning back an individualizing termination process while groping for new forms of self-government and self-direction. Language is not an abstract symbol of an abstract identity so much as a site and object of group activities for reclaiming and remaking past and present.

NOTES

1. "Calling out" occurs when members of the audience shout out for specific dancers to leave the line they are in and step forward, performing special steps. Drucker reports *tsɛna'sɛt na: 'gaʎ* "in front walk" as a calling out phrase (1937, 265); "Bobby, out in front . . . out in front!" would be a contemporary English equivalent. "Calling out" is an old practice, though only in some kinds of dance. It is reported for the more sociable Wealth Display dance, though not at the more somber Girl's Puberty dance (Drucker, 1937).

2. Criteria for membership that have been put forward and argued about include, in declining inclusivity, (1) anyone with any amount of Tolowa blood, (2) anyone currently residing at or able to trace descent from those residing at the How-on-quet or Elk Valley Rancherias, and (3) anyone currently residing at or able to establish direct descent (siblings, children, and grandchildren) from those residing at How-on-quet.

3. World Renewal was a widespread revivalist movement among Northwest California Indians. It apparently began at the turn of the century. The ceremonies occurred annually, featured initiating and conlcuding prayers, and were held in particular places with built structures that were embued with holiness during the ceremonies. Dance was a central aspect of ritual activity, and in the Northwest region it was often the Jumping and Deer Skin dances which were performed. Within these general constraints, there was and continues to be considerable variation in the carrying out of Renewal ceremonies (Kroeber and Gifford, 1949).

4. That funding is uncertain in the wake of California's economic problems. In the spring of 1992 the Tolowa language class was slated for cancellation from regular high school offerings. It was reinstated after a letter-writing campaign by locals and concerned outsiders.

REFERENCES

Anderson, Benedict. 1983. *Imagined Communities: Reflections on the Origin and Spread of Nationalism.* London and New York: Verso.

Bommelyn, Loren, and Berneice Humphey. 1989. *Xus We-Yo': Tolowa Language,* 2d ed. Crescent City, Calif.: Tolowa Language Committee.

Bureau of Indian Affairs. 1961. *Report to the Secretary of the Interior by the Task Force on Indian Affairs,* July 10. Excerpted in Spicer 1969.

Clifford, James. 1988. "The Mashpee." In *The Predicament of Culture.* Cambridge, Mass.: Harvard University Press.

Collins, James. 1992. "Our Ideologies and Theirs." In P. Kroskrity, B. Schieffelin, and K. Woolard, eds., *Language Ideologies,* special issue, *Pragmatics* 2(3): 405–16.

Deloria, Vine, and Clifford Lytle. 1983. *American Indian, American Justice.* Austin: University of Texas Press.

Drucker, Philip. 1937. "The Tolowa and Their Southwestern Oregon Kin." *University of California Publications in American Archeology and Ethnology* 36: 221–300.

DuBois, Cora. 1936. "The Wealth Quest as an Integrative Factor in Tolowa-Tututni Culture." In R. Lowie, ed., *Essays in Anthropology: In Honor of A. L. Kroeber*. Berkeley, Calif.: University of California Press.

Fabian, Johannes. 1983. *Time and the Other: How Anthropology Makes Its Object*. New York: Columbia University Press.

Gould, Richard. 1966. "The Wealth Quest among the Tolowa Indians of Northwest California." *Proceedings of the American Philosophical Society* 110(1): 67–89.

———. 1978. "The Tolowa." In I. Goddard, ed., *Handbook of North American Indians, 10: California*. Washington: Smithsonian, 128–36.

Hobsbawn, Eric, and Terrence Ranger. 1983. *Invented Traditions*. New York: Cambridge University Press.

Jorgensen, Joseph. 1972. *Sun Dance: Power for the Powerless*. Chicago: University of Chicago.

Kroeber, A. L., and E. W. Gifford. 1949. "World Renewal: A Cult System of Native Northwest California." *Anthropological Record* 13(1): 1–153.

Norton, Jack. 1979. *When Our Worlds Cried: Genocide in Northwestern California*. San Francisco: American Indian Historical Society.

Slagle, Allogan. 1985. *Huss: The Tolowa People: A Petition for Status Clarification/Federal Recognition Prepared for Submission to the United States Department of Interior*. Arcata, Calif.: Center for Community Development, Humboldt State University.

———. 1987. "The Native American Tradition and Legal Status: Tolowa Tales and Tolowa Places." *Cultural Critique* 7: 103–18.

Spicer, Edward. 1969. *A Short History of the Indians of the United States*. New York: D. Van Nostrand Co.

United States Congress. 1953. House Concurrent Resolution 108. *Congressional Record*.

12

"Word-Sound-Power": Language, Social Identity, and the Worldview of Rastafari

John W. Pulis

INTRODUCTION

Some time ago I asked a Rastafarian, a back-country "rootsman," what the worldview of Rastafari was all about: "Jus words-sounds-paawa, bradda, dat wha I-n-I [Rastafari] a-deal wit, jus words-sounds-paawa," was his reply. As I learned, word-sound-power was by no means as simple as suggested, but was bound up with local ideas of knowledge concerning history, identity, and the power or political efficacy of talk.

The Rastafarian Brethren resemble what anthropologists refer to as a millennial, a revitalization, or a syncretistic cult.[1] They first emerged or "invented themselves" during the interwar decades in Kingston, Jamaica, but are now active in Africa, Asia, Europe, and North America. Their proclamations concerning Haile Selassie, their mediation of contemporary and biblical events, and their unique way of speaking, known as "I-ance," "I-yaric," or "Dread Talk" have been dismissed as the false or irrational prophecies of a soon-to-disappear cult (see Wilson 1973; Post 1978, for millennial cults; Alleyne 1988; Nettleford 1970, 1979, for cultural formation; Pollard 1984, for Dread Talk; Chevannes 1994; Yawney 1978, 1979; and Homiak 1987, 1995, for I-ance and I-yaric).[2]

This chapter discusses the importance of language, speech, and communication to practitioners of Rastafari in Jamaica. Rather than false or irrational prophecy, it suggests that word-sound-power is a way of speaking in which Rastafarians bring a tension or antagonism between Creole and Standard-English words, sounds, and meanings to bear on contesting traditional constructions of identity.[3] The writer contends that theories that render worldviews and beliefs as mirrors or reflections fail to consider language as a material or constitutive practice. They not only overlook the relationship between language and social life, but they gloss or background the way linguistic expressions are constructed, performed, and negotiated in everyday life. This essay opens with a background survey of language in Jamaica, proceeds to the presentation of reported speech, a "reasoning" or dialogue about the politics of language, speech, and communication in which the writer participated, and follows with a discussion of how Rastafarians brought their understanding of word-sound-power to bear on reshaping folk or traditional understandings of history, identity, and agency.[4]

BACKGROUND

The island of Jamaica was the crown jewel of the eighteenth-century British Caribbean. African laborers and Anglophile planters created a unique Creole or West Indian culture expressed by festivities such as Jonkonnu, the belief-system of Afro-Christianity, and a spoken language, a form of Creole-English known as Jamaica Talk (see Brathwaite 1978 [1971] for Creole culture; Schuler 1980 for Jonkonnu; Cassidy 1982 [1961]; Cassidy and Le Page 1967 for Jamaica Talk).[5]

Creole languages were long considered to be baby talk, slangs, or broken dialects of European languages, be they French, English, or Dutch. Recent studies of syntax, phonology, and vocabulary have demonstrated that West Indian Creoles are not baby talk or slangs, but bona fide languages that originated in Africa and were reconstituted in the yards and plantations of the New World (see Hymes 1985 [1971]; Bauman and Sherzer 1989 [1974]; Holm 1988; and Roberts 1988).

Such is the case of Jamaica Talk. As Alleyne (1988) and Cassidy (1982 [1961]) have argued, Jamaica Talk constituted the discourse or unofficial language of the colony. It was spoken by Africans and Europeans alike in the sugar plantations, the villages or yards, and the local markets. The vocabulary of Jamaica Talk contained African loan words and incorporated various performative genres, from African proverbs to the talking drums and the abengs or horns sounded during slave rebellions and maroon wars.[6]

Although Jamaica Talk was the discourse of everyday life, it was not a natural, neutral, or apolitical means of communication. On the one hand, it was subordinated to Standard English as the official spoken and printed language of the colony. Lady Nugent, the North American wife of Governor George Nugent of Jamaica (1801–6), made the following observations: "The Creole language is not confined to the Negroes. Many of their [European] ladies, who have not been educated in England, speak a sort of broken English, with an indolent drawling out of their words, that is very tiresome if not disgusting. I stood next to a lady one night, near a window, and, by way of saying something, remarked that the air was much cooler than usual; to which she answered, 'Yes, ma-am, him rail-ly too fra-ish'" (Wright 1966 [1907], 98).

On the other hand, the drums and horns sounded during slave rebellions and maroon wars were by no means a hidden transcript or secondary genre, but were means of communication clearly understood by Africans and Europeans alike. Just as Jamaica Talk was reconstituted in the yards and plantations of the eighteenth century, so the word-sound-power of Dread Talk was transformed into a discourse of resistance in the urban enclaves or dungles of the twentieth century.

Balm Yards and Dungles

As Hart (1989) and Post (1978) have illustrated, the interwar decades were turbulent years in Jamaican history. Events set in motion in the nineteenth century transformed involuntary laborers into a disenfranchised working class by the 1930s. Landless peasants and unemployed workers migrated to Central America to dig canals and build railroads. The population of Montego Bay and Kingston trebled, and urban enclaves, balm yards, and dungles became focal points of social and political unrest (see Bryan 1991).

Pan-Africanists, trade unionists, and street preachers alike were active in Kingston contesting British colonialism. Labor leaders such as Alexander Bustamante and nationalists such as Norman Manley organized unions and laid the foundation for what became the People's National and Jamaican Labor Parties. Similarly, pan-Africanists such as Marcus Garvey, "native Baptists"[7] such as Alexander Bedward, and advocates of Rastafari such as Leonard Howell were also active; but they drew upon a tradition of prophetic oratory and biblical interpretation to probe, contest, and subvert the signs, symbols, and cultural practices associated with British hegemony (see Elkins 1977 for street preachers; Hill 1981, 1983; Campbell 1987; and Chevannes 1994 for history of Rastafari and interwar politics).

Both mounted formidable challenges. On the one hand, street preaching and biblical interpretation expressed a continuity with the political and linguistic praxis of Afro-Jamaican culture. Relegated by colonial historians to witchcraft, "obeah" (Long 1774, 2:416–17; Edwards 1801, 2:107–8), considered by missionaries to be "mental delusions" (Underhill 1862: 179; Waddell 1863: 195), and associated with events such as the Baptist War (1831) and the Great Revival (1860), slave leaders and native Baptists fused religion and politics into an Afro-Jamaican worldview expressed not in the grammar and rhetoric of English, but in the words and sounds of Creole or Jamaica Talk (see Nettleford 1979 for religion and politics).[8]

On the other hand, international events such as the coronation of Haile Selassie and the pan-African movement provided the text and context for the reconstitution of Jamaica Talk into Dread Talk. As Moore (1969), Elkins (1977), Hart (1989), and others (Ramchand 1983; Chevanes 1994), have demonstrated, it was the tonal semantics of Creole and the worldview of Afro-Christianity that inspired the publications of West Indian poets, historians, and political activists. Jamaica Talk became their "chosen tongue," the means of communication through which trade unionists and street preachers alike assaulted British hegemony (see Martin 1984, 1987; Robinson 1983, and Magubane 1987 for Ethiopianism, literary Garveyism, and black Marxism).[9]

It was not the printed word, however, that inspired the word-sound-power of Dread Talk, but the spoken. The events that unfolded in Africa substantiated a linguistic praxis that subordinated spoken and printed English to the sound-based or tonal semantics of Creole. As we shall see here, the sound or phonic structure of English words and the grammatical structure of printed texts were "penetrated," that is, sounded out loud, broken apart, and reassembled into a discourse that renegotiated traditional understandings of history and identity. If the words and sounds of this discourse were first spoken in Kingston, by the end of the twentieth century they were heard in Africa, Asia, Europe, and North America as a generation of Rastafarians matured, a number of organizations or "houses" were established, and a local music industry expanded globally (see Yawney 1978; Homiak 1985 for "elders"; Smith et al. 1976; Campbell 1987; Chevannes 1994 for societies, houses, and colonial politics).[10]

FOREGROUND

The proper way to frame a presentation of language and language use by Rastafarians is not to focus on the sentence or the word as such, but on the context of communication. As important as grammatical analyses are, they tend to background the speakers, the setting, and the scene. Backgrounding the speakers and hearers is understandable in analyses of historic texts, but not in studies of spoken languages, where meaning is embedded within the context and subject to negotiation by participants.[11]

As with all spoken languages, Dread Talk cannot have a history apart from those who speak it. The writer of this chapter engaged in a series of discussions or "reasonings" with a Rastafarian, a rootsman we shall know as Bongo. The name Bongo is a pseudonym for a Jamaican who "turned dread" or became a Rastafarian during the 1960s. Bongo was not an elder or an ancient, that is, a member of the prewar generation of Rastafarians. He was born in a rural community during the 1940s and migrated to Kingston in the early 1960s. He established a residence in a local camp, where he learned or became "grounded" in the "words" and "works" of Rastafari. Bongo remained in Kingston until the 1980s when the "tribalism" or politically sponsored violence led him to reestablish a rural residence or "back country gates" in the parish of Manchester. It was in the parish of Manchester that the writer first encountered Bongo.[12]

Although Bongo was not an elder, he was recognized by Rastafarians and non-Rastafarians alike as a rootsman whose "countenance shined," that is, his "words" or rhetoric did not contradict his "livity" or way of life. He refused to consume alcohol, animal protein, or commercially processed foods, and he rejected the "sport" or social behavior associated with the "karna" or local rum bars. His household or gates were open to all, dread and non-dread, African and European, and were noted for their lively debates or reasonings. It was at Bongo's back-country gates that the writer was introduced to or became "grounded" in the relationship between words, sounds, and power.

As we noted earlier, word-sound-power is a linguistic construct that expresses local ideas concerning identity, agency, and the power or political efficacy of language, speech, and communication. Just as Dread Talk cannot have a history apart from those who speak it, the power of words and sounds is not to be found in the ink and letters of print, but in the dialogics of linguistic interaction and communicative exchange. While Bongo's back-country gates framed the scene or physical setting, the dynamics or politics of our encounter were subject to negotiation. The following conversation was the first in a series of dialogues in which we negotiated the political context, the power, efficacy, or dynamics of interaction and exchange. Through the dialectics of this exchange, the ongoing and shared dynamics of a speech event known as reasoning, the writer became grounded in the worldview of Rastafari.

Butta and Watta[13]

"So da man move among dread?" Bongo asked as I arrived at his "gates" or household.

"Well, I would like to learn about Rastafari," I replied, as he plucked an orange from one of his trees, sliced off the skin, and offered me half.

"How long da man been in a Jam-roc [Jamaica]?"

"Only a few months, but I was here last year."

"So de man know de runnings?"

"Well..., not really, I mean, I've heard reggae and Bob Marley tunes in New York, but I don't know the ropes."

"Claudi tell I da man cite-up [read from the Holy Bible] in Town [Kingston]?"

"Somewhat, but I really want to talk to country people, you know, grass roots, get a feel for Rasta in the rural areas."

"Yes I, de movement rooted here," he replied, adding, "still Town de center, times hard now, de beast ina KON-trol, Michael gone."

"You mean Manley?"

"DAT what I seh, MICHAEL. Rea-gan install Seaga said why Tatcher install him, ana de Pope install her, da man no see!"

"Are they all connected?" I asked, as we moved over and sat on some rocks in the shade.

"I na seh de connected, dem part of de system, said way."

"You mean Babylon?"

"Yes I, da system."

"Interesting...."

"...Na INTERESTING, REALITY, da man no see it."

"Well, reality yes, but only one view...."

"...Only ONE reality, I-aya, na VIEWS. Da man's vision no clear, or maybe da man see images dat not exist, See-la-sie-I [Haile Selassie], dat reality."

"This is what I want to find out, about...Sel..las...sie-I and Babylon and what the consciousness...[of Rastafari is all about]."

"...I-n-I [Rastafarians]," he interjected, "no deal wit no KON-sciousness [pronounced with an emphasis on KON], I [Bongo] deal wit trut, rights, WIZ-MON, na KON no one, Jah seh, 'Him dat have ears,...HEAR! Him dat have eyes,...SEE!' I-n-I no KON no one, if dem wan see, dem mus jus open dem selves an dem see."

"Well, I didn't mean KON, but..."

"...WELL, ha! dat fa water, BUT-TA, ha! dat fa bread, mon, dem na UP-FULL sounds, I-n-I deal wit dem," he interjected once again, as he smiled and shrugged his shoulders.

"So," I asked, responding to his criticism and his shift or change in the conversation to language, "you drop out certain words."

"I nat seh I-n-I DROP dem, cause, if dem bust [are spoken], dem mus bust, I na bust sounds dat deal wit down-press-ion or kon-sciousness, cause, how I lif-up, if I reason down, I-n-I deal wit UP-press-I, I-sciousness, dem sounds UP-FULL, deal wit livity [life] not death. I-n-I no KON no one, jus words, sounds, power, bradda, words, sounds, power," he declared, adding, "Tell I, Da man mus cite-up more time?"

"Well, not really. I mean, I've heard biblical expressions but never really read anything."

"I tell da man, WELL ... is fi water, BU-TA ... fi bread, dem na UP-FULL sounds."

"Why are they not ... UP-FULL?"

"Dem not heartical. I-n-I no deal wit Babylon words dat con-fuse I, make I look in-a-da wrong place [pointing up to the sky and down to the ground]. I deal wit I-scious words dat over-stand, cause how can I reason [talk] wit da man an under-stand," he declared, explaining, "dat mean ta seh da man over I. Dat wishy-washy slave ting, when I-n-I mus humble I-self before dem false gods, an dem preacher, an dem bukkie-massa, no I-aya, times faawod. Da man mus know dis if him move among dread?"

"Well...," and before the sounds passed through my lips I pulled them back and said, "ah..., I mean, I've only been here a short time and have a lot to learn."

"Yes, I Sel-lassie different. How da man come to do dis?"

"What do you mean?"

"I na YOU, hail I [refer to me as] dread or da I or Bongo. Na YOU, or HIM, or HE da man no see?"

"Cause they're not up-full?"

"Ah..., YES I! Still, da man no know da runnings, da movements."

"I'm afraid not."

"What da man fear? I-n-I deal wit knowledge and wiz-mon, de trut na hurt no one, I-aya, I-n-I da source, da man mus acknowledge dat. True, de bee-ble [Holy Bible] culture, dem change it to KON-fuse I, I cite cause I know, bee-ble support I knowledge. Yes I, it de word of Jah [Selassie]. De system change de word, I-aya, mix em up, KON-fuse I-n-I, so I look in der wrong place. More times I rest pon hill top an di I reveal h.i.m. [his imperial majesty] self. Da man no see it."

"How does Sel-las-sie reveal himself?"

"Jah work differently, h.i.m. mystical, Sel-lassie I give tanks [thanks] wit blessings—da rain, h.i.m. put pon de ert all creation, come I show da man, look pon dat, what da man see," he asked pointing at what appeared to me as a barren patch of his garden.

"Dirt, ground, weeds..."

"...Ground? Yes, cause I-n-I trod pon de firmament. Dem na weeds, dem herbs! Dat na dirt, da ert [the earth]! Creation dat. Dem spring fort from de ert, I na do noting, da man see? Herbs spring fort from de I, Yes I-aya, de ert de lord and de fullness der of. Dat how Jah reveal himself to I. Look pon de hillside, da man see dem trees, dem bushes, farms too?"

"Yes, I see them."

"Sel-lassie I put dem pon de ert for I-n-I, for I livity, da man see?"

"I think ... [so]"

"...Da man na TINK, Jah seh dem dat have eyes, see and dem dat have ears, hear, dis here no duppy business, I-aya, no little spirit from above KON-FUSE-I, jus word, sound, paawa, bradda, jus word, sound, paawa, da man no see?"

UP-FULL SOUNDS

Dread Talk, like all spoken languages, incorporates various genres, styles, and discursive practices. The preceding dialogue was presented to illustrate the importance of language to Bongo, to demonstrate how meaning is embedded within the context and subject to negotiation, and a means to express the dynamics of interaction and exchange, the dialogics of a shared experience. The remainder of this chapter discusses the formation of up-full sounds and their relationship to history, identity, and the dialogics of reasoning.

We heard as Bongo spoke or "busted" words that sounded like English. For Bongo, and for all Rastafarians, language is an arena, a site of political struggle and personal transformation. Since English was associated with the enslavement of African people, its syntax, phonology, and semantics were not considered by Bongo to be "heartical," that is, capable of expressing a reconstituted understanding of African culture and consciousness. The phonological structure of English words was "penetrated," that is, sounded out loud and broken apart to expose contradictions between sound and meaning, and then reassembled into new words described by Bongo as "up-full" sounds. For example, the "de" sound prefix in the word dedicate (pronounced as DEAD-di-kate) was deleted because of its sound-sense similarity to the "de" sound in the English words death and destruction. The "de" prefix was replaced by a sound that signified its opposite, not in Creole, but in English, life, creating the up-full sound "liv-i-cate." The "un" sound in words such as understand was replaced by the "o" sound of over as in "overstand," implying that all speakers are competent, that is, no speaker of Creole, English, or Dread Talk is under, beneath, or below another. The "up" sound in the word oppression was replaced by "down," as in "down-press-I," because, as Bongo stated, few people are "pushed up" in social or economic mobility but many are pushed down. The "con" sound in words such as conscious and control was associated with the "k" sound in the Creole word "kunni," meaning clever. It was replaced by the first-person pronoun "I" as in "I-trol" and "I-scious." Similarly, the suffix "dom" was deleted from the word wisdom because of its similarity to the word dumb. According to Bongo, the formation of English words from oppositional or contradictory meanings was not natural or neutral, but was a political practice intended to create and spread confusion or "kon-fuse-I." How, Bongo reasoned, can a man be both wise and dumb at the same time? The Creole "mon," that is, man, replaced the suffix "dom," creating the word-sound "wiz-mon" (see Cassidy 1982 for cunni or cunning).

Transforming what Bongo referred to as "Babylon" words into "heartical" sounds was not a local, an idiosyncratic, or a stylistic convention, but a social, political, and linguistic praxis. While the various changes are suggestive of phonological rules unique to Atlantic Creoles in which syllables are omitted from the beginning, the middle, and the end in Creole word formation (see Holm 1988:105), Rastafarians such as Bongo brought the tonal semantics of Creole to bear on transforming both Jamaica Talk and Standard English into Dread Talk. Dread Talk departs from Jamaica Talk, but does not replicate English, in its use of personal pronouns. The pronouns "him" "she," "we," "you," and especially the use of "me" as a first-person pronoun in Jamaica Talk, were replaced by the singular "I" and noun phrase "I-n-I." The first-person "I" replaced the "u" or you-sound, the second-person derivative, in words such as unity and human creating the words "I-nity" and "I-man" similar to the word-sounds "I-trol" and "I-scious." The noun phrase "I-n-I" is a homophone. When used to signify a plurality, the first-person "I" replaced the "me" and "we" of Jamaica Talk with "I-n[and]-I." When used in reference to person or self, the "I" signified the cornerstone or "foundation" of a renegotiated identity known as "I-n[within]-I."

Breaking apart English, the sign-signifier relation, enabled Rastafarians such as Bongo to key or link the meaning they attached to up-full sounds to historical events and cultural constructs. Bongo was careful to stress that the word-sound-power of Rastafari was not to be confused with "duppy business." The word "duppy" or "dupe" is African in origin. It refers to a social construction in which identity is composed of multiple souls. What was known as a "dupe" was considered to be a spiritual force and what was referred to as a "shadow" was considered its external expression. The multiple soul concept constituted the core of Afro-Jamaican constructions of identity. Each individual was born with a character (duppy-soul) and an accompanying personality (shadow-spirit) that communicated during ecstatic trances in glossolalia or "tongues" with a pantheon of Afro-Christian spirits in folk religions such as Revival and Pocomania (see Bascom 1969; Field 1960 for West African usage; Cassidy 1982:247 for Afro-Jamaica meaning; Beckwith 1969:97; Simpson 1956:336; Moore and Simpson 1957:8 for Revival and Pocomania).[14]

The ecstatic trance, ritual embodiment, and "tongues" associated with traditional expressions of identity were superseded by the multiple speaking voices of I-n[and]-I, the up-full sounds of Dread Talk, and a social or cultural knowledge known as "wiz-mon." As we mentioned earlier, the word-sound wiz-mon was used by Bongo to signify a wise as opposed to a dumb man. The knowledge associated with wiz-mon was not a historical but was keyed to international events. According to Bongo, the coronation of Haile Selassie broke or opened the seventh seal as recounted in the Book of Revelation (Ch. 19, verse 6), releasing knowledge. Rather than a knowledge born of printed texts, the seven seals signified sight, sound, speech, smell, and wiz-mon—a knowledge located in what Bongo referred to as the "foundation" in a "foundation-structure" embodiment.

The foundation-structure embodiment renegotiated traditional constructions of identity and agency. According to Bongo, the personas and
caricatures associated with duppies and spirits controlled body and
mind, thought and activity, or the relationship between foundation and
structure. Known in the anthropological literature as possession-trance
and ritual dissociation, "getting in the spirit," the culturally learned and
socially performed embodiment, epitomized by the "trumps," "groan-
ings," and "shouts" of Revival, reproduced "knowledge" about the
structure. Groundation in the rhythms and semantics of up-full sounds
renegotiated the traditional call and response, sender-receiver dyad.
Rather than a pantheon of Afro-Christian spirits who resided in the
heavens, communicated in tongues, and controlled the structure,
Selassie was a living Messiah associated with a knowledge or literacy
that emerged from the foundation. Inverting the sender-receiver dyad,
placing foundation over structure, challenged accepted convention
concerning the relationship between history, identity, and social behavior. To Bongo and the dreads with whom he reasoned, the Christian
millennium was superseded by an apocalypse associated with Haile
Selassie, a discourse of up-full sounds, and renegotiated identity known
as I-n-I.[15]

In addition to renegotiating local or traditional knowledge concerning history and identity, breaking apart or transforming Babylon words
into heartical sounds enabled Bongo to bring the agency, efficacy, or
power of up-full sounds to bear on the dialogics of reasoning, the
dynamics of linguistic interaction and communicative exchange.
Bongo's comments concerning my use of "but" and "well" and his
discussion of the word-sound "overstand" expressed a concern for
context and contextualization. On the one hand, they were attempts to
gauge how our identities would mold and shape our ability to "bust
sounds" and take our reasonings "to the heights." As I learned, the
performance of up-full sounds was an everyday practice, a multivocal
speech event. The ability to channel or direct the dialogics of speech
was an aspect of language and language-use that distinguished reasoning as a speech event or discursive practice from the "argument," the
"boasting," and the "cursing," ways of speaking associated with language and language-use on the corner. My failure to bust such sounds
told Bongo that I did not as yet "move among dread."

On the other hand, incorporation of up-full sounds entailed a radical
restructuring of our relationship. While use of the word *overstand*
indicated fluency or competence on the part of Bongo, inclusion of
such expressions in everyday discourse were calls for linguistic
compliance that set the stage, establishing a political context in which
power or "I-trol" in reasoning was subject to negotiation. It not only
called for a reflexive posture, but mandated that I privilege the

ethnographic encounter, that is, that I discuss the importance of language and language-use to Bongo not in terms of a monological exchange, linguistic or otherwise, between an abstract interlocutor and an equally abstract other, but reproduce it for what it was, the dialogics of a shared experience.

CONCLUSION

It is critically important not to reduce up-full sounds to grammatical categories or to classify them as irrational prophecy or false consciousness. In addition to glossing the way linguistic expressions are constructed, performed, and negotiated in everyday life, theories and approaches that fail to consider language as a material or constitutive practice background the ongoing and open-ended relationship between language and social life. The problem, to paraphrase Williams (1977:20–44, 92), is not that they are overly or too materialistic, but that they are not materialist enough. In their reduction of culture to a secondary or mechanical reflex, they overlook the way linguistic expressions are constructed, performed, and renegotiated in everyday life. Whether transmitted over radio waves, performed by musicians, or spoken in local reasonings, the word-sound-power of Dread Talk has inspired a society, creating a national identity, a national culture, and a national consciousness from a legacy of colonialism. To render cultural production as false not only fails to consider language as a constitutive practice, but glosses the indeterminate relation between language, social life, and political practice. While the vocabulary of Dread Talk contains both Creole and English loan words, it is not the word that constitutes the focus of their agenda, but the decolonization of thoughts and ideas, actions, and behavior. It is likely to be an ongoing process.

ACKNOWLEDGMENTS

An abbreviated version of this paper was presented at the 87th Annual Meetings of the American Anthropological Association. The author wishes to thank the Inter-America Foundation for a field research fellowship; the Right Honorable Rex Nettleford and Dr. Carl Stone of the University of the West Indies, Jamaica, for their assistance; Michael J. Harner, John P. Homiak, Carole Yawney, and Richard Blot for their comments; and the "rootsmen" of St. Elizabeth and Manchester.

NOTES

1. "Syncretistic," "nativistic," "revitalization," and "millenarism" are terms used to define a subfield of the anthropology of religion concerned with the formation and transformation of religious movements. See the Smith-Wallace

exchange in *Man* (1959) for an earlier, and in many ways still relevant, debate concerning classification and typology. For a bibliographic compilation see La Barre (1971); for a cross-cultural survey see Lanternari (1965) and Wilson 1973.

2. "I-yaric," "I-ance," and "Dread Talk" are terms that refer to the first-person pronoun or "I" usage characteristic of the language spoken by Rastafarians. I-yaric and I-ance emerge from the spoken language of everyday speech (see Owens 1976; Yawney 1985; Homiak 1995; Roberts 1988). In her grammatical analysis of taped conversations, Pollard expanded upon Cassidy's descriptive term Jamaica Talk and referred to language and language-use by Rastafarians as "Dread Talk." I have followed that convention here (see Pulis 1993, 1999). As with all spoken languages, Dread Talk cannot have a history apart from the setting, the scene, and those who speak it.

3. Our use of the term "ways of speaking" is based on Hymes (1974), Bauman and Sherzer (1989), and Bauman (1977).

4. Our understanding of identity, agency, and the power or political efficacy of talk is based on statements by Marx and Engels in the *Economic and Philosophic Manuscripts of 1844*, *The German Ideology*, and *The Eighteenth Brumaire of Louis Bonaparte*; E. P. Thompson's *The Making of the English Working Class*; and Raymond Williams's *Marxism and Literature, Problems in Materialism and Culture*, and *Culture*.

5. It is beyond the scope of this chapter to discuss Creole languages as such. For extended discussions of Creole language studies and Jamaican Creole see Cassidy (1982 [1961]), Cassidy and Le Page (1967), Hymes 1971, Roberts (1988), and Holm (1988); for language as resistance see Devonish (1986) and Alleyne (1988).

6. The Maroons were semi-autonomous communities of escaped slaves established in the seventeenth century. An abeng was a cow horn and/or conch-shell horn sounded during the Maroon Wars.

7. Native Baptists was the term applied to itinerant or folk preachers epitomized by the activities of the Afro-Americans Moses Baker and George Liele in the eighteenth century and by the Afro-Jamaicans Sam Sharpe in the nineteenth century and Alexander Bedward in the twentieth century.

8. For an illustration of the struggle between Afro-Jamaican and European Christianity see the discourse published by Hope Masterson Waddell (1863, 26, 35–36, 46) and James Phillippo (1843:188–89, 270–71). For obeah and myal see Brathwaite (1974) and Schuler (1980). For Revival and Pocomania see Simpson (1956), Moore (1965), and Morrish (1982).

9. The British West Indies has produced, as Brathwaite (1970), Ramchand (1971, 1983), and Wynter (1971) have noted, two distinct but interrelated literary traditions; one codified in the printed accounts of histories, travels, and journals, and a second in a spoken tradition of oral literature-history. While they are committed to contradictory means of communication, they share a mutual context, plot, and character. For oral-social history see Brodber (1984); for the West Indian novels see Moore (1958) and Gilkes (1981); for literature and resistance see Cudjoe (1980) and Lewis (1979); for poetry and the oral tradition see Brown (1984).

10. Since their emergence in the 1930s, two generations of Jamaicans have listened to the discourse of words-sounds-power. For a discussion of elders and ancients see Yawney (1978) and Homiak (1985). For a review of Rastafarian bibliography see Chevannes (1977) and Owens (1976).

11. As a spoken language, Dread Talk cannot be submitted to any form of analysis that excludes those who speak it. I was introduced or "grounded" in

the "I" language not as individual words or grammatical rules, but as a way of speaking known as "words-sounds-power." Learning to "bust sounds," speak with word-sounds, was undertaken by participating in a communicative event known as "reasoning." The terms "grounding" and "groundation" refer to both a means of introduction and a mode of response to word-sounds-power. For similar understandings of groundation and reasoning see Yawney (1978, 1985) and Homiak (1985).

12. Bongo's household was located in what was once a nineteenth-century Moravian mission-village. While he was neither an "elder" nor an "ancient," he was without question a "rootsman," a Rastafarian who rejected the way of life associated with contemporary Jamaican society.

13. This conversation occurred on January 14, 1982. The author has followed the guidelines outlined by Fine (1984:166–203) for transliterating oral into printed dialogue and the pronunciation guides of Cassidy (1982). I have upper-cased words and sounds that were overdifferentiated or stressed in speech and hyphenated word-sounds that were inverted, deleted, or substituted. All such guides are relative.

14. It is not my intention to gloss the importance of this concept. "Duppi," "duppi ting," and "duppy business" are words used to signify the multispirited world of Revival, Pocomania, and obeah. The term dupe is West African in origin and refers to a cultural tradition of multiple souls. A "dupe" was considered the spiritual force inside a person's body and what is referred to as a "shadow" is considered its external expression. The multiple soul concept embodies the Afro-Jamaican cultural construction of social being. Each individual is born with a unique character (duppy-soul) and an accompanying personality (shadow-spirit) associated with socially defined understandings of good and bad. When a person dies, a duppy travels to an otherworldly realm while a shadow is believed to lurk behind. In a series of rituals, the shadow is dispatched below the earth, insuring it can not be used malevolently by an obeahman. For West African word usage see Bascom (1969) and Field (1960); for Afro-Jamaican word meaning see Cassidy and Le Page (1967, 164) and Cassidy (1982, 247); for Revival, Pocomania, and obeah see Beckwith (1969, 97), Simpson (1956, 336), Moore (1954, 1965), Moore and Simpson (1957, 1958), Hogg (1967), Barrett (1977), Schuler (1980), and Moorish (1982).

15. The foundation-structure mediation stands in opposition to the embodi-ments, that is, constructions, offered by Revival and Pocomania. The ritual performances are social activities that express and reproduce "knowledge" associated with the relationship between thought and activity. For example, "getting in the spirit," the culturally learned and socially performed embodi-ment of a god, duppy, or spirit, is enacted by drumming, dancing, and hyper-ventilation in a variety of "workings," that is, exhalation and/or inhalation to patterned drum rhythms known as "trumps," "groaning," "laborings," or "shouts" that can include ingestion of alcohol mixed with various herbs. Known in the anthropological literature as ritual dissociation and possession-trance the caricatures associated with Lucifer, Michael, and/or ancestor duppies are be-lieved to control body movements and personality. Duppies, gods, and spirits are summoned by special drum rhythms, songs, and dances. Individuals enact the persona they embody; some are threatening, others are friendly, some speak in unintelligible tongues, while others engaged in dialogue. Both Moore (1954, 59–60) and Hogg (1967, 263) described "Bongo-men" who recognized Christian deities but who only enacted the caricatures (duppies) of powerful obeahmen and maroons.

REFERENCES

Abrahams, Roger. 1983. *The Man of Words in the West Indies*. Baltimore: Johns Hopkins University Press.

Alleyne, Mervyn. 1988. *Roots of Jamaican Culture*. London: Pluto Press.

Asprey, G. F., and Phyllis Thornton. 1953. "Medicinal Plants in Jamaica, W. I." *West Indian Medical Journal* 2: 233–52.

Austin, Diane. 1984. *Urban Life in Kingston, Cambridge Jamaica*. New York: Gordon and Breach Publishers.

Bailey, Beryl L. 1966. *Jamaican Creole Syntax*. Cambridge: University Press.

Barrett, Leonard. 1977. *The Rastafarians*. Boston: Beacon Press.

Bascom, William. 1969. *Ifa Divination*. Bloomington: Indiana University Press.

Bauman, Richard. 1977. *Verbal Art as Performance*. Rowley, Mass.: Newbury House.

Bauman, Richard, and Joel Sherzer, eds. 1989. *Explorations in the Ethnography of Speaking*. Cambridge: Cambridge University Press.

Beckwith, Martha. 1969. *Black Roadways*. New York: Negro Universities Press.

Bilby, K., and Elliot Leib. 1986. "Kumina, the Howellite Church, and the Emergence of Rastafarian Traditional Music in Jamaica." *Jamaica Journal* 19: 22–28.

Brathwaite, Edward Kamau. 1970. "Creative Literature of the British West Indies during the Period of Slavery." *Savacou* 1: 46–74.

———. 1974. "The African Presence in Caribbean Literature." In Sidney Mintz, ed., *Slavery, Colonialism, and Racism*. New York: Norton, 73–110.

———. 1978. *The Development of Creole Society in Jamaica 1770–1820*. Clarendon: Oxford University Press.

Brodber, E. 1984. "Oral Sources and the Creation of a Social History of the Caribbean." *Jamaica Journal* 16: 2–12.

Brodber, E., and J. Edward Green. 1981. *Reggae and Cultural Identity in Jamaica*. Kingston: ISER.

Brooks, Walter H. 1922. The Evolution of the Negro Baptist Church. *Journal of Negro History* 7: 11–22.

Brown, Beverly. 1975. "George Liele: Black Baptist and Pan Africanist 1750–1820." *Savacou* 11/12: 58–67.

Brown, Lloyd. 1984. *West Indian Poetry*. Port of Spain: Heinemann.

Brown, Samuel. 1966. "Treatise on the Rastafarian Movement." *Caribbean Studies* 6: 39–40.

Bryan, Patrick. 1991. *The Jamaican People, 1880–1902*. London: Macmillan.

Campbell, Horace. 1987. *Rasta and Resistance*. Trenton: Third World Press.

Caplan, Pat. 1987. *The Cultural Construction of Sexuality*. London: Tavistock.

Carnegie, James. 1973. *Some Aspects of Jamaica Politics: 1918–1983*. Kingston: Institute of Jamaica.

Cashmore, E. 1983 [1979]. *Rastaman*. London: Unwin.

Cassidy, Frederic. 1982 [1961]. *Jamaica Talk: Three Hundred Years of the English Language in Jamaica*. London: Macmillan.

Cassidy, F. G., and R. B. Le Page. 1967. *Dictionary of Jamaican English*. Cambridge: Cambridge University Press.

Chevannes, E. Barrinton. 1971. "Revival and Black Struggle." *Savacou* 5: 27–37.

———. 1977. "Revivalism: A Disappearing Religion." *Caribbean Quarterly* 24: 1–17.

———. 1977. "The Literature of Rastafari." *Social and Economic Studies* 26: 239–62.

———. 1978. *The Social Origins of the Rastafari Movement*. Kingston: Institute of Social and Economic Studies.

———. 1994. *Rastafari: Roots and Ideology*. Syracuse: Syracuse University Press.

———. 1995. *Rastafari and Other Afro-Caribbean Worldviews*. New York: Macmillan.

Cudjoe, Selwyn. 1980. *Resistance and Caribbean Literature*. Athens: Ohio University Press.

Davis, John W. 1920. "George Liele and Andrew Bryan: Pioneer Negro Baptist Preachers." *Journal of Negro History* 4: 119–27.

Devonish, Hubert. 1986. *Language and Liberation: Creole Language Politics in the Caribbean*. London: Karia Press.

Eaton, George E. 1975. *Alexander Bustamante and Modern Jamaica*. Kingston: Kingston Publishers Ltd.

Edwards, Bryan. 1801. *The History, Civil and Commercial, of the British Colonies in the West Indies*. London: John Stockdale.

Elkins, W. F. 1977. *Street Preachers, Faith Healers and Herb Doctors in Jamaica, 1890–1925*. New York: Revisionist Press.

Erskine, Noel. 1982. *Decolonizing Theology*. Maryknoll: Orbis.

Fabian, J. 1979. "The Anthropology of Religious Movements: From Explanation To Interpretation." *Social Research* 46: 4–35.

Faristzaddi, Millard. 1982. *Itations of Jamaica and I Rastafari*. New York: Grove Press.

Field, M. J. 1937. *Religion and Medicine of the Ga People*. London: Oxford University Press.

———. 1960. *Search for Security*. New York: Oxford University Press.

Forsythe, Dennis. 1983. *Rastafari: For the Healing of the Nation*. Kingston: Ziaka.

Gardner, William James. 1971 [1873]. *A History of Jamaica*. London: Frank Cass.

Gayle, Clement. 1982. *George Liele: Pioneer Missionary in Jamaica*. Kingston: Jamaican Baptist Union.

Gilkes, Michael. 1981. *The West Indian Novel*. Boston: Twayne Publishers.

Hart, Richard. 1989. *Rise and Organize*. London: Karia.

Hill, Robert. 1981. "Dread History: Leonard P. Howell and Millenarian Visions in Early Rastafari Religion in Jamaica." *Epoche* 9: 30–71.

———. 1983. "Leonard P. Howell and Millenarian Visions in Early Rastafari." *Jamaica Journal* 16: 24–39.

Hogg, Donald W. 1967. *Jamaican Religions*. Ann Arbor: University Microfilms.

Holm, John. 1988. *Creole Studies, Vol. 1*. London: Cambridge University Press.

Homiak, John. 1985. *The "Ancient of Days" Seated Black: Eldership, Oral Tradition, and Ritual in Rastafari Culture*. Ph.D. Dissertation, Brandeis.

———. 1987. "The Mystic Revelation of Rasta Far-Eye: Visionary Communication in a Prophetic Movement. In E. B. Tedlock, ed., *Dreaming*. Santa Fe: School of American Research Press, 220–45.

———. 1995. "Dub History." In E. B. Chevannes, ed., *Rastafari and Other Afro-Caribbean Worldviews*. Chapter 6.

Hymes, Dell. 1971. *Pidginization and Creolization of Languages*. London: Cambridge University Press.

———. 1974. *Foundations in Sociolinguistics*. Philadelphia: University of Pennsylvania.

———. 1974. "Ways of Speaking." In R. Bauman and J. Sherzer, eds., *Explorations in the Ethnography of Speaking*. New York: Cambridge University Press, 433–53.

Jekyll, Walter. 1966 [1970]. *Jamaican Song and Story*. New York: Dover.

Kitzinger, Sheila. 1960. "Protest and Mysticism: The Rastafari Cult of Jamaica." *Journal for the Scientific Study of Religion* 7: 240–63.

———. 1966. "The Rastafarian Brethren of Jamaica." *Comparative Studies in Society and History* 9: 33–39.

La Barre, Weston. 1971. "Materials for a History of Crisis Cults: A Bibliographic Essay." *Current Anthropology* 12: 3–44.

La Guerre, Michel. 1986. *Afro-Caribbean Folk Medicine*. Hadley, Mass.: Bergin and Garvey.

Lanternari, Vittorio. 1965. *The Religions of the Oppressed*. New York: Mentor Books.

Lewis, Maureen W. 1979. "The African Impact on Language and Literature in the English-Speaking Caribbean." In M. Crahan and F. Knight, eds., *Africa and the Caribbean*. Baltimore: Johns Hopkins University Press, 102–23.

Long, Edward. 1970 [1774]. *The History of Jamaica*. London: Frank Cass.

Long, Joseph. 1973. *Jamaican Medicine*. Ann Arbor: University Microfilms.

Magubane, Bernard M. 1987. *The Ties That Bind: African-American Consciousness of Africa*. Trenton: Africa World Press.

Makonnen, Ras. 1973. *Pan-Africanism from Within*. London: Oxford University Press.

Martin, Tony. 1984. *The Pan-African Connection*. Dover: Majority Press.

———. 1987. "International Aspects of the Garvey Movement." *Jamaica Journal* 20: 10–19.

Marx, Karl, and Frederick Engels. 1969. *Selected Works in Three Volumes*. Moscow: Progress Publishers.

Mau, James. 1968. *Social Change and Images of the Future*. Cambridge: Schenkman Publishing Company.

Moore, Gerald. 1969. *The Chosen Tongue*. New York: Harper and Row.

Moore, Joseph. 1954. *Religion of Jamaican Negroes*. Ann Arbor: University Microfilms.

———. 1965. "Religious Syncretism in Jamaica." *Practical Anthropology* 12: 63–70.

Moore, J., and George E. Simpson. 1957. "A Comparative Study of Acculturation in Morant Bay and Kingston, Jamaica." *Zaire* 11: 979–1019.

———. 1958. "A Comparative Study of Acculturation in Morant Bay and Kingston, Jamaica." *Zaire* 12: 3–87.

Morrish, Ivor. 1982. *Obeah, Christ, and Rastaman: Jamaica and Its Religion*. Cambridge: James Clarke and Sons.

Nettleford, Rex. 1970. *Mirror Mirror: Identity, Race, and Protest in Jamaica*. Kingston: William Collins.

———. 1979. *Caribbean Cultural Identity*. Los Angeles: University of California Press.

———. 1987a. "The Spirit of Marcus Garvey." *Jamaica Journal* 20: 2–10.

———. 1987b. "Cultivating a Caribbean Sensibility." *Caribbean Review* 15: 4–8, 28.

Newton, V. 1984. *The Silver Men*. Kingston: ISER.

Ong, Walter. 1967. *The Presence of the Word*. New Haven: Yale University Press.

Owens, Joseph. 1976. *Dread*. Kingston: Sangster.

Phillippo, James. 1843. *Jamaica: Its Past and Present State*. London: Dawsons.

Pollard, V. 1980. "Dread Talk." *Caribbean Quarterly* 26: 32–42.

———. 1982. "The Social History of Dread Talk." *Caribbean Quarterly* 28: 17–40.

———. 1984. "Word Sounds: The Language of Rastafari in Barbados and St. Lucia." *Jamaica Journal* 17: 57–62.

Post, Ken. 1978. *Arise Ye Starvelings*. The Hague: Martinus Nijhoff.

Pulis, John W. 1993. "Up-Full Sounds: Language, Identity, and the Worldview of Rastafari." *Ethnic Groups* 10: 285–300.

———. in preparation. *Gates to Zion: An Ethnography of an Afro-Jamaica Religious Movement*. London: Gordon and Breach.

———. 1999. "From Revelations 'faawod' to Genesis: Reading Scripture in Jamaica." In J. Pulis, ed., *Religion, Identity and Diaspora*. New York: Gordon and Breach, 357–402.

Ramchand, Kenneth. 1971. "History and Novel." *Savacou* 5: 103–14.

———. 1983. *The West Indian Novel and Its Background*. Kingston: Heinemann.

Reckord, V. 1977. "Rastafari Music: An Introductory Study." *Jamaica Journal* 1: 6–8.

———. 1982. "Reggae, Rastafarianism, and Cultural Identity." *Jamaica Journal* 46: 70–79.

Roberts, R. 1988. *West Indian Languages*. London: Cambridge University Press.

Robinson, Cedric J. 1983. *Black Marxism: The Making of the Black Radical Tradition*. London: Zed Press.

Rodney, Walter. 1983. *The Groundings with My Brothers*. London: Bogel'Ouverture.

Schuler, Monica. 1980. *Alas, Alas, Kongo*. Baltimore: Johns Hopkins University Press.

Semaj, Leachim. 1980. "Rastafari: From Religion to Social Theory." *Caribbean Quarterly* 26: 22–31.

Sheridan, Richard. 1989. *Doctors and Slaves*. Cambridge: Cambridge University Press.

Simpson, George Eaton. 1955a. "Political Cultism in West Kingston, Jamaica." *Social and Economic Studies* 4: 135–49.

———. 1955b. "The Rastafari Movement in Jamaica: A Study of Race and Class Conflict." *Social Forces* 34: 167–170.

———. 1955c. "Culture Change and Reintegration Found in the Cults of West Kingston, Jamaica." *Proceedings of the American Philosophical Society* 99: 89–92.

———. 1956. "Jamaican Revivalist Cults." *Social and Economic Studies* 5: 321–434.

———. 1962. "The Rastafari Movement in Its Millennial Aspect." *Comparative Studies in Society and History*, Supplement 2: 160–65.

Smith, M. G., Roy Augier, and Rex Nettleford. 1976 [1960]. *The Rastafari Movement in Kingston*. Kingston: ISER.

Smith, Marian W. 1959. Towards a Classification of Cult Movements. *Man* 59: 8–12.

Tafari, I. Jabulani. 1980. "The Rastafari: Successors of Marcus Garvey." *Caribbean Quarterly* 26: 1–11.

Taylor, Patrick. 1989. *The Narrative of Liberation*. Ithaca: Cornell University Press.

Thompson, E. P. 1968 [1963]. *The Making of the English Working Class*. London: Penguin Books.

———. 1978. *The Poverty of Theory and Other Essays*. New York: Monthly Review Press.

Underhill, Edward Bean. 1862. *The West Indies*. London: Jackson, Walford, and Hodder.

Waddell, H. M. 1863. *Twenty-Nine Years in the West Indies and Central America*. London: T. Nelson and Son.

Wallace, Anthony F. C. 1956. "Revitalization Movements." *American Anthropologist* 58: 264–81.

———. 1959. "Towards a Classification of Cult Movements: Some Further Contributions." *Man* 24/25: 5–8.

Wedenoja, William. 1978. *Religion and Adaptation in Rural Jamaica*. Ann Arbor: University Microfilms.

Williams, Raymond. 1977. *Marxism and Literature*. Oxford: Oxford University Press.

———. 1981. *Culture*. London: Fontana Paperbacks.

Wilson, Bryan. 1973. *Magic and the Millennium*. New York: Harper and Row.

Wright, Philip. 1966. *Lady Nugent's Journal*. Kingston: Institute of Jamaica.

Wynter, Sylvia. 1971. "Novel and History, Plot and Plantation." *Savacou* 5: 95–103.

Yawney, Carole. 1978. *Lions in Babylon*. Ph.D. dissertation, McGill University.

——. 1985. *Don't Vex Then Pray*. Paper prepared for Qualitative Research Conference, University of Waterloo, May 15–17.

13

Passionate Speech and Literate Talk in Grenada

George Mentore

Literacy gives agency to the system of education in Grenada. Through this means, it serves to form the social category of a dominant but intellectually sycophantic minority. Historically charted by British imperial rule of the colonized Grenadians, the way to literate identity became the symbolic property of the local elite.[1] Not surprisingly, literacy now molds the social category of privilege in the image of its cosmopolitan masters. Particularly through the ritual of formal schooling, literacy functions to legitimize high rank; it gives academic authority to social power. Much of this authority derives from conferring upon individuals specific kinds of literate knowledge associated primarily with European culture. The act of conferring, that is, the *literizing* of the individual, legitimizes the recipient, expresses the force of literacy and provides the donor with one means of confirming social power. (Throughout this chapter I use the term *literizing* in much the same way as Brian Street [1984, 101] does when he considers it to be, following Jacques Derrida [1978, 8], a "literary act" of constraint with restrictive capacities for manifesting experience.)

On its own literacy has no *a priori* disposition for privileging the cultural property or status of one group over another. In the service of the modern nation state, for example, it has come under the control of central governments seeking the "homogenization and standardization" of their citizens (Hobsbawn 1990, 93). To counteract competing Caribbean images of community, state patriotism has employed mass literacy programs in the "national language" of the colonizer. This has facilitated state governance, and, at the same time, has politicized literacy. Susceptible to political control, in its privileging of the colonizing state and the colonizing person, literacy stands against an alternative "nation language," one filled with the "noise" of resistance (Brathwaite 1984, 17). I shall refer to literacy's competitor in Grenadian society as the voice of creolese.

Initially primed on an African canvas of utterances, subsequently mixed with the colonial hues of French and English, the Grenadian creole voice currently exhibits the influences of its eclectic past. Retaining these influences, as opposed to shedding them for the standard English of the current "master's voice," has clothed creolese locally with linguistic inferiority. In fact, the creole voice has been accused of lacking any resemblance to language. Yet Grenadian creolese, like other Caribbean creole languages, clearly displays certain rule-governed features. It proposes the use of an *a/iz* topicalizer (e.g., "iz di mango we want"),[2] the application of *does* to convey habitual meaning, and the prevalence of *wi* (tag)[3] (following Roberts 1988, but see Bickerton 1981, Fishman 1972, Hymes 1971, Romaine 1988, Stewart 1962). It also displays a "verb-centered" syntax. It has adjectives functioning as verbs. It uses double negatives. It can have as many as four verbs without an intervening conjunction. It has a prevalence for "front focusing" sentences (e.g., "iz foreday-morning he come"). It renders standard English short vowels as long, and many English long vowels as short. In addition, it has many orthographic omissions and insertions, for example, the regular apocope of past participles, as in *sellin* (selling); metathesis, as in *flim* (film); syncope, as in *tin* (thin); epenthesis, as in *athalectic* (athletic); prothesis, as in *hegg* (egg); and aphaeresis, as in *ooman* (woman). Yet, in Grenada, literacy ignores all of these principles, ones which, if given literacy's support (as in parts of the Dutch and Francophone Caribbean) certainly could be consciously recognized if not actually embraced by state authority.

In this brief essay, I attempt to raise the question about why Grenadian creolese, as the audible voice of the lower classes and the oral mark of their social category, falls on the deaf ears of the state and its agents. My inquiry will be guided by the understanding that radically different moral codes underscore the competitive social classes, and that it is this difference which motivates the specific manifestations of power and domination in Grenadian society. After identifying and briefly discussing the significant groups, institutions, and symbols of social being, the literate and nonliterate groups, the school and the state, the textual and oral symbols of identity are my main focus. I begin, however, by considering the principal causes, functions and effects of literacy achievement in Grenada. I argue, perhaps controversially, for speech over race as the primary inscriptive of social identity and suggest that what influences elite speech the most is the "literacy event," here considered as a strategy of inequality beginning with a belief in the autonomy of literacy. Two examples of literate inscriptives which act to implant legitimacy in the dominant voice support my argument. In contradistinction to the dominant voice, the subordinate creole voice seeks out emotional orality to assert its own speech routines. The speech routine of "cursing" (obscene language), for example, demonstrates how the social logic of the subordinate creole moral order gains its internal coherence. I then present four distinct teaching styles, used in the pedagogical production of literacy, each actively engaged with alienating the creole voice from its own moral base. My conclusion will be that while the state empowers its own voice with literizing strategies these same strategies result in an oppression of the impassioned creole voice.

LITERATE ACHIEVEMENT AND RECRUITING THE ELITE

The 1981 Grenada Population Census reports that "about 87 percent of the adult population have never passed any examination" (Vol. 3: 32).[4] Exams have provided state officials with what they consider to be an obvious means of measuring literacy achievement. Yet, because definitions of literacy have varied, resulting in fluctuating figures of 15 percent (World Bank Report 1979), and 60 percent (People's Revolutionary Government 1980), what examinations actually gauge appears to be less than apparent. Examinations certainly provide evidence, to the satisfaction of the state, that success rates have been low for a large proportion of the Creole-speaking population. In the creole speech community, contrary to what some local educational pundits have claimed, non-literacy does not stem from natural stupidity (The Grenadian Voice 7(37) (1988): 4; The Informer 4(37) (1988): 4). And while the low number of teachers and their inadequate training, as well as lack of facilities and funding, may contribute to low levels of literacy achievement, I would contend that they are not the principal cause. I would argue instead that the criteria of literacy favor those already socialized by the cultural forces of reading and writing and disfavor those whose meaningful social world happens not to be governed by such standards.

Literacy achievements serve, as manifest in national and regional examinations, as well as school grades, to establish rigorous grounds for the recruitment of new literate persons. In the process, they place control in the hands of those with vested interests in reproducing in their own image the marks of literate identity. Such control and bias result in not only validating the form of literate identity, but also in some persons receiving no recognition for their efforts and others receiving certified proof of low literate achievement. In either of the latter two cases, "underachievers" are banished to the waste ground of "poor" career choices and low social status. Because wealth and power have been forged to literacy, non-literate identity prescribes poverty and class victimization. Set upon acclaimed principles of merit, which allow many to partake but few to succeed, the achievement process provides in itself the legitimacies for excluding large portions of the population from the advantages of literate enlightenment, economic wealth, and social power. In advance of themselves, the actual agreements of participation offer logical and reassuring accounts for any case of exclusion; recognized failure to achieve the set standards furnishes "objective" evidence for denying membership. This process of including and excluding fits well with the much avowed rational tendencies of the state. Integrated into the state, that is, into its governing apparatus, whereby governing can no longer function without literacy, literate achievement now implies the continuance of state power. With dialectic force, the state and its literate agents insure their mutual continuity. In this respect, as the handmaiden of state power, literate achievement secures the form and the rank of its members. It functions, in fact, as an integral aspect of their identity. In addition, literate elite personhood possesses the intonations of the standard English voice. All of which stand in contrast to the creole voice, which has been disqualified for literate inscription and expelled to the lower ranks of society.

SPEECH INSCRIPTIVES OF IDENTITY

The category of the non-literate lower class person is formed primarily with the speech of creolese. Given the immense emphasis on race in Caribbean studies, this may seem an imprudent statement to make regarding social status in Grenada. Yet, while I do indeed consider racial diacritica to play a large part in giving form to Grenadian notions of class difference, I judge them as doing so with secondary impact to that of speech. Admittedly, in Grenada today, many effective symbols combine to produce the social person. Skin color, residence, profession, and education, for example, all work to define social identity. Nevertheless, speech occupies a special place of primacy in the configuration of personhood. For example, coming principally from the rural Mount

Moritz community in the parish of St. George, the *Monmon* (lower class whites) speak only creolese. Similarly, some individual blacks, particularly those in high status jobs associated with the capital city and the urban areas, speak only standard English. These latter are in fact identified with the social category of the privileged *Bake* (brown-skin elite) whose image of exclusiveness relies strongly upon speaking standard. English. Known locally as *Townee*, the small proportion of black and large percentage of brown literate urbanites comprise the upper classes of Grenada. It is, however, the large Creole-speaking population, defined variously as "uneducated," "under-educated," "illiterate," "rustic," and/or "black" who are most often recognized as the under-privileged. Known locally as *Country Bookie*, the predominantly black, nonliterate, rural, Creole-speaking peasant constitutes the fundamental image of the lower class person.

"LITERACY EVENTS" AND THE *TOWNEE*

The *Townee's* world is filled with the events of literacy—I am here following the supposition that literacy's predetermined and shared assumptions are inculcated during what Shirley Brice Heath (1983, 386) calls "literacy events" (but see also Anderson, Teale, and Estrada 1980). The representation of the *Townee's* social being relies upon the rule-governed social interactions pertaining to the production and/or comprehension of graphically coded messages. These literacy events involve one or more persons focused on the sequential act of writing and reading. Obviously, such action does not take place solely in the context of formal schooling. That they do not may be understood as a strategy of inequality; if the criterion of schooling is set by literacy achievement then those predisposed to the literizing process will have an advantage over those who do not. The *Townee* grabs, generates, and prescribes conditions for interacting with text, interpreting text, and talking about text. The *Townee's* social being depends upon the practice of literacy and the control of literacy's productive means.

The literizing process is, for the *Townee*, a generalized occurrence, that is, it is not restricted only to formal schooling. My understanding about why this should be begins with the assumption that the *Townee* perceives literacy as being an autonomous manifestation in the world (Street 1984). In other words, literacy is ideologically understood as having its own force outside of and independent to society. It occupies an almost mystical domain where human influence appears as the effect rather than as the cause of its energy. Hence, by presenting literacy as an aspect of what it means to be *Townee*, a link is made between this category of person and the forces which seem to exist beyond it. Such linkage to autonomous literate forces confers upon *Townee* personhood the credentials for evoking superiority over those detached from the source. Literacy's pervasive independence in the world suggests that any successful engagement it makes with individuals will not be indiscriminate. The *Townee*'s coupling with literacy can therefore be interpreted as resulting from an independent and natural (perhaps even supernatural) source which recognizes only superior receptive beings. Impersonal and external, this source of proof extends through *Townee* personhood and superiority to instill preeminence in the institutions dependent upon literate power.

Yet, with literacy's pervasiveness and its discerning intimacy with the *Townee*—reinforcing belief in the latter's intellectual superiority—why would there be the need to insist upon the moral virtues of schooling? Acting as the formal institution for channelling and distributing the generally accepted norms of literacy conduct, schools become the ritual space for valorizing the elitist content of literacy and the liminal ground for dramatizing the inferiority of the non-literate. Because literacy conveys the elite's moral code of order, the non-literate appear as the threat of chaos. They are like the witchery of "counter-society" (Balandier 1972, 111), or the enemy within who wars against the norms of conduct (Foucault 1979, 90). Of course, from the point of view of the dominant, this chaotic community of non-persons must have, if not literacy, at least discipline, for they must recognize leadership and follow commands. Schooling operates as ritual discipline to bring this chaos under control. In the way I understand elite *Townee* culture to bring its project into effect, it uses schooling like the phase of "antistructure" in rites of passage, where initiates become innocuous or so bound-up with "communitas" they no longer present themselves as a threat to society (Turner 1992, 1969).

A certain fiction must be propagated to sustain credence in the autonomy of literacy however; those who believe in literacy's independence in the world-at-large must deny its culturally constructed character. Broadcasting the fiction, to deny the human genius of culture, is to effect a public concealment of literacy's bias toward *Townee* personhood. The *Townee*'s dominant category and the advantage this gives it in the education system stems from literacy's predisposition towards its own cultural markings. Without the denial which conceals, the claim cannot be maintained (without the realization of a contradiction of course) that "natural" intellectual ability will find justified success and reward in a "meritorious" system of education. Hence literacy's bias cannot be part of the collective conscious. I would argue that literacy achieves denial by being instrumental in the makeup of the dominant culture. For not only does the event of literacy instill the abilities to encode and decode graphic text, it also verifies the empirical reality of its own existence. It does so through enforced actions. The cultural construction of literacy finds effective denial in the "truth" of its material existence.

LITERATE INSCRIPTIVES AND THE *TOWNEE*

To intensify the cultural and social distances between themselves and the *Country Bookie*, Townees frequently mark their speech with literate inscription. This involves a "way of speaking" (Hymes 1974) which exhibits bookish knowledge. It requires placing efficacy in text and identifying textual power in the voice. The effective literate voice relies upon the textual origin of speech. Such a voice has no coercive force without this source. Grenadian listeners seek constantly to establish a reason for giving their attention to a particular voice. They recognize the literate inscriptives of speech as one authoritative source. What they comprehend is a speaker's identification with authorial experience; it is as if the voice speaks the text and, in so doing, places the speaker in the category of literate dominance. Here experience is an indirect one *through* the text of the author. To speak with literate inscriptives depends upon the ideological convictions that text communicates and that it does so through knowing how to decode its message.

EXAMPLE ONE

Location:	Belmont, St. George's, Grenada
Time and Date:	Late morning, 26 April 1989
Scene:	The assembly hall of the Grenadian Boy's Secondary

School on the occasion of "The Principals' Fourth Annual Seminar."

During the first intermission, a group of teachers huddle in conversation, eager to discuss the points just presented by the Chief Education Officer. Three of them hold posts at prominent institutions in St. Georges, while the other two do so at obscure primary schools in the provinces.

Town Teacher One:	"Well man, what you think? Do you thing govern ment can get the money to restructure the whole system?"
Town Teacher Two:	"I don't know, but I was reading the Belamy Report the other day, and it says quite clearly that Government expenditure on restructuring would be misplaced."
Town Teacher Three:	"Why?"
Town Teacher Two:	"Because it considers the Tanteen Complex part of the teaching system."
Country Teacher One:	"I don't know how dey expect us to fill de National College with students if dey don't support the elementary structure better."
Town Teacher One:	"What ya talking about man? You an know by now that Government don't care about elementary

> education no more? If it did, it would give our
> teachers more money."
Country Teacher Two: "I have been doing some work on dis very
> subject, and my research shows that even if
> Government could put more money into salaries, the
> system would not improve by much."

Stunned silence, as the others collect their thoughts to consider this source of authority and new line of argument.

The opening query by the Town Teacher solicits the opinion of the gathered colleagues and, at the same time, invites them to confirm the exclusiveness of their professional community. The conference was already functioning to solidify, through their participation, the teachers' membership in one of the state's highest-ranked status groups. Nevertheless, the opening query clears the way for an introduction of membership's more tangible qualities; it introduces to personal scrutiny the technical means for expressing the nature of head teacher membership.

Belonging possesses a quality of textuality; a quality largely imparted to head teacher membership by means of an exclusive circulation and knowledge of government documents among state-employed principals. Note in the dialogue the use of such terms as "restructure," "system," "complex," and "research," suggesting familiarity with the kind of social science prose commonly found legitimizing state literature. By speaking such terms and in the context of the conversation recognizing and acknowledging such terms, the teachers display not only a sharing in the textually bestowed knowledge of government, but also a sharing in the legitimacy of government's identity. Note also the other distinct ways in which the conversing teachers evoke knowledge of text to add authoritative force to their voice. These appear most noticeably where Town Teacher Two mentions he has read the "Belamy Report" and where Country Teacher Two cities his own research. In each case, the teachers draw on an acknowledged intimacy between author, text, and reader, a condition ideologically knowable and confirmable through literacy—the technique of knowledge broadcast in speech as evidence of high social rank.

It should be evident, however, that the cross-cutting differentiation of status between urban and rural identities and the insular similitude of being a Head Teacher complicate our case example. In their speech acts, the teachers sought to acknowledge both the cultural closeness among members of their teaching profession and the social distance between town and country. Neither contingent of the conversing group wished to devalue the professional category to which all belonged; yet to inscribe difference in the status given to teaching in the different locations, speech took on the role of helping to configure such difference. Recruited to give high status to urban teachers, or, better still, to assist in identifying the urban teacher as the fully developed ideal type of Head Teacher, literate inscriptives served to mark their speech routines.

Standard English speech facilitates recognition of authority's textual source. The lingua franca of Grenada emulates the speech of the British upper classes. For most Grenadians, a "well spoken" individual is an educated person, and, consequently, an individual who speaks "badly," i.e., creolese, is an uneducated person. This culturally imposed dogma perpetuates a symbolic correlation between literacy and standard Grenadian English speech. It initially derives from a taught notion that reading and writing influence speech to the degree that they increase vocabulary and correct poor grammar. The fact as to whether they do or do not is not at issue; what I am working with here is the local opinion of the large majority who believe quite strongly that they do. This has been reinforced by historical and social realities. For Grenadians, the British colonial experience was implemented primarily by a highly literate civil administration. Thus, to them, British society was indeed perceived as being a literate one. The fact that the British and the Grenadian elite spoke in standard English assisted the view that power has a rather distinctive literate sound. Within the Grenadian speech community, standard English speech and literacy have come to be closely associated with each other. A voice marked in such a fashion carries authority.

The use of low, moderate tones of the voice can be thought of as another significant literacy inscriptive. A soft modulation of voice is the ideal for standard Grenadian English speakers. Soft tones attempt to connote a reduction of expressive emotion. The desired effect is for one's argument to be "rational" in order that it may be accepted. Rationality here depends upon an avoidance of any turbulence which would detract attention away from the "logical" development of one's argument. For the standard Grenadian English speaker, a soft, calm voice forces argumentation to rely upon "objective" textual sources and not upon subjective validations signaled by loud, emotional utterances. Clearly the belief here is that strong sentiments reduce credibility in the speaker's statements. Because literacy inscriptives supposedly bring rationalist validity to the standard Grenadian English speaker's voice, it is believed that obscuring such legitimacy with extraneous emotions reduces the sought after effect of vocal authority.

EXPRESSIVE EMOTION AND THE *COUNTRY BOOKIE*

A rather different situation exists for the creole voice. The Creole-speaking *Country Bookie* has infrequent encounters and, at times, altogether lacks the literacy event. Literacy seldom marks the *Country Bookie*'s voice. Precisely because of what could be construed as dislocation and distancing from literacy, the creole voice commands no authority outside its own speech community. I visited many such communities in the rural areas. In their environment, I found very few instances of the textual circumstances which filled the world of the *Townee*. Invariably, there was either no printed matter whatsoever or very little of it in homes. There were no visible signs of text in the villages, for example, no street names, no house numbers, and no road signs. Except in the capital city of St. George's and in the three major towns, newspapers were rarely seen. In addition, poor lighting or no lighting at all frequently hindered leisure time writing and reading. After school, at the end of the daylight hours spent working in the fields or on domestic chores, children could hardly see to read; in the fading light of day, those with books could be observed sitting on their front steps squinting at the text on a dim page. Considering these observations and more, it is quite understandable why "talk" about, "interpretation" of, and "interaction" with writing are either scarce of absent among Creole-speakers. However, while being of immense interest for any thorough understanding of the political economy of text, concern about lack of access to the supportive mechanisms of literacy is not here my main point of departure. It is rather that the Creole-speaker hardly ever seeks out legitimacy for his or her own voice in the objective criteria of literacy. The fact is that even with the set desires for and alienation from literacy, nurtured primarily in schools, the literacy event is not a generalized features of *Country Bookie* identity. It is hardly surprising, therefore, that when asked to perform in a schooling system defined by literacy achievement the *Country Bookie*'s success rate is extremely low. Yet elite society continues to blame this category of person for the poor educational performance of the nation. And, more distractingly, rather than this poverty of performance having the effect of galvanizing officials radically to alter the education system, it has instead become a major symbol of the *Country Bookie*'s social inferiority.

Dislocated and set adrift from the primary vehicle of ruling class epistemology, the creole voice has to rely upon its own form of oral legitimacy. Its validity rests not in an ideology of objectified text or in any distant exclusive center, but in an emotionally expressive orality.[5] The authority of Grenadian creolese counts on the open expression of assertive feelings, yet it is this very feature, stemming from internal causes, which excludes it from the "national" language of the state. While the standard Grenadian English voice receives its support from the more generally accepted actions and artifacts of reading and writing, the creole voice sustains its own valorization with dynamic emotional oral emphasis. The effect of dominance, by the standard English voice and its instruments of power, has influenced the creole speaker to think of his or her expressive voice as being invalid outside of its authoritative speech community, in other words, of being alienated from the "correct" national standards of discourse.

EXAMPLE TWO

Location:	The Registrar General's Office, St. George's, Grenada
Time and Date:	Late afternoon, 25 January 1989
Scene:	The Chief Registrar has her small private office at the

back and to the right of large open-plan room where several secretaries
work at their individual desks. A high counter separates the secretaries'
space from the public. In front of the counter, in the cramped public
area, people mill around waiting to be attended to by the Receptionist.
The lack of space forces most of them out into the cobbled courtyard,
where they can see into the building through the glass-latticed windows.

From out of the Chief Registrar's office storms an angry, burly woman.
She stumps through the secretaries' room, lifts the hinged section of the
counter, steps out into the public area, turns, and raises her voice, directing
her words back toward the office she has just vacated.

Angry Woman:	I gun air-rout NOW, ya dyam red-skin BITCH.
	ya mek me walk till I green. And fa what?
	You're a LIAR. You're WICKED. You're a EVIL 'oman.
	Ya t'ink I stupid? Ya t'ink ya could pull de wool over me eyes? I spen FIVE years in school. Ya dyam BITCH.
	"Forward, ever backward." (an ironic play on a once very popular Revolutionary slogan) [Laughter from the audience]
	One 'and can't clap and one yam can't tie. [more laughter]
	I'm goin SEE da Minista AND de Prime Minista. I'm goin SHINE me show NOW. I not waitin fa cock to crow.

With this last threat, the Chief Registrar sends the Angry Woman's
damaged birth certificate to be replaced. The damaged certificate was the
source of the dispute. The woman's anger had been directed at the
Registrar's initial refusal to provide another certificate, after the first had

been cut through by the excessive pressure placed on it while being stamped with the official seal.

On leaving the Registrar's office, it would appear the Angry Woman felt so frustrated by her efforts to replace the document that she began to "air-rout"/air out (release) her passion by verbally attacking the Registrar. Convinced that the Registrar was the tangible cause of her frustration, she vented her fury on this official. In seeking support for her position in the eyes of her immediate audience (in other words, to present herself as the victim and the Registrar as the assailant), she began by retelling how much trouble the Registrar had put her through in trying to replace the damaged document. In fact, by taking the dramatic step of openly confronting the Registrar in this fashion, the Angry Woman had already received a certain amount of sympathy. It was immediately understood by those present that only a person who had been pushed to extreme anguish would resort to such dramatic means of redress. Her open expression of emotions in such a staid officious environment meant, to those around her, that a basis for grievance must exist. For anyone to challenge the bureaucratic authority of the state so flagrantly and with such an isolated personal force was either the sign of madness or the legitimate action of a grievously hurt individual. In addition, from the way she had masterfully unpacked, assembled, and fired her attack—with the claim of being educated and with the use of the political slogan and proverbs—the audience had decided against her insanity. The shift in tide of sympathy either from its neutral position or from its support of the Registrar to the Angry Woman, showed itself when the audience—among both the gathered public and working secretaries—began to laugh at her well-placed jokes. For those around her, the Angry Woman's expressed passion was proof enough of her sincerity; it was legitimate because it exhibited the tenable grounds of her rage.

The audience had recognized the authority of her voice from the presence of its loud, rhythmically intense explosions. The resonating impact of her voice exposed the trajectory of her passion and the detonating device of her discomfort. While being propelled at their target, her words supplied vivid proof, to the audience, that her emotions had not been repressed inside her body. Grenadians believe that to restrain strongly felt feelings makes the body physically ill; to release pent-up emotions maintains well-being and hence gives authority to the vocal expression of emotions. It should be added that by showing signs of being hit—in this case, by the Registrar publicly giving in to the demands of the Angry Woman—the target exposed itself as the detonating device for explosive words and as the legitimate object for verbal aggression.

I should make it patently clear that when I say expressive emotion is the distinctive feature of the subordinate Creole-speaking person, it is not that individuals of the dominant culture do not or cannot express strong, passionate feelings, or in fact that Creole-speakers are incapable of subduing passion. It is rather that the collective representation of expressive emotion holds a position of high value in one category of the person and, in fact, has come to be identified with that category more so than with any other. It is, therefore, from no arbitrary decision that language and the community of speakers come to be revealing markers of cultural difference. Being the edifice in which the individual lives, language both provides and protects the means by which identity is constructed. In Grenada, orality becomes the cultural instrument for constructing the Creole-speaking person and the actuality of that constructed distinctiveness. In addition, the orality of the Creole-speaker's constructed identity defends its vulnerability with emotionalism.

The *Country Bookie* says, by means of the creole voice, that internal sentiments should not be artificially suppressed. When one speaks, it should be with spontaneous exuberant emotions verifying the sincerity and conviction of one's ideas. Within the speech community where literacy inscriptives conventionally pertain, expressive emotion reduces the credibility of the voice, but, within those marked by assertive feelings, expressive emotion increases the voice's credibility. It is this feature of emotionality in the assertive voice which pervades the creole speech routines of *commess* (gossip), *melee* (malicious gossip), "beating *la vie*" or "beating *combos*" (throwing words or arguing), "teasing," "boasting," "cursing" and many more. But, in creole speech, the most significant aspect of expressive emotion is that far fewer restrictions exist for this source of legitimizing the voice than for the literacy inscriptives of standard Grenadian English. For creolese, everyone has the prerogative to assert his or her voice; all those present can and should be heard. This gives rise to what has been called, rather ingeniously, the "contrapuntal conversation" (Reisman 1974), that is, a multi-vocal counterpoint of assertions in spontaneous self-expression. An aggressive egalitarianism stems from the personal source of the equalizing voice: an emotional voice sustained by cultural process to engage and to proclaim inner feelings.

"CURSING" AND THE *COUNTRY BOOKIE*

If, by being the source of their legitimacy, literacy sustains standard Grenadian English, the dominant culture, and the state, then emotional orality supports the moral order of the subordinate Creole-speaking community. With the speech routine of "cursing," for example, the emotion of embarrassment results in a conscious sense of shame. How this operates can be understood in light of the symbolic system that underpins the social relations between mother and child within the Creole-speaking community. It is the meaningful symbolic connections between womanhood as other (that is, the sexual domain of birth) and personhood as progeny (that is, the status domain of honor) which make obscene language an effective instrument of the moral order within the Creole-speaking community.

In 1970 "[o]bscene and insulting language [wa]s the single most common offence recorded at the police station in Gouyave," Grenada (Macdonald 1973, 94). In 1988, although I witnessed no official reports or recorded no court convictions for verbal abuse, "cursing" still occurred "as an everyday commonplace of great frequency" (ibid). "Shit," "ass," "fuck," and "cunt" continue to be used regularly in the genre of speech known as cursing. Corroborating Macdonald's 1970 observations, my field material has "Ya mauder kunt" (your mother's cunt) as the most frequently used and most devastating phrase in the cursing repertoire. Men, women, and children in the Creole-speaking community use it all the time. The impact of the words and the seriousness of their intent are context dependent and historically specific to the relations between the curser, the cursed, and their audience. Depending on the perceived view, a verbal attack can be justified or unjustified. When the curser is viewed as a victim, the verbal assault is considered justified. When the curser is viewed as an offender, the assault is considered unjustified. Justified cursing is defensive. Unjustified cursing is clearly offensive language. What serious intentional cursing does is harm the moral character and identity of the person(s) being cursed.

EXAMPLE THREE

Location: Hermitage, St. Patrick, Grenada
Scene: A middle-aged woman, smoldering with rage, stands in the street in front of her neighbor's "bottom house." It is late in the afternoon on a Saturday. The neighbor, having just finished her domestic chores, has retired to her front room, which overlooks the street. As the woman in the street begins her tirade, the neighbor moves to close her windows. Because the other houses in the village are closely situated to each other and to the street, every word from the woman outside can be heard by the entire community.

Woman in Street: "BRING ya mauder kunt out here."
                              "Ay wan see ya UGLY face."

                              "Is when ya tek it pon yaself to be so brazen as to tek me man?"

                              "Bring ya stink self out here, I gun BUS ya tail with ONE beating."

                              "Ya mauder kunt."

"I lef' me money in de jar, fa buy food fa me chil'ren.
Next ting I know, I hear he buying ya dress fa
carnival."

"Wha'is this RASS?"

"Ya always got ya mout on de ground."

This verbal battering continues for about an hour, with everyone listening but taking no active part in the engagement. When she completes her
cursing, the woman in the street turns and dramatically marches to her
own home, apparently satisfied with her task.

To make sure her aim would not be misdirected or her words assume
some other person as target, the woman in the street placed herself directly
in front of the house of the woman she wanted to curse. Being at home and
unable to leave her house, the cursed neighbor had been made into a fixed
target; she had become a captured audience for what the curser wanted to
say to her. By positioning herself in the street, the curser additionally
ensured that what she had to say would be heard by the entire village—a
crucial feature for negotiating her cursing as an act of legitimate defense.

The woman in the house remained where she was and did not respond
to the attack because, at one level of interpretation, to have done so would
have confirmed the curser's accusations. From the cursed woman's point
of view, to have responded would have been proof—to the rest of the
village—that her attacker's words, by drawing a retort motivated by guilt,
had hit their mark; after all, apart from the victim only a guilty person
could know the details and circumstances of the accusations and thus be
able to respond. In addition to justifying the curser's use of lethal speech,
however, a response would have activated what, to the cursed woman,
would have been a technique of redress understood to be the last means
of resource in a dispute. Certainly a face-to-face confrontation would have
meant the total breakdown of any further relations between the women.
The indirect relation, which they shared through sexual ties to the same
man, could no longer be sustained. Given the degree of obliqueness operating
to preserve the social honor and the moral code of their separate roles, a
direct confrontation would have forced them to consider the irreconcilable
differences of their relationship. Thus, in this instance, not coming out to
rebuke her assailant and not saying a word while the attack was in
progress function as available ways for the cursed woman to claim innocence and maintain relations beyond the act of a cursing. She quite rightly
interpreted the curser's goading—to come outside—as a hostile strategy
for confirming her guilt and terminating their relation. Refusing to be
provoked into a confrontation may not only be construed however as
innocence and an unwillingness to jeopardize relations with the implicated man (and, consequently, oblique ties to the curser), but also as an
act of passive resistance. Indeed, if her reluctance to confront her attacker
does suggest innocence, it can also, from the cursed woman's point of view,
indicate an unjustified attack on the part of the curser.

The fact, however, that the curser went away apparently satisfied with the result of her cursing may imply that she had presumed justified recompense from the cursed woman's silence—the cursed woman's silence functioning here as compensation for the injury felt by the curser—the injury, that is, which had triggered her passion into the use of obscene and abusive language. The curser had little need to justify her actions because this was already being catered for within her public display of anger. However, implementing obscene speech within the genre of cursing allows the curser to reassert her damaged self-esteem and to parade her pride and courage to the world. She had after all not taken the option of calling the police, but stayed within the confines of village custom and personally set in motion the sanction of cursing. The knowledge that her adversary showed no signs of being hurt by the assault could have confirmed, for the curser, that the cursed woman had no moral values to be damaged. This would then not only substantiate the latter's guilt (of hoarding rather than sharing the products of the implicated man's social relations), but also explain why the crime was committed in the first place. From the curser's point of view, only a woman with no social morals could influence another woman's man to take household earnings for the purchase of a carnival dress. Certainly, in this context, only a person without moral values could be seriously hurt by an attack of obscene and abusive words.

The audience, that is, the listening villagers, were drawn into the dispute both to witness the moral character of the disputants and to help establish one or the other as the aggrieved victim. The victim would be the one who would convince the audience that she had been unjustifiably hurt or violated by an attack on her personal moral being. As it turns out, the passive participation of the audience—listening but making no commentary—allowed both disputants to defend their respective positions and to claim innocence and recompense. The audience's impartiality came into effect because the listening villagers were unable to establish whose moral character was suffering from the most shame. It is because obscene speech injured the moral character of both the individual and the community that the hurt it inflicts can serve as an effective indicator or victimization. The individual and the community share in the same moral qualities; as such, when one or the other receives an attack, both suffer the same hurt; the violence of obscene words directly wounds shared moral values. A symptom of such social pain would be that of shame, a shame emanating from the embarrassment of exposed private knowledge.

Speaking in public about a mother's "private parts" exemplifies the Grenadian adage of *"Bombon la plass"* (Cake in the market). In other words, it places in public view, like an object of sale, that which is considered to be private, personal, and inalienable. A sense of violation pertains. Such flagrant disregard contaminates by public utterance the privacy of the home and the sanctuary of a mother's body. It inverts a highly valued moral imperative which draws a sharp distinction between house/close relatives and street/non-relatives. In particular, it places on the street the category of the closest relative a person possesses in the Creole-speaking community—the mother. In addition, cursing conveys a lack of respect for the cursed person's social being and does violence to that being. By mentioning, in public, the cursed person's mother's "private parts," the curser frustrates the former's wish to preserve, uncontaminated, the single undisputed family tie constructing social personhood. In the context of cursing, "wish-frustration" (Gordon 1990) disrupts the social composure of the cursed. It embarrasses and, thus, dishonors. But, for cursing to be effective, there must be a conscious sense of shame.

Not to be aware of shame is to be what Grenadians call "ignorant," that is, not to care about what others think or say about your actions. Knowing the moral order by which one lives is to be wise and respected (Sanders 1987; Wilson 1973). Not to be hurt by the disgrace brought about by the public mention of one's mother's most private part, the origin of one's existence, is to be impervious to the differences between right and wrong and, thus, to be morally bankrupt and, therefore, useless to society.

THE HEGEMONY OF THE CLASSROOM

I have mentioned that the nurturing ground for obedience to the state begins in the schools. I would now like to state quite explicitly that the alienation of creole emotionality takes place most effectively within formal education. Homogeneity and ranked differentiation are qualities of submission which aid state control of citizens. Such engendered features of obedience begin with the edifice of school and its allocation of space separate from home and domestic life. Loyalty to the greater cause, encouraged by competition between schools and within schools, buries the individual beneath the group. School uniforms, mottos, badges, and emblems instill a sense of identity to a stronger force than individual will. Some schools even have parade-group drill and marching bands to facilitate regimented behavior and to sharpen group response to command. A liberal use of and belief in corporal punishment prepares the student for institutional violence. But it is the routinized behavior, implemented through the daily time-table of every school, which drives home the point of homogeneity. The unchanging curriculum, the constancy of classroom formality, the regularity of playground relaxation, the fixed times of study and play, all help to enforce conformity. As the suppression of individual will clears the ground in the ideal situation, the reconstruction of a new order of differentiation takes form. It is based upon rigid ranking prescribed by rules of promotion. The central authority of the teacher in the classroom, the stratified hierarchy of the teachers and students within the school, attempt to replicate a moral order of merit. Here control becomes a major consideration of authority to the extent that its various forms are set against the impassioned character of the creole student.

It is actually within the classroom that expressive emotion becomes most exposed to the process of oppression. I recorded four distinct teaching styles in Grenadian schools which worked unconsciously to achieve this goal. All four have been identified by researchers in other countries. "Monologuing," for example, is when a teacher continues to speak by herself and/or to herself, and thus successfully excludes the student from the lesson even while actively soliciting a response from the student (Hernandez 1986, 84). With the use of "irony," teachers initially encourage student response, but then, if the response is incorrect, they ridicule it with an ironical tone of voice (de Texanos 1986, 68). A teacher's "intermittent deafness" ignores an incorrect answer and functions as a form of punishment by rejecting the response of a child seeking reassurance from the central figure of authority in the classroom (ibid). "Repetitive nominalism" features a teacher constantly repeating the words of a student who has responded to a question (ibid., 69) This has an effect of nullifying the student's efforts and canceling out the student's creative input. These various styles of teaching produce the submissive child. And that feature of the creole child most susceptible to such forms of repression is expressive emotion. In other words, the alienation of this central component of the Creole-speaking person takes effect through the process of schooling and its efforts at literacy production.

The emotional orality of the creole voice is set apart and held in constant contrast to the "rational" literacy of dominant society. It has no space of legitimacy in the hallways of state power, while in comparison the culture of writing fills every nook and cranny in the administrative structure of Grenada's polity. The two culture's variant sources of authority sustain different forms of moral behavior. Literacy and schools, orality and families hold ground on legitimacies that are concerned with divergent moral values. It is, however, revealing that while the subordinate category of the Creole-speaking person maintains its own integral moral order and values, while aspiring to those of the dominant culture, the latter trivializes the former and alienates its source of authority within the context of formal schooling. The strange irony is of course that while the social elites of Grenada oppress their own society's alternative culture, they are at the same time oppressing themselves with the moral ideals of the foreigner.

CONCLUSION

The dominant and the Creole-speaking cultures sustain variant moral values reliant upon different forms of knowledge. Within the context of formal schooling, however, it is the morality and emotional authority of the creole voice which suffers most from alienation and subordination. As a result, the system of education has been unable to evolve out of a debilitating cycle of redundancy. By persistently refusing to accept the viability of its own society's alternative culture and the credibility of this alternative culture's body of knowledge, formal schooling has produced a strange paradox in Grenada. Its constant denials have squandered a real opportunity for releasing the system from its tautological cycle.

Formal schooling produces reading and writing as fundamental instruments of knowledge. During the process, however, these instruments become not only the means but also the object of knowledge. In other words, reading and writing become knowledge itself. The production of an intellectual acquaintance with literacy gives literacy an impression of autonomy. But this autonomy, or neutrality, blurs the view that knowledge privileges some "truths" and denies others altogether. Thus, during schooling, the experience of "knowing" obscures literacy's loaded ideology. And it does so through the communicative success of literacy which depends upon predetermined and shared assumptions. Literacy claims its meaning through cultural tradition and, thus, is content dependent.

In Grenada, formal schooling is in the hands of the state, and the state is in the grip of the dominant culture. In recent years, the disappointment that the state and its benefactors have incurred has not been the schools' inability to transmit the favored paradigm of literacy to those in the lower ranks; its greatest frustration has been the schools' lack of success in producing sufficiently acquiescent citizens. The system of education was set up as an artifice of British colonial rule to produce obedient servants for the Empire. Independent Grenada and Revolutionary Grenada both continued, in varying degrees, the same structure that feeds the highly stratified state bureaucracy with its servile labor force. Even today the state is the major employer. Academic qualifications are an imperative passport to placement within the ranks of the civil service, but deferential servility keeps the ranks in their stratified order. Ideal school and classroom behavior, organization, and structure replicate the order of the state. In essence they prepare the student for good citizenship. The analogy being of course that the school is a miniature state and the state is but an enlarged school. The least that is demanded of participants is that they obey commands. One of the most efficient ways to accomplish this relies upon having participants recognize that the voice of command has authority. It is this lack of training in recognizing and then accepting the authority of the literate voice of command which has caused social elites to despair over the inefficiencies of schools.

Instead of accepting a viable alternative source of knowledge, the schools, the dominant culture, and the state assume that no knowledge or an inferior knowledge exists within the subordinate culture. Consequently, they work against, instead of with, the Creole-speaking person. Thus, ironically, the most immediate means of transcending the institutions and ideas which have kept the local elites in intellectual bondage continues to be squandered. The local elites persist in mechanically mimicking the Occidental and, in their obsequious role, have maintained the cultural oppression of the periphery by the center.

ACKNOWLEDGMENT

I wish to thank the Spencer Foundation for the sponsorship supporting the project from which this research was carried out during the period 1988–89. I would also like to take this opportunity to express my gratitude to Lambros Comitas and Mike Smith for including me in the team of field workers on the project "Education and Society in the Creole Caribbean." Philip Burnham and Josep Llobera were of tremendous support to me and my family while we were in the field. To R.I.S.M., the University of the West Indies, and the people of Grenada, I acknowledge my great debt.

NOTES

1. Grenada was granted independence from British rule on 7th February 1974. On 13th March 1979 Grenada came under the Marxist administration of the People's Revolutionary Government. On 19th October 1983 its Central Committee gave orders to turn the army against the people. Six days later the U.S. Armed Forces were on the island. Currently the country is back to the British system of a bicameral parliament.

2. Of the eleven countries compared by Roberts, only Barbados is without the "indispensable West Indian Creole feature" of the *a/iz* topicalizer.

3. Like the sentence structure shaping the common Grenadian phrase, "How many years you have?" (How old are you?), the *wi* syntax tag is evidence of the past French-creole influence in Grenada. Roberts wishes, however, to highlight that it is not just the persuasion of French or indeed the geographical proximity of the more dominantly affected Francophone islands like St. Lucia and Dominica which play a part in the current construction of Grenadian English-creole. He draws attention to the fact that, with regard to similarity in linguistic development, Trinidad and Grenada are much closer to each other than to the Francophone islands. Nevertheless, in its own right, Grenadian English creole stands as a viable and vital language.

4. Of the remainder, some 3.5 percent have the "School Leaving Certificate," the lowest ranked qualification, while the rest have General Certificate of Education (G.C.E.) "O" levels or better. About 5 percent have either 1–4 "O" levels or 1–3 Caribbean Examinations Council (C.X.C.) "General" passes. 1.3 percent

of males and 0.4 percent of females have a degree (ibid). ("O" levels are "ordinary" while "A" levels are "advanced.")

5. I owe much of my technical interpretation on the emotionality of the Grenadian creole voice to the work of Thomas Kochman (1981).

REFERENCES

Anderson, A. B., W. B. Teale, and E. Estrada (1980). "Low-income Children's Preschool Literacy Experience: Some Naturalistic Observations," *The Quarterly Newsletter of the Laboratory of Comparative Human Cognition* 2(3): 59–65.

Balandier, G. (1972). *Political Anthropology*. Harmondsworth: Penguin Books.

Bickerton, D. (1981). *Roots of Language*. Ann Arbor, Mich.: Karoma.

Brathwaite, E. K. (1984). *History of the Voice: The Development of a Nation Language in Anglephone Caribbean Poetry*. London: New Beacon Books.

Derrida, J. (1978). *Writing and Difference*. Chicago: University of Chicago Press.

de Texanos, A. (1986). "Styles of Teaching in Colombian Classrooms," *Teaching the Children of the Poor: An Ethnographic Study in Latin America*, ed. B. Avalos. Ottawa: International Development Research Centre.

Fishman, J. (1972). *Language in Sociocultural Change: Essays by Joshua Fishman*, ed. A. S. Dil. Palo Alto, Calif.: Stanford University Press.

Foucault, M. (1979). *Discipline and Punish: The Birth of the Prison*. New York: Vintage Books.

Gordon, R. M. (1990). *The Structure of Emotions: Investigation in Cognitive Philosophy*. Cambridge: Cambridge University Press.

Heath, S. B. (1983). *Ways with Words: Language, Life, and Work in Communities and Classrooms*. Cambridge: Cambridge University Press.

Hernandez, I. (1986). "Schools and Teaching in Venezuela," *Teaching the Children of the Poor: An Ethnographic Study in Latin America*, ed. B. Avalos. Ottawa: International Development Research Centre.

Hobsbawn, E. J. (1990). *Nations and Nationalism since 1780: Programme, Myth, Reality*. Cambridge: Cambridge University Press.

Hymes, D. (1974). "Ways of Speaking," *Explorations in the Ethnography of Speaking*, eds. R. Bauman and J. Sherzer. Cambridge: Cambridge University Press.

Hymes, D. (ed.) (1971). *Pidginization and Creolization of Languages*. Cambridge: Cambridge University Press.

Kochman, T. (1981). *Black and White Styles in Conflict*. Chicago: University of Chicago Press.

Macdonald, J. S. (1973). "Cursing and Context in a Grenadian Fishing Community." *Anthropologica* 15: 89–128.

Reisman, K. (1974). "Contrapuntal Conversations in an Antiguan village," *Explorations in the Ethnography of Speaking*, eds. R. Bauman and J. Sherzer. Cambridge: Cambridge University Press.

Roberts, P. A. (1988). *West Indians and Their Language*. New York: Cambridge University Press.

Romaine, S. (1988). *Pidgin and Creole Languages*. London: Longman.

Sanders, A. (1987). *The Powerless People: An Analysis of the Amerindians of the Corentyne River*. London: Macmillan Caribbean.

Stewart, W. A. (1962). "The Functional Distribution of Creole and French in Haiti," *Georgetown Monograph Series on Language and Linguistics 15*. Washington: Georgetown University Press.

Street, B. V. (1984). *Literacy in Theory and Practice*. Cambridge: Cambridge University Press.

Turner, V. (1969). *The Ritual Process: Structure and Anti-structure*. Chicago: Aldine.

Turner, V. (1992). *Blazing the Trail: Way Marks in the Exploration of Symbols*, ed. E. Turner. Tucson: University of Arizona Press.

Wilson, P. J. (1973). *Crab Antics: The Social Anthropology of English-speaking Negro Societies of the Caribbean*. New Haven, Conn.: Yale University Press.

Index

About the Contributors

RICHARD K. BLOT is coordinator of the interdisciplinary program in linguistics at Lehman College of the City University of New York, where he teaches anthropology, linguistics, and education. He has done fieldwork in Ecuador under a Fulbright fellowship and taught at the Escuela Politécnica del Littoral in Guayaquil and the Pontificia Universidad Católica in Quito. He has also taught at Ignatius College of Fordham University, the University of Alaska, Fairbanks, and the State University of New York at Albany. He recently published (with John Lofty) "Covering One's Tracks: Respecting and Preserving Informant Anonymity" in Kirklighter et al., *Voices and Visions,* and with James Collins, *Literacy and Literacies: Texts, Power and Identity* (2003).

CHARLES L. BRIGGS is professor of ethnic studies at University of California, San Diego. The recipient of numerous honors and fellowships, most recently Guggenheim, 1994–95 and Woodrow Wilson, 1997–98, his work makes significant contributions to anthropology, sociolinguistics, folklore, and Southwestern studies. He is the author or editor of nine books including: *The Woodcarvers of Cordova, New Mexico* (1980); *Learning to Ask: A Sociolinguistic Appraisal of the Role of the Interview in Social Science Research* (1986); *Competence in Performance* (1988); and *Disorderly Discourse: Narrative, Conflict, and Social Inequality* (1996).

Based on extensive fieldwork among the Warao of Venezuela, he, along with Clara Mantini, M.D., is preparing *Stories in Times of Cholera: Race and Death in a South American Epidemic*. He is co-editor of *Pragmatics* and serves on the editorial boards of *American Quarterly, Text,* and the Studies in Interactional Sociolinguistics series for Cambridge University Press.

JANET M. CHERNELA is a professor of anthropology at Florida International University, Miami. Her research interests include language and identity, social and political organization, and local-global interactions. She is author of *The Wanano Indians of the Brazilian Amazon: A Sense of Space* (1993); her recent publications include "Ideal Speech Moments: A Woman's Narrative Performance in the Northwest Amazon" (*Feminist Studies* 23, 1997); "Cross-genre Talk: Expanding the Ground" in *Reviews in Anthropology* 26; and "Death, Memory and Language: New Approaches to History in Lowland South American Anthropology" (*Latin American Research Review* 33, 1998).

JAMES COLLINS is a professor of anthropology and of reading at SUNY Albany. His primary research efforts have been in the study of Native American languages and cultures, especially those of the Pacific Northwest Tolowa, and in the study of language and education, especially studies of literacy in urban America. His *Understanding Tolowa Histories: Western Hegemonies and Native American Responses* has recently appeared, and together with Richard Blot he has written a book on the anthropology of reading and writing, *Literacy and Literacies: Texts, Power, and Identity* (2003).

GARY H. GOSSEN is Dean at Deep Springs College and formerly distinguished teaching professor of anthropology and Latin American studies at SUNY Albany and former chair of the anthropology department there. His field work has focused on the Tzotzil Maya of Chiapas, Mexico, where he has studied diverse aspects of their verbal arts, oral history, religion, and cosmology. His more general interests concern problems in ethnic identity, popular religion, and oral traditions of Latin America. His published works include *Chamulas in the World of the Sun: Time and Space in a Maya Oral Tradition* (1974); *Symbol and Meaning Beyond the Closed Community: Essays in Mesoamerican Ideas* (ed., 1986); *South and Mesoamerican Spirituality: From the Cult of the Feathered Serpent to the Theology of Liberation* (ed., with Miguel Leon-Portilla, 1993); and *Telling Maya Tales: Tzotzil Identities in Modern Mexico* (1999).

JERRY KELLY teaches language arts at Exeter Area High School in Exeter, New Hampshire. Since 1991, he has worked in southern Belize with Belizean educators, a collaboration that led to his doctoral research on the moral dimensions of Belizean storytelling. He is co-editor with Louis Cucul and Thomas Teul of *Stories in the Air*, a collection of Kekchi and Mopan Mayan traditional narratives, produced for the Belizean indigenous textbook program. Most recently, he has been invited by the Ministry of Education, Sports, and Culture of Zimbabwe to develop a teacher-to-teacher partnership similar to the Belize–New Hampshire Teacher Program.

MARÍA L. LAGOS is an associate professor of anthropology at Herbert H. Lehman College and at the Graduate Center of the City University of New York. She has done extensive field and archival research in Cochabamba, Bolivia on processes of agrarian transformations and cultural and political struggle. Her current interests, in addition to agrarian issues and Latin America, include history and anthropology, popular culture and the politics of identity. She is the author of *Autonomy and Power: The Dynamics of Class and Culture in Rural Bolivia* (1994) and of "'We Have to Learn to Ask': Hegemony, Experience, and Antagonistic Meanings," *American Ethnologist* 20, 1993.

ERIC J. LEED is emeritus professor of history at Florida International University, North Miami. His is the author of three books: *Nomansland: Combat and Identity in World War I* (1979), a study of how the experience of industrialized war shaped combatant identities and solidarities; *The Mind of the Traveler: From Gilgamesh to Global Tourism* (1991), which examines the literature of European travel to see how travel has been felt to alter mobilized selves and mentalities; and, *Shores of Discovery: How Expeditionaries have Constructed the World* (1996) which deals with military, missionary, commercial, scientific, and touristic expeditionaries and the connections they form to the lands and peoples along their passage.

MICHAEL H. LONG is a professor of English as a second language at the University of Hawai'i at Manoa, where he teaches in the M.A. in ESL and Ph.D. in second language acquisition programs. He is the author of over 100 articles and several books, and in 1999 was recipient of TESOL's International Research Prize. He serves on the editorial boards of Studies in Second Language Acquisition, Language Teaching Research, and Estudios de Linguistica Aplicada and is co-editor of the Cambridge Applied Linguistics Series. Recent and forthcoming publications include *Task-Based Language Teaching*, *Problems in SLA*, and (co-edited with Cathy Doughty) *Handbook of Second Language Acquisition*.

GEORGE MENTORE is an associate professor of anthropology at the University of Virginia. He has done fieldwork in the rainforests of Southern Guyana, and in the Caribbean on the islands of Puerto Rico,

Grenada, and Jamaica. His recent research on the anthropology of the body has resulted in a number of significant publications: "Tempering the Social Self: Body Adornment, Vital Substance, and Knowledge among the Waiwai"; "Epilepsy as Social Power, Silent Pain, and Episodic Memory"; and "Peccary Meat and Power among the Waiwai Indians of Guyana."

JOHN W. PULIS is assistant professor of anthropology at Hofstra University. He has done fieldwork in Africa, the West Indies, and in North America. Extensive fieldwork in Jamaica led to a number of articles on the topic of Rastafari. He has contributed entries to the *Historical Encyclopedia of Slavery* (1997) on Afro-Christianity and on the role of missions in Jamaica and has edited a volume of historical essays entitled *Moving On: Black Loyalists in the Afro-Atlantic World* (1998). He has also edited *Religion, Diaspora, and Cultural Identity: A Reader in the Anglophone Caribbean* (1999). His monograph *Gates to Zion: Texts, Voices, and the Narrative World of Rastafari* will be completed next year.

ELLEN M. SCHNEPEL is a research fellow at the Research Institute for the Study of Man in New York and a consultant in applied anthropology. She has conducted ethnographic research in the French Antilles, Indian Ocean, Belize, and Andorra on language and nationalism, gender issues, and ethnic identity. Her writings have appeared in *Plantation Society in the Americas, New West Indian Guide, Ethnic Groups, High Plains Applied Anthropologist, Etudes Creoles, Recherches Feministes,* and *Anales del Caribe.* She co-edited Creole Movements in the Francophone Orbit, a special issue of *The International Journal of the Sociology of Language* (1993).

BONNIE URCIUOLI is professor of anthropology at Hamilton College. A recipient of numerous awards and grants, her extensive research among New York Puerto Ricans resulted in a major monograph, *Exposing Prejudice: Puerto Rican Experiences of Language, Race, and Class* (1996). Among her many articles are "The Political Topography of Spanish and English: The View from a New York Puerto Rican Neighborhood," *American Ethnologist* 18, 1991, "Representing Class: Who Decides?" *Anthropological Quarterly* 66, 1993, and "Language and Borders," *Annual Review of Anthropology,* 1995.

MARÍA EUGENIA VILLALÓN is associate professor at the Escuela de Anthropologia of the Universidad Central de Venezuela. She specializes in Carib languages and culture and has been doing fieldwork among Indian communities of the Orinoco Basin since 1970. Her research interests include linguistic anthropology, historical linguistics, applied anthropology, and sociolinguistics. Among her publications are *Aspectos de la organizacion social y la terminologia de parentesco E'ñapa* (1978); "Do Differences Engender Rights? Indian and Criollo Discourses over Minority Rights at the Venezuelan National Constituent Assembly" (2002, *Social Justice: Anthropology, Peace and Human Rights* 3(1–2): 8–42), and, with Tania Granadillo, "Los marcadores de persona de la lengua mapoyo" in Hein van der Voort and Simon van de Kerke, eds., *Indigenous Languages of Lowland South America*, Leiden Research School CNWS, Universiteit Leiden, 2000, 197–211.

KATHRYN A. WOOLARD is professor of anthropology at the University of California, San Diego. She has published on the politics of language and ethnicity in Catalonia and in the United States, and her current research is on language and ideology in the Spanish colonial empire. Woolard is author of *Double Talk: Bilingualism and the Politics of Ethnicity in Catalonia* (1989), co-editor with Susan Gal of a special issue of *Pragmatics* on "Constructing Languages and Publics" (1995), and co-editor with Bambi Schieffelin and Paul Kroskrity of *Language Ideologies: Practice and Theory* (1998). Among her most recent publications is "Simultaneity and Bivalency as Strategies in Bilingualism" (1999, *Journal of Linguistic Anthropology*).